THE
MOURNING-LIBERATION
PROCESS

THE MOURNING-LIBERATION PROCESS

Volume I

George H. Pollock, M.D., Ph.D.

INTERNATIONAL UNIVERSITIES PRESS, INC.
Madison   **Connecticut**

Library of Congress Cataloging-in-Publication Data

Pollock, George H.
  The mourning-liberation process / George H. Pollock.
    p. cm.
  Consists primarily of reprints of articles from various sources.
  Includes bibliographies and index.
  ISBN 0-8236-3485-X (v. 1) . ISBN 0-8236-3486-8 (v. 2)
    1. Bereavement—Psychological aspects. 2. Loss (Psychology)
3. Adjustment (Psychology) 4. Bereavement—Psychological aspects—
Case studies. 5. Loss (Psychology)—Case studies. 6. Adjustment
(Psychology)—Case studies. I. Title.
    [DNLM: 1. Adaptation, Psychological—collected works.
2. Bereavement—collected works. 3. Grief—collected works. BF
575.G7 P777m]
BF575.G7P63 1989
155.9'37—dc19
DNLM/DLC
for Library of Congress
                                        88-13628

                                                CIP

Manufactured in the United States of America

DEDICATION AND APPRECIATIONS

I wish to dedicate these volumes to the memory of my mother, whose sudden, unexpected, and untimely death was the stimulus for my ongoing research in the mourning-liberation process these past thirty-three years. I have learned much about myself and this fundamental process since that time. This knowledge has been of personal benefit and also has greatly contributed to my understanding and to the assistance offered to my patients and my friends. I am grateful to my patients for what they have taught me and what I could then further apply to helping them and others.

I also wish to thank Anne P. Lederer, whose generous support has enabled me to study, think, read, discuss, and investigate the mourning-liberation process. I am also very grateful to Jacqueline Miller, who continues to assist me in so many ways in the preparation of my manuscripts and speeches.

My deepest affection and greatest appreciation is reserved for my dear wife, Beverly. She has helped me through various life crises; she has been the liberating force in my life. She has encouraged me whenever I needed this booster and she patiently read, criticized, and raised critical questions that helped me elucidate what was unclear or incomplete. Her very active participation in the care of our five children freed me to carry on my investigative work. Our children's subsequent development is mainly due to Beverly's devotion, dedication, and active involvement with them. I contributed some, but the major positive influences were from their mother.

George H. Pollock, M.D., Ph.D.
October, 1988

CONTENTS
VOLUME I

Contents Volume II

PREFACE

The reports in these volumes of my investigations of the mourning-liberation process allow the reader to follow my thinking and research step by step. Observations gave rise to new questions and further observations which resulted in other queries and studies. At times, introspection, clinical observations, reading literature, looking at paintings, or hearing music stimulated thoughts which seemingly diverted me from the straight direction I was pursuing, but I did not lose the trail, even though an interesting detour allowed me to explore a new area. This process still is ongoing. In a sense my work for over thirty years in this general area allows me to "collaborate" with my past investigative self, my present investigative self, and with my forebearers who set the stage for me; when I arrived on the scene I could benefit from what they had already discovered and observed. Since scientific inquiry goes on continuously, the link just described is an essential part of the process. As Cannon (1945) has noted, "no research can be final, every publication is a progress report" (p. 94).

Cannon's concept of homeostasis of biological states has been of great importance to me since my earlier days as a physiologist. He indicated that various physiological mechanisms were "purposive" and these evolved to facilitate adaptation to changes internally and externally and so protect the organism against possible harm and to aid in "survival in the struggle for existence" (Cannon, 1945, p. 112). These adaptive devices appeared in the course of evolution and had utility. Cannon believed that these biological mechanisms were related to natural selection, which accounted for their development and continued persistence. Thus the "concept of utility and purposiveness" has significance in biological activities. It is my belief that this is also true in psychological research. My initial contribution to the central subject of my research, the mourning–liberation process, related to the utility, purpose, possible evolutionary development, and current adaptive significance of this process. The mourning–liberation process evolved and became part of the psychological adaptive processes of the mind in order to maintain a constant state within the mind so as to maintain the organism in a stable state. Cannon called this maintenance of the steady-state homeostasis. Earlier Claude Bernard (1865) described a similar operation when he called attention to the constancy of the internal milieu, referring to biological constancy.

It is my belief that the mind, using various psychological agencies, evolved with its many elaborations to maintain the constant state of man. Some of these agencies, such as memory, future planning, aesthetic appreciation, creativity were not immediately connected with conflict resolution or maintenance of psychological homeostasis in the face of serious disruptions of the prior stable state, but were derivations from such mechanisms. Cannon suggests that there may be homeostatic control of social conditions; and I would extend this to include homeostatic control of psychological changes, either normative and/or catastrophic. As he notes:

1. There is evidence that agencies in the body act or are prepared to act to maintain constancy of the internal biological state;
2. Change is automatically met by factors which resist change, and corrective measures are instituted when threat to the steady state of balance appears;
3. "The regulating system which determines homeostasis of a particular feature may comprise a number of cooperating factors brought into action at the same time or successively" (1945, p. 114); and
4. There are reactions to shifts in homeostatic balance which act in a direction opposite to the initial disruption. These homeostatic righting reactions are not accidental or random.

Again, I emphasize the parallels Cannon describes for biological mechanisms of adaptation to similar psychological mechanisms. However, the individual has his or her own developmental unfolding and there may be different psychological mechanisms that achieve prominence at different periods of the life course.

Cannon's research and wise conclusions regarding biological mechanisms strongly influenced me from my earliest days as a college and medical student. His researches on the bodily changes resulting from various emotional states were precursors to my later interests in psychosomatic–stress disorders and particularly the specificity of reactions to disturbed psychological homeostatic balances and the increased vulnerability to later psychophysiological disruptions. As our knowledge increases, it is apparent that there are multiple factors present in what were seen as relatively simple correlations not so many decades ago. Nonetheless, certain basic principles still have validity, applicability, and can be extended to realms of knowledge that were not part of the initial formulations; that is, extension to psychology from biology, and recognition that individual developmental variables are not the same throughout the life course but differ in different periods of life. Complicated processes must be appreciated for what they are and care must be taken to avoid oversimplification and reductionism while still retaining what has more general utility.

Cannon has noted that the efforts of an investigator are far from impersonal "disinterested research." I can confirm this observation. I believe all research articulates at one level with the personal needs, characteristics, and curiosity of the investigator. As indicated above, observations and new ideas may come to the fore in the course of pursuing a given study. These leads can be pursued, examined, and further studied. They may result in new researches that elaborate aspects of the original research. One can go back to this initial work, but the observations on the new side streets may give rise to newer perspectives that were not present before the "excursions" stimulated the interest of the investigator. As the reader examines the various chapters in these volumes the validity of the "excursion discoveries" will become apparent. Here again the intensely personal serves as a motivation and stimulus for research pursuits. Through introspection and insight the investigator can discover the sources of his curiosity and then further scientifically pursue questions and hypotheses so stimulated. Not all research, however, is solely directed by or for self-exploration. Scientific research can become more autonomous and separated from the initial motivations. These considerations obviously may have greater significance in the pursuit of psychological and social studies than in other fields of science. Nonetheless research pursuits of many if not all varieties have an intensely personal component.

Although Cannon suggests that planning for research can stifle "the unique foresight and personal drive of the investigator, whose eagerness for discovering leads him deeper and deeper into the elucidation of hidden meanings" (1945, p. 149), one must be aware of the dangers of pursuing an investigation that is heavily subjective. Hypotheses can be generated from such experiences, but they then must be carefully examined to determine their validity by comparison with the observations of others, and tested in accordance with established canons of scientific method; that is, reality testing. This is not always possible for all hypotheses and for all disciplines. In some, it is possible to set up controlled experiments and the results can be useful in establishing the validity of the hypotheses. In some disciplines, other methods for testing can be employed, when the body of knowledge is such that such reality tests are possible. In some fields, observations have to suffice until more data, techniques, and approaches develop which can permit such testing. In some fields (for example, aesthetics, the humanities, and depth psychology), such testing may never be possible or precise. We can still recognize the importance of such attempts at reality testing of hypotheses and look forward to a time when it may be possible to examine such data and ensuing hypotheses.

An illustration of this idea that has applicability to the mourning–liberation process is the recent research on the role of the immune system in a stress–strain–coping process. From all indications we now may have biological markers for such psychosocial disruptions. As the adaptive processes occur, changes in the immune markers can give us an indication of the efficacy of these adaptive processes. When we have obtained sufficient baseline data we may hope to detect deviations from the adaptive process that may require more active intervention. When the adaptive process is successful, the immune markers will so indicate. This very promising research may provide us with a window to monitor and study a variety of psychosocial activities, such as, aging, therapeutic responses, stress–strain reactions. Until such observations and methods were available to us, we relied mainly on clinical course, comparative observations, and more or less systematic follow-up and outcome studies. We now enter a new era of research and testing of hypotheses. This will help us in our quest for validity verification.

The exciting research on the relationship of the mourning–liberation process and the immune system has now been extended to other major life transitions; for example, marital separation, examinations, loneliness, loss of support systems, divorce, job loss, serious illness of family members, and serious surgical procedures and aging. This correlation lends support to my thesis that the mourning–liberation process is a universal transformational adaptive process to loss and change throughout the life course. It has biological, psychological, emotional, and social consequences. It has a developmental progression from earliest life onward. It is found throughout man's history, in every culture, in every class, and a subclass of it, bereavement, relates specifically to reactions following the death of a significant individual. The process involves not only detachment from internal representations and external absences, but reattachments and freedom (i.e., liberation) at the concluding adaptation. I report on four possible outcomes of the mourning–liberation process: (1) a normal process with a "creative-liberating" outcome leaving memory traces, and in which I assume there is a return to normal immunologic functioning; (2) an arrest in the development of the mourning–liberation process with assumed immunologic abnormality; (3) a fixation of certain aspects of the mourning–liberation process with a periodic return to the fixation level as seen in anniversary reactions. Here again I assume abnormal immune responses; (4) pathological mourning–liberation processes, such as, melancholia, suicide, and severe psychosomatic symptoms. Here again I envision immune abnormalities. My initial studies of (1) adults who lost one or both parents through death in childhood or adolescence; (2) adults who lost through death one or more siblings during childhood or adolescence; (3) adults who lost their spouse or partner through death; and (4) adults who lost one or more children through death not only provided me with clinical data for understanding the mourning–liberation process and its variations, but stimulated a further ongoing study of the changing psychoemotional meanings of significant individuals, who bear the same kinship label but who take on different significances through the life course. Seeming gender differences have been observed in spouse loss bereavements and bereavement reactions in mothers and fathers.

My studies of creativity and loss, aging, and Bertha Pappenheim are further paths I pursued in the course of this research to date. The research continues in many directions and I hope to present some of this work in future reports.

George H. Pollock, M.D., Ph.D.
June 1988

Part I
INTRODUCTION

1
MOURNING AND ADAPTATION

ADAPTATION

Claude Bernard (1813–1878), the French physiologist, was the first to advance the concept that animals exist in two environments: an external milieu in which the organism is actually situated, and an internal milieu in which the tissue elements are present. Although Bernard was concerned mainly with the physiological and biochemical aspects of the organism, he concluded that the "primary condition for freedom and independence of existence" was the constancy and stability of the internal milieu and the mechanisms that allowed this state to continue. Bernard felt that the organism had to be "so perfect that it can continually compensate for and counterbalance external variations." The equilibrium had to be constantly maintained and all vital mechanisms had "only one object: that of preserving constant the conditions of life in the *milieu intérieur*" (Bernard, 1865, foreword).

I am taking the liberty of extending Bernard's ideas to the psychological environment. Here too we find an external and an internal milieu. In both we find definite regulatory devices designed to deal with various alterations that may occur. Freud extensively studied the internal psychological milieu and advanced various theoretical constructs which allowed conceptual framework to be formulated. As early as 1892, Freud alone and with Breuer proposed the idea of the constancy of excitation. When the nervous system had difficulty in dealing with increases in excitation through associative thinking or motor discharge, Freud and Breuer suggested that a "psychical trauma"

The author wishes to acknowledge the support given him by the Foundations' Fund for Research in Psychiatry during the preparation of this paper.

Reprinted by permission from the *International Journal of Psycho-Analysis*, 42:341–361 (1961).

occurred. In 1911, Freud advanced his understanding of psychological processes with his "Formulations on the Two Principles of Mental Functioning." Here he introduced two modes of constancy adaptations—the immediate energetic discharge or avoidance of the pleasure-pain principle, and the capacity, oriented to external reality, for discharge delay of the reality principle. This later type of adaptation used mechanisms involving consciousness, attention, notation, and memory storage as well as decision making with action to alter external reality and thought, as means of coping with new and potentially disrupting situations. In *Beyond the Pleasure Principle* (1920), Freud once more emphasized the principle of constancy and its relationship to the mental apparatus. We can see that Freud's idea of the psychological constancy of the internal milieu paralleled Bernard's model of the physicobiochemical stability. In both the internal milieu was optimally maintained within a certain range. Less variation could occur here in contrast to the external milieu, and various defense mechanisms were necessary to maintain this constancy of the inside.

Walter Cannon (1871–1945) extended and elaborated this concept of stability by his principle of homeostasis, which emphasized the various biological processes tending to reestablish steady states of equilibrium and constancy when disturbing elements upset the state of balance. As biologists have continued their investigations, various optimal ranges for particular body processes have been discovered. With disease interferences, these ranges vary in accordance with the degree of impairment imposed upon the organism, as well as with the restitutive capacity operative within the organism.

Cannon envisioned the extension of his homeostasis idea to include "some general principles for the establishment, regulation and control of steady states" (p. 24) which could be applicable to social and industrial organizations. He wrote that "Perhaps a comparative study would show that every complex organization must have more or less effective self-righting adjustments in order to prevent a check on its functions or a rapid disintegration of its parts when it is subjected to stress" (Cannon, 1932, p. 25).

Although Freud was aware of defensive maneuvers utilized in psychological adaptation early in his work, it was in 1923 that he first presented us with the structural organization of the mental apparatus in *The Ego and the Id.* The ego's integrative role was elaborated and its relationship to the external milieu (reality) as well as to the psychic internal milieu explained. In 1936, Anna Freud developed in further detail the protective and sustaining aspects of the ego's function. In 1939, Hartmann's classic work on *Ego Psychology and the Problem of Adaptation* first appeared. These last two contributions focused the direction of later psychoanalytic developments and investigations upon ego activities.

It was Cannon who noted that "the perfection of the process of holding a stable state in spite of extensive shifts of outer circumstance is not a special gift bestowed upon the highest organisms but is the consequence of a gradual evolution" (1932, p. 23).

Charles Darwin (1809–1882), in *The Origin of Species* (1859), suggested that, by a process of natural selection, less well adapted forms of life would have on the average a heavier death rate and a lower multiplication rate. Again dealing with physical characteristics, he postulated his idea of the "survival of the fittest." Undoubtedly the homeostatis stabilizing mechanisms came into being through a process of gradual evolution and natural selection. These included both psychological and physiological processes for reintegrating and reestablishing the self-regulating internal equilibrium. It was Bernard who wrote that "the phenomena of living beings must be considered as a harmonious whole" (1865, p. 226).

We can thus see that a fundamental property of every living organism, at every stage of its existence, is the capacity for adaptive response to its external environment which allows for a state of balance in its internal milieu. Natural selection seems to have favored those individuals and species that possess the greatest power of responsive plasticity of the individual within the optimal range of adaptation. Both the theory of evolution and that of the dynamic steady state or homeostatic adaptation are necessary to the understanding of human responses to psychological and physiological stresses both external and internal. We must have adaptation to the environment now, and the capacity for it in future, if smooth functioning is to be secured.

Adaptation involves a series of processes that are goal-directed and designed to facilitate the establishment of a state of equilibrium between the organism and its environment. In some instances the optimal level of equilibrium is fixed and various mechanisms attempt to adjust to this constancy. In other situations, devices are utilized to allow for a state as close to the optimal as possible. In any event the adaptational process is a dynamic one, having its roots in the biological structure and constantly attempting to balance intersystemic and intrasystemic tensions by way of the ego (Hartmann, 1939).

Phylogenetic evolution has been directed toward allowing the organism increased independence of its environment, but this freedom is operative only within a certain range. As biological evolution has proceeded there has been a concomitant internalization of vital structures and functions. This applies to essential physiological, anatomical, and psychological process and structures. We may view the appearance of intrapsychic structures along this continuum of evolving internalization. The simplest unicellular organism operates on the uncomplicated stimulus-response level. Man also may in some instances do this, but he can perceive many stimuli which can be internally understood and stored without any immediate external response. Hartmann (1939) suggests that animals may have some kind of ego, though it is not comparable to that which we think is present in man. He feels that, in lower animals, reality relationships provide the patterns for the aims and means of pleasure-gain to a greater extent than they do in adult man. In view of Freud's "Formulations on the Two Principles of Mental Functioning" (1911), this statement can be elaborated to indicate that certain infrahuman species, as well as the egos of very young children, operate primarily on the basis of the pleasure principle, whereas more mature and integrated human egos function in accordance with the reality principle and utilize secondary process thinking which includes intrapsychic representations of external objects and memory. Pleasure principle operations view the object mainly in terms of the function it performs for the individual being, namely that of the reduction of tension. Only with greater maturation and development does the object become differentiated as an individual entity with distinct personal characteristics of its own in addition to those that are overtly functional. We see that psychological adaptation may occur at levels which have phylogenetic significance as well as ontogenetic importance.

Hartmann differentiates the state of adaptedness from the adaptive process which brings this state about. In this adaptive process, various defensive techniques are utilized. But "adaptation achievements may turn into adaptation disturbances" (1939, p. 54), when reality situations are altered. Thus when an object relationship is interrupted by the death of one of the significant participants, a new ego-adaptive process has to be instituted in order to deal with the altered internal-external psychological situation. Where there is a possibility of substitution with little difficulty, the adaptive task may be easily accomplished, as is the case with certain animals and very young infants. But when the lost object has taken on psychic significance in addition to functional fulfillment, the adaptive process involves in part an undoing of the previous adaptational equilibrium established with that object, and the gradual reestablishment of new relationships with reality-present figures. The complex adaptive process instituted in such a situation is called mourning.

A process may come about in one of two ways. There may be the stepwise series of consecutively followed specific stages, or the situation where many stages exist simultaneously and concomitantly. Even in this latter type of process, where varying intermediate phases are present at the same time, there are quantitative differences between the varying stages, but definite starting and end points may be ascertained. In the intermediate phases of the process, reactions and interactions may have inhibitory, facilitatory, or neutralizing effects.

It is only by carefully studying each component part that we can gain an approximate appreciation of the complex relationship of the entire process. For the sake of simplicity, this second type of process may be described as if it occurred in seemingly isolated consecutive steps, although this may not be so in fact.

The mourning process consists of a series of operations and stages whose appearance seems to follow a sequential pattern. In line with the above, however, it is necessary to indicate that although certain aspects of the process are more apparent at particular times, the succession of one stage by another does not necessarily indicate that a former stage may not be present later in time, or that a later one was not in evidence earlier.

THE MOURNING PROCESS IN MAN

Psychological lesions result when there is a disruption of the state of equilibrium that is established to allow for optimal functioning. As indicated above, reactions evoked by the upset in adaptation give rise to a process designed to reestablish an intrapsychic homeostatic steady state. Characteristically, mourning refers to the response following the death of a meaningful figure. As will be postulated below, this mourning reaction is an ego-adaptive process which includes the reaction to the loss of the object, as well as the readjustment to an external environment wherein this object no longer exists in reality. The mourning process is not species specific, and is obviously intrapsychic, as the external loss cannot be undone. Usually we assume that mourning and the reaction to permanent loss without death are equivalent. This equation, though not rejected, requires further demonstration. Differences may be present which allow for more precise description.

The antemortem nature of the relationship between the bereaved and the deceased will be an important factor in the resultant mourning process. The type of ego development, maturation, and the level of integration and organization, however, will be the crucial variables in determining the course and extent of the mourning process. Thus an ego that has developed to the point where reality is correctly perceived, and objects distinctly and uniquely differentiated, will mourn differently from an ego that is poorly integrated and immature.

Historical Considerations

In a discussion attached to the case history of Fraulein Elisabeth von R, which appeared in the *Studies on Hysteria* (1893–1895), Breuer and Freud described[1]

[1] Acknowledgment is made to Sigmund Freud Copyrights Ltd., the Institute of Psycho-Analysis, and the Hogarth Press for permission to quote from *The Standard Edition of the Complete Psychological Works of Sigmund Freud*, translated and edited by James Strachey.

a highly-gifted lady who suffers from slight nervous states and whose whole character bears evidence of hysteria, though she has never had to seek medical help or been unable to carry on her duties. She has already nursed to the end three of four of those whom she loved. Each time she reached a state of complete exhaustion; but she did not fall ill after these tragic efforts. Shortly after her patient's death, however, there would begin in her a work of reproduction which once more brought up before her eyes the scenes of the illness and death. Every day she would go through each impression once more, would weep over it and console herself—at her leisure, one might say. This process of dealing with her impressions was dovetailed into her everyday tasks without the two activities interfering with each other. The whole thing would pass through her mind in chronological sequence. I cannot say whether the work of recollection corresponded day by day with the past [p. 162].

An editorial comment in the *Standard Edition* at this point indicates that this account of the "work of recollection" anticipated Freud's later concept of the "work of mourning" (p. 162).

Freud goes on to say that "in addition to these outbursts of weeping with which she made up arrears and which followed close upon the fatal termination of the illness, this lady celebrated annual festivals of remembrance at the period of her various catastrophes, and on these occasions her vivid visual reproduction and expressions of feeling kept to the date precisely" (1893, pp. 162–163). Freud gives a specific instance of this woman crying actively on the occasion of her husband's death which had occurred three years earlier.

This careful clinical description not only presented Freud's precursory ideas referable to the mourning work, but also was the first conceptualization of what we now call anniversary reactions. This type of reaction, more currently rediscovered and elaborated upon, is clearly a variation and an incomplete form of the mourning process. In the patient described by Freud, these observations are made only in passing, but in retrospect they already predict some of his later significant contributions.

In 1895 in Draft G on Melancholia, Freud related depression and melancholia to mourning and grief. He spoke of a "longing for something that is lost," and "a loss in the subject's instinctual life." Again anticipating his later formulations, he also commented that "the uncoupling of associations is always painful." In Draft N, written on May 31, 1897, Freud not only gave us the first hint of the Oedipus complex, but also connected mourning with melancholia. This comparison he further commented on in his 1910 discussion of suicide, where he referred to the "affect of mourning."

Freud described mourning as a normal emotional process in his *Five Lectures on Psycho-Analysis* (1910 [1909]), and in the same year in his "Notes Upon a Case of Obsessional Neurosis" (1909), he states that "I told him, a normal period of mourning would last from one to two years" (p. 186). The essays on *Totem and Taboo* (1912–1913) further develop Freud's ideas on the mourning process. He writes that "mourning has a quite specific psychical task to perform: its function is to detach the survivors' memories and hopes from the dead. When this has been achieved, the pain grows less and with it the remorse and self-reproach" (p. 65). In the same work Freud points out that after a death both affection and hostility to the deceased exist. The mourning relates to the positive feelings, while satisfaction is the reaction of triumph related to the hostile feelings. The hostility, however, is repressed and becomes unconscious, because the mourning process which derives from an intensification of the loving feelings does not allow of any satisfaction. But this hostility may be dealt with by projection onto the dead object, and this gives rise to the fear of the dead. This phenomenon also is related to the feelings of anger which will be discussed below.

In January 1914, Freud spoke to Jones about his paper on mourning and melancholia, and in December of that year he presented his ideas to the Vienna Psychoanalytic Society. He wrote his first draft in February 1915, and the manuscript was finished in May 1915. In March and April 1915, Freud wrote his paper "Thoughts for the Times on War and Death." In November 1915, Freud's "On Transience" was written, and published the following year.

In attempting a correlation of events in Freud's life with the appearance of these papers, we note that Freud's father died on October 23, 1896. In July 1897 Freud began his self-analysis, and on October 15, 1897, in a letter to Fliess announced his discovery of the Oedipus complex. Draft N, it seems, was written at a time when Freud himself was in the midst of working out his own mourning for his dead father. In 1910 the difficulties with Adler were increasing, and in 1911 the break with him actually occurred. In 1913 the dissension with Jung was very painful to Freud, and in 1914 came Jung's resignation from psychoanalytic associations. The distress these oppositions caused to Freud is well known. Although it is speculative, his more formal conceptualization of mourning may have been related to his grief over the loss of Jung and what Jung represented to him. The 1913 Congress was an unpleasant experience for Freud, and in 1914 Jung's formal separation occurred. In November 1914, Freud's beloved brother Emmanuel died in a railway accident. Jones states "eighty and a half, the age at which both his [Freud's] father and his brother Emmanuel had died" (Jones, 1957, p. 213). In December 1914, "Freud's spirits were low, and he begged Abraham to come and cheer him up" (1955, p. 176). It was in the same month that Freud spoke to the Vienna Society on mourning and melancholia in a discussion of a paper by Tausk on melancholia.

In 1915 Freud's two sons were actively involved in the war and he was quite concerned over them. Jones notes that "Freud had several dreams about calamities to his sons, which he interpreted as envy of their youth" (1955, p. 180). Many of his close associates (Abraham, Ferenczi, Rank, Sachs) were also on army service during this period. It was in 1915 that the three major works referred to above were written. We may infer that all the losses, disappointments, and threats undoubtedly influenced Freud, so that his introspective activities yielded insights on mourning that were reflected in his papers on this theme.

In his essay "On Transience" (1915b), Freud notes that individuals "recoil from anything that is painful," and so there is "a revolt in their minds against mourning." Thus thoughts about the transience of an object involve "a foretaste of mourning over its decease" with resultant avoidance of thoughts on this theme. Until the early 1960s surprisingly few investigations had been made of the mourning process per se by psychoanalysts and others involved in psychological research. Perhaps Freud's statements quoted above are in part an explanation of the apparent lack of study of this normal and omnipresent phenomenon.

In "Mourning and Melancholia" (1917 [1915]) Freud states that "mourning is regularly the reaction to the loss of a loved person, or to the loss of some abstraction which has taken the place of one, such as fatherland, liberty, an ideal, and so on" (p. 243). He indicates that a mourning process as such can occur after varying losses. The loss of the abstraction, however, is reacted to as if it were the intrapsychic object that is lost. In this investigation, the loss following the death of a significant figure will be the major source of clinical data, and the major definition of the mourning process. In the various clinical and theoretical reports appearing on this subject some terminological differences seem to confuse aspects of the mourning process. Thus grief is an affect that may follow on a multitude of situations. It is seen in the mourning process, but grief as such may be seen in situations where there is no such process. Transitory object loss in time and in space may give rise to various reactions that are components of the mourning process, but this again must be differentiated from the permanent loss in time and space of a significant object.

In *The Ego and The Id* (1923), Freud states that "the character of the ego is a precipitate of abandoned object-cathexes" as well as the recording of past "object-choices" (p. 29). Thus all prior frustrations and renunciations were seemingly followed by mourning processes. When viewed in this broad way, the mourning process becomes very significant, as it is apparently one of the more universal forms of adaptation and growth through structuralization available to man. Not all aspects of this process necessarily occur with every loss. In studying the response to the death of meaningful figures, various facets not usually seen in other types of frustration and loss may be described and delineated. Mourning may result when there is rejection by an object not by death, but the important focus here is on the resulting process and not necessarily on the precipitating event. We mourn something that is lost but previously had been strongly cathected, and through this process the ego is built.

Klein (1938) has commented on the close connection between the testing of reality in normal mourning and the early mental processes. It is her contention that the early mourning characteristic of the child's reactions to frustrations is revived and reexperienced whenever grief occurs in later life. Just as Freud has stressed the importance of reality testing as the most important part of the adult mourning work, so Klein emphasizes this ego activity in overcoming a mourninglike process seen in young children where in external reality no death has occurred.

In this paper an attempt will be made mainly to delineate and discuss more specifically the various stages of the mourning process as it customarily occurs in man after the death of an object. These findings will then in the final section be related to observations made on infrahuman responses to death. More deviant types of mourning reactions will be briefly mentioned.

Stages of the Mourning Process

In the mid-1950s, while intimately involved in a mourning adaptation of his own, the author had occasion to experience and observe more closely the changing aspects of the mourning process in himself and also in family members of various ages and developmental levels. As the mourning continued it became apparent that different aspects of the process could be distinguished. These stages consisted of a series of reactions occurring in a temporal sequence, having distinct degrees of acuteness and chronicity, and seemingly divided into component parts. Stimulated by these observations, a more systematic study of the mourning process was undertaken, and the following conclusions were arrived at.

When a death occurs, the first response is that of shock. This results from the sudden upset in ego equilibrium, and is related to the initial awareness that the object no longer exists in space, time, or person. The particular emotional orientation to this being is disrupted, and initially there is excessive stimulation due to this initial awareness that cannot be integrated. The overwhelming task may unsuccessfully be dealt with and result in a panic response, which includes shrieking, wailing, or moaning, or may be manifested by a complete collapse with paralysis and motor retardation. The behavior in this shock stage indicates acute regression to a much earlier ego-organizational level. The narcissistic loss, related to the resulting shock, is connected with the suddenness of the event. The phenomenon of narcissistic mortification is applicable to this shock state. There is "a sudden loss of control over external or internal reality, or both, by virtue of which the emotion of terror is produced, along with the damming up of narcissistic libido or destrudo" (Eidelberg, 1959, p. 163). The shock phase results when the ego is narcissistically immobilized by the suddenness and massiveness of the task that confronts it.

The response noted in this initial stage varies in intensity according to the suddenness of the death and the degree of preparation the ego underwent prior to the death. Thus death following chronic and prolonged serious illness is reacted to differently from the acute unexpected demise of a close object. Nonetheless, a shock response will be present in both situations, although the intensity will vary. Previous shocks of a similar kind may suddenly be catapulted into this most recent one and can result in a total regressive immobilization. In susceptible individuals this shock can be of such magnitude as to precipitate a serious somatic dysfunction such as thyrotoxicosis (Alexander, Ham, and Carmichael, 1951). In instances where death is anticipated as a result of a long-standing debilitation, acute mourning reactions may occur prior to the actual death. In several patients, whose parents were dying of malignant conditions, the shock response came when the patients first heard of the hopeless malignant diagnosis, and only very slightly when the actual death occurred. In these persons, the ego was able to react to the upset in present reality more gradually, so that when death supervened much preparation had already been done.

It is the sudden impingement of reality on the unprepared ego that results in an overwhelming of the stimulus barrier and the integrative capacity of the organism. Massive regression with panic can ensue until further restitutive activities take over. The duration of this shock phase is usually short, although the immobilization may persist owing to faulty later reparative reactions. It may be that the degree of shock ranges through a spectrum of responses depending upon the type of ego stimuli barriers that have previously been integrated.

The second stage in the mourning process, very closely

following the shock response, is the grief reaction. Darwin describes the physical aspects of this response in his *Expression of the Emotions in Man and Animals* (1872). He indicates that early grief is characterized by much muscular hyperactivity such as hand wringing, aimless wild walking, pulling of hair and clothes. Darwin interprets this behavior as indicative of the impotence the bereaved feels in terms of undoing the death that has just occurred. This frantic movement changes when it is realized that nothing can be done. Then deep despair and sorrow take over, and the sufferer becomes very quiet, sits motionless or gently rocks to and fro, sighs deeply, and becomes muscularly flaccid. All the facial features are lengthened and the characteristic grief appearance results. Darwin especially calls attention to the grief muscles, whose innervation results in the typical obliquity of the eyebrow and the depression of the corners of the mouth. As grief lessens, the change may be detected in muscular alterations even before feelings are altered. Lindemann has described the feelings of fatigue, exhaustion, and anorexia seen in this acute grief phase. The energy impoverishment seen in grief has been related to the mourning process by Freud in his *Inhibitions, Symptoms and Anxiety* (1926).

As the shock stage merges into the grief phase a subjective feeling of intense psychic pain is felt. The suffering ache is initially of much greater intensity than what subsequently follows in the later chronic grief phase. Accompanying this psychic pain may be the sudden screaming, yelling, and other nonverbal but vocal manifestations of this grief reaction. This acute initial response later becomes the more characteristic depression. The spasmodic crying changes to tearful lamentations, and gradually verbal communications become more frequent, though still accompanied by much sobbing.

What explanations can we seek for the phenomena described in this phase? Initially we must consider the "Formulations on the Two Principles of Mental Functioning" (1911) of Freud. The pleasure ego, operating under the pleasure-pain principle, strives for the release of tension and excitement. In the very young child this is completely related to the external object. Thus when there is an increase in excitation without release because the object is absent, pain results. With the death of the object, there is temporary ego disruption with regression to an ego state where the pleasure-pain principle is the chief axis of mental functioning. Since reality-principle functioning is temporarily abrogated, the capacity to wait for discharge and the ability to seek alternative ways of handling the increase in tension is very much diminished.

Thus the external reality loss so overwhelms the ego that immobilization and shock occur with regression to the earlier pleasure-pain principle operation. This pain may result from the heightened nondischarged "energic cathexis" due to the absence of the object. As greater ego integration occurs, reality-principle functioning and secondary process thinking return with the resulting amelioration of the psychic pain. Freud has noted the feeling of pain that occurs in mourning in his "Mourning and Melancholia" (1917 [1915]). In this paper, however, Freud initially refers to the pain as *Schmerz* and not *Unlust*, the "mental antithesis of pleasure," also translated as pain. Later he calls the pain that is present *Schmerz-Unlust*. It is my contention that this pain is both *Schmerz* and *Unlust*, and represents the regression to the earlier phase of mental functioning. The idea that the lost object can no longer hopefully fulfill the needs of the mourner seems to be the key point. This reality awareness, however, is more characteristic of the later chronic mourning process. This early intense pain is seemingly more closely tied to the reaction of frustration at not having the object there.

In his paper "On Narcissism" (1914) Freud notes that as libidinal interest and investment is withdrawn from a love object into the ego, there is a damming-up of libido in the ego. With this increase in tension, pain is experienced. This conceptualization allows us to view this aspect of the mourning process as analogous to the model of the actual neuroses. When the libido is discharged, the pain diminishes.

The pain phenomenon may alternatively be approached from the point of view of Federn (1952). Thus the object is gone and temporarily libido may be avulsed along with it. This can result in an ego impoverishment and an inability to bind stimuli so that withdrawal is the emergency adaptation to conserve libido by avoiding stimuli that additionally tax the ego. Regression to an earlier ego state requires less expenditure of ego cathexis. Utilizing this concept of ego depletion in mourning may assist in differentiating the reaction after the death of an object from that on the loss of an object not through death but through growth. Thus in analysis mourninglike reactions occur when childhood objects are given up. The grief involved in losing all retained relationships revived in the transference neurosis is not due to impoverishment. This latter is a living process leading to a particular goal of detachment. This process is different from the mourning following the actual death of a significant being. I cannot say whether the avulsion hypothesis or the "swelling" hypothesis causes the pain. Either phenomenon can result in this reaction, and further study is necessary to find specifically which is more significant.

Convergent evidence for the presence of pain is to be found in understanding the rather "animal-like" crying seen in the earlier phase of mourning. The cry is an alarm signal that is vocalized very early in life. In addition it expresses unpleasurable feelings and emotions. The cry is not only a proclamation of pain or some other nonpleasurable state, but is also the earlier form of vocal communication and command. It seems to announce that something undesired is present, and it usually arouses the simple and appropriate response on the part of those who hear it. Thus as "pain" occurs, it is accompanied initially by the primitive crying that is indicative of this pain. As the local communications become more verbal, the crying also seems to be less primitive and less wail-like, and the needs are expressed in more advanced ways.

With separation we get crying. This is commonly seen when a young child is spatially and temporally removed from its mother. It is also seen in adults on various occasions of parting. French (personal communication) has postulated that underlying the crying is the wish for reconciliation. In certain of the anthropoids this seems to be the case; initially, however, it is the cry of distress that accompanies separation from the mother. When the child becomes aware of the mother's respone to the crying, it may then become the signal for reconciliation in addition to its earlier significance.

In "Mourning and Melancholia" (1917 [1915]), Freud states that mourning work involves the testing of reality that shows that the loved object no longer exists and requires "that all the libido shall be withdrawn from its attachment to this object" (p. 244). Thus when reality-principle operation takes over, there is a consciousness of the external world without the departed object. This absence is not only perceived but is confirmed by repeated confrontations of the external world, and is finally noted and remembered. There may be a partial repression of the pain involved in the loss. This pain will be reexperienced periodically throughout the mourning process and the experience integrated in the later stage of mourning work. As the ego passes judgment on the truth and permanence of the loss, action and thought processes are utilized to facilitate appropriate alterations of reality with subsequent adaptation.

Fantasy making and daydreaming, however, not being dependent upon real objects and reality testing, still remain subordinated to the pleasure principle alone, and so repression remains as the all-powerful defense. Thus fantasies and daydreams concerning the deceased object can interfere with the mourning work, and in instances where the death of the object is not realistically appreciated, the object may continue to exist as an unassimilated introject with whom internal conversations can be carried on. This phenomenon has been observed in several patients who lost their parents in childhood. The use of fantasy defensively in ignoring reality is commonly seen in various clinical pictures. But the fantasied monologue and interior dialogue is quite frequently found in this phase of the mourning process.

In the "Formulation on the Two Principles of Mental Functioning" (1911), Freud relates a repetitive dream of a man whose father died after a long illness, the dream occurring months after the death. In it the father was alive again and the patient talked to him as of old. But as he did so "he felt it exceedingly painful that his father had really died, only without knowing it" (1911, p. 225). Freud in 1911, involved in working out problems of id psychology, related the pain to the dreamer's death wishes toward the father when he was alive. This pain, however, may have resulted from the awareness of the death as it has been described above, and in the dream we can see how the reality of the father's death is avoided by portraying him as alive, and yet the dreamer is simultaneously aware of the fact that he is dead. In other words, this dream represents the mourning work involved in partially accepting the father's death, yet at the same time avoiding this recognition.

In his paper on "Fetishism" (1927a), Freud discusses two male analysands who lost their fathers at the age of two and ten respectively. He mentions that each patient had refused to acknowledge his father's death, yet neither of them had developed a psychosis. On further investigation, Freud found that "only one current of their mental processes" had not accepted the father's death. "There was another which was fully aware of the fact; the one which was consistent with reality stood alongside the one which accorded with a wish" (p. 156). One of these cases was a severe obsessional and "in every situation in life he oscillated between two assumptions: the one, that his father was hindering his activities; the other, opposite, one, that he was entitled to regard himself as his father's successor" (p. 156). We can infer here that the patient's mourning process was such that he still could not accept the reality of the father's death. Freud (1938) points out that in certain states of conflict the synthetic function of the ego is abrogated and both reality and instinct may be satisfied at great cost. This type of non-synthetic ego functioning related to isolation may be the adaptive technique utilized by this patient.

In the chronic mourning stage, pain may continue to be felt. It is, however, less intense, less generalized, and less continuous, related to specific recollections or perceptions, and gradually extinguished. In the acute mourning phase the pain does not have these buffering characteristics.

In instances of chronic illness, these painful grief responses may antedate the actual death, as we have said above for the shock responses. The reaction here is that the loved person is already lost in the internal milieu, even though death has not yet occurred in reality. An individual speaking of a close relative who had recently been diagnosed as having a fatal illness, referred to the ill person in the past tense throughout the conversation. Spontaneously the speaker remarked, "You know he is dead for me already." This indicated that the internal loss and mourning process was already in motion. Mourning work is still required, however, after the actual death has occurred. If there is no evidence of it, it may represent a defensive short-circuiting of the process to avoid pain, and hence does not allow for full resolution and integration.

To be sure, any previous ambivalent feelings, conflicts, or

hostilities with death wishes can play an important part in the mourning process. The magical belief in the causality of the death with great guilt may be the major contributor to subsequent serious psychopathology. Freud discussed this point in his paper on "Dostoevsky and Parricide" (1928 [1927]). There he clearly related the predeath wish for the object's demise to the actual death of the object followed by a transient period of triumph and joy. This, however, quickly gave rise to guilt, and the self-punishing attitude persisted. In his biography, Jones mentions that when Freud was nineteen months old, his next younger sibling, a brother, died aged eight months. "In a letter to Fliess (1897) he [Freud] admits the evil wishes he had against his rival and adds that their fulfilment in his death had aroused self-reproaches, a tendency to which had remained ever since" (1953, p. 8). These self-reproaches can in susceptible persons result in abnormal mourning reactions, which may include melancholia and psychosis.

The third phase of the acute mourning process is that of the separation reaction. This may manifest itself in various ways, and will be more intense in individuals with earlier unresolved conflicts in this sphere. The reality of the loss intensifies this reaction, and initially recognition of the traumatic event may be avoided. Thus the absence of grief described by Deutsch (1937) may be involved in this inability to recognize that the object's absence is not temporary but permanent, and that the object is dead.

A patient talking of her inability to face the idea of her mother's death reported in an analytic session that to face it was "too difficult." Not only had she become aware of her grief and pain, but she was attempting to defend herself against what she described as feelings of "nothingness and emptiness." She gradually recognized that to mourn was to acknowledge the nothingness of her mother, and this meant emptiness inside her. Defensively she kept her mother alive in heaven and used "religion" as an aid to her ego in avoiding the "total nothingness of death."

The ego-adaptive task in this aspect of the mourning process requires a reorientation in the perceptual sphere involving both self and object. In order to master that part of the early anxiety experience related to separation, a total internalization is required, or a greater dependence on previously internalized and integrated relationships in the ego of object representations. Anna Freud (1936) has described this as object constancy. Where internal object representations are not well integrated, where tensions exist in the form of ambivalences unsolved and with nonneutralized aggression, the energy balance is seriously disturbed. The integrative task becomes greater at reconciling external reality with internal structures where the prior developmental pattern was defective or distorted.

The representation of the lost object is recathected because the instinctual energies that would have been discharged in actual relationship to the object, being now undischarged, recathect the internalized object image. Where there is poor differentiation between self and not-self, where there is poor ego integration, the hypercathected internal object may be projected and hallucinated as an external figure. The hallucinatory process in this instance is a manifestation of what happens when instinctual tension is not discharged because the real object is lost, and we have a primitive type of ego organization. Separation is not accepted and the lost object is hallucinatively retained.

Introjection and identification in terms of psychic structural formation relate to this point. Both, however, are internalization operations. If we view introjection as a process, mode, or technique, and identification as the end-result of the process in which introjection is initially present, the confusion between these two terms may be clarified and may shed light on subsequent mourning processes.

In a healthy object relationship, where there has been total assimilation or identification, the mourning process is comparatively short-lived, and comes to a spontaneous end. It may reflect whatever unresolved components of incorporation without identification are still present, but a comparatively healthy ego integration allows reality to be perceived, accepted, and dealt with appropriately without lasting ego immobilization. Grief is present, but is of such intensity and duration that it is not considered pathological. When an object has been introjected without identification, it exists as an encapsulated image in the ego as the result of the lack of assimilation. This introjected object retains characteristics of the original object, in many ways intensified as a result of the ambivalent feelings connected with the object. When the external object dies, an abnormal mourning process ensues. This may be reflected in the inability to accept the actual death of the object, and the retention of the introjected image with responses indicative of the fact that this introjected object still exists. Because of the lack of completeness of identification and ego integration, the ambivalences directed toward this object enhance the mourning process, if it occurs, with the formation of severe symptoms of melancholia or self-destruction, or both. When the actual death of the external object is totally denied with the absence of grief, what is found is a retention of the introjected object as an entity of the relationship, and this object is perpetuated externally by means of secret internal "communications" with this object. An example of this phenomenon has been observed in three adult patients, one of whom has been briefly discussed above.

In all the cases a parent had died prior to the patient's sixth birthday. Throughout the years there had been a retention of the deceased parent in the form of a fantasied figure who was in heaven; to whom the patient could talk and tell whatever he or she wished; who never verbally or actively responded to the patient; and who was always all-seeing and omnipresent. The fantasies about these retained figures came out with great caution and difficulty lest the patients be shamed for retaining these images. In all three instances the patients denied ever visiting the cemetery where the deceased parent was buried, and there was a period of amnesia that extended from the moment when the patient was told of the parent's death until many months later.

In one of these cases, the man's father died when he was a very young child, and his mother died when he was an adult. The process described above was observed in connection with his father's decease. In the case of his mother, however, he was able to accept her death, but continued to visit her grave regularly and to speak to her. He still envisioned her as alive, but not able to answer him.

This retention of the object as a figure that can be spoken to and envisioned, and the denial of its demise, interferes with mourning. When there has been incomplete identification, that is, when the identification process has not come about or has been arrested at a preliminary stage owing to immaturity or arrest of development, there is either a melancholic depressive response, or a denial of the death of the deceased with ego arrestation, distortion, or defect.

Patients report that following particular analytic hours they continue to talk to the analyst even though they have left his office. In these reports the analyst rarely answers, and as the analytic process proceeds, this "talking to the analyst as analyst" gradually diminishes and finally ceases with the integrated assumption of a "communication with self." It is maintained that in these instances a process occurs similar to that mentioned above, namely initial introjection of the analyst as an object with later identification and assimilation. He is retained in a somewhat encapsulated form with whom internal communication proceeds. When identification is complete, the introject is assimilated and the presence of the separate imago disappears.

In "Group Psychology and the Analysis of the Ego" (1921), Freud discusses the relationship of identifications to object cathexes and object relations. Object cathexis implies an object that is outside and energized. Identification is the process and end result wherein changes occur in the ego and actions take place without reference to the assimilated object. "Identification with an object that is renounced or lost as a substitute for that object" occurs through the "introjection of it into the ego" (p. 109). We assume that "identification is the earliest and original form of emotional tie with an object." Thus, "in a regressive way it becomes a substitute for a libidinal object-tie" by introjection. In identification with an object, the result is being like the object; in choosing the person as an object, the result is having the object. Identification may appear regressively and defensively in lieu of "object-choice." In mourning this defensive wholesale identification with the lost object can be used to avoid the painful resolution of mourning work.

In Freud's monumental *Inhibitions, Symptoms and Anxiety*, (1926), the last seven pages are directed to a discussion of anxiety, pain, and mourning. In this section, Freud differentiates mourning from anxiety, in that the former results from the loss of an object, while the latter is "a reaction to the danger of losing the object" (p. 169). In both responses there is pain, although it may be more clearly identified in the mourning reaction of the adult. Freud, citing the infant's response to the loss of the mother, even on a temporary basis, states that "the first determinant of anxiety which the ego itself introduces is loss of perception of the object (which is equated with loss of the object itself)" (p. 169). This antedates the fear of loss of love which has not as yet appeared. It is regression to this early stage of separation and its defenses that characterizes this phase of the mourning process.

The response to recognizing the separation and its permanence gives rise to anxiety and also to anger. Both these affects are experienced in the acute mourning stage. Defenses to deal with these threatening affects may quickly come into existence. Freud states that pain is "the actual reaction to the loss of the object, and anxiety is the reaction to the danger which that loss entails, and in its further displacement a reaction to the danger of the loss of the object itself" (1926, p. 170). This differentiation, though valid, need not be mutually exclusive. The object is dead and is no longer externally present. This results in pain, but also in anxiety. The ego cannot completely accept the reality and finality of the separation in time and space, and so anxiety about the loss is experienced. That part of the ego which regresses to pleasure-principle operation does feel the pain owing to the absence of the object. The later chronic mourning work is not characterized by excessive anxiety, as the object is more and more accepted as permanently gone. Instead pain continues "in view of the high degree and insatiable nature of the cathexis of longing which is concentrated on the object of the bereaved person during the reproduction of the situations in which he must undo the ties that attach him to it" (Freud, 1926, p. 172).

The anger at being left and frustrated is also characteristically part of the acute separation reaction. Typically it comes out in an undisguised fashion in children. They are frustrated and enraged. In adults, however, this anger may be displaced onto others, as hostility to the dead is not easily tolerated by the mourning ego. Thus physicians, hospital personnel, undertakers become the focus of displaced hostility. There may be accusations against close relatives, or even self-accusations about what the mourner could or should have done. This anger is usually unrealistic and unwarranted, and in the adult may not be present in identifiable form. It may fuse with the grief, and in the chronic mourning work be indicated by feelings of depression or through various guilt-expiating rituals.

When there is anger about the loss, it is indicative that the separation is recognized and acknowledged. In this sense anger is restitutive, as cathexis can be discharged through the affective experience of anger. Thus the anger is in the service of mastery of the shock, panic, and grief. As to the reasons for the anger, we must recognize that the rage is a narcissistic rage. It is as if the child is screaming "It happens to me and I have no control over it. It is the parents' fault and they should have prevented it." When the rage is discharged diffusely, frustration at being left is avoided, as is the feeling of helplessness.

Clinically, the frustration consequent on the death of a parent or spouse is due not only to the factors mentioned above, but also to the increased demand made upon the bereaved by the other survivors. Thus the child who loses a parent and is expected to fulfill the needs of the bereaved surviving parent suffers a double loss and is angry at this. The handling of the bereavement by the various mourners, as well as by the social mores and religious customs, can aid or reinforce various expressive and inhibitory activities involved in the mourning process. This latter point will be discussed elsewhere.

Separation anxiety may manifest itself in various ways. There may be a reluctance to be separated from the corpse. Thus one may look longingly and fixedly at it, at the coffin, or at the grave. There may be the false perception that the dead person is still breathing or moving. Afterwards there may be an inability to accept that the lost object is permanently gone. Thus, Queen Victoria ordered that her husband's study must not be disturbed in a single detail after his death. It almost seemed as though the reality of permanent separation could be avoided by keeping the room ready for occupation. Variations of this denial of separation may be manifested by displacement of cathexis from the object onto auxiliaries which are reminders of the departed. Thus old letters, keepsakes, portraits, eyeglasses, bits of hair, clothing, and other intimate possessions are treated as if they have to be constant reminders of the existence of the object. In some instances this reflects the inability to let the object die, be buried, and let life go on. In "Mourning and

Melancholia" (1917 [1915]), Freud notes that the struggle involved in abandoning a libido position previously occupied by a loved object could be so intense that "a turning away from reality" can result and the object "clung to through the medium of an hallucinatory wish-psychosis" (p. 244). Eventually, however, in the normal individual reality gains the day.

In mourning, libido detachment or object decathexis occurs topographically in the system unconscious. The process then proceeds through the preconscious into the conscious. It is here that reality perception can occur. When this path is blocked owing to ambivalence, as Freud pointed out in "Mourning and Melancholia," repression continues to operate and pathological mourning results.

The task of mourning consists of internal object decathexis with the freeing of energy for later recathectic activities. As Freud pointed out, this process may be stopped at the level of a hallucinatory wish-psychosis which denies the death of the object, or it may go on to completion wherein the ego becomes free and uninhibited when the mourning work is finished. The mourning process end result may stop at various intermediate steps short of completion. Thus one may get total or partial undifferentiated identification with the object, as was seen in the clinical data cited above, or on the side of completion of mourning, partially unneutralized cathexis that is only moderately changed though still bound and ego-inhibiting.

To recapitulate briefly, the acute stage of the mourning process refers to the immediate phases following the loss of the object. These phases consist of the shock, grief, pain, reaction to separation, and the beginning internal object decathexis with the recognition of the loss. The reaction to separation brings with it anxiety as the perception of the loss in time and space is integrated, as well as the anger reaction.

As the acute stage of the mourning process progresses, the chronic stage gradually takes over. Here we find various manifestations of adaptive mechanisms attempting to integrate the experience of the loss with reality so that life activities can go on. Adaptation in the chronic stage of mourning involves the further integration of newer reality demands which include newer functional need gratifications and demands. The ego is able to withstand the more immediate effects of the loss of the object and to begin the reparative aspect of the more lasting adaptation. Freud has described this chronic stage of the mourning process as the mourning work. This work is a continuation of the process that began more acutely immediately following the loss.

The sequential dreams occurring during the mourning process are indicators of this work of the ego. Changes occurring in the perception of the lost object in the dream reveal the gradual withdrawal of cathexis from the object and its associations. Thus in one instance, initial dreams of the departed object immediately after the death still kept the object alive, functioning, and communicating. Gradually the object disappeared from the dreams per se, and in late phases of the chronic mourning process, a dream was reported wherein an individual spoke of a funeral and burial that had occurred several months previously. Associations to the dream dealt with "finally accepting" that the figure was dead, buried although still remembered. Here the acceptance of the reality of the loss came about, and secondary process reality-principle–oriented behavior utilizing memory was in evidence.

Another patient reported that as he accepted the reality of the death of his father, his dreams began to lose color. Gray was the predominant shade, until one day a gray dream was reported as having a "sprig of green" in it. His associations dealt with "something coming to life again." It was as though the freed energy heralded "the arrival of spring, when things began to grow again after a long cold gray winter."

In analysis the mourning work can be followed by noting the varying restitutive ego activities. One of the patients mentioned above was unable to mourn, as it was indicative of the acceptance of the death. If the death was not accepted, then mourning was not going to occur. This patient at times even wondered if she had ever had a real mother. As the analysis proceeded, her great guilt toward her mother came out. The mother had died when the patient was four and a half. The multiple ambivalences overwhelmed the patient with excessive guilt and anxiety. This was strongly reinforced by the strong oedipal feelings toward the father. As the analysis continued, the mourning process gradually began and proceeded in the fashion described above. The transference neurosis provided this woman with objects that rekindled her repressed conflicts. Various shades of her mixed feelings emerged, and her dreams began to deal with meaningful figures. In a similar way to the dreams mentioned above, her early dreams dealt with the deceased object as being alive. This woman actually retained her mother in heaven as a live figure. Each night she spoke to her, and the patient "knew that mother" heard her. As the analyst was cathected, he became the replacement for the mother, and thus it was with him that conversations took place by night. With the energizing of the introject of the analyst, the mother was allowed to die, and the patient began to grieve, feel anxious, cry, and dream of meaningful figures who had died. This long and interesting analysis clearly indicated that the degree of ambivalence toward the dead object before the death occurred was related to the stage of psychic development achieved at the time of the loss. This ego distortion in part determined the length of the mourning work as well as the type of mourning reaction. In instances where melancholia or absent mourning occurs, we must look for the pathological interferences with the mourning process. It is not within the scope of this paper to discuss the effect of therapy on the mourning process. This problem has been dealt with by Fleming and Altschul (1959), and also by the present author elsewhere.

Any death in childhood, especially that of a parent, interferes with the growth and developmental processes of the gradual detachment of libido from infantile images of the object. These parental internalizations are important in the integration and structuralization of the ego and superego.

In considering the mourning process, it is imporant to note that similarities can be observed in all such adaptational activities. But there are significant differences also. First, the type of loss suffered must be considered. A permanent loss through death may be quite different from a temporary separation that is time-limited and not absolute. A sudden unexpected death results in a more acute response than a chronic loss due to institutionalization or even death. Second, we must recognize the significance of who or what is lost. The death of a parent in childhood differs from the death of a parent in adulthood. The death of the mother during the oedipal stage of a girl may have a different effect from what it has for an oedipal boy. The death of a sibling in childhood differs from the death of one's own child. The death of a spouse may be more significant than the loss of a political election in which there may be great involvement. It is difficult to generalize in this field, but further precision and delineation are necessary in our study of different types of losses and of the different objects that can be lost.

We must also recognize that the degree of maturity of the psychic apparatus of the mourner will be another important variable to investigate in the mourning process. Ego defects, distortions, or arrests cannot result in healthy mourning processes. The function of the lost object to the mourner is closely related to object replacement after the mourning process has ended.

In all probability the purest form of the mourning process occurs in mature adults. Even here, however, the loss of a child can never be fully integrated and totally accepted by the mother or the father. In an exchange of letters with Ludwig Binswanger (1957), Freud (letter dated April 11 and 12, 1929) wrote on the anniversary of his dead daughter's thirty-sixth birthday, "We know that the acute grief we feel after a loss will come to an end, but that we will remain inconsolable, and will never find a substitute. Everything that comes to take the place of the lost object, even if it fills it completely, nevertheless remains something different" (p. 84). In another note, Freud recalls that he cannot forget the younger child of his deceased daughter, who also had died several years earlier. About this child Freud wrote, "to me this child had taken the place of all of my children and other grandchildren, and since then, since Heinele's death, I don't care for my grandchildren any more, but find no joy in life either. This is also the secret of my indifference—it was called courage—towards the danger to my own life" (letter of October 15, 1926, quoted in Binswanger, 1957, pp. 78–79).

Freud touches on the possible different mourning reactions that may occur in later life and senescence. Energies may not be so freely available as internal objects may not be so easily decathected. What one can do with these liberated energies in older age differs from what may result earlier in life. Personal observations made on this point reveal that external objects may not be invested with the decathected libido, if it is available, by older people. More frequently, economic investments of less object-directed activities are made, and more narcissistic with-drawal occurs. Where there is an inability to make such shifts, too much ego depletion results and death may occur. It is not infrequently observed that shortly after the death of a long-standing marital partner, the survivor also succumbs. In these instances adaptation to life without the object is not possible.

The acute mourning reactions gradually become less in-tense and more distanced. As the ego is able to perceive reality correctly, various discharge techniques become more apparent. Little episodes that are suddenly recalled may serve as poignant reminders of the past. They may rekindle the dying fire of grief and tears for a short time. The response, however, is short-lived. There may be gradual acceptance of the fact that someone is not in a particular place at a specific time. Slips in conversation may indicate that the death of the object is still partially un-accepted. With the disposal of the dead figure's possessions, and having to deal with the alterations in practical reality, the ego begins to cathect new activities. True, the need to give up a house, a social group, or the like as a result of the separation may serve to institute new mourning processes and increase the integrative task of the ego, but these also are gradually worked through.

As personal possessions are dispersed, living arrangements altered, decisions made without reference to the lost object, the ego recognizes that narcissistic supply can be had elsewhere. Newer external objects become the focus of "give and take." These newer objects are seen not as exact substitutes for the lost objects, but as figures which permit reality relations that are mutually satisfactory. The loss of the dead object is assim-ilated, accepted, and the bereavement can come to an end.

Intrapsychically the object that is lost becomes part of the ego through identification. This may be manifested by activity such as a woman showed after the death and mourning for her husband. When confronted with a problem one day she said, "I deliberately looked at this in a way that my husband might have done had he been alive. I was surprised that I could hon-estly face it and deal with it in a way I never could have pre-viously." This identification with facets of the lost object is frequently seen after the death of a close relative. In part it may be due to an increased cathexis of the internalized object to overcome the effects of the external loss, and thus take over some of the functional activities that the dead object previously provided.

Identification with the analyst after the termination of analysis allows the process of self-analysis to continue. The observing ego of the patient becomes sufficiently expanded and integrated for observation, interpretation, and experiencing to occur autonomously and nonvolitionally. This healthy development is the end product following termination of a successful analysis. The mechanism is similar to though not the same as that following the successful completion of a mourning process. The ego is enriched and different, and can take over functions that were previously handled by the strongly cathected external object.

In the essay "On Transience" (1915b), Freud notes that mourning comes to a spontaneous end "when it has renounced everything that has been lost, then it has consumed itself, and one's libido is once more free (in so far as we are still young and active) to replace the lost objects by fresh ones equally or still more precious" (1915, p. 307). The lost object is not forgotten, nor is the new object identical with the lost one if the mourner's ego is capable of differentiation. The end of mourning occurs with a resultant identification in the form of a consciously decathected memory trace.

Sporadic episodes of mourning may still occur in connection with specific events or items, but these become fewer and less time-concentrated. New mourning experiences can serve to revive past mourning reactions that may still have bits of unresolved work present. In the instance of the loss of a very significant object, the total mourning process may never be completed.

Various religious rituals, when divested of their theological implications, emphasize the cultural evolution of mores and folkways which can defensively assist the ego in the adaptation involved in the mourning process (see chapter 12).

Mourning as a process of adaptation to a significant loss occurs in the attempt to maintain the constancy of the internal psychic equilibrium. The process consists of an acute and chronic stage. Various phases of these stages as well as their characteristic defensive operations have been presented. The ego's ability to perceive the reality of the loss; to appreciate the temporal and spatial permanence of the loss; to acknowledge the significance of the loss; to be able to deal with the acute sudden disruption following the loss with attendant fears of weakness, helplessness, frustration, rage, pain, and anger; to be able effectively to reinvest new objects or ideals with energy, and so reestablish different but satisfactory relationships, are the key factors in this process. The process has certain phenomena, utilizes certain mechanisms, and has a definite end point. Pathological interferences with it result in maladaptations with resultant psychopathology.

INFRAHUMAN RESPONSES TO DEATH

As mentioned in the first section of this presentation, the evolution of adaptive mechanisms and processes is related to survival of the species. When attempting to find information dealing with the phylogenetic roots of the mourning process, we quickly realize that little has been reported about the response of infrahuman animals to death. When accounts have appeared, they have usually been either anecdotal or detailed observational reports and inferences by field workers. Systematic investigations of this problem have not been made. In the examples cited below, the reported data will be presented and comparisons will be made to note any similarities with various component phases of the human mourning process.

Death is a universal biological phenomenon from which no individual animal other than certain protozoa escapes. Although a biological event, with the evolution of familial organization, and psychological internalizations and structuralizations, it has taken on psychosocial significance. Involved in this is the need to differentiate the mourning response for a meaningful deceased object from the significance of death as an event that may invovle the survivor himself. It is not my intention here to deal with the latter area except as it relates to the mourning response. Nature has seemingly evolved a homeostatic process to cope with the event of separation through death in the form of the mourning process in man. Investigating the responses of certain animals to the death of meaningful figures, I feel that the mourning process is an adaptation that has evolved phylogenetically. Although we cannot equate the responses observed in infrahuman animals to the events of the mourning process as it is characteristically seen in man, the strikingly parallel reactions in nonhuman animals to certain phases of the mourning process in man seems to indicate phylogenetic evolutionary anlage for the human mourning process.

Systematic observations and investigations of animals' responses to the death of a previously meaningful object have not been carried out. Reports of such events are found with great difficulty, and these are mainly behavioristic observations. Dr. Theodore C. Schneirla (personal communication), of the American Museum of Natural History, informed the author that behavior described as depression occurring after the removal of a meaningful figure has been observed in certain mammals and birds, but not in reptiles, amphibians, or fish. This would seemingly set a phylogenetic base for the development of this adaptational process. In this chapter, only the mammalian references will be cited.

It is common knowledge that dogs attached to their owners go through various grief and "mourning" responses when separations occur. A description of such an event, quoted from a newspaper account, stated that

> Corky, a small, forlorn fox terrier, ran away three times to sit in front of Our Lady of the Angels School, waiting for his mistress, Angelene. Angelene, 14, had died in the fire-scarred building. But Corky could not comprehend this. Three times the runaway dog was brought home to Angelene's mother, Mrs Julia Lechnik. Finally, she locked Corky inside the house. Mournfully the dog wandered to Angelene's room and crawled under her bed. Corky did not come out for four days. He neither ate nor slept. Towards Christmas, Corky at last began to perk up. "He'd still go to the front door in the afternoon, looking for Angie," Mrs Lechnik said. "But at least he began eating again."

Another report concerned a Japanese dog named Hachi:

> Born on 20 November, 1923, Hachi was sold a month later to a professor at Tokyo University. Hachi soon formed the habit of going to the railroad station with his master each morning, and waiting there until he returned from the university on the afternoon train.

When the professor died in 1925, his family moved to an-other part of Tokyo. Hachi, however, returned to the railroad station each day to await the master who would never return. He set out for the station in the morning and remained there until evening. Hachi made his daily trip to the station for ten years, until he died on 8 March, 1935.

Interestingly, a statue of Hachi was erected in front of the Tokyo railroad station with the inscription "The Faithful Dog, Hachi." In 1953, Japan issued a stamp in his honor.

Konrad Lorenz (1952, 1954), has also reported his own experiences of the faithful devotion shown him by his lupus-derived dogs. His pet, Stasi, refused to return to her young puppies when it interfered with her being with Lorenz. Lorenz has noted that a lupus dog (wolf-derived) who has once sworn his allegiance to a certain man, is forever a one-man dog. No stranger can take the master's place, and if the master leaves, the animal becomes "literally unbalanced," obeying no one and acting like "an ownerless cur." Lorenz has observed that lupus bitches seem to have a monogamous type of fidelity to a par-ticular dog, and in chows especially the oath of fidelity is seem-ingly irrevocable. Lorenz has advanced a theory that explains the difference in this fixed type of object relationship charac-teristic of wolf-derived dogs as contrasted with other canine varieties. It would carry us far afield to elaborate his hypo-thetical premises here. Instead it is interesting to note that the behavior described as grief, denial, and time-limited anorexia following the death of Angelene seems similar to what we see in man during acute phases of the mourning process. Corky seems to have been able eventually to accept his mistress's ab-sence, but Hachi (wolf-derived no doubt) presumably could not adapt to the change in his life.

Jones (1958) has described the behavior of a ewe when her lamb has died. The ewe does not wish to leave her dead lamb, and if she loses sight of it she "will race around and bleat in demented searching." In order to effect the adoption of another lamb by the "bereaved ewe," the farmer

quickly ties a length of twine to the lamb's neck and then, when the ewe is near, gives it a little tug. The ewe sees movement, fancies her lamb is alive, and makes to follow. The lamb is kept

moving with little tugs of the string until the ewe is following it
into the barn, where it is quickly whisked out of sight round the
corner and as rapidly as possible a live lamb is presented to the
questing mother [pp. 1512–1513].

We can infer from this report that the anxiety attendant
on the separation of the dead lamb from its mother is short-
lived when a viable substitute is carefully introduced as a new
object. Movement as an indicator of life is quite important in
sheep. When a viable moving lamb could be substituted for the
dead one, the ewe presumably did not know the difference
provided no delay occurred. The primitiveness of this response
is one that is akin to the functional substitution that is possible
for the human neonate in the early months of life. The association of life with bodily movement is also not limited to sheep.
We know it is frequently used as evidence of life or death by
man as well. Dr. Schneirla described the behavior of a cat,
reared with a rat, when the two were separated. The cat yowled,
cried, ate very little, and lost weight. Similar accounts for various
birds have been recorded by Lorenz and others. The reports
of the dogs, unlike that of the ewe, seem to indicate a reaction
that includes greater specificity and differentiation of the object.

Spitz (1946) writes that substitution of the mother or absence from the mother prior to the sixth month does not give
rise to anaclitic depression. If the mother was a "good" object,
removal after the sixth month for an unbroken period of three
months gave rise to anaclitic depression, whereas if the mother
had been a "bad" one, the incidence of depression was markedly
reduced, as was its severity when it occurred. Spitz relates these
findings to the ego organization in the second half of the first
year. The ego then can coordinate "elementary perception and
apperception," can coordinate elementary volitional motility,
and has "a capacity for elementary differentiation of affect as
is involved in the capacity to produce distinctly discernible positive or negative affective reactions on appropriate stimulation"
(p. 325). Before six months, the infant has achieved no loco-
motion and so is quite passive in its social demands from the
environment. The adult initiates all activity. In the sheep, the
response seemingly is that of the young child before the sixth

month of age. In both, substitution and equivalence are possible without difficulty.

The reports of simian responses to death are more impressive in connection with an evolutionary concept of the mourning process. Professor Sherwood L. Washburn, of the University of California at Berkeley, has sent me the following direct account of his observations of baboons:

> I witnessed one case of the relations of a mother to a dead baby baboon. One day I heard a tremendous scream of a kind I had not heard before. When I located the troop of baboons (a troop which I had seen repeatedly and knew well) I saw that one of the larger babies was dead. A baby of this size jumps on its mother's back when the troop moves and takes care of itself pretty well. The mother walked away from the baby, but the largest male of the troop refused to leave it and set up a terrific noise of screaming and barking until the mother came back. She then picked up the baby and carried it while walking on three legs. This process was repeated at least four or five times until the troop finally reached their sleeping trees.
>
> I believe this case is unique in that it was the leader of the troop who urged the mother back to the baby after she had left it. Small babies who die are carried by the mother without the urging of other baboons. I never saw this, but it has been observed many times [personal communication].

The need to deny death and effect separation is inferred from this first-hand report. Zuckerman (1932) also in studying baboons has found similar behavior indicative of the denial of death. Thus, young animals would cling to the carcasses of their dead mothers, or mothers would cling to their dead young, and in the London Zoological Gardens baboons as well as apes tried to prevent the removal of a dead animal as if it were the abduction of a live one. Even in the sexual sphere, "when a female baboon dies in a 'sexual fight' on Monkey Hill, the males continue to quarrel over her dead body, which they also use as a sexual object until it is forcibly removed by the keepers" (p. 298). This retention of the dead and attempt to treat it as still living is characteristic only for the higher anthropoids and man. Other species may show some response to the death of the object, but deal with the actual dead body as dead and having no functional appeal. Zuckerman concludes that "monkeys and apes . . . react to their dead companions as if the latter are alive but passive" (p. 298). This may be the manifestation of the primitive denial of death mechanisms relating to separation anxiety that is seen in early stages of mourning in man. Eissler (1955), however, feels that only the human species knows of death and that the apes are ignorant of it. This may be so; animals, however, can discern things that are not alive, so that responding to nonliving animals as if they were alive seems rather to involve a denial-like mechanism.

Chimpanzees seem to show even more dramatic responses to death. Brown in his paper "Grief in the Chimpanzee" (1879),[1] writing about the behavior of the surviving chimpanzee after his partner died, states:

> With the chimpanzee, the evidences of a certain degree of genuine grief were well marked. The two animals had lived together for many months, and were much attached to each other; they were seldom apart and generally had their arms about each other's neck; they never quarrelled, even over a pretended display of partiality by their keeper in feeding them, and if occasion required one to be handled with any degree of force, the other was always prepared to do battle in its behalf on the first cry of fright. After the death of the female, which took place early in the morning, the remaining one made many attempts to rouse her, and when he found this to be impossible his rage and grief were painful to witness. Tearing the hair, or rather snatching at the short hair on his head, was always one of his common expressions of extreme anger, and was now largely indulged in, but the ordinary yell of rage which he set up at first, finally changed to a cry which the keeper of the animals assures me he had never heard before, and which would be most nearly represented by hah-ah-ah-ah-ah, uttered somewhat under the breath, and with a plaintive sound like a moan. With this he made repeated efforts to arouse her, lifting up her head and hands, pushing her violently and rolling her over. After her body was removed from the cage—a proceeding which he violently opposed—he became more quiet, and remained so as long as his keeper was with him, but catching sight of the body once when the door was opened

[1] Permission to quote from this work has been granted by the University of Chicago Press.

and again when it was carried past the front of the cage, he became violent, and cried for the rest of the day. The day following, he sat still most of the time and moaned continuously—this gradually passed away, however, and from that time he has only manifested a sense of a change in his surroundings by a more devoted attachment to his keeper, and a longer fit of anger when he leaves him. On these occasions it is curious to observe that the plaintive cry first heard when the female died is frequently, though not always, made use of, and when present, is heard towards the close of the fit of anger. It may well be that this sound having been specialized as a note of grief, and in this case never having been previously called into use by the occurrence of its proper emotion, now finds expression on the return of even the lesser degree of the same feeling given rise to by the absence of his keeper, and follows the first outbreak of rage in the same manner as the sobbing of a child in the natural sequence of a passionate fit of crying. It may be noted too, that as his attachment to his keeper is evidently stronger than when there was another to divide with him the attention which they received, the grief now caused by the man's absence would naturally be much stronger and a more exact representation of the gestures of grief would be made.

Notwithstanding the intensity of his sorrow at first, it seems sufficiently evident that now a vivid recollection of the nature of the past association is not present. To test this a mirror was placed before him, with the expectation that on seeing a figure so exactly like his lost mate, some of the customary signs of recognition would take place, but even by caressing and pretending to feed the figure in the glass, not a trace of the expected feeling could be excited. In fact, the only visible indication of a change of circumstances is that while the two of them were accustomed to sleep at night in each other's arms on a blanket on the floor, which they moved from place to place to suit their convenience, since the death of the one, the other has invariably slept on a cross-beam at the top of the cage, returning to inherited habit and showing, probably, that the apprehension of unseen dangers has been heightened by his sense of loneliness.

On looking over the field of animal emotion it seems evident that any high degree of permanence in grief of this nature belongs only to man; slight indications of its persistence in memory are visible in some of the higher animals and domesticated races, but in most of them the feeling appears to be excited only by the

failure of the inanimate body, while present to the sight, to perform the accustomed actions.

The foundation of the sentiment of grief is probably in a
perception of loss sustained in being deprived of services which
had been of use. An unrestrained indulgence in an emotion so
powerful as this has become in its higher forms would undoubtedly prevent due attention to the bodily necessities of the animal
subjected to it; in man, its prostrating effects are mainly coun-
teracted by an intelligent recognition of the desirability of re-
pairing the injury suffered, and in him, therefore, the feeling
may exist without serious detriment to his welfare, but among
the lower animals it would seem probable that any tendency to
its development would be checked by its own destructive effects—the feeling, for instance, would most frequently occur on
the death of a mate—a deep and lasting grief would then tend
to prevent a new association of like nature and would thus impede
the performance of the first function of an animal in its relation
to its kind—that of reproduction [pp. 173–175].

We can see illustrated here the shock, grief, and separation
anxiety stages characteristic of the acute mourning responses
of man. The sustained mourning work seemed, however, to be
absent. This phase of the mourning process seems to be
uniquely human. Brown suggests this is because of memory
differences. The difference in type of object relationships with
intrapsychic representation of specific objects and structuralizations would be the more precise explanation. The apparent
anger of the chimpanzee at his inability to rouse his dead companion is seemingly connected with the impotent grief activity
described above for man. To be sure, we might postulate that
this could be reflective of anger at being left or frustrated, but
this would be only a speculative interpretation of these data. In
our patients this anger response is often found, though concealed by the depression that is present.

Garner[1] (1900) has also reported extensively on the history
and observations made on a particular chimpanzee, Aaron,
which he studied extensively from the time of the animal's capture in the jungle until his death in captivity. I shall quote parts
of Garner's report, as they pertain to our present interest.

[1] Material from *Apes and Monkeys: Their Life and Language* by R. L. Garner
is reprinted by permission of Silver Burdett and Ginn.

At the time of his capture his mother was killed in the act of defending him from the cruel hunters. When she fell to the earth, mortally wounded, this brave little fellow stood by her trembling body defending it against her slayers, until he was overcome by superior force, seized by his captors, bound with strips of bark, and carried away into captivity [p. 145].

After he was captured, Aaron was placed with another chimpanzee, Moses. In time Moses fell ill, and the following reaction was reported:

At night, when they were put to rest, they lay cuddled up in each other's arms, and in the morning they were always found in the same close embrace.

But on the morning Moses died the conduct of Aaron was unlike anything I had observed before. When I approached their snug little house and drew aside the curtain, I found him sitting in one corner of the cage. His face wore a look of concern, as if he were aware that something awful had occurred. When I opened the door he neither moved nor uttered any sound. I do not know whether or not apes have any name for death, but they surely know what it is.

Moses was dead. His cold body lay in its usual place; but it was entirely covered over with the piece of canvas kept in the cage for bed-clothing. I do not know whether or not Aaron had covered him up, but he seemed to realize the situation. I took him by the hand and lifted him out of the cage, but he was reluctant. I had the body removed and placed on a bench about thirty feet away, in order to dissect it and prepare the skin and the skeleton for preservation. When I proceeded to do this, I had Aaron confined to the cage, lest he should annoy and hinder me at the work; but he cried and fretted until he was released. It is not meant that he shed tears over the loss of his companion, for the lachrymal glands and ducts are not developed in these apes; but they manifest concern and regret, which are motives of the passion of sorrow. But being left alone was the cause of Aaron's sorrow. When released he came and took his seat near the dead body, where he sat the whole day long and watched the operation.

After this Aaron was never quiet for a moment if he could see or hear me, until I secured another of his kind as companion for him; then his interest in me abated in a measure, but his affection for me remained intact . . . (pp. 151–152).

The new companion, Elisheba, a female, became ill and once more the opportunity to observe Aaron's reactions presented itself. Hour after hour Aaron sat holding her locked in his arms. He was not posing for a picture, nor was he aware how deeply his manners touched the human heart. Even the brawny men who work about the place paused to watch him in his tender offices to her, and his staid keeper was moved to pity by his kindness and his patience. For days she lingered on the verge of death. She became too feeble to sit up; but as she lay on her bed of straw, he sat by her side, resting his folded arms upon her and refusing to allow anyone to touch her. His look of deep concern showed that he felt the gravity of her case in a degree that bordered on grief. He was grave and silent, as if he foresaw the sad end that was near at hand. My frequent visits were a source of comfort to him, and he evinced a pleasure in my coming.

On the morning of her decease I found him sitting by her as usual. At my approach he quietly rose to his feet and advanced to the front of the cage. Opening the door, I put my arm in and caressed him. He looked into my face and then at the prostrate form of his mate. The last dim sparks of life were not yet gone out, as the slight motion of the breast betrayed; but the limbs were cold and limp. While I leaned over to examine more closely, he crouched down by her side and watched with deep concern to see the result. I laid my hand upon her heart to ascertain if the last hope was gone; he looked at me, and then placed his own hand by the side of mine, and held it there as if he knew the purport of the act.

At length the breast grew still, and the feeble beating of the heart ceased. The lips were parted, and the dim eyes were half-way closed; but he sat by as if she were asleep. The sturdy keeper came to remove the body from the cage; but Aaron clung to it and refused to allow him to touch it. I took the little mourner in my arms, but he watched the keeper jealously and did not want him to remove or disturb the body. It was laid on a bunch of straw in front of the cage, and he was returned to his place; but he clung to me so firmly that it was difficult to release his hold. He cried in a piteous tone and fretted and worried, as if he fully realized the worst. The body was then removed from view, but poor little Aaron was not consoled.

After this he grew more attached to me than ever. When I went to visit him he was happy and cheerful in my presence; but the keeper said that while I was away he was often gloomy and morose. As long as he could see me or hear my voice, he would fret and cry for me to come to him. When I had left him, he would scream as long as he had any hope of inducing me to return.

A few days after the death of Elisheba the keeper put a young monkey in the cage with him, for company. This gave him some relief from the monotony of his own society, but never quite filled the place of the lost one. With this little friend, however, he amused himself in many ways. He nursed it so zealously and hugged it so tightly that the poor little monkey was often glad to escape from him in order to have a rest. But the task of catching it again afforded him almost as much pleasure as he found in nursing it.

Shortly after Elisheba's death, Aaron himself died. Not having been present during his short illness or at the time of his death, I cannot relate any of the scenes accompanying them; but the kind old keeper who attended him declares that he never became reconciled to the death of Elisheba, and that his loneliness preyed upon him almost as much as the disease [pp. 170–173].

The description of Aaron's reactions, though colored by the sentimental terms used by Garner, could seemingly be a behavioristic account of the acute mourning phase in man. Again we have no evidence of mourning work per se, but we have ample evidence of grieflike reactions following what seems to have been some form of meaningful object relationship. The possible utilization of Garner as a new object after Moses' death bears some similarity to the recathectic phase following the completion of the mourning work.

Yerkes (1925) has described the screaming responses of survivors in gorillas and monkeys, as well as in chimpanzees. In other reports (Yerkes and Yerkes, 1929), surviving animals insisted on following the body of the deceased companion when it was removed, and on being prevented from doing this, cried for a while, and then became listless and spiritless for several days. They further state "that depression, grief, and sorrow are occasionally manifested by the chimpanzee is beyond dispute. Definitely established also is the fact that weeping in the human sense does not occur. The typical approach to it is whining, moaning, or crying in the manner of a person in distress. Tears we have never observed" (p. 299).

This tearless moan has been reported to the author by two patients. In one instance when the patient first saw the corpse of his mother, he cried and screamed in what was described as "an inhuman howl." He had no tears. In the second case, the patient on hearing of the death of her mother screamed and shrieked "like an animal" but without tears. In both instances the tears occurred after the shock period passed and the grief phase came into focus. This crying response, unlike the tears accompanying grief and depression, is very rarely recovered in any but the original stimulating situation. It is transitory, but undoubtedly is a most primitive means of communication of the unpleasant affect accompanying the first awareness of the death of the object. This initial human reaction, though infrequently reported in man, seems to be more common in anthropoids.

The cry heard in the howling monkeys when there is an acute separation from the mother has been described by Carpenter (1942). It serves initially to indicate distress in the young animal and can signal retrieving activity. Concomitantly, the mother wails and groans until recovery of the infant occurs. The cries of the infant serve as cues which localize it for the other animals that might retrieve it, while the mother's wails not only express her distress, but focus the activities of the clan on recovery of the infant, while also producing stimulation to which the infant may orient and move. Carpenter has been able to distinguish and categorize these cries so that they can be identified.

Carpenter, studying gibbons, has also identified the separation cry of the infant. In gibbons, the family groupings are monogamous, and are inferred to be relatively stable. Thus the tie between infant and mother may more clearly approximate to that of the human infant. Carpenter has reported an interesting observation on the mother–dead child interaction. He states: "I have observed two rhesus mothers which carried dead babies until only the skin and skeletons remained. They guarded these remains persistently for over three days and seemed confused by the lack of normal responses on the part of the dead infants" (1942, p. 355). He reported no crying on the part of the mothers, but Garner has noted that monkeys do not talk when alone, so perhaps the auditory signals between the mothers were sufficient stimuli and this more distressed response was not evoked.

On the basis of the above data and discussion, the hypothesis is advanced that infrahuman mammals do show responses to the death of significant figures in their environment. The anthropoids and chimpanzees particularly seem to react in a fashion similar to those of the acute mourning stages as seen in man. No data or evidence exists that true mourning work occurs after the acute reactions. The level of ego functioning in these animals would be comparable to that of a very young pleasure-seeking child. Further investigations of mourning responses in children of various developmental levels of integration are needed to complete our ontogenetic picture of this process of adaptation. It is to be hoped that anthropologists and psychologists may also assist in providing us with additional facts that can confirm or refute the propositions presented in this section.

SUMMARY

The mourning process as an adaptational adjustment of the internal psychic milieu to an altered external milieu has been discussed. This process involves the series of responses to the loss of the object as well as the later reparative aspects of the process. Adaptation must include the capacity to adjust to the failure of a prior adaptation, as well as the capacity to make the initial adaptation. One example of this situation is seen in the response to the death of a significant object. In man, the object relationships that existed prior to death can become antiadaptational after that object is no longer in existence. In order to reestablish ego equilibrium, a mourning process begins. This process consists of an acute and a chronic stage. The first stage may seemingly be seen in mammalia and birds, especially in chimpanzees and baboons. The chronic mourning stage, consisting mainly of the mourning work of object decathexis, is predicated on a qualitatively different type of psychic organization characteristic of the more mature human ego (intrapsychic differentiation and object representation, memory, reality-principle secondary process thinking). Apparently phylogenetic evolution has allowed, through natural selection, for additional adaptation with new object ties after reality has interfered with a prior object relationship. In man object replacement after death depends upon the instinctual needs of the mourner, the degree of energy liberation or replenishment resulting from the mourning process, and the maturity of the ego and the superego. The cathexis of new objects is not part of the mourning process per se, but an indicator of its degree of resolution. The objects newly chosen may be substitutes or replacements, but are rarely exact equivalents for the lost object.

2
CHILDHOOD PARENT AND SIBLING LOSS IN ADULT PATIENTS: A COMPARATIVE STUDY

Stimulated by the report of Hilgard (1960), in which she called attention to the temporal coincidence of anniversary reactions in hospitalized patients with histories of childhood parent loss, and by the psychoanalytic observations of Fleming and her collaborators (Fleming, Altschul, Zielinski, and Forman, 1958) who have investigated the effect of orphanhood in childhood on ego development and the formation of a transference neurosis, the author undertook the review of all of the cases that he had seen in his office practice over an eight-year period, where there had been either parental or sibling deaths prior to the patient's nineteenth birthday. The purpose of this communication is to present and briefly discuss the results of this survey and to indicate areas for future study.

METHOD OF INVESTIGATION

The general population in this investigation consisted of all patients personally evaluated by the author over an eight-year span in his private psychiatric office practice. These patients were unselected by the author and were referred by other physicians (psychiatrists and nonpsychiatrists), by auxiliary medical

Support given by the Foundations' Fund for Research in Psychiatry during the preparation of this manuscript is gratefully acknowledged.

I wish to thank Dr. Donald W. Fiske of the University of Chicago for his statistical consultations on this project.

Reprinted from the *Archives of General Psychiatry* 7:295–305 (1962). Copyright 1962, by American Medical Association.

personnel, by community and private agencies, and by former patients or their relatives and friends. These were not, however, patients randomly distributed in the general population. They were referred for a private psychiatric evaluation and recommendations because they could financially afford this and because the referring source felt that the patient could benefit from this consultation and subsequent therapy if it was indicated.

Either at the time of the initial interviews or shortly thereafter a written anamnesis was prepared. This case record included pertinent historical and actuarial information, data concerning the patients' difficulties, defensive activities, and prior adaptational accommodations. A preliminary diagnostic evaluation was appended to the written record as was the summary of recommendations when the patient was referred elsewhere. These case records have been filed consecutively. In instances where the patients were treated by the author for varying periods of time beyond the initial evaluation, subsequent data were obviously obtained and in selected instances recorded in great detail. In this paper, however, the information utilized is mainly from the initial anamnestic records.

All of the records were reviewed, and those patients who had lost one or both parents and/or siblings prior to their nineteenth birthdays were selected for the statistical tabulation to be presented below. Parental and sibling deaths were the variables studied. It is understood that death of parents or siblings is not a single isolated variable but that the adaptations that the child had to make prior to the loss and as a survivor might be crucial determinants of later adjustments. However, in this survey death occurring at a particular stage in the child's development was selected as a reality trauma to be investigated. The death is not viewed as the causation of psychopathology. The emotional difficulties may have preceded the actual decease of the close relative. However, the death required additional adaptations. These obviously involved intrapsychic mourning or denial of such, along with the altered external reality factors resulting from the reality loss and its impact on the total milieu of the child.

In this study, parental or sibling loss is defined as confirmed biological death. This death resulted from acute or chronic disease, accident, murder, or suicide. Excluded from the experimental population, but included in the general patient population, were instances of permanent parental separation due to abandonment, desertion, hospitalization, divorce, or permanent political detention without proof of death. Miscarriages were not included in the sibling death category. It is fully appreciated that all of these latter situations dynamically may be equated to death in the mind of the child; however, for purposes of this investigation the noted limitations were followed. In some instances distortion and repression of dates with retrospective amnesia or falsification occurs. In this series, however, those patients who were intensively treated, usually tended to confuse events or repress feelings in connection with the deaths rather than markedly misconstrue ages. However, this consideration is noted as a possible source of error.

Correlational studies will be made of the socioeconomic level of these patients at the time that they were initially seen as well as of the income and educational standards existing in their childhood families to note if these are of any significance. In the main, this patient grouping was of the middle-middle and upper-middle class at time of the original consultation, and in most instances the patients came from similar backgrounds. Additional investigation will be made of the patient's exact position in the family at the time of the loss, the presence or absence of a replacement for the deceased relative, the type of relationship existing with the surviving parent or sibling after the loss, as well as the type of psychopathology presented by the patient when he was initially seen. An attempt will be made to describe and delineate further any similarities and contrasts noted in patients whose losses occurred during the same developmental period. For now, however, the following results are presented.

RESULTING DATA

A total of 380 patients were seen in the eight-year period covered by this survey. There were 183 women and 197 men. In Table 2.1, the actual numbers of parent loss and sibling loss cases are given, as are the equivalent percentages of the total patient census. It will be noted that 16.9 percent of the women

TABLE 2.1

	Combined Total	Female	Male
No. Patients	380	183	197
Father Loss Only	42	31(16.9%)	11(5.6%)
Mother Loss Only	16	6(3.3%)	10(5.1%)
Father & Mother Loss	6	2(1.1%)	4(2.0%)
Father & Sibling Loss	4	2(1.1%)	2(1.0%)
Mother & Sibling Loss	4	2(1.1%)	2(1.0%)
Sibling Loss	20	5(2.7%)	15(7.6%)
Total Parental Loss	72	43(23.5%)	29(14.7%)
Total Sibling Loss	28	9(4.9%)	19(9.6%)
Total Parental & Sibling Loss	92	48(26.2%)	44(22.3%)

were father-loss cases in contrast to 5.6 percent of the men. These figures exclude cases involving more than one loss. The women showed 3.3 percent having lost their mothers, in comparison to the 5.1 percent of the men. Thus we find a 3:1 ratio of father loss for women to men, and approximately a 3:5 ratio for mother loss for female to male patients. The proportions of father loss for women and men are significantly different ($p < 0.001$). The proportions for mother loss are not.

When sibling loss alone is considered, we find 2.7 percent of the women lost siblings, while 7.6 percent of the men reported this. The ratio here becomes approximately 3:8 for female:male patients. This difference is also significant ($p < 0.05$). Since some patients lost both parents and siblings during childhood, these combined figures are presented in the table. It will be observed that the female patients had an appreciably higher rate of parent loss than the male patients, whereas the male patients had twice the number of sibling deaths as the female patients.

In Table 2.2, the age range of the loss population at the time of the initial evaluation is presented. More than half of the women seen were in the nineteen to thirty-year range. Almost half of the male patients, however, were in the thirty to forty-year bracket. This data permits us to compare it with statistical information from the 1959 *Statistical Abstract of the United States*

(Table 2.3). The 1920 figures are applicable for males in the thirty to forty range. The government figures are for orphanhood under age eighteen in contrast to the age of nineteen which is used in this study. Also, the government statistics are for the entire population, while the survey figures are for an ambulatory psychiatric office population. Keeping these limitations in mind we find that for 1920 there were 8.5 percent of the child population that were paternal orphans, 5.9 percent that were maternal orphans, and 1.9 percent that were full orphans. This is in contrast to 6.6 percent of the male experimental population who were paternal orphans, 6.1 percent who were maternal orphans, and 2.0 percent who were total

TABLE 2.2
Age Range of Loss Population at Time of Initial Appointment

Age		
19-30	25	11
30-40	11	21
40-50	10	5
50-60	2	7
Total	48	44

TABLE 2.3
No. 378*: Orphans,† by Type, 1920 to 1958, and by Age, 1958

Date, Item	All Orphans	Paternal Orphans Only	Maternal Orphans Only	Full Orphans
1920:				
No.	6,400	3,350	2,300	750
% of child population	16.3	8.5	5.9	1.9
1930:				
No.	5,050	2,700	1,900	450
% of child population	11.7	6.3	4.4	1.1

* *Statistical Abstract of the United States, 1959*, 80th Annual Edition, U.S. Department of Commerce, Social Insurance and Welfare Services, p. 292.
† In Thousands. Orphans refer to children under age eighteen who have been orphaned at any time; full orphan refers to loss of both parents, paternal orphan to loss of father, maternal orphan to loss of mother. Age on last birthday.

orphans. The only difference to be pointed out is that the male experimental population does not differ significantly from the census figures using χ^2. To be sure, not all of the male patients were comparable to the 1920 figures, but when reference is made to the 1930 statistics, the percentage of father loss is still less than the figures for the general child population.

When one examines the experimental female population one notes that the incidence of paternal orphanhood is twice that of the 1920 statistics and almost three times that of the 1930 figures. This difference is highly significant ($p < 0.001$). The maternal loss figures are lower in the experimental population (but not significantly so) than either set of comparable figures for the general population.

On this basis, the conclusion seems warranted that in female patients with parent loss through death in childhood there is a significantly higher incidence of father death and a not statistically significant lower incidence of mother death when compared with the general population. It is appreciated that the government statistics were gathered on children, whereas the present data were collected on adults; however, this discrepancy should only reduce the general statistics, since a certain percentage of these children did not survive beyond age nineteen themselves.

The different age level of the male and female population is brought out in Table 2.2. This is not necessarily a factor in accounting for the varying results seen; however, it cannot be overlooked as a potentially significant determinant. Although one can speculate about its meaning, only comparable data from the patient populations of other male and female therapists can establish its reliability and then lead to more precise conclusions about its validity.

In Table 2.4, the sibling loss data are presented. Nine women patients lost siblings in childhood, in contrast to nineteen male patients. (The difference is not significant: $p < 0.10$.) However, five women and fifteen men lost siblings but neither parent. (This difference is significant: $p < 0.05$.) The significant finding here is that eight of the nine women who lost siblings in childhood lost older siblings. However, of the nineteen male patients with twenty sibling losses in childhood (one patient lost an older and a younger sister), there were seventeen younger

TABLE 2.4
Sibling Loss

	Female	Male
Younger Brother	1	10
Older Brother	5	1
Younger Sister	0	7 (1)
Older Sister	3	2 (1)
	9	19 (20 siblings died)

siblings lost and only three older siblings who died. Again the sharp contrast between female and male patients is highly significant (excluding the double loss: $p < 0.002$). The difference is also significant for brother loss cases ($p < 0.02$) and nearly so for sister loss cases ($p < 0.07$). In the females, older brothers were the largest grouping of deceased siblings. This might be pertinent in view of the higher percentage of paternal orphanhood in female patients. In male patients, younger brothers' deaths was the largest category of the sibling deaths.

In Table 2.5, there is a breakdown of the male and female patient data into mother, father, or sibling loss along a time axis. In Table 2.6, there has been a condensation of the data in particular age categories that allows for a clearer presentation. In Table 2.6, the data presented in Table 2.5 are grouped into six developmental periods. The average number of deaths per year per developmental period is presented along with the total figures.

Starting with the data of the female patients in Table 2.6, we notice that three developmental periods stand out significantly in the parent loss figures. These are the Developmental Age Range Periods (DARP) that correspond to period A (birth–1 year), C (ages 3, 4, 5, 6), and F (ages 15, 16, 17, 18). It will be noted that this is equivalent roughly to the first year of life, the oedipal period, and the late adolescent period. In the female patients, the significant figures seem to be in the parent loss data. We observe that of the forty-five parental deaths, twenty-six, or 58 percent, occurred in adolescence, and ten, or 23 percent, occurred during the oedipal period. The

TABLE 2.5
Tabulation of Data*

Female Patients

Age at Loss	0	1	2	3	4	5	6	7	8	9	10	11	12	13	14	15	16	17	18
Mother Loss				1	2	1	1	1		1	1	1	1	1		1	1	1	1
Father Loss	4		2	1	2	2	1	1		1	1	1	2		2	3	5	4	5
Total	4		2	2	4	3	2	2		2	2	2	3	0	2	4	6	5	6
Sibling Loss		2	2		1	1	1	1		1	1	2	2	2	3	2	1	1	
Total		2	2		1	1	2	2		2	2	2	3	2	3	5	7	6	6

Male Patients

Age at Loss	0	1	2	3	4	5	6	7	8	9	10	11	12	13	14	15	16	17	18
Mother Loss	2	2	2		2	2	1		1		1	1	2	2	1	2	2		3
Father Loss	1	1		2	2	2	1	1		1		1	2	1	3	2	2	3	3
Total	3	3	2	2	4	5	2	2	1	1	1	2	4	3	4	5	2	3	6
Sibling Loss	2	2	4	2	2	3	1	1		1	2[B]	2	2	1[B]	1	2	2	2	2
Total	3	5	4	5	5	5	2	2	1	3	3	4	3	3	5	5	3	2	6

* The letter B indicates two sibling losses.

highest average figure occurred during the late adolescent period. When we refer back to Table 2.5, we find that of the twenty parental deaths occurring during late adolescence, seventeen were father deaths and three were mother deaths. Of the ten parental deaths occurring during the oedipal period, six were father deaths and four were mother deaths. The four parental deaths in the first year of life were all father deaths.

In Table 2.6, the figures for the male patients' parental loss present some discrepancies. The highest average figure is DARP B (ages 1, 2 years). This is not found in the female patients, and if significant, it may reflect a varying developmental capacity between male and female children. The next highest average figure is that of parental loss during late adolescence (DARP F). This average figure however is exactly half

TABLE 2.6
Tabulation of Data

Developmental Age Range Periods	Total Parent Loss	Ave., Yr.	Total Sibling Loss	Ave., Yr.	Total Loss	Ave., Yr.
Female Patients						
A. Birth-1 yr.	4	4.00	0	0	4	4.00
B. 1, 2	2	1.00	0	0	2	1.00
C. 3, 4, 5, 6	10	2.50	3	0.75	13	3.30
D. 7, 8, 9, 10	3	0.75	3	0.75	6	1.50
E. 11, 12, 13, 14	6	1.50	1	0.25	7	1.80
F. 15, 16, 17, 18	20	5.00	2	0.50	22	5.50
Total	45		9		54	
Male Patients						
A. Birth-1 yr.	2	2.00	1	1.00	3	3.00
B. 1, 2	6	3.00	1	0.50	7	3.50
C. 3, 4, 5, 6	7	1.80	7	1.80	14	3.50
D. 7, 8, 9, 10	2	0.50	4	1.00	6	1.50
E. 11, 12, 13, 14	6	1.50	3	0.75	9	2.30
F. 15, 16, 17, 18	10	2.50	4	1.00	14	3.50
Total	33		20		53	

Two female patients lost both parents.
Four male patients lost both parents; one male patient lost two siblings.

that for the corresponding DARP in female patients. Of the ten parental deaths occurring in late adolescence in male patients, five were mother losses and five were father losses. Of the six parental deaths occurring during ages one and two, four were mother losses and two were father losses. This pattern shows differences in the parental distribution between male and female patients.

If one contrasts the distribution of parental deaths during the oedipal period, we find that the women had six father deaths and four mother deaths during this period. The male patients, however, had six father deaths but only one mother death in the corresponding period. In the female, father deaths far exceed mother deaths in late adolescence, and slightly exceed mother deaths during the oedipal period. In the male patients, father deaths far exceed mother deaths during the oedipal period, but are equal during late adolescence, although the average figure is half that of the female patients. In the first year of life, there were only father deaths in the female patients, whereas the males showed an equal father-mother death distribution for this period. In DARP B (ages 1, 2), only fathers were lost in the female group, but double the number of mothers compared to fathers were lost in the male group.

The exact significance of these findings is as yet not worked out; however, the inference is made that the death of a father during the oedipal period seemingly is more traumatic for the male child, whereas the death of a father during late adolescence is very traumatic for a female child. In both males and females late adolescence is a very sensitive period. The first two to three years of life also are crucial periods as far as parent loss is concerned. The pathology that these patients present is quite different from that seen in the patients with later loss.

In Table 2.6, we can note additionally that of the twenty sibling losses for males, the highest average number occurred during the oedipal period and was more than twice the average for sibling loss in female patients during the corresponding DARP.

When one compares the averages for the total losses, the highest figure noted is that for female patients in late adolescence. The total number of losses for male and female patients is quite the same, but the distribution is much different. In female patients, the three highest average losses occur during periods F, A, and C, in that order. In male patients, the three highest average losses occur during periods F, B, and C. It will be noted that even here there is a great similarity in final average figures, though distribution is much different.

COMMENT, INTERPRETATION, AND IMPLICATIONS

One of the simplest statistical devices is that of simply counting and comparing. Essentially this has been the procedure followed in this study. The anamnestic data were collected without reference to any particular hypothesis and before the author was familiar with or interested in aspects of this problem area. It is understood that the patient population of this study was not a randomly unselected one. These were not specially chosen patients in that all who were seen in the specified period were counted. However, they came for specific reasons and to a particular person. Fortunately the essential factual data were obtained in every instance. This unique patient population makes comparison with statistics gathered by other investigators, whether in or out of hospitals, somewhat inexact. Nonetheless, some trends may be observed when the findings of other authors are compared with the results presented above.

Hilgard and Newman (1959), studying 3,909 hospital admissions, found 122 cases of parent loss between ages two and eighteen (inclusive). These adult patients were under fifty years of age and sufficiently ill to require hospitalization. Their experimental sample consisted of eighteen men (1 percent of total men admitted) and 104 women (5.5 percent of total women admitted). Women who lost mothers in childhood totaled forty-three cases, and women who had lost fathers totaled fifty-four. An additional seven women had lost both. The variance of these figures with those obtained in the current study shows significant differences. The ratio of father loss to mother loss in women is more nearly equal (though not equal in Hilgard and Newman's investigation) than in that of the author. The number of parent loss cases in the ambulatory group is much higher than that of the state hospital population proportionally, and the number of male patients in the author's parent loss census is much higher than that found by the California investigation.

In 1961, these investigators further compared their previous results with another sample, although they used somewhat altered criteria for patient selection. They did conclude that there was a significant age coincidence between parental age at death and the patient's age at the first admission to a mental hospital for psychosis. In addition they state that this first hospitalization is likely to occur when the patient's oldest child is within one year of the age the person was when the parent died. The important identification of the patient with the deceased parent is mentioned as a basic mechanism in these patients.

Bowlby (1961a) and Gregory (1958) have reviewed the literature on the incidence of childhood loss of parents in psychiatric patients and delinquents. Gregory feels that this incidence is appreciably higher in the case of psychiatric patients (psychoneuroses and psychoses) than it is in the general population. Felix Brown (1961) studied 216 unselected adult depressive clinic patients (61 males and 155 females). In his study he compared these patients with a matched control group and found that in his depressive patients, 41 percent had lost a parent in the first fifteen years of their life. The loss of mothers was equally significant at each five-year period of childhood (birth to 15 years of age), but the loss of the father was more significant in later childhood. Brown feels that the loss of a father is as severe a trauma as loss of a mother and is considerably commoner. He concludes that a person may be sensitized by a severe loss in childhood and in adult life a subsequent rejection or loss can provoke a depressive illness. This has been confirmed by the author and others and is especially seen during anniversary periods.

Barry, alone (1949) and with Bousfield (Barry and Bousfield, 1937), also studied the incidence of orphanhood among institutionalized patients. Their findings were mainly made on psychotic patients. The incidence of psychosis was quite low in the experimental population reported upon in this paper. Most of my patients were nonpsychotic, and very few required hospitalization. In a study of psychoneurotics, Barry found that in female patients, maternal deaths before the patient reached three years of age were four times the expected figure. This finding was not confirmed in the present investigation. In a more recent study Barry and Lindemann (1960) reaffirm their earlier conclusions that the death of the mother before the child is five years old is more frequent in psychoneuroses than in the total population. They feel that the most critical age for maternal death in little girls who later develop neuroses is from birth through age two. Although maternal bereavements reach a peak for female patients before the age of three, they find no such corresponding peak for males. They further find that the loss of the mother during childhood is more common in women psychoneurotics (12 percent) than among males (7 percent). These findings are at variance with those of the present investigation. The authors state "the evidence indicates that the death of the father does not have the same impact on a child as the death of the mother" (p. 178). The author cannot agree with this. At different developmental periods the father may be a most important figure in the child's further growth and maturation. It is true that this differs for the little girl and the little boy. The observations of Hilgard and others also raise questions about Barry and Lindemann's conclusion that "the age of the patient when first seen does not seem to be related to incidence of bereavement during childhood" (1960, p. 175). The explanation for these differences may lie in the different population used, since nonrepresentative samples cannot be compared and may yield inferences that are not generally valid.

Rosenzweig and Bray (1943), studying 356 histories of male schizophrenics, found that 39 percent had experienced sibling deaths. The majority of such deaths involved siblings younger than the patient, and they occurred before the patient reached the sixth year of life. This incidence of sibling death in males is much higher than that found in the current study; however, the finding that male patients tend to lose younger siblings in contrast to older ones coincides with the findings reported in this study.

At this point, perhaps a more specific discussion of the findings in this study is in order. The death of a parent in childhood is always a traumatic event affecting the development of the survivor's personality. The trauma is not only mediated through the separation, loss, and absence of the deceased parent, but also through contact with the surviving parent and family members who themselves have mourning reactions that may alter their contact with the child. The trauma of the death of a sibling also affects the child's development, though in a different fashion than that of parental death.

Hilgard, Newman, and Fisk (1960), studying a nonhospital population of individuals who lost a father in childhood but who were reasonably well adjusted in their adult life (living in an intact home, satisfactory marriage, adequate relationship with their children), found that the following factors were important in maintaining the ego strength of these adult individuals: (1) the home was kept intact by the mother who served the dual role of homemaker and breadwinner; (2) a network of support existed outside of the house which the mother made use of; (3) the preloss relationships were stable, well defined, compatible, and generally healthy; (4) the development of a tolerance for separation before the loss had occurred; and (5) grief and mourning occurred at the time of loss. These individuals presumably had no psychiatric illness. It is important to study childhood parent loss patients who come to us from the points of emphasis delineated by these authors. They further note that although some women recalled their mother's reactions to the father's death, which occurred before they were nine, none recalled their own grief. If the father died in the nine-ten-eleven-year age range, the recall could be either of the maternal grief and mourning or of the individual's own grief. When the loss occurred after the age of eleven, identification with the maternal grieving ceased, and the individuals spoke more of their own sensitivity to the father's death as such. Only in women whose fathers had died before eleven was there an identification with the maternal loss reactions. Men who lost fathers showed vivid recall of the death or funeral in all instances when they were over nine years of age at the time of the death. Men did not identify with the mother's grief as the women did. The structural and personality changes in this nine-ten-eleven-year prepubertal period undoubtedly are the crucial factors in the differential responses noted. Sylvia Anthony (1940) has written about the stage of development where the idea of death can be assimilated in the face of an actual loss. She feels that the eighth year is a turning point for most children having this experience. By the twelfth year she finds that the assimilation is commonly completed. The coincidence of her findings with those of Hilgard, Newman, and Fisk is striking and should focus our attention on what crucial developmental changes are occurring in this apparently critical period of maturation.

In the present study, significantly for both male and female patients, there is a clustering of parental and sibling deaths in the oedipal and late adolescent periods. However, the preponderance of paternal deaths in the oedipal period for male patients is not found in female patients. On the other hand, a similar preponderance of paternal deaths in late adolescence is seen in female patients, while male patients show an equal incidence of maternal and paternal deaths in late adolescence. The implication of these comparisons seemingly points to the different role the fathers have for their sons and daughters at different developmental eras. Thus the boy needs a father to assist him in resolving his castration anxieties and oedipal conflicts as well as setting up various nucleii for later identifications in adolescence. In adolescence, when the developing female comes into active conflict with her mother, she needs a father who can healthily encourage her budding sexuality in an appreciative fashion. The adolescent boy, however, usually conducts his sexual experimenting outside of the parental home, therefore his is the more independent or less scrutinized course than that of the girl.

In late adolescence, the girl's budding femininity can threaten the mother, but appeal to the father. This may cause conflict with the mother, but it aids in solidifying the identity of the feminine self-concept in the adolescent. If the father dies at this point in the child's development, it leaves the two contenders alone, and a male is gone for both. Male adolescents in our culture are given social license to act out and experiment. When they do this, it usually is away from home, and the conflict may be minimal. There may actually be identification of the father with his late-adolescent son. The castration threat is not in evidence for either father or son, and the son's sexual object is a girl who is his peer and not his father's wife. If parents wish to infantilize the male adolescent or are fearful of their own unresolved difficulties involving sexuality and aggressivity, conflict occurs. In the male, however, the conflict is more in the spheres of dependence and aggressivity. With the female, the conflict usually involves genital sexuality more directly. Competition between mothers and late-adolescent daughters usually is more keen than that of the fathers with their late-adolescent sons.

The author is aware of the fact that more father losses occur in later years, since men tend to be older than their wives and males have a higher death rate than females of the same age (Gregory, 1958; Barry and Lindemann, 1960). Nonetheless, the comparative differences between male and female patients are significant and cannot be ignored.

In the oedipal period, the conflict is mainly between the phallic male child and the threatening father. Girls' oedipal conflicts are more in the background, as castration anxiety is not present. The fear of loss of love and aggressive drives toward mother as well as to the nonfulfilling father is present, but castration anxiety with bodily harm is not strongly in evidence. Since castration anxiety in its primitive form is a major anxiety for the oedipal male child and his father, father loss at this developmental phase would be highly significant for the child.

The identification process with healthy differentiation of self and others requires the presence of both a mother and a father throughout the developmental periods. Heretofore little attention has been paid to the different stages in the adolescent period. In this study the seemingly important differentiation between early and late adolescence is indicated. It is in late adolescence that we finally get the resolution of the various conflicts which allows for consolidation, integration, and the commencement of a comparatively smooth adulthood. Even this, however, does not indicate total resolution of difficulty. Benedek (1959) has recently written about "Parenthood as a Developmental Phase," and Eissler, in 1947, noted stresses that test the integration of the ego in later life. These include the ego's reaction to internal changes resulting from the aging process, the effect on the individual by his developing progeny, and his influence on their progress.

It is in late adolescence that mature object relations begin. This involves sexual object selection of a peer-aged partner, commitment to marriage and future children, choice of and progress toward achieving independent economic existence with work as a meaningful, effective, and gratifying experience. In later adolescence the developing organism is more externally directed than the earlier adolescent who is much more internally preoccupied with the radical hormonal and body ego alterations. The integrative task in early adolescence requires much internal rearranging and solidification. In late adolescence, the activities become more externally directed with realistic object relationships resulting.

In the early years of life parents fulfill functions for the young child that later internal psychic structures take over. Parental absences at that time can give rise to various difficulties. Spitz and Wolf (1946) have described the effect of mother loss in infants after six months of age. With loss there is both a direct and indirect effect. The effect of the absence of a father on the mother's psyche can have great importance in that mother's relationship to her young child. The effect may not be comparable to the actual loss of the mother; nonetheless, maternal depressions during a child's infancy have later serious consequences. The role and function of parents in the child's development takes on different significance at different periods in the child's life. In this study an attempt has been made to note any correlations that exist between parental death and age of the child at the time of death. The crucial periods that were focused upon by this investigation have been delineated above.

The significance of the distribution of a higher incidence of older sibling deaths for female patients in contrast to the higher incidence of younger sibling deaths found for male patients is not easily explainable. Older siblings frequently are identified as parental figures, whereas younger siblings represent the envied, more protected, and preferential position in the family. Perhaps the male child who is culturally expected to be more aggressive and active would be more in conflict about his relationship with the younger sibling. Since the feminine role in our culture has been a receptive one, the conflict might not be of a descending sibling type, but more with the older sibling who is given more opportunities and responsibilities and who is more closely identified with the adult.

Older siblings can symbolically represent parental transference love or competitive objects. Thus the significance of the death of older siblings may relate to displaced feelings from the parent, particularly if the parent was an insignificant figure. Similarly, younger siblings are at times identified not as siblings but as fantasied children of the patient with the parent of the opposite sex. Their death can be viewed as punishment for forbidden sexual wishes or impulses.

Although not reported statistically in this paper, the number of cases seen in which there had been death of a spouse or child was quite small in comparison to the childhood parent-sibling deaths. It is postulated that this may be due to the different significance these deaths, occurring during adulthood, have as contrasted with deaths of parents or siblings occurring during the crucial periods when the development and structuralization of the psychic apparatus occurs. The meaning of these spouse and child deaths for adults as compared with childhood bereavements is another area requiring further study.

Factors which produce events are termed *causal determinants*. In this study the author is not proposing that parent and/or sibling loss are the causal determinants for the patient's emotional difficulties. These losses may be of critical or peripheral importance, but, as indicated, they undoubtedly had some effect on the personality development of these patients. Not all parent-sibling losses during childhood result in severe pathology. Future investigations may reveal what conditions occur which allow these traumatic events to have later etiological importance. Only the careful study of individual cases can allow for more specific hypotheses.

SUMMARY AND CONCLUSIONS

A total of 380 patients were seen consecutively by the author in his private practice during the eight-year period covered by this survey. A written anamnesis including pertinent actuarial and historical information in addition to evaluative impressions was prepared for each patient. Those patients who either had parental and/or sibling loss prior to their nineteenth birthdays were investigated further in this study.

The resulting data have been analyzed in terms of the age of the patient when the loss occurred, the age of the patient at the time of the initial psychiatric evaluation, the distribution of younger and older sibling loss, and the contrasts presented between male and female patients.

It was found that:

1. Of the total women, 16.9 percent were father loss cases in contrast to 5.6 percent of the male patients.

2. Of the total women, 3.3 percent were mother loss cases in comparison to 5.1 percent of the total male patients.

3. Of the women, 2.7 percent lost siblings, while 7.6 percent of the male patients reported this information.

4. In the females, older brothers were the largest grouping of deceased siblings, whereas younger brothers' deaths was the largest category in male patients.

5. Six developmental periods for the first nineteen years of life are postulated. The average number of deaths per year per developmental period is calculated. (a) In female patients, the highest incidence of parental death occurred in adolescence. In male patients, the highest incidence of average parental deaths occurred when the patients were one or two years old. (b) The highest average of sibling deaths for male patients occurred during ages three, four, five, and six. This was more than twice the average for sibling loss in female patients during the corresponding period.

Not all parent-sibling losses during childhood result in severe pathology. In this study the author is not proposing that these losses are the crucial determinants of the patients' emotional difficulties. Nonetheless, when a correlational comparative study of consecutively unselected private patients is made, significant differences are noted based upon the variables of age, sex, and type of childhood loss.

3
CHILDHOOD SIBLING LOSS: A FAMILY TRAGEDY

A bereaved mother dedicated her book *The Bereaved Parent* to the memory of her son, who died when he was ten years old (Schiff, 1978). She wrote of her experiences, as well as those of her family and friends who had similar losses, in order to help those who confront a similar tragedy, recognizing that though each such catastrophic occurrence has its own individual significance there are some commonalities that can ease some of the pain and the burden. I begin my presentation with a tale that she uses in the introduction to her volume.

> There is a tale about a prince fleeing from revolutionaries determined to kill him and take away his throne. The prince, terrified, sought shelter in a peasant's cottage.
>
> Although the peasant had no idea the frightened man was a member of the nobility he gave the prince refuge by telling him to hide under the bed. The prince had no sooner done so when his pursuers battered down the door and began to search the cottage.
>
> The revolutionaries searched everywhere. When they came to the bed they decided to prod it with knives rather than move the cumbersome piece of furniture. At last they left.
>
> The prince, pale but alive, crawled from under the bed after

Presented at "Perspectives on Sibling Loss," a conference celebrating the opening of the Rothman-Cole Center for Sibling Loss of the Southern School, cosponsored by the Barr-Harris Center, Institute for Psychoanalysis of Chicago, and Department of Psychiatry, Northwestern University Medical School, June 8, 1985.

Permission has been granted by Brunner/Mazel, Inc., for the quotation from J. M. Patterson and H. I. McCubbin (1983), and by the Crown Publishing Group for the quotation from H. S. Schiff (1978).

Reprinted from *The Annual of Psychoanalysis*, 14:5–34 (1986). Madison, CT: International Universities Press.

hearing the pursuers depart. He turned to the peasant then and said, "I think you should understand that you have just saved the life of your prince. Name three favors and I will grant them."

The peasant, a simple man, thought for a while and said:

"My cottage is in great disrepair and I have not had the money to fix it. Can this be done?"

"Fool!" cried the prince. "Of all things in the world, why did you ask so small a favor? I will honor your wish, but what is your next request?"

"Sire, my neighbor sells the same wares as me in the marketplace. Would it be possible to change his location so both of us could make a better livelihood?"

"Idiot," said the prince. "Of course I will do as you wish. What foolishness, when you could have riches, to ask such nonsense! Take care that you do not anger me with another silly request."

No longer able to restrain his curiosity, the peasant said, "As my third request I ask only that you tell me how you felt as the knives were being pushed through the bed."

The prince, infuriated, shouted, "How dare you offend majesty by asking of my emotions? For this act I will have you beheaded tomorrow!"

The prince called in a few of his retainers and had the hapless man carried off to the local jail.

All through the night the man wept for his folly and feared what would happen on the morrow.

When the sun rose his jailers came to him and led him into a courtyard where an executioner with his black hood stood awaiting a terrified man.

Forced to kneel on the block he heard a soldier call "One, two . . ." but before he could say three, another soldier on horseback came tearing into the courtyard calling "Stop! The prince commands it."

With those words the executioner, whose blade had been resting on the peasant's neck, withdrew the sword. The shaking man arose and faced the soldier who had saved his life.

"His Highness gives you his pardon and orders me to give you this note," said the soldier.

The peasant, relieved to the point of tears, began to read the few terse words:

"As your final favor you wanted to know how I felt under that bed when the revolutionaries came. I have granted your request because now you know!"

The prince had shown the peasant more graphically than words could possibly have done just what the horrendous ordeal had been like.

The prince, no fool, had realized that some things are beyond describing. No matter how eloquent the words, their impact can fall flat when not accompanied by a similar experience.

And so it is with bereaved parents [Schiff, 1978, pp. ix–xi].

Although Schiff writes from the perspective of the parent who has lost a child—an unexpected crisis, as parents are supposed to die before their children—she indeed poignantly but carefully addresses the issue of the loss of a child and how it affects the mother, the father, and the siblings. In other words, childhood loss is a tragedy for every member of the family, though for each individual it takes on a different meaning. For the mother, it can give rise to guilt, severe melancholia, a lifelong bereavement. For the father, we may find similar though somewhat different responses. For the siblings, we again find varied reactions—some having lifelong significance and others in which the impact is less. For grandparents, the response can vary from great despair to quiet, contemplative mourning. Our focus here is on the sibling who "loses," but since the sibling does not relate in a vacuum, we must at the outset recognize how the surviving child or children are confronted by the reactions of the parents and other siblings, as well as their own responses when the death occurs.

Let me return to some of Harriet Schiff's observations. She notes that because of her protective maternal inclination, she made a massive error in judgment at the funeral of her son. She did not let her twelve-year-old son view the body of his dead brother because of the horror she felt in seeing it. In retrospect she indicates that she harmed him "because it took many years for him to lay his brother's ghost to rest" (Schiff, 1978, p. 14). Her then four-year-old daughter did not attend the funeral, and "She is resentful after all these years that she was cheated of the experience" (p. 14). I might suggest that the cheating may relate to a blockage of the mourning-liberation process that is always so necessary in adapting to loss and change, even when death is not the cause of the disruption.

Schiff describes how difficult it is for parents to continue in their roles as mother and father to the surviving children. Parenthood carries with it an additional burden—having to deal with one's own pain and yet comfort the living children. Achieving a balance between too much and too little communication is truly a task requiring herculean strength. The loneliness, the emptiness, the void left by the child who shared games, television programs, toys, hopes, joys, and hurts—these are gone and yet responsibility remains to the survivors. When parents cannot fulfill their responsibilities to the living children, and when the focus is too concentrated on the dead child, the effects on these surviving children can be lifelong. These survivors can feel unloved, alone, ignored during the bereavement period, *or* they may become overprotected, overinvested with care and apprehension. The children may feel pushed aside, ignored, abandoned at a crucial time. In the family upheaval created by the dead sibling, unless the parents are aware of the entire situation, the surviving children may be ignored.

The mourning process for a dead sibling, especially in childhood and adolescence, is similar to other mourning processes (e.g., the loss of a parent), and yet there are differences.

The crying mother and father, the at times devastated household, the lack of opportunity to talk about the dead, the feeling of helplessness–powerlessness, the guilt—these responses and behaviors can be seen in both childhood parent loss and childhood sibling loss situations. But the loss of a parent presents a potential pathogenic trauma that seemingly more often interferes with development than an appropriately handled childhood sibling loss.

Mrs. Schiff notes the guilt reactions of her two children to the death of their brother. " 'I used to have nightmares that he died because I punched him. . . . It took me years to understand that I had nothing to do with his death' " (1978, p. 87). Another childhood sibling survivor I came to know felt she was punished by God because of her jealous feelings. Still another child, whose brother became profoundly depressed and withdrawn after the death of their father, though previously they had been close and communicative, felt when this brother was killed in an automobile accident that there would never be an opportunity to "patch things up." Like the survivors of the Nazi concentration camps, some children lose their faith in God. "How can you trust Him? Are prayers only a bunch of words?" The dis-illusionment with the omnipotent and omniscient deity can be a cover for the deeper mistrust of parents: How can they be expected to protect, to ensure life, to know what to do? If the parent, especially the mother, feels she could or should have done more and holds herself, her husband, or the doctors re-sponsible, a vicious cycle can be set up that reverberates between parent and child and does indeed have the potential for creating psychological difficulties in later life. Normative developmental transitions become excessively stressful and straining and fur-ther complications ensue. When the child finds it impossible to communicate with the parents and siblings, to receive or give pleasure with respect to parents and siblings, we indeed find lifelong impacts that get carried over into the next generation, if there is one, as survivors possibly do not marry or, if they do, elect to have no children.

Not all children and adolescents emerge from this family tragedy with psychopathology or distorted personalities. Some become very creative and deal with their mourning for the dead siblings in a positive way; for example, Gustav Mahler, Edvard Munch, Käthe Kollwitz, Thomas De Quincey, Jack Kerouac, Bertha Pappenheim, Nietzsche, Goethe, Oscar Wilde, Lenin, Van Gogh, Heinrich Schliemann, and James Barrie, to mention a few.

Clinically, I have worked with adults who were "replace-ment children," even to the extent of being named after the dead siblings. The Cains (1964) have written about this. The comparison with the dead child, the idealization of the dead child, the inability to compete with a ghost—these can become insurmountable developmental tasks and can lead to identifi-cations with the dead sibling, even to the point of expecting to have a similar death or to have one's future child die as did the sibling. Anniversaries, holidays, pilgrimages to the cemetery, enshrined keepsakes can become the focus of uncompleted mourning. Healing cannot occur and at times one even seeks a sibling replacement. I have observed this in two male hom-osexual patients—both looked for partners that they could pro-tect, feed, love, and who had physical characteristics of the dead brothers. I do not wish to suggest that the sibling deaths in adolescence were the only etiologic agents for the later life-style and pathology, but one cannot ignore the significance of the object choice, the mode of sexual activity, and the linkages that emerged in the analytic treatment situation, especially the sibling transference.

I wish to add parenthetically at this point, since I will not elaborate on this issue at this time, that studies of sibling loss throughout the life course seem to indicate thus far that with older adults the response to such deaths is different from, and far less pathogenic than, those of younger individuals. Older adults who lose a sibling realize that their family of origin is following the expected course of life and that they themselves are much closer to the end of their life. They do not fear death though they are saddened by its greater probability. Younger individuals are also threatened by death, but for different reasons; for example, they wish to be with their spouse and children and see the latter grow and develop. Young children fear the darkness and "permanent sleep" that death connotes, especially the loss of parents before they are ready for this permanent and irretrievable separation.

Solnit (1983) has noted that "sibling experiences are always significantly shaped by two interacting, profound dynamic forces . . . there is first, the nature of the mutual relationships of parents and child; and second, the child's developmental capacities and preferences that are formative in sibling relationships and experiences" (p. 283). One might add the relationships the parents have with each other and how the children fit into this constellation. For example, we do see transferences from parents to children that complicate the relationships in the family. Solnit focuses on the mutual attachments, identifications, and empathic resonances in the parent-child relationship. However, we do see in abusing and abandoning parents the other sides of the positive attachments. Identifications of children with one or another of these facets of the parent's personality and aggression can be acted out toward siblings. For example, a mother who was very conflicted over her deep sibling competition with her older sisters and brothers had three children who duplicated her sibling rage and competition in the next generation to such an extent that all ties between the siblings were severed and no contacts continued although the father attempted to effect reconciliations without much success—this despite the fact that as young children the three did very well together.

Loewald (1980) described how a patient "appeared to be the victim of his father's denial of the death of the father's beloved brother. The patient became the substitute for the brother and the father now clung to him with all the force of this never-relinquished attachment. The patient had great difficulty in emancipating himself from his father because of the guilt involved in severing this tie . . . this was only one aspect of the patient's neurotic attachment to the father" (p. 261). This does suggest, however, a variant of the lifelong separation-individuation process that goes beyond that of mother and child. Children can bear the burden of their parents' conflicted, strained, or inadequately mourned-for sibling relationships.

Morawetz (1982) has studied the impact on adolescents who lost an older sibling in the Israeli Yom Kippur War. Joanna Fanos of the University of California, San Francisco, is involved in a major research on the developmental consequences of the death of a sibling following a chronic illness. She affirms that the death of a child is generally considered to be one of the most stressful events encountered by families in our society and that when medical advances extend the life of a child stricken with such disorders as leukemia and cystic fibrosis, we find an additional dimension to the sibling loss problem. What are the effects of living with a child who has a fatal illness on the mother, father, and siblings? Dennis Farrell (1987) studied the impact of childhood sibling loss on the life of Hermann Hesse. Let me mention a few current research studies in progress.

A current study of mine which I will now discuss deals with the impact of having a chronically sick or disabled sibling on one's childhood, and the impact on adult personality as studied during psychoanalytic treatment. Patterson and McCubbin (1983) have discussed the sources of stress when there is chronic illness in a family who have a chronically ill child. They delineate the following hardships:

(1) *Strained family relationships* often reflected in (a) overprotectiveness, jeopardizing the child's development of independence; (b) coalitions between the primary caretaker (usually mother)

and the child, with other family members feeling left out; (c) scapegoating and blaming of the child or possibly blaming a parent believed to be genetically responsible; (d) overt or covert rejection of the child, which affects the child's physical and emotional development; (e) worry (possibly resentment) about extended parenting/caretaking responsibilities; (f) sibling competition for parental time and attention; (g) sibling comparisons and discrepancies regarding uneven physical, emotional, social, and intellectual development; and (h) an overall increase in intrafamily tension and conflict. . . .

(2) *Modifications in family activities and goals*, such as (a) reduced flexibility in the use of leisure time and restricted options for family vacation; (b) less opportunity for both parents to pursue careers; and (c) worry and uncertainty about whether to have more children when the illness is related to genetic factors.

(3) *The burden of increased tasks and time commitments*, such as providing special diets (diabetes, cystic fibrosis); extra cleaning of equipment or of the house (asthma); providing daily therapy or treatment; extra appointments to medical facilities, and hospitalizations resulting in family separations.

(4) *Increased financial burden* due to medical specialist consultations, hospitalizations, medications, equipment needs, therapy, with variability of insurance coverage affecting direct costs to families.

(5) *Need for housing adaptation* in terms of geographic proximity to adequate medical care, optimal climatic conditions for certain illnesses, and fitting the house with special features (e.g., ramp for wheelchairs).

(6) *Social isolation* because of (a) friends' and/or relatives' reactions to and expectations regarding the chronically ill child; (b) family embarrassment when there are visible abnormalities; (c) limited mobility of the ill or handicapped child; (d) unavailability of adequate child care; (e) fear of accidents, or exposure to infections or conditions which might exacerbate the illness; and (f) limitations on social life as a result of the above factors.

(7) *Medical concerns* related to (a) obtaining competent medical care; (b) understanding, clarifying, and verifying medical information; (c) the family's ability to follow through with prescribed home treatment; (d) the child's willingness to comply; (e) how to help the child endure or minimize pain; and (f) worry and uncertainty regarding the child's prognosis.

(8) *Differences in school experiences* where special needs must be met in a regular school environment, special schools must be

found, or education must occur in the home environment regularly or periodically—all of which require ongoing monitoring.

(9) *Grieving* associated with developmental delays or abnormalities, restricted life opportunities for the child, and, for some illnesses, anticipation of an early or painful death [Patterson and McCubbin, 1983, pp. 25–26].

What I am suggesting is that children can experience various kinds of losses that include events other than death: prolonged hospitalization, divorce with split custody, abandonment, separations during war and other disaster experiences, migrations to other countries resulting in family breakups. The multiple meanings of these complicated events and the influence of these sibling losses on later patterns of behavior, feelings, fantasies, and object choices can be observed best, I believe, when such individuals are in psychoanalytic treatment.

The bedrock of data for psychoanalysis comes from the clinical situation. From it and from observations in therapeutic and naturalistic settings we have evolved our theories about development. Some of these theories about "normal" development mesh with our ideas about pathogenic causation, some become generalized and universalized, and some stimulate further research and investigation. Nonetheless, psychoanalysis depends upon illness for its data base, and one might ask if extrapolation to the "healthy" individual without further observation and testing is warranted. A fruitful area for study is that of crisis and trauma. A useful distinction is one that differentiates between expected normative crises associated with developmental changes and unexpected catastrophic crises which are traumatic and which can result in pathology in the individual, his or her siblings (born or as yet unborn), the parents, and even in the grandparents. We see these latter individuals in our consulting rooms and in treatment situations.

The augmentation of observations of childhood normative and catastrophic crises, from the analyses of children and from reported cases of others by data derived from the psychoanalytic treatment of adults who suffered similar catastrophic crises due to serious illness or injury to younger siblings can be useful in our further clinical understanding and theoretical formulations. I wish to report data from the analyses of adults.

The patients were physically healthy and their physically ill siblings, in two cases, were younger than my patients. Let me summarize their situations.

Adam, a successful married lawyer, is three-and-a-half years older than his only sibling, a brother I shall call Richard. Richard has had Hodgkin's disease since he was ten years old (patient was thirteen-and-a-half). This disease, treated "successfully" with medication, had three "crises"—the first when the disease was initially diagnosed and treated, the second episode several years later, and the third, in 1984, six years after the second exacerbation. My patient, reacting to his brother's current exacerbation, has been able to recall and reenact much of what occurred in the two earlier periods of acute disease. When the brother currently becomes very despondent and threatens passive suicide by stopping his medical treatments, my patient is filled with guilt, rage, and then shame at his reaction to his brother's regressions, sense of hopelessness, and despair. The brothers received supportive treatment while undergoing the medical regime, which is painful, debilitating, and filled with the most uncomfortable side effects.

Adam had no conscious recollection of Richard before Richard was four years of age. Two years ago Richard broached the idea to Adam that he, Adam, must have had a severe sibling rivalry which was repressed. My patient explored this and concluded his brother was correct. Mother had always fostered a "healthy competition" between her sons as she felt this would bring out the best in both of them. Adam recalled how he would seek to control and have "power" over Richard. I asked if he ever wanted Richard "out of the way." He said, "I never wanted him dead—because then I'd be in trouble with my parents . . . they were the law. By the way, do you think this could have contributed to my becoming a lawyer?" Adam described how his brother was overweight, did poorly in school, and acted out in petty ways. When Richard's illness was first diagnosed, the patient was out of the city in an Eastern boarding school. Mother called him and asked him to return to Chicago—he refused. He felt unconcerned, denied that Richard had a serious illness, and felt confirmed in this belief when Richard had a remission. When the second attack came on, he understood his mother's anguish for the first time and then the "devastating effects of the chemotherapy" on Richard, his mother, and on him. His father was dead. His mother suffered two heart attacks in quick succession and he no longer could deny what the medication was doing to Richard's body—he "looked awful." The patient got very depressed, had several financial crises, and suddenly felt the burden of his brother's care and life in a way he had never experienced previously. Adam thought of suicide but realized it might kill his mother and his brother. "Richard, my mother, and I were sunk low in the morass of life." Richard had another remission, mother recovered, and Adam came out of his "blue state" and went on again to fulfilling his life goals in a very successful way. He finished his education, began his practice, married, and even though his mother had subsequently died, his life seemed in balance.

Last year Richard had his current exacerbation and again chemotherapy was recommended. The course this time has not been smooth—side effects, liver biopsies, and bone-marrow studies were accompanied by anger on Richard's part. Finally Richard told Adam that he, Richard, hated him and always had. Now Richard calls Adam, insists that Adam or his wife drive him to the hospital for his treatments, needs money constantly as he cannot work and has had little in savings. Adam says, "I am his surrogate mother and father. He borrows money from me, he is so profligate with friends, he upsets me. [Voice loud] I can't stand it any longer. I now realize he always bugged me. I hate him. I finally got so angry with him I blew up. He hates me, despises me, that's why he harasses me." The patient calmed down and then went on, "I am not rivalrous with him. I am not jealous of him. I am winning every battle—health, money, sex, marriage, the future." I asked if he always felt triumphant. He went on, "Mother understood his competition with me and so spent more time with him socially. She wanted me to do this, too. When I would not she said I had an obligation to him and to her. I had a responsibility that I was not meeting. Since our father died when he was quite young, he had fewer years with him and I had to take over. Actually when Daddy died, she fell apart and I actually did care for Richard—we were close then. But I thought just now—why me? Care for him, care for her, I am so mad at Richard now and at you [pause]. . . . That's crazy. You make no demands of me. Are you Richard, or Mother, or Daddy? I get so terrified that something will happen to you—to him—I'll be alone [crying]. I have not been a very good brother to Richard. I did not pay enough attention to him, I wasn't supportive enough of him when he was younger. I should have written him more letters when I was away at school. I should have called him. I should have been interested in what he did—his music, theater, ballet. I never made him important to me. He was low, very low on my totem pole of values and importance."

In the next session, he returned to the theme. Again, in his words, "Sibling rivalry—sibling failure—triumphs over Richard. This is a big ugly black monster that lurks in my mind and it creeps out like the Loch Ness monster. It causes me to have so many reactions. It is wrong to compete with him, with anyone. One should only compete with oneself—exogenous competition is bad. I realize I was very competitive in school—it started before kindergarten. My parents both encouraged it. I had to win in marbles, I had to win in hide-and-seek. When I began to swim the teacher said we were tadpoles. I remember telling my mother and father I wanted to be a shark or a flying fish. They laughed and said, "Go do it." My teachers in kindergarten, first grade, all pushed me to compete. I got the gold stars, I won the athletic contests, I won the athletic honors. I got into the best schools. You know I am the super Type A—time is the second most important commodity. Maybe health or money comes first. The striving for excellence is actually number one; preservation of my health is number two; optimum time utilization and success are tied for number three [pause] . . . I guess happiness is number four. My German ancestors—compulsive, hard working, no compassion—my grandparents, my parents—they are not dead. They live inside of me and still control me. I guess I saw Richard as a loser and tried to keep him out of my life." He then began to talk of his competition with me, how little he has accomplished compared to me; he is unimportant even though he is well-to-do. "If I left the world I would not be missed. If you died the world would be a bigger loser than if I died. I guess Richard's illness, my mother's death, my father's death—they all are related."

It should be noted that there is a difference between what

I call premorbid sibling rivalry, or the rivalry that is seen nor-mally between siblings, and postmorbid sibling rivalry, a rivalry that results from parents "giving more" or paying more atten-tion to a chronically ill or disabled sibling. This latter type of sibling rivalry is more fraught with guilt and at times builds on the premorbid rivalry, but not always. Another area needing study relates to the question of whether different illnesses and/or different deaths (acute-unexpected versus chronic, with premorbid mourning) affect survivors in different ways. I have clinical data that suggest that there are critical differences, but we need more systematic studies of these issues.

I will now briefly describe the second analysand:

When Harold first came to see me, he was thirty years old, still living at home, inhibited sexually and socially, unable to complete his education, and fighting furiously with his parents and his four-year-younger sister, Susan—his only sibling. He had a severe case of infantile and childhood eczema and recalled his mother applying various salves regularly to all parts of his body—it felt very good. However, when his sister was born, the rubbing by mother diminished markedly and then ceased. Though his skin was clear, he recalled asking his mother to rub him some more, especially when she was caring for Susie, but mother was unable or unwilling to do this, telling him he was a "big boy" and did not need to have this done. He presumably had a normal childhood, traversing the normal developmental crises until tragedy struck the family when he was almost thir-teen and sister was almost nine years old. The sister had left the bus that brought her to school and was crossing the street when a car suddenly swung out to bypass the stopped bus. It was traveling very rapidly and struck Susan, breaking both of her tibias and fibulas. The right leg had compounded fractures, the left multiple fractures but without penetration through the skin. The patient, who was in the eighth grade, was already in class. The principal called him out of the room, saying, "We think your sister was hurt in an accident but we want you to stay in class." The patient recalled laughing and saying, "You must be wrong. My sister is fine—there is nothing wrong with her." He returned to the class but felt uneasy. When the class was over he ran down to Susie's room, did not see her, and asked her shocked-looking teacher where she was. The teacher said Susan was ill and went home. He called home, got no answer. He called his father's furniture store and got no answer. He found himself crying, feeling tension in his chest, and running home. When he got there the front door was ajar and he realized his mother must have left in a hurry—her coffee cup was on its side, coffee was over the table, and things in a state of disarray which was not very characteristic. A neighbor who saw him running out, looking distraught and in panic, called to him and told him his mother was rushed to the hospital by the police as his sister was seriously hurt. In a short time, although he recalled it as interminable, an aunt arrived and told him what had happened. He could not believe her, and yet he found himself crying and moaning.

To summarize the medical course, the sister was treated surgically, both legs had open reductions, and in order to prevent one leg from being longer or shorter than the other, the bones were "filed down" and made equal in size. Susie spent three months in the hospital—the patient did not see her as the regulations forbade a minor from visiting the orthopedic unit. After returning home, the child was in a full body cast for four more months, then in a wheelchair. Mother initially slept in the hospital room with Susie, then slept at home, but left early in the morning and returned exhausted late at night. Father had an equally full day—he had to open and close the store and then went to the hospital. The routine was the same on weekends. My patient had cold suppers alone, felt abandoned, concerned, confused, angry, guilty, and depressed. When Susie returned home mother moved her bed into Susie's room and devoted herself to teaching Susie how to walk again. To this day, mother still sleeps in the same room as Susie, leaving father to sleep alone. My patient's resentment, displaced from his own oedipal longings, is directed toward his sister, who he feels has successfully kept his parents from "sleeping with each other." He also expressed his great resentment at being separated from his mother by his sister—this condensed anger stemmed from feelings that were related to the birth of Susie but were exacerbated by his being a "latchkey" child when she was in the hospital.

His sister was a "preemie," born seven months after conception. She was always treated with great care. She was and is very attractive, but as a result of the surgery has stunted growth (i.e., she is under five feet). He described her as a good student, a young woman who was determined, for example, to learn to drive, which she did and does. But she lacks confidence, is still a virgin, has no boyfriends, and despite her "special treatment" feels the parents have favored my patient. Harold does not disagree with this, but feels it was he who was left alone and that although he has "made it," the cost was high. He felt left out. At one time he thought of becoming a physician specializing in orthopedic surgery. In this way he thought he could help his sister or children like her, as well as get his parents' attention and praise.

Many defenses could be dated to Susie's accident: denial which covered great anxiety over her possible death or serious disability (she has none); detachment in order to deal with his sense of isolation; premature self-sufficiency and autonomy; a repression of all excessive affect; especially against basic rage at his mother, sister, and father (who become very overprotective toward my patient after the accident to the point of intrusive control and excessive caring).

In the third clinical illustration we address another dimension of the problem under discussion. The youngest of three brothers—let us call him Alfred—was born after the older siblings had their physical difficulties. The oldest was ten years older than Alfred, and the middle brother was seven years older. Before the patient's birth, the oldest brother had poliomyelitis which left him paralyzed from the waist down. When Alfred was three to four, he recalled witnessing the removal of his brother's cast with a shears. He was so anxious he vomited in the cast room. His fantasy was that his brother's legs were going to be cut off. The personal meaning need not be spelled out. The second brother was in a serious auto accident in which he was propelled through the front windshield. His face was badly scarred. As Alfred grew up, he realized how specially his brothers were treated and wondered if he, Alfred, needed a disability or disfigurement to also get such special care. Nonetheless, his parents were so fearful that Alfred might be injured that he was treated with great caution, and was rarely allowed to be out of his parents' sight or contact. He himself, as an adult, has similar feelings about his own children. If they are out of contact with him, he still gets apprehensive.

Thus the disabilities and disfigurements of his siblings, even though the actual illness and accident occurred before his own birth, exerted a marked influence upon his character. This very interesting clinical case suggests the significance of chronic illness in a sibling without visible external signs of the infirmity, as compared to an externally visible disfigurement or disability interfering with normal motoric behavior.

In these patients, concerns over the possible genetic basis of the chronic illness of the sick sibling were expressed and served many functions including displacement of responsibility for the illness and fear of retaliation in kind. I have attempted to indicate briefly the organizing and crystallizing effects of a traumatic situation on the personality and character structure of adult males who suffered the "traumata" as very young adolescents. In a sense these clinical reports are follow-up/outcome studies as seen in psychoanalytic treatments during early adult life. Changes in external events coming at crucial times provide possible explanations of alterations in normative forms and structures. Substantial change in external family structure may result in or serve as triggers for subsequent internal psychological development. We do find that many marriages either "break up" or become noncohesive when a child develops a serious life-threatening illness such as leukemia, or after a serious, sudden, accidental death of a child, at which time blame can be placed on the marital partner. This immediately adds to the burden of the surviving, healthy children. Disguised predeath tensions can no longer be hidden or denied, and the preexisting family pathology emerges into the open. Thus the illness or death of a child can precipitate many tensions and issues which add to the burdens of the children already beset with many other internal crises.

Let me present another clinical example that may illustrate the difference between disability and chronic illness without disability. Perhaps the distinction can best be seen in a chronically ill individual with diabetes mellitus, who is not disabled or does not show or give indication of overt physical impairment. Barney, a physician in psychoanalytic treatment, reported that his five-year-younger brother, Sam, had been a sickly child. When Sam was born, Barney was very jealous of mother's attention to the baby. Barney recalled having conscious thoughts dealing with Sam's death. They were reinforced when Sam developed a severe pneumonia at six months of age and several recurrent bouts of scarlet fever followed by a serious attack of rheumatic fever which produced structural cardiac damage. The parents were distraught, expecting Sam to die at any time. They became overprotective of him and curtailed his activities, even though there were no overt functional limitations. Barney's intense sibling rivalry was suppressed and his death wishes were repressed. He felt guilty about his academic triumphs but partially dealt with this through his restitution wishes—a manifestation of this was his choice of medicine as a life work. We find many individuals who are physicians, mental health professionals, or caregivers who as children have either a sick parent, a sick sibling, a serious illness themselves, or a significant childhood loss. The choice of work does have its determinants in childhood traumata. Sam's envy of Barney became overt in their adult years and eventually led to a rupture in their relationship. Though both have survived these unpleasantries the scars remained. Barney recognized his "sibling transferences" in and out of the analytic situation. Interestingly, Barney's special interest in medicine dealt with issues of prevention, especially as these related to young children, and epidemiologic studies of incidence of illness as it relates to prognosis and mortality.

In another psychotherapeutic situation, my patient in her late sixties recalled the death of her three-year-older sister when the patient was fourteen. She still expressed much resentment at this sister's special role in the family as a result of a chronic illness. My patient never went to the cemetery to see her sister's grave, did not go to the funeral, and refused to name her daughter after her dead sister as was the family's custom.

I will report on a young physician specializing in infectious disease who told me that his parents lost a son from meningitis before his birth. He was conceived as the replacement child. He was named after his dead sibling, whom he never knew but in whose shadow he lived throughout his childhood and adolescence. The brother's illness "steered him" to medicine and to the subspecialty of infectious disease. He recalled his parents' great concerns over his health, safety, and activities. Even though he understood and felt liberated, he still finds himself quite anxious when one of his children becomes ill.

I worked with a young woman whose parents divorced when she was a relatively young child. She recalled her parents constantly arguing. Before the divorce, her mother became pregnant and despite her father's wish to have the child, the mother induced an abortion at home. The father was furious and took the three-month fetus, placed it in a jar of formaldehyde, and kept it in the kitchen on a shelf in front of the breakfast table. The fetus was male, but in the abortive process, its head became detached from the body and lay on its side in the jar. The mother had a hemorrhage as a result of the abortion and needed a hysterectomy. In later life, the patient feared pregnancy and when she had a miscarriage went into a panic, expecting to deliver a decapitated male fetus and then require a hysterectomy. This did not occur and she subsequently had two normal children.

I have worked with individuals who themselves as children had physical illnesses, later sequelae, and in some instances actual disability, disease, or chronic illness. From them I learned of their siblings' responses. I have also worked with individuals who had siblings with epilepsy, spasticity of limbs, diabetes mellitus, and in one instance with an individual who had a sibling who was a Mongoloid child. In a few instances, I have worked with parents of disabled and/or chronically ill children, suffering, for example, from the crippling effects of serious neurological disease, congenital heart problems, muscular dystrophy. My data indicate that these tragic illnesses have an impact on all members of the family. The different reactions depend on many variables. Kenneth Newman (personal communication) has suggested that a child who wishes for a sibling and does not "get one" can be considered as a special instance of a childhood loss for which the parents are blamed.

Perhaps we should now begin examining in greater depth the effects of pathogenic and nonpathogenic trauma on later development. Just as tree rings show traumatic effects without impairing growth, so can we now by combining psychoanalytic work with children, adolescents, and adults throughout the life course have new researches. I know that serious and even catastrophic illness in a seventy-year-old sibling does not evoke the same reactions in an eighty-year-old healthy sibling as it would if this occurred when both were children. We need more normative studies from which to obtain baseline data that can then be compared to deviation data. Normative crises are traumatic without being pathogenic. Catastrophic crises are traumatic and possibly pathogenic for the individual and other members of the family.

In summing up this presentation, some general remarks are in order. The loss of a significant object, the loss of a home (security, personal possessions, familiar space that has emotional meaning), the dislocation from one's home or land as occurs in wars or disasters gives rise to stress-strain responses that may have short- or long-term effects (e.g., post-traumatic stress disorders). The hidden or neglected victims of such occurrences frequently are children—be they siblings or direct descendants. In childhood sibling loss, the effects of the loss are mediated through different members of the family. The acute stressors can give rise to later adversity unless it is recognized that there is a social context in which life-and-death events occur. Recognizing these individual responses in the family can lead to interventions that may prevent later difficulty. Understanding the meaning of the events to the child, appreciating the fact that events are not just single occurrences but interact with what existed before as well as with other concomitant events, helps in our therapeutic recommendations and interventions. Exciting new biological studies of bereavement and mourning (e.g., immunologic alterations) promise a new tracking method for following the course of mourning; T-cells may undergo alterations that parallel the mourning process. As normal mourning occurs, the immune indicators may return to the prebereavement state. This allows for the monitoring of a psychological process with a physiological indicator. If the indicator points to an abnormal response, intervention may be instituted to prevent later difficulties.

Sibling loss, though initially related to the death of a sibling, can now be expanded to include the loss of a sibling through chronic illness (emotional, medical, surgical) or long-term hospitalization, birth injuries, disabilities (accidents or illness with body changes), chronic illness with visible as well as nonvisible

changes that require special parental and nursing care, medication on an ongoing basis, restrictions in diet and activities.
The impacts of these losses without death can have devastating
effects. Sibling loss, from whatever cause, occurs throughout
the life course. We have little data about these stressful events
in the various age groups and how they affect emotional, behavioral, physiological, and psychological states. Sibling loss
takes various forms, has different precipitants and different
outcomes, and relates to the meanings and fantasies of the loss
events.

In sibling loss through death or in holocaust events, we
find many reactions; for example, identifications, guilt, inability
to mourn, the paralysis of the future because of the past, a
sense of foreboding and expectation of dire consequences, anger, envy, responsibility, shame and stigma, overcompensations,
resentment, and so on. Variables I have observed as they relate
to causes of the death can be broken down into acute (accidents,
unexpected illness, sudden catastrophes) and chronic (childhood diabetes, renal disease). Various coping-defensive measures are utilized (e.g., mourning-liberation, projection, denial,
splitting, transference, depression and withdrawal, delin-
quency, psychosomatic complaints including sleep disorders,
school failures, or learning difficulty).

Breslau and her colleagues (1981), in studying the psychological functioning of siblings of disabled children from an epidemiologic perspective, found that such siblings did not
manifest higher rates of severe psychologic impairment or
greater overall symptomatology when compared with control
subjects. On measuring interpersonal aggression with peers and
within school settings, such siblings scored significantly higher,
indicating greater pathology in these psychological domains.
The type and severity of the disability bore *no* relationship to
the psychological functioning of the siblings. Sex and age were
not related to psychologic functioning nor was birth order per
se. However, birth order was found to have a statistically significant interactive effect with gender; that is, "among siblings
younger than the disabled children, male siblings had greater
impairment than female siblings, whereas among siblings older
than the disabled children female siblings were psychologically
worse off" (Breslau, Weitzman, and Messenger, 1981, p. 350).

It is time to study siblings who lose a sibling utilizing various points of view and different methodologies. Research and careful investigations will help us reconcile the differences that seemingly emerge from the Breslau work and from our clinical experience. Not all siblings suffer from parental inattention following loss. If we can identify those who are especially vulnerable and at high risk we will be able to intervene successfully and prevent later personality pathology.

A few concluding comments summarize the three tasks required of the "normal" surviving siblings.

(1) They must perform for the parents, especially the mother (see chapter 24);
(2) they must perform for the impaired or deceased sibling; and
(3) they have their own needs and feelings that are independent of, unless interfered with by, the above two considerations.

These children cannot make up for the emptiness, defects, or losses over which they have had no control. We have seen this type of situation in an as yet unpublished study of childhood duodenal ulcer—as it affects children and their parents.

It is my impression that children with childhood sibling loss, especially due to death, do not get married, and that, if they do, they may elect not to have children of their own. Or, they may marry early and have many children, at times in an overcompensatory fashion.

In this paper I have explored various aspects of sibling loss resulting from accidental tragedies, disasters, or chronic-disabling illness. The focus has been on how various members of the family react to the victim and some of the family stress-strains that have mental health consequences. The importance of short-term crisis intervention, long-term individual treatment, family therapy, social-support systems, and coping mechanisms, though dealt with, requires a much more in-depth discussion.

Bank and Kahn (1982) have discussed the importance of "frozen images" of the dead child which allow for little or no change if reinforced externally and/or if a mourning-liberation process cannot take place which allows for new and healthier adaptations to loss. These "frozen images, positive or negative, created by death or prolonged geographical separation" (p. 74) are very difficult to relinquish and can become stagnant and fixed—or can exert a powerful shaping influence on the as yet unformed personalities of the sibling-survivors. In the case of Lenin, I found a partial identification with his executed brother set the adolescent on a path that had a powerful impact on the history of man. This identification included elements of loyalty, revenge, wish to avoid mourning, denial that the ideal was gone even if the brother was no longer here, as well as other components that interacted with the socioeconomic-cultural stage to yield a revolution against the czar. The devaluation of the dead brother, the aggression against him, the depreciation of his tactics—all present before the brother's death—became submerged and redirected against the oppressive political system.

I agree with the emphasis Bank and Kahn (1982) place on the factors that affect the sibling bond beyond the grave. These include (1) the parental influences on the mourning of the surviving siblings; (2) the silence and secrecy of the ghost siblings who are still omnipresent; (3) the parental reactions of preciousness and overprotection or the counterphobic reactions toward the remaining siblings; (4) the risks involved in psychological replacement and resurrection—thus, the surviving siblings live two lives, one for the parents, the other for themselves, which obviously is affected by the former consideration; (5) the circumstances of the sibling's dying, (e.g., sudden or chronic), the psychological age of the survivor, the premorbid or preillness relationship with the dead sibling (e.g., rivalry, negative identification, positive identification, love, degree of parental transference to the dead sibling); (6) the direction of creativity caused by the sibling's death (e.g., Mahler, Stalin, Barrie, Kerouac, Van Gogh, and others).

In my work with political leaders, I have been very interested not only in Lenin's sibling loss and Stalin's father loss when he was nine, but also in the case of Hitler, who lost three siblings before he was born; the death of his brother Edmund at age six, when Adolf was eleven, may have had a serious impact on his later fascination with death (Bank and Kahn, 1982). His bedroom overlooked the cemetery in which Edmund was buried, and neighbors noticed him frequently staring at the burial ground. After Edmund's death, "he became a brooding misfit, a spiteful, defiant troublemaker, who despised authorities" (Bank and Kahn, 1982, p. 291). He withdrew into fantasies, began drawing, and became openly hostile. His disappointed and strict father may have played a role in his sadism and arrogant claim to superiority and invulnerability. After all, he survived four siblings, but had no children of his own.

Levine (1984) has written, "most live as though life was something yet to come. But as John Lennon pointed out, 'Life is what happens while we are busy making other plans'" (p. ix). I have touched on some of the sibling catastrophes that we encountered in our clinical work—perhaps we will be more sensitive to these in the future.

4
PROCESS AND AFFECT: MOURNING AND GRIEF

INTRODUCTION

The psychoanalytic instrument, which includes method, setting, and existing theories, uniquely allows for depth investigations over time of many psychological phenomena. Our focus here is on depression and other painful affects as they relate to the psychoanalytic situation.

The study of fundamental phenomena, processes, and laws is as basic for any science as it is for psychoanalysis. We deal with fundamental phenomena every day—in our work, in ourselves, and in those who are close to us or with whom we are intimately involved. Phenomena can be described in simple terms and their presence can be confirmed by other careful observers. These are the facts or realities of existence with which we are involved. In psychoanalysis we relate to many phenomena, both internal and external, stemming from the varied relationships in which we are immersed. However, phenomena must be distinguished from the labels and the theories that may have explanatory, causal, etiological, or pathological meanings and significance. Confusion between factual descriptions, designations, and theory can give rise to serious difficulties, methodological and ideological. Since our science is concerned with

Presented in an abridged version as part of a Dialogue on "Depression and Other Painful Affects" at the 30th International Psycho-Analytical Congress, Jerusalem, August 1977.

This study comes from the Barr-Harris Center for the Study of Separation and Loss During Childhood of the Chicago Institute for Psychoanalysis; supported in part by the Anne Pollock Lederer Research Fund of the Chicago Institute for Psychoanalysis.

Reprinted from the *International Journal of Psycho-Analysis*, 59:255–276 (1978).

more than ontogenetic descriptions, we must be constantly aware of the historical and developmental dimensions of the individual as well as of the various forces that have shaped outcomes at critical stages and of process itself. Process has its own developmental history. It can be continuous or discontinuous, and even when fully developed has a progression of stages. We are particularly invested in the sequence, alteration, vicissitude, and outcome of process and change as we see it clinically and observationally. Our involvement with change is fundamental to the applications of our science to therapeutic work and to our understanding of the individual over time, and through the many layers of functioning at a given time. Since we pay particular attention to feelings, emotions, and affects, it is useful to consider them and their changing patterns as being specific indicators of change as process is progressing. Affects are a class of indicators of change. In the course of processual progression, we find different affects present at a single stage (assuming one can theoretically isolate such a stage for study) as well as different affect states at the different stages of the process. For simplicity, I am presenting these considerations as if we are dealing with a single process at a particular time. This of course is not what actually exists. There are many interacting systems and processes during development and at later points in time after the organism has achieved maturity, which influence each other as well as have their own outcomes. Interactions occur at many levels within the individual and between the individual and the external world. Processes and systems have their own developmental histories, their own paths of progression, and their own end points. It is my contention that in man these processes additionally have an evolutionary history and, using a Darwinian approach, have or had survival value for the entire species and for the reproducing individuals of the species. In man, with his highly developed psychic and neural apparatus, we obviously go beyond the simpler models used in less highly developed and structured beings, but the interacting processes, interacting systems, and structures can still be studied as if they operated independently. Since I maintain that affects are signals or indicators of processes, it can be useful to begin from this perspective.

At the outset I again wish to emphasize the distinction

between empirical and conceptual problems. I believe the lack of clarity about this difference gives rise to difficulties in communication, understanding, meaningful application, and further research. One could discuss the scientific and philosophical aspects of such distinctions but I will refrain from this now. Since science is essentially a question-oriented and problem-solving activity, we can consider theories insofar as they provide adequate solutions to problems, and answers to questions, as an end result of scientific activity (Laudan, 1977). Laudan suggests that "the function of a theory is to resolve ambiguity, to reduce irregularity to uniformity, to show that what happens is somehow intelligible and predictable" (1977, p. 13). He further distinguishes between two different kinds of problems which scientific theories attempt to solve: *empirical* and *conceptual* problems. Empirical problems, or first order problems, are those questions that directly relate to phenomena for which we seek an explanation. Anything in our natural world that is in need of explanation is an empirical problem. The second type of problem-solving and question-answering activity deals with conceptual or nonempirical issues. Laudan notes: "if empirical problems are first order questions about the substantive entities in some domain, conceptual problems are higher order questions about the well-foundedness of the conceptual structures (e.g., theories) which have been devised to answer first order questions" (p. 48). Since a conceptual problem has broader and at times deeper significance than an empirical problem and its immediate solution, the conceptual formulation or theory is more serious than the empirical solution. The overall effectiveness of a theory is ascertained "by assessing the number and importance of the empirical problems which the theory solves and deducting therefrom the number and importance of the anomalies [questions] and conceptual problems which the theory generates" (Laudan, 1977, p. 68). As theory is changed in one dimension the change becomes meaningful "if and only if the later version is a more effective problem solver than its predecessor" (Laudan, 1977, p. 69).

Freud, ever mindful of such concerns, was constantly involved in the relationship of empirical problems to conceptual problems. He himself changed his theories when they did not fit the data of observation, and as new data have come to the fore, he modified, extended, or even in some instances contracted the scope of a given theory.

The distinction between empirical and conceptual problems is obviously not a clear one and should be seen as a continuum. Conceptual orientations influence what we consider empirical questions. "Problems of all sorts (including empirical ones) arise within a certain context of inquiry and are partly defined by that context" (Laudan, 1977, p. 15). Put another way, "whether something is regarded as an empirical problem will depend, in part, on the theories we possess" (Laudan, 1977, p. 15).

When we speak of painful affects, including depression, what are we investigating? It is well known that depression is a feeling state that may be of short- or long-term duration, reactive to a trauma or stress or strain, and with or without pathological significance. Depression may be a characterologic state, a disease or syndrome of varying degrees of seriousness, or a concomitant state of another pathological entity. The affect has psychological, behavioral, emotional, cognitive, biochemical, and physiological correlates. The affect itself can occur at different stages of development, can be seen in its relationship to other affects, and in the psychoanalytic situation may be a transference experience that may not be capable of being remembered and linked to the past. Its meaning may be inferred and reconstructively interpreted by analyst and/or analysand. When we consider the meaning of affects, we can recognize that affects may serve as (1) communications in the intimate bonding situation and in reaction to stimuli which disrupt or threaten the unity of such symbiotic states (Pollock, 1964); (2) manifestations of internal psychological processes either externally or internally precipitated and having a sequential and temporal dimension; and as (3) indicators of crisis, illness, resolution, or satisfaction.

The depression spectrum has been a topic of inquiry from the earliest days of psychoanalysis. The pioneering empirical and conceptual studies of Freud and Abraham are still of great value. But we know that despite the marked accumulation of clinical empirical data and the increase in the number of conceptual formulations and theories, the clinical problem of depression still remains, and we are challenged to review and integrate the findings of many investigators and theoreticians in the hope of uncovering additional unsolved problems. Competing and alternative theories are welcomed. They stimulate new researches and inquiries. Ambiguity, though frustrating, can facilitate the transformation of unsolved problems into solved ones. We know that "what one generation of scientists will accept as a perfectly adequate solution will often be viewed by the next generation as a hopelessly inadequate one" (Laudan, 1977, p. 25) even though predecessor contributions may still be valid even though they have less general application than was originally believed. We also must be aware, as Laudan reminds us, that a theory usually involves an entire network of theories. Consequently, if a prediction or explanation turns out to be erroneous or inadequate, we may not be able to locate quickly the error in the theoretical network. To abandon the entire theory complex may be unnecessary and can in and of itself be an error. If we can ascertain what still had validity and what may be wrong or applicable only to specific instances and not to a general population, we can advance our science and open the doors for further crucial and important study and problem solving. It is unfortunate if we become emotional partisans or antagonists when we disagree or cannot accept a particular hypothesis. For we no longer have scientific challenge but polarization when each side attempts to seek only confirmation of its own views and attacks the other. When we distinguish between empirical and conceptual problems, we may have a clearer understanding of where differences occur and how they can be resolved.

Pierre Duhem (1954), the French physicist-philosopher, has observed that the testing of theories is more complicated than one might imagine. He pointed out that individual theories do not usually allow for that which can be directly observed in the laboratory and, I would add, in the clinical observational situation. Duhem maintained that only a complex conjunction of a variety of theories can lead to predictions about the world. We should recognize that theory complexes cannot be tested but that individual theories only can be empirically tested. One can rarely claim that an entire theory is either proven or refuted. In our theory appraisal activities, be they in the clinical situation, the laboratory, or in any other observational setting, we act as if we are dealing with only one theory and one set of circumstances, yet we can appreciate the fact that "the successful prediction of an experimental outcome leaves us in as much doubt about how to distribute credit, as an unsuccessful prediction leaves us unclear where to locate blame" (Laudan, 1977, p. 41). Laudan believes it is "entirely appropriate to talk about the appraisal of individual theories—with the proviso that such appraisals concern problem solving effectiveness and not truth or falsity" (p. 41). It is hoped that the relationship of these considerations clarifies some of the issues which previously led to error, incompleteness, controversy, and confusion.

ON AFFECTS AND THEIR CLASSIFICATION

In 1877 Charles Darwin published his fascinating essay "A Biographical Sketch of an Infant" in which he reported on the observations he made of one of his own children thirty-seven years earlier (in 1840). His empirical data on the reflexes, perceptions, and bodily movements in relationship to external stimuli are succinctly described and have the ring of authenticity. His descriptions of emotional reactions, antedating his classic 1872 study, *The Expression of the Emotions in Man and Animals*, provide us with some of the first systematic empirical data dealing with affects and infancy.

The observational data, some presented on a longitudinal developmental axis, are of great interest, but I bring this pioneering essay to the reader's attention because Darwin presents us here with one of the first observational classifications of affect. He notes that "pleasurable sensations" are associated with sucking, looking at mother, and are accompanied by smiling at forty-five days of age. Aesthetic pleasure in his four-month-old child was associated with hearing the pianoforte. Affectionate behavior was seen when the infant was under two months of age. At about six months of age, depression was identified. Fear, believed by Darwin to be one of the earliest feelings experienced by infants, was seen when the infant was a few weeks old and was followed by crying. "Moral sense," shame, anger come after the first year, and shyness was observed during the second year.

Darwin could distinguish between crying due to hunger,

pain, and suffering as early as eleven weeks of age and even earlier in one of his other children. Darwin (1877) writes:

> The wants of an infant are at first made intelligible by instinctive cries, which after a time are modified in part unconsciously, and in part, as I believe, voluntarily as a means of communication, by the unconscious expression of the features, by gestures and in a marked manner by different intonations, lastly by words of a general nature invented by himself, then of a more precise nature imitated from those which he hears; and these later are acquired at a wonderfully quick rate. An infant understands to a certain extent, and I believe at a very early period, the meaning or feelings of those who tend him, by the expression of their features [pp. 473–474].

In addition to a classification of infantile affects, Darwin gives us longitudinal observational data on a single infant, his own, over a period of time—truly a superb study and one that relates to current research on facial expression as a means of communication. One might add that his data suggest an evolved series of mechanisms designed very early to facilitate mother-infant bonding or attachment behavior and to form the matrix for later bonding relationships which I include under the general term *symbiosis* and which I believe extends throughout the entire life cycle (Pollock, 1964). Obviously when bonding, symbiosis, or attachment behavior is present, that which early threatens separation or effects separation evokes states of disease which include anxiety, fear, sadness, and other painful affects including anger. The process that is initiated by such "separating experiences" and which can eventuate in the adult in a satisfactory rapprochement internally and externally, I call the mourning process. The various phases of the process occur sequentially although the borders of each stage are indistinct and each phase has various affect states, not all different from each other. Although already observed in its earliest forms in young infants, the entire process has its own developmental progression and can be arrested or deviated into pathological directions. The mourning process progresses developmentally; that is, each phase comes into being at different developmental stages. In the adult we may find the fully mature mourning process with its various stages telescoped into a sequential progression. Arrests or deviations of the process may occur at the various developmental stages of the process. Thus we can get arrest, fixation, or deviation at any mourning process stage that has already come into existence. This consideration will be discussed below in another context (i.e., differences in the conceptualizations of when mourning is possible). I do wish to emphasize again that I believe the mourning process is a universal adaptational and transformational process having sequential phases and stages, phylogenetically evolved, and present as a reaction to loss, but not solely to object loss or object death. Bereavement is a subclass of the mourning process related to external object death. Furthermore, I believe each phase or stage of the mourning process has varied affect states and that three outcomes of a mourning process are possible: successful completion with a creative outcome; an arrest at various stages of the process; and a pathological or deviated process that is closely, though not exclusively, related to melancholia, the depressive disorders, and their potentially lethal outcome. These considerations have been elaborated in publications (chapters 1 and 8; Pollock, 1977a). The mourning process is related to specific historical or biographical contexts, which may or may not be remembered, recollected, or cognitively experienced. In the psychoanalytic situation, however, emotional recapitulation does occur and requires understanding by the analyst before interpretations can be offered.

Engel (1963) has noted that transitions between states of health and disease are regularly accompanied, if not heralded, by affect changes. In a sense, the affect change can be viewed as a signal of an internal balance shift. In order to understand the meaning of different affects, Engel attempted his classification of the phenomenology of affects within the framework of psychoanalytic theory. As others have noted, Engel understands the behavioral expression of affects as a means of communication to and with others of needs, distress, or degree of comfort. This communicative aspect of affect is particularly important for the helpless infant who depends on adult caretakers for its needfulfillment and reestablishment of equilibrium. The affect communications include internal signals or messages as well as external behavioral manifestations.

Typically the overt expression of affect evokes a complementary affective response in others. We consider empathy as related to this internal and external communication network and we are now able to describe more precisely the cues utilized in this affective exchange. Such cues are essential to bonding, symbiotic, or attachment exchanges. Although concerned with crises, Engel suggests that affects are present at all times, even during sleep. Their internal communicative expression can be observed in dreams.

The earliest affect experiences are relatively undifferentiated and are called *primal undifferentiated affects* by Engel. They usually indicate satiety or need, pleasure or unpleasure, and are communicated to the outside environment as well as within the organism. As the mental apparatus develops with progressive internalization of the environment and differentiation of self and object representations occurs, distinctive affect qualities appear. These are designated as *differentiated affects* which can be further subdivided into *signal scanning affects* and *drive-discharge affects*. The signal scanning affects are further subdivided into those indicating *unpleasure* (e.g., anxiety, shame, guilt, disgust, sadness, helplessness, and hopelessness); and those indicating *pleasure* (e.g., contentment, confidence, joy, pride, and hope).

The drive-discharge affects show less signal activity and more releasing activity. Drive-discharge affects are not classified as either pleasant or unpleasant, but are categorized in relation to the major drive tendencies; that is, anger and rage being the affects of aggression, and love, affection, tenderness, and sexual feelings being the affects of the libidinal drive. In addition, Engel considers the *affects of partial or fused drives*, such as envy, greed, sympathy, pity, impatience, and stubbornness. He emphasizes that the two major divisions of affects, signal-scanning and drive-discharge, are not mutually exclusive; each has qualities of the other, but in one or the other there is a relative prominence of the respective phenomenological features. Although the equilibrium-maintaining aspect of affects as normal phenomena is emphasized, we are clinically aware of affective disorders and syndromes where affective imbalance is indicative of disease processes. In discussing affects, additional considerations include possibilities of affect equivalents, defenses, facilitators, and inhibitors.

The primal affects of unpleasure include *primal anxiety* or fight-flight patterns, and *primal depression–withdrawal* or the *con-servation-withdrawal pattern*. Primal anxiety evolves gradually into more differentiated anxiety as the distinctions between self and not-self and later between self and the other occur. For example, a generalized crying fit begins to be linked more specifically as a response to actual separation, the absence of the familiar facial configuration, darkness, strange places, or to a strange face. Engel examines anxiety in terms of ego, self object, and drive, and traces the developmental paths that finally culminate in the specific affectual quality that differentiates anxiety from other affects.

Depression-withdrawal as an identifiable affect state appears early in life, but is much less well defined than anxiety. He suggests that the psychic elaboration of depression-withdrawal as affect may develop around the same time in infancy as it does for anxiety. Depression-withdrawal is less likely to be vocally expressed than anxiety and much has to be inferred from the manifest visible behavior of the child. Depression-withdrawal as an undifferentiated affect indicates loss of supplies and the need for conservation of energy. Other more complex affects, such as helplessness and hopelessness, may evolve from depression-withdrawal. Depression-withdrawal is self-preservative. It conserves energy, and includes a reinforced stimulus barrier which reduces incoming stimuli. The reduction of activity (withdrawal), for example, sleep, saves energy. Unless the environment responds appropriately and actively, such a state is not compatible with life for long.

As development of the mental apparatus takes place, affective experiences become more differentiated, and distinctive affect qualities can be identified. The signal-scanning affects, more involved in the control and regulation of psychic equilibrium, serve as signal systems for the initiation of defensive and integrative processes within the ego in terms of pleasure and unpleasure (pain). Affects that are pleasurable (e.g., joy, pride), and those that are painful (e.g., anxiety, shame, guilt, sadness), are indicators of internal reactions. Sadness indicates object loss, real, threatened, or fantasied, but not yet a giving up. Sadness as a transitional affect includes nostalgia, longing, and hope for eventual reunion. The image of the self is felt to be in varying degrees impoverished, deprived, empty, weakened, or in some way deficient. Engel's descriptions suggest a continuum with sadness at one end of the spectrum and despair at the other.

Anger and hope are the painful affects considered under the drive-discharge affects, especially of aggression.

Spitz (1963) has also suggested that early unpleasure is a response to experiencing pain, discomfort, or a failure of the stimulus shield to protect the infant against overload. Negative emotions appear later than somatic pain or discomfort. "The first unequivocal psychological manifestations of unpleasure in the infant occur when he begins to cry when left by the adult with whom he has been in contact. This behavior appears after the third month of life and is the counterpart of the smiling response" (Spitz, 1963, p. 54). "The infant will react to the adult's moving away by expressing negative emotion in antici-pation of being deprived of the gratification of this quasi need" (p. 54). Before three months the experience of discomfort and pain is manifested mainly as a physiological upset. The later counterpart in the adult is a general somatic reaction such as nausea. In general Spitz's conceptualizations closely correspond to those of Engel, but his emphasis is on the importance of the mother-child relationship in organizing the original discharge of unpleasure into recognizably different expressions linked to specific emotions. "The unfolding of the individual child's ob-ject relations parallels closely the ontogenesis of the expression of his emotions" (Spitz, 1963, p. 57). Later emotions are dif-ferentiated in response to specific object relations.

Several additional affect classifiers should be briefly men-tioned before concluding this section. Shand (1920) in his classic work, *The Foundations of Character*, described and discussed in great detail his organization of primary emotions such as fear, anger, joy, sorrow, disgust, and repugnance and surprise. Al-though phenomenologic and not psychoanalytic in orientation, Shand's ideas are worthy of note.

Glover (1939) suggested various ways of classifying affects. He believed the pleasure-pain criterion was unsatisfactory. Among his categorizations, he considered the division of affects into fixed and labile, primary and secondary, positive and re-active, tension and discharge, simple or compound, and so on. Glover believed depression to be an exceedingly complicated affect. "Some states of depression are certainly simpler and more primitive than others" (p. 302). The affective matrix of depression includes "a feeling of impoverishment due to internal loss of love, feeling of deadness due to the action of internal anger directed against the love-object (with which the ego is partly identified) together with reactions of anxiety, guilt and remorse . . . an overwhelming feeling of hurt, the ultimate expression of frustration" (p. 302). This depressive matrix may be an overriding entity that is seen throughout healthy and pathological states of being. Thus to Glover depression was a pathological entity that was unique and specific.

Jacobson (1971) also presented a classification of affects. She criticized Glover's schema and replaced his classification with one employing more current structural concepts. Jacobson distinguished between simple and compound affects arising from intrasystemic tensions; for example, between and from the drives, the id, the ego, and those induced by intersystemic tensions between ego and id, and between ego and superego. Although she used the term *tension* rather than *conflict*, she recognized that affect and affective states might be expressive of conflict. What comes through from the attempt at classifying affects is the necessity to differentiate affects from disease entities, to consider distinctions of affect as developmental proceeds, to recognize the possible adaptive significance of affects, and to continually reexamine affect theory from the perspective of ongoing advances in our conceptualization about the psychic apparatus. The distinction between empirical and conceptual problems is clearly applicable when we address the questions of affect in its normal and pathological dimensions. The monumental contribution of Rapaport (1953), "On the Psycho-Analytic Theory of Affects," will be noted here without further discussion. Rapaport's encyclopedic review and his contributions to the theory of affects is a core contribution that should be studied by all students of our discipline.

Brenner (1974a) has reexamined affect theory with the purpose of reformulating our ideas about this significant area of human behavior. He distinguishes affects on the basis of their pleasurable or unpleasurable content. He recognizes that unpleasurable affects (e.g., depressive), can have differing origins and differing ideational content from patient to patient.

Based primarily on data derived from the psychoanalytic situation, he offers a unified theory of affects. In summary he states:

> Affects are complex mental phenomena which include (a) sensations of pleasure, unpleasure, or both, and (b) ideas. Ideas and pleasure/unpleasure sensations together constitute an affect as a mental or psychological phenomenon.
>
> The development of affects and their differentiation from one another depend on ego and, later, superego development. Indeed the development and differentiation of affects is an important aspect of ego development.
>
> Affects have their beginnings early in life when ideas first become associated with sensations of pleasure and unpleasure. . . . They constitute the undifferentiated matrix from which the entire gamut of the affects of later life develop [p. 554].

In a later paper he compares the affects of anxiety and depression and relates these to the pleasure principle (Brenner, 1975). Brenner's contributions are clarifying and useful, but he seemingly ignores the relationship of affects to our more current ideas about the self and its ongoing development. Furthermore one might ask if the affects associated with conflict are the same as those which are present in a unified selfhood when there is minimal pathological conflict. One might even ask if anxiety itself is an affect. Perhaps if we consider anxiety as a special category of response, we can then consider painful, painless, and agreeable-enjoyable affects from a different perspective than has heretofore been the case. Anxiety, the response and/or signal, can be viewed as a general reaction. Affects can in turn be viewed as specific indicators of various internal processes and of different stages of a process. Perhaps there is not one unitary theory of affects but several theories. As affects are different in quality, they may also be different in ontogenesis, and in meaning in different age groups and under different circumstances.

In his essay "Some Observations on Depression, on Nosology, on Affects, and on Mourning" Brenner (1974b) doubts if patients in analysis exhibit mourning as Freud described it. He has never observed this and he does not know if other analysts have seen it. Brenner, working with psychoanalytic patients, comes to a conclusion different from that of Freud. He believes the basic issues are anger, triumph, and hatred—feelings that are intolerable to the mourner. Instead, the "painful, compulsory preoccupation with memories of a dead person serves a largely defensive function" (p. 18). In contrast to Brenner, I have observed what Freud originally described as mourning behavior, including what we would consider libido detachment and libido reattachment. If one considers mourning as a process, composed of various component phases each with varied affects, then what Brenner observed in his patients can be viewed as one aspect of the process, along with the more traditionally described behaviors and affects. It may also be important to distinguish observations made on patients in active psychoanalytic treatment from nonpatients, and to also consider additional variables such as chronicity or acuity of the death process, significance of the dead object, as well as other factors.

ON THE MOURNING PROCESS AND DEPRESSION

In the mid-1950s, following the sudden and unexpected death of my mother, I began my study of the mourning process. As my own mourning work proceeded, I was able to observe the subjective experiencing part of myself in a more objective fashion. My dreams, varied affect states, and beginning resolutions of my shock, pain, sadness, and other painful feelings became muted and were then succeeded by affective states and activities that were more positive than what had been present previously. I could discern sublimations, and also new directions for my endeavors. As an outcome of this study of myself, I began to study the process in which I was involved, which was very meaningful to me, and which brought forth new insights into myself and for my understanding of mourning theory. The continuing inquiry into the specific subject led to a broadening of my clinical and conceptual knowledge. I found my research moved into more discernible areas that were distinct in and of themselves (Pollock, 1966; and see chapters 17, 18, and 19). One begins with a particular study of a specific topic or experience but soon finds many different paths that lead from the original stimulus and investigation. This has been my experience in my research on the mourning process. Beginning with the subjective and then attempting to objectify what I learned I pursued different strands. Newer ideas took form and these shaped my further clinical and theoretical investigative efforts. This process is still ongoing, but on occasions such as this, one can pause, examine the state of one's knowledge, attempt to relate and synthesize the empirical and conceptual findings of others with one's own positions, and then present a statement which reflects where one is at, keeping in mind that much remains of the journey of further exploration. I shall not review my already published reports further at this time but, as indicated above, I see the mourning process as a universal adaptational series of intrapsychic operations occurring in sequential successive stages involved in the re-establishment of a new level of internal and related external equilibrium (see chapter 12). The stages, though somewhat unidirectional, do on occasion oscillate and revert back temporarily to earlier stages as part of the back and forth transformational process. The mourning process occurs in the lives of all and is not the same as bereavement, which, as I noted above, I see as the specific subclass of the mourning process occurring after a meaningful person has died. I do not absolutely link the mourning process with object loss, although object loss has been most characteristically associated with mourning and I myself have studied object loss as the example par excellence to investigate the mourning process. The subject of the external and internal meaning of the object and its loss is one that psychoanalysis has and will continue to study. But there are other avenues available to study the mourning process. Recently I have suggested that all change involving the "loss" of something and the "gain" of the new entails a mourning process that may be brief, nonconscious, and in telescopic fashion including affects associated with the process. On the basis of my research I have been able to distinguish clinically between three outcomes of the process. In the optimal resolution, the mourning work allows for the acceptance of reality and a subsequent deployment of psychic investment in other more acceptable and gratifying activities, relationships, or objects. In some, there is an arrest of the mourning process itself and sublimatory and creative resolution remains either in limbo or does not take place until the process can be resumed and carried to completion. Fleming and Altschul (1963) have written about how mourning can be activated during psychoanalytic treatment in order to facilitate further work. The third outcome is one that we are more familiar with and which clinically is associated with diagnosis of melancholia, depressive disorders, and other disturbances clustered around the clinical condition of depressive disorder. I believe this description is insufficiently precise and should be replaced with other diagnostic terminology. I believe the actual diseases called depression are many and have different etiologies even though presenting symptoms include depression. Furthermore, depression, as Glover (1939) has noted, can be found in almost all disease entities.

In my research on creativity, I have not found that creative work or play is only found when there has been a successful mourning process per se, although clinically I have seen this occur. I have observed that creative work at times is used in the service of the mourning work itself. The relationship of creativity to the mourning process is one that requires much more careful study. Our present formulations, some of which will be presented in the next section, will undoubtedly be revised, extended, and reexamined in the light of newer future discoveries in our science. I also believe that although the mourning process has its own developmental history that can be linked to other developmental accomplishments, in its earliest form it must have evolved phylogenetically in order to facilitate survival of the individual and the group; that is, self-preservative and species preservative. When one approaches the mourning process from the developmental perspective, the question of whether mourning is possible in infancy, childhood, or adolescence becomes one concerning the stages of the process as they come into being at particular times of overall development. Thus in the early infantile period, the earlier and more primitive stages of the mourning process are in evidence. These may correspond in some ways to what has been observed in higher mammals (see chapter 1). As the psychic apparatus develops further, later stages of the process come into being and are utilized in the mourning process when it is set into motion. Studies of infants, children, and adolescents provide empirical data for this assertion. To be certain we do not have one system or process operating in isolation—it is related to and linked with what is ongoing in the many developments of the psychic apparatus. But for research, we on occasion attempt to study the process as though it existed by itself. In the mourning process, the linkages extend to all aspects of psychic functioning, some more and some less significant than others.

One theoretical position concerning the depressive syndrome repeatedly stressed suggests that during infancy a constellation appears which is the prototype or model for all depressive reactions that occur in later life. Mahler (1961) has called our attention to the importance of grief and mourning as the immediate precursor to the psychotic break with reality in vulnerable children. She also suggests that sadness and grief can have positive importance for the child when there is restoration of the libidinal object. Anna Freud (1965) suggests, however, that mourning is the painful, gradual process of detachment of libido from an internal image and so cannot be expected to occur before object constancy has occurred. For her mourning is not the same as the various manifestations of anxiety, distress, and malfunction which accompany object loss in the earliest phases of development. In the ambivalence conflicts present in the older child, reunion with the parents is only palliative and only analytic work can truly cure the disorder. This is in contrast with the infant separated from the parent, where reunion with the parent relieves the distress. Miss Freud (1942) notes that grief in the young child is short-lived, as its "life is still entirely governed by principles which demand that he should seek pleasure and avoid pain and discomfort" (p. 184). The child cannot bear discomfort as it is unable to foresee that pleasure can once again be reached. The child's memories of the past and his future outlook are not sufficiently established so as to maintain an inner relationship with loved objects and in this way help it bridge the painful period until reunion is possible. The child's "needs are so urgent that they require immediate gratification; promises of pleasure do not aid him" (1942, p. 184). In her discussion of John Bowlby's work on separation, grief, and mourning, she again questions the use of the term *mourning* in its technical sense for the separation reactions of the infant because the infant's reactions are governed by the pleasure-pain principle. She does not link early separations with later depressive or melancholic illness. The chronological age of the child is of less importance than the level of ego maturity and the level of object relationship reached by the child before separation, especially as it bears on the length of loss reactions. She observes that the nearer to the object constancy state, the longer the duration of the brief reactions and its closer correspondence to the adult internal process of mourning. In the separation reactions of children she had observed: psychosomatic disturbances (e.g., sleeping upsets, feeding upsets, constipation, increased tendency to develop respiratory infections); regression in the libidinal and aggressive spheres; regression in ego development (e.g., loss of speech, bowel, and bladder control); and upsets in libido distribution. The longer the separation, the more difficult it becomes to reverse these pathological developments. In another study Anna Freud (1958) compared the states of mourning, the reaction to an unhappy love, and the libidinal position of adolescence. She notes all may have mental suffering, all have an urgent wish to be helped with their pain, and none responds well to analytic therapy as the immediate object lost must first be given up before analytic treatment can become effective.

Anna Freud's conceptualizations based on her empirical studies and her theoretical understanding introduce alternative considerations as they relate to the mourning process. In a related position Mahler (1961) has also noted that systematic affective disorders are unknown in childhood as the immature personality structure of the infant or the older child is not capable of producing a state of depression as is seen in the adult. But as soon as the ego emerges from the undifferentiated state, the behavioral signs of grief appear, albeit in rudimentary form. Children seemingly recover from transient reactions of grief with lesser or greater scar formation. Mahler, like Freud (1926 [1925]) sees "grief as the reaction specific to object loss, and anxiety as the reaction specific to the danger which loss entails" (Mahler, 1961, p. 343). Furthermore, the subjective feeling of longing is viewed by her as a precursor of the affect of sadness and grief. Only if there has been a libidinal object can sadness and grief occur when the object is lost. Thus, according to Mahler, grief is late in its appearance and is dependent upon the gestalt of the need-satisfying mother.

Anna Freud and Mahler have described for us the earliest

developmental aspects of the mourning process as they have empirically observed them. These features can be seen in the early phases of the mature mourning process in adults where initially regression to early pregrief states occurs. It seems that what is developmentally early also appears in the early phases of the full-grown and fully completed adult reaction. As the mourning process in the adult proceeds, it grossly seems to recapitulate the developmental history of the process itself. The findings of Anna Freud and Mahler are at variance with those of Bowlby (1960) and to some extent with the conclusions reached by Melanie Klein (1940) who also indicates that the young child's reaction is similar to mourning in adults.

On a developmental time axis, Melanie Klein (1940) connects the very early depressive position with later normal mourning activity. Bowlby (1960, 1961b) considers the response of infants and young children from six months onward to the loss of an object as being the same as grief and mourning in adults. The position of Anna Freud and Mahler is close to that of R. Furman (1964), who believes that mourning can occur quite early in childhood if the child has a concept of death, has attained the stage of object constancy, and has reached the phallic level of object relationships—this corresponds roughly to chronological age four. R. Furman writes: "if the representation of the object cannot be maintained in the object's absence, the decathexis cannot occur" (p. 325). In a clinical study of twenty-three children who had lost a parent through death and were intensively treated by child psychoanalysts, Erna Furman provides us with an up-to-date formulation of Robert Furman's conceptualizations. In this volume, Mrs. Furman (1974) also discusses many of the crucial topics of grief and mourning as well as a review of the pertinent literature. Wolfenstein (1966) holds that adolescence constitutes the necessary developmental condition for being able to mourn. In her work with latency children and adolescents who had lost a major love object, she found her subjects: denied the finality of the loss; expected the dead parent to return; and hypercathected the representation of the lost object instead of decathecting it. Wolfenstein compares adolescence to mourning, as Anna Freud (1958) and J. Lampl-de Groot (1960) had done earlier, and she suggests that the trial mourning of adolescence is a critical precursor for the more mature mourning process. There are questions one could raise about Wolfenstein's comparisons and requirements for the operation of the mature mourning process. In adolescence the process of detachment is internal and self-regulated, while in mourning, there usually is an external precipitant (e.g., an object loss, a disappointment, a lack of attainment of an aspirational ideal, and the process is not under one's control). Wolfenstein's descriptions of her patients' reactions seem to describe defensive attempts to deal with the overwhelming trauma of the losses. Perhaps this is all her children could do. Her distinction between adaptive reactions to major object loss in childhood from mourning itself is useful. These adaptive reactions may be seen as part of a mourning process that either is arrested, deviated, or not fully developed. For example, denial through the substitution or replacement of the lost object is different from cathecting a new successor object following a mourning process. Substitution and replacement is a means of arresting the mourning process and so avoiding the painful work of accepting the new reality. Identification globally with the lost object may also be indicative of a deviant mourning process. In my study of anniversary reactions including suicide I found such pathological identifications of great importance (chapter 13). H. Deutsch (1937) in her classic paper on the absence of grief has noted that

> the process of mourning as reaction to the real loss of a loved person *must be carried to completion*. As long as the early libidinal or aggressive attachments persist, the painful affect continues to flourish, and *vice versa*, the attachments are unresolved as long as the affective process of mourning has not been accomplished [p. 21].

There are, however, some instances where the mature mourning process may not be able to be fully concluded; for example, maternal mourning for the death of a child, or when the mourning process cannot be completed because of the immaturity of the psychic apparatus at the time of the loss. Deutsch has also noticed children's indifference following the death of a loved person. She proposes that this occurs because "the ego of the child is not sufficiently developed to bear the strain of the work of mourning and that it therefore utilizes some mechanism of narcissistic self-protection to circumvent the process" (1937, p. 13). "This mechanism . . . may be a derivative of the early infantile anxiety which we know as the small child's reaction to separation from the protecting and loving person" (1937, p. 13). In Deutsch's pioneering report she proposes that the ego has to be strong enough for mourning to take place. If this is not the case, two courses are possible; either there is regression to earlier states and anxiety is present, or there is a mobilization of defensive forces which attempt to protect the ego from disintegration. In her view, the most extreme expression of this defensive operation is the omission of affect.

The above conclusions of the psychoanalytic investigators of the mourning process might be integrated if one views the mourning process as a sequential process that is intimately related to the maturation of the psychic apparatus. The early phases of the process are linked to earlier developmental periods and occur early in the ontogenetic process in the adult who mourns. Perhaps it is only with the completion of adolescence that one is capable of completing the entire mourning process as we characteristically see it in the adult. In younger individuals they may only have attained and are capable of experiencing that part of the mourning process that the development of their psychic apparatus allows. Arrests, deviations, and regressions from and to the various phases of the mourning process are possible and their assessment can be of diagnostic value. Working analytically with such arrested, regressed, or deviated mourning process individuals one can obtain data that allows for a more precise diagnosis of where and when mourning arrest, fixation, regression, or deviation occurred. The analytic work can then assist the patient to carry the mourning process further and in accord with adult reality, even though the loss, disappointment, or failure to attain the aspirational ideal had taken place at an earlier period.

Bowlby's pioneering studies, empirically and conceptually, have been stimulating and helpful. His comprehensive reviews of pertinent psychoanalytic and other research and theory are to be commended. His critiques, though not universally accepted, are in the true tradition of science. As others have noted, I, too, would wonder if his phases of the mourning process,

Protest (separation anxiety), Despair (grief and depression), and Detachment and Reorganization, are truly the same for all individuals from six months of age onwards. Are the reactions, phases, and even processes identical in infant, young child, and adult? Bowlby and perhaps Klein seemingly do not consider developmental maturations beyond infancy in their published reports. Bowlby's data, especially as they relate to the affects of sorrow and anger in the mourning process are of great value to the empirical phenomenologist. His attempts at terminological precision are also to be appreciated. He proposes that mourning denotes the psychological processes set in motion by the loss of a loved object and commonly leads to the relinquishing of the object, though not always so. Grief, on the other hand, denotes the sequence of subjective states that follow loss and accompany mourning. Bowlby's definition of grief is too broad for utility as I believe this compound affect can be more carefully delineated and described. He himself notes (Bowlby, 1961b) that "grief . . . is a peculiar amalgam of anxiety, anger and despair following the experience of what is feared to be irretrievable loss" and that

> Mourning is best regarded as the whole complex sequence of psychological processes and their manifestations, beginning with craving, angry efforts at recovery, and appeals for help, proceeding through apathy and disorganization of behavior, and ending when some form of more or less stable reorganization is beginning to develop [p. 332].

This general affective progression mixed with more abstract purposeful explanation is useful in describing the young child's reaction to loss—but is this the same as the mature, fully developed mourning process seen in adults?

In 1963, Bowlby described four phenomenological forms of pathological mourning that are not completely exclusive but yet distinct. These include (1) anxiety and depression where a persistent and unconscious yearning to recover and reunite with the lost object is present; (2) intense anger and reproach, frequently unconscious, directed toward various objects including the self; (3) absorption in caring for others who have been bereaved; and (4) denial that the object is permanently lost, especially through the mechanism of splitting. Bowlby sees pathological mourning as giving rise to clinical conditions and anxiety and depressive illness, fetishism, and hysterical and psychopathic behavior. I have also seen pathological and arrested mourning in anniversary phenomena and psychosomatic conditions. The question remains, however, whether we are seeing pathology stemming from deviant mourning, object loss, or a combination of both of these factors.

Klein's classic 1940 paper describes her theoretical position which, though different from Bowlby, asserts that there is a close connection between normal mourning and the early processes of the mind, specifically what she called the infantile depressive position. The ability in later life to mourn and recover is contingent upon the resolution of this infantile depressive position. Klein's theories, though useful in explaining some clinical phenomena, are not buttressed by empirical observational data from normal children. Her conceptualizations of internal good and bad objects, again useful in an explanatory fashion, need further verification. Perhaps current laboratory research on infant-mother interactions will provide the empirical data that can be used to test various of her hypotheses. Klein (1940) writes: "the mourner is in fact ill, but because this state of mind is common and seems so natural to us, we do not call mourning an illness" (1940, pp. 136–137). Instead she sees the adult mourner going through the processes which the child normally goes through in his early development though in different circumstances and with different manifestations. Klein's insights and clinical descriptions are very stimulating. In fact we can confirm some of her clinical and empirical observations. Some of her theoretical explanations also have a feeling of authenticity. However, her attempts to equate early infantile states, which are deduced and inferred—perhaps correctly, but not necessarily so—with adult functioning does not seem to take into account the developmental progression and unfolding of the psychic apparatus that seems to take place on the road to maturity. Her discussion of reparative drives, restitution for destructive impulses in early childhood, and their relationship to creativity and sublimation, will be discussed in the next section.

Before closing this discussion, the work of Edward Bibring

should be mentioned. Although Bibring (1953) suggested that all depressions are affective states and are reactivations of an infantile structured ego state of helplessness, his position is different from that of Klein. He viewed depression as an intra-ego conflict. Rapaport (1967) has noted that Bibring's is a "structural theory which treats depression as the reactivation of a structured state" (p. 765). The Bibring theory of depression is not at variance with the theory that it is essential for a structured ego to be present for depression to appear. We might add that Bibring does not deal with mourning per se, but his ideas suggest he views depression as a process. Perhaps Rochlin's (1953) loss complex, in which he includes the relationship of object loss, depression, and dread of abandonment, can be viewed, as one might the work of Bibring, as pathological mourning.

THE MOURNING PROCESS, THE CREATIVE PROCESS, AND THE CREATION

My thesis, stated earlier, is that the successful completion of the mourning process results in creative outcome. This end result can be a great work of art, music, sculpture, literature, poetry, philosophy, or science, where the creator has the spark of genius or talent that is not related to mourning per se. Indeed the creative product may reflect the mourning process in theme, style, form, and content, and it may itself stand as a memorial. In the less gifted—and we have seen this in many clinical situations—a creative outcome may be manifested in a new real relationship, the ability to feel joy, satisfaction, a sense of accomplishment, or newer sublimations that reflect a successful resolution of the mourning process. In some individuals, great creativity may not be the outcome of the successfully completed mourning process but may be indicative of attempts at completing the mourning work. These creative attempts may be conceptualized as restitution, reparation, discharge, or sublimation. Though they may not always be successful in terms of mourning work solutions, the intrinsic aesthetic or scientific merit of the work still may be great despite the failure of mourning completion.

   Let me illustrate my thesis by examining the resolution of a piece of mourning work by the founder of our science, Sigmund Freud. Freud's father, Jakob, died on October 23, 1896. Although Jones (1953) notes that Freud first fully analyzed one of his dreams in July 1895, his "casual analyses became a regular procedure with a definite purpose" in July 1897 (Jones, 1953, p. 323). In thanking Fliess for the condolences he sent him after his father's death, Freud wrote:

> By one of the dark ways behind the official consciousness my father's death has affected me profoundly. I treasure him highly and had understood him exactly. With his peculiar mixture of deep wisdom and fantastic lightness he had meant very much in my life. He had passed his time when he died, but inside me the occasion of his death has reawakened all my early feelings. Now I feel quite uprooted [Jones, 1953, p. 324].

Jones reminds us that Freud told us it was this experience, his father's death and his mourning for him, that led Freud (1900) to write *The Interpretation of Dreams* in 1898. The writing of this classic went hand in hand with the first year or two of his self-analysis.

> In the Preface to the Second Edition, written in 1908, Freud said he only recognized the connexion with his father's death after finishing the book. "It revealed itself to me as a piece of my self-analysis, as my reaction to my father's death; that is, to the most important event, the most poignant loss, in a man's life" [Jones, 1953, p. 324].

Freud's father's death was the stimulus for the transformation of Freud's scientific interest and research into the mechanism of dreams and of mental life, as well as for the composing of his monumental book. In the February after his father's death, Freud questioned the seduction hypothesis and there were the first hints of his discovery of the Oedipus complex.

On October 15, 1897 (almost a year after his father's death), Freud announced two elements of the Oedipus complex, the love for one parent and jealous hostility to the other, in a letter to Fliess. These insights came directly from his self-analysis (Jones, 1953, p. 356). "The aftereffects of his father's death had been slowly working in those months between it and the decisive reaction to the event" [the writing of *The Interpretation of Dreams*]

(Jones, 1953, p. 356). It is my suggestion that we see here in dramatic fashion a superb illustration of my hypothesis that the successful completion of the mourning process results in a creative outcome—in Freud's life, a creation that has influenced all of our lives. I have elsewhere written about such creative outcome as related to the mourning process in the lives of Lenin (see chapter 20), Mahler (see chapter 27), De Quincey, James Barrie, Käthe Kollwitz, Jack Kerouac (Pollock, 1978), and am investigating the relationship of the mourning process in other writers, poets, artists, scientists, musical composers, philosophers, religious leaders, political and historically significant royal figures, in individuals whose accomplishments are not so widely known, and in patients who in the course of their analytic mourning work have the energy and motivation to lead productive, happy, and fulfilling lives. Although I have studied the biographies of creative individuals where there was an object loss through death, my research focus has been on the mourning process and not just on the object loss. It is my belief that the mourning process may be a critical factor in the creative process even without object loss through death. This hypothesis will require additional investigation.

Psychoanalysts have studied well-known individuals who have had childhood losses through death and reported their findings, but the focus usually is on either object loss or a preoccupation with death. Dr. P. Rentchnick (1975) states that, after studying over 350 biographies of political and religious leaders in history, a common denominator emerges, namely that "all the great leaders in history have been orphans, abandoned children, illegitimate children, or children who have rejected their father" (p. 50). I can confirm this correlation, though perhaps not agreeing that "all" such leaders are orphans. I have found similar mourning–object loss correlations in many writers and other gifted individuals. William Niederland, Bernard Meyer, Phyllis Greenacre, and others have discussed the relationship of creativity to object loss and grief in particular writers, scientists, explorers, and artists. Tor-Björn Hägglund, a colleague from Helsinki, has actively pursued research on mourning and has recently published a most interesting monograph. Hägglund (1976) concluded that "creativity is a continuation of mourning work"; however, when "creativity replaces mourning work, it is manifested in compulsory repetition" (p. 134).

Gay (1976) believes we can distinguish between three kinds of causes in works of art: the impact of the surrounding culture of the artist; his craft; and his personal psychological configuration. For different artists, and I would use the term *artist* in the broad sense and not just one dealing with visual spatial representations, one or another of the "causes" noted by Gay may be the predominant feature. With regard to the first cause, we may ask how we can assess the relative dominance of cultural impact or personal urgency, since both are present. One might additionally ask how one can compare the external and internal significances of cultural determinants in an individual creator. Conversely, one may query what impact the personal elements have on shaping the culture. For example, the personality of a Stalin, Hitler, Churchill, or Roosevelt can and I believe did have an impact on the political-sociocultural state of the world during a critical period of our history. Furthermore, can we discern in the creative product, through an analysis of the content, which elements are represented? We may not be talking about causes and effects but about antecedent elements that are woven together in unique ways to result in conditions, responses, reflections, and creations. To try to isolate the antecedent elements may be impossible or at least difficult. Analogously it would be like a qualitative-quantitative chemical analysis—we might determine which elements are present and in what amounts, but the unique configurations resulting in reactivity may not be so easily ascertained. The psychological reflections, definitions, and reworkings, additions and reflections, involvements, and choices that went on in the creator's mind in the preparation and production of the creative work are usually unavailable to us. Thus our speculations, even buttressed by seemingly appropriate correlations and significant repetitions, are at best approximations. This we should state, repeat, and emphasize.

We need also to separate explicitly the questioning of the psychoanalytic historian from the appreciation of the critic. As Gay notes, "The historian does not render critics redundant; his most exhaustive and most satisfactory causal explanation remains mute on the aesthetic properties, let alone aesthetic value, of a landscape or a symphony" (p. 3). Gay deals with art, not as an aesthetic object, but as a "piece of history." Too often our colleagues overlook this important distinction. We lose sight of the aesthetic value of a creation in our pursuit of understanding the psychological factors in the creator that may have played a role in its genesis. Both can be and are useful, but we must with humility address both considerations. Why a story, painting, musical composition, or poem, appeals to us can be as useful a contribution as is the approximate understanding of the creator's psychology or psychopathology. To be sure, we have not as yet fully addressed the question of aesthetics from a psychoanalytic vantage point. Perhaps we should begin thinking about this as an area for further study. In addition, to investigate the genetic determinants of the creator, it may be useful also to explore the historical factors associated with the particular creative work. This is to be contrasted with the search for the psychological meaning of the artistic achievement for its creator. At times we may easily detect the self-revelations in the creative product, at times what is formally expressed is less easily or at times impossible to discern and outside the domain of psychoanalytic study.

When we look at craft we are at a disadvantage unless we are truly students of the discipline in which the artist works. We need to know more about technique, style, and sensitivity, and so again with humility decline to conjecture about that which we know only superficially.

With regard to personality and psychological configuration, we recognize that multiple determinants and outcomes can be puzzling. Different psychoanalysts may focus upon one or another aspect of the same event or the same manifestations. Insofar as they ask different questions, use different theoretical approaches, look for different etiological antecedents, different features will assume a saliency that at times borders on exclusivity. Analogies or models may be treated as actualities. Fancy can become fact and caution is not in evidence. The theoretical approach and the question addressed may, if not put into appropriate perspective, appear to be the sole variable responsible for whatever is the subject of the report. It is true that some factors are more important, more serious, more meaningful than others. But such distinctions can be made more explicitly as well as the reasons for the choice and evaluation.

An artistic work undoubtedly represents some aspect, narrow or broad, shallow or deep, simple or complex, of its creator. But as is well known, understanding the creator, the meaning of the work, is speculative and probabilistic, unlike the data and explanations we can offer about individuals with whom we have had contact directly. This notwithstanding, I do not advocate abandoning the investigation of artists and their creations as I believe artists do give articulation to their personal perceptions, understandings, ideas, and values in their products. We may attempt to give meaning to these works but we have the responsibility to present evidence not just subjective impression, which has some significance. Perhaps repetitive patterns of response or style, correlations of thematic content with life events—past or present, observing similarities and connections—all of these should push the answerable questioning further and make the formulations more convincing. We should discriminate between instances where all we can do is speculate or broadly approximate from those where meaning and significance can be traced in fine detail. Purpose and motivation can usually only at best be inferred. These should not be avoided in discussions. They should be labeled as conjectures based on evidence more significant than chance explanations.

Before concluding this section of my essay I wish to acknowledge the contributions of Melanie Klein, Hanna Segal, and Ella Freeman Sharpe to our deeper understanding of the relationship of deeper psychological processes to creativity. M. Klein's theories are well known. Her suggestion that reparative drives restoring loved internal and external objects for the basis of creativity and sublimation is a cornerstone of her theories (Klein and Riviere, 1953). Restoration preserves the lost object and gives it eternal life. She noted in 1929 that drawing and painting could be used to restore and repair a psychological injury. In 1935, reparation was seen as a central concept in relation to the depressive position. In 1940, reparation was emphasized as being of specific special significance in overcoming states of mourning. She writes that in acute mourning

suffering can become productive. We know that painful experiences of all kinds sometimes stimulate sublimations, or even bring out quite new gifts in some people, who may take to painting, writing or other productive activities under the stress of frustrations and hardships. Others become more productive in a different way—more capable of appreciating people and things, more tolerant in their relationships to others—they become wiser [Klein, 1940, p. 143].

Hanna Segal (1952), in her paper "A Psychoanalytic Approach to Aesthetics," builds on the work of Klein, especially that dealing with loss and infantile depression and its relationship to later reparation and restoration through sublimation and creativity.

Utilizing the works of Proust, Segal calls our attention to his statement that "the artist is compelled to create by his need to recover his lost past. But a purely intellectual memory of the past even when it is available, is emotionally valueless and dead." Through chance associations filled with vivid emotions remembrances of the past occur and then the experience of loss and mourning process is activated. Yet Proust observes that the past remains elusive as such memories are transient. Segal translates and quotes Proust when he states: "I had to recapture from the shade that which I had felt, to reconvert it into its psychic equivalent. But the way to do it, the only one I could see, what was it—but to create a work of art" (p. 198). Through his memory work, Proust's past is revived, including his parents, his beloved grandmother, his Albertine. Proust comments that it is only the lost past and the lost or dead object that can be made into a work of art. To Segal, "It is only when the loss has been acknowledged and the mourning experienced that re-creation can take place" (p. 199). I would question whether the piece of art is only a re-creation. My view is that it is a new creation deriving its energy and perhaps inspiration and direction from the past, but still a successor creation and not just a replacement creation. Furthermore, I have evidence that suggests that at times the creative product is not the end result of the mourning process, but represents an attempt at mourning work through creativity. At times the mourning is pathological with a suicidal outcome, and yet the creative works have an aesthetic validity nonetheless (e.g., Virginia Woolf, Anne Sexton, Sylvia Plath, John Berryman). Segal does suggest that writing for Proust could be seen as mourning work. As his past objects are gradually given up, "they are re-instated in the ego, and re-created in the book" (p. 199). Furthermore, she believes that in the unconscious of all artists

> all creation is really a re-creation of a once loved and once whole, but now lost and ruined object, a ruined internal world and self. It is when the world within us is destroyed, when it is dead and loveless, when our loved ones are in fragments, and we ourselves in helpless despair—it is then that we must re-create our world anew, re-assemble the pieces, infuse life into dead fragments, re-create life [1952, p. 199].

Linking the wish and capacity to create to the successful working through of the depressive position, she conversely sees inhibitions of artistic expression as indicative of an inability to acknowledge and overcome this early depressive anxiety. When I think of Segal's explanations as nonabsolutes I can confirm some of her assertions. But I have found creativity at times where little mourning process was evidenced or where it was grossly distorted or arrested. I also maintain that the mourning process is distinct from the infantile depressive position. Actually, Segal discusses how an assimilated or renounced object or its equivalent becomes a symbol which is differentiated from the lost, recovered, or changed object, is a creation of the self—a creation that has personal meaning but also in the talented has aesthetic significance to others. In Segal's (1952) view, "all aesthetic pleasure includes an unconscious re-living of the artist's experience of creation" (p. 204). I would also add the conscious and unconscious response to the artistic product itself. If the artist touches a universal affective theme, each of our individual responses, coming from our own specific sources, having unique meanings, could still have a commonality that is stimulated by the product itself. Perhaps in order for us to enjoy, appreciate, or be moved by the creative product we ourselves must have undergone our own mourning processes and so can empathize with that process and its outcome in the artist. "All artists aim at immortality; their objects must not only be brought back to life, but also the life has to be eternal. And of all human activities art comes nearest to achieving immortality; a great work of art is likely to escape destruction and oblivion" (Segal, 1952, p. 207).

DATA AND RESEARCH METHODS

There have been many sources of data utilized in my research. The primary sources have directly related to the psychoanalytic situation—by this I refer not only to the work with analysands, but also self-analytic work—which in one form can be thought of as the self-psychoanalytic situation (introspection, dream analysis, self-insight, and recognition are chief agents in this data understanding). In addition to self-work following a sudden loss of my own, I also was able to observe members of my immediate family when the trauma occurred and over a period of time. Dreams, fantasies, and affects were of great significance. Gradually resolutions occurred, acute affects were replaced by memories and reminiscences, and life was resumed with even more zest in some ways than ever before. As I observed the process of change, I began the systematic investigations of loss and the mourning process.

I studied four specific loss situations from my own cases: (1) adults who had lost one or both parents through death prior to age nineteen; (2) adults who had lost one or more siblings through death during childhood; (3) adults who had lost a child through death; and (4) adults who had lost a spouse through death (see chapter 2).

I will now briefly present a clinical example that will illustrate my thesis that the resolution and completion of the mourning process can result in a creative product, activity, or change in one's life. The solution of the problems of mourning are to be distinguished from the attempts to cope or defend oneself against the impact of the problem. These latter attempts, if unsuccessful, are usually the presenting symptoms our patients bring to us.

Clinical Example

June, a twenty-five-year-old single woman, a secretary in a medical college dean's office, first contacted the clinic in which I worked because she was "nervous, trembly, and easily upset over little things at work." She spoke in a hushed mousy tone, blocking and blushing frequently. She was raised on a farm in northwest Nebraska. Her father, forty-eight years old, was described as a "quiet farmer, highly moral but who, despite his not personally drinking, would not vote for prohibition." The patient consciously identified with him and this included his "nervousness." Her mother, aged forty-seven, was seen as more emotionally labile than father. She "shows her affection and other feelings more easily" than father. When June was nine years old, her two years older sister, Jane, died after a six-month paralytic illness. Both parents were very upset, but the patient was especially affected as she and sister were very close, played constantly with each other, and, being on a farm without any other children close by, they "were everything" to each other. In the period shortly before contacting the clinic, June began to dream of Jane coming back in a white uniform. June asks her sister in the dream: "Why didn't you come back before?"—Jane does not respond. In telling me this dream, June mentions that Jane had wanted to be a nurse and that she had been a very active and lively girl. June was very lonely after Jane's death.

Two years prior to seeing me, June's mother had an unexpected pregnancy—a menopausal baby. A little girl that I shall call Jean was born. June, who professed to love this little sister, was concerned that she, Jean, would be very lonely on the farm, or that she (Jean) would grow "too fond" of my patient and so be very upset when they could not be together.

Although the patient had a degree in education and some graduate work in social science, she did not get an advanced degree or teach. Instead she worked as a secretary. She left Nebraska to "protect" Jean; and this was the reason offered for her moving to Chicago.

There was no sexual experience except masturbation, and she expressed fears of "becoming too involved with one man." As a result of this fear, she was hypercritical of all men and discouraging of dates. She lived in a girls' rooming house and was especially fond of one girl there, who was two years older than she. When asked if this girl friend had any recent changes in her life, the patient blushed and indicated that her friend had recently become engaged and she felt she would "lose" her friend. Diagnostically I saw the patient as an inhibited obsessive-compulsive character having an intact ego, good contact with reality, high level of intelligence, and some depression and unconscious guilt over her sister's death.

We began our treatment on September 13, 1949. The patient related well and entered into an active therapeutic process. She spoke easily, brought out negative feelings with ease, and early evidences of a paternal transference appeared.

On November 2, 1949, she had her first dream. Before telling it to me, she said: "I was reading a book by Faulkner about a boy who was thinking of committing suicide. I got to thinking, should one eat beforehand and enjoy the last meal or not." She then told me the dream.

> "Jane's body and a baby's body lying there. I was there—felt unconcerned—no feeling whatsoever." When she awoke she wondered how she could have no feelings. Her associations were: "I never looked at the body—but I knew it was her body. I am sure the other body wasn't Jean—just a baby—had no features—a short body. Jane always seems as big as I am to me. I never think of her as being as little as she was when she died. I don't want to talk of this. I am getting a pressure in my head." She then mentioned that mother recently wrote that she, June, was a happy-go-lucky child until Jane died. She then became serious and withdrawn. Later in the session she returned to the dream and recalled Jane's last day. "Jane seemed slightly better—but all of a sudden things became worse. I got scared and began to pray—I said, 'Save her for us.' After she died I got the idea that the goal of life was to die and go to heaven. That disgusts me now—[voice low] when she died, she died so peacefully, she smiled." At that point the patient began to sob hysterically. After sometime, she mumbled: "I don't seem to have much self-control—I always can control myself and not show it—but something is happening to me." Again more embarrassed crying and then the patient indicated that her parents were always so sorry for her because she was so lonely being an only child. In fact, she felt they were more concerned about her than about her dead sister. She left and at the last session reported she slept very soundly after the last appointment. She also felt an indescribable change and that was accompanied by thoughts about becoming a social worker in a children's agency or hospital instead of remaining as a secretary.

There soon were more dreams of dead sisters, recollections and memories of Jane that she had not thought about for years. For example, she recalled finding a little envelope of Jane's, after Jane's death, on which was written "Do not open." When the patient read the contents, she was surprised to read Jane's definition of love, and of her interest in and fantasies about boys.

I will stop with this clinical example and report that my contact with this patient continued until mid-1956. At the end of our work, she had returned to school, obtained an advanced degree in education, was teaching in an elementary school. (Interestingly, her classes were mainly of nine-year-olds.) She had begun to date actively, gradually became orgastic, thought of marriage, and seemed on the road to a more fulfilling and satisfying life.

SOME UNANSWERED QUESTIONS AND CONCLUSIONS

1. Mourning is a normal transformational adaptive process, found in all people and throughout history.

2. This mourning process has its own line of development, beginning in early life and reaching its maturity after adolescence when the psychic apparatus is fully developed.

3. The mourning process has evolved phylogenetically as an adaptive means of dealing with loss, disappointment, and change.

4. Bereavement, the specific reaction to the death of a meaningful object, is a subclass of the mourning process.

5. The mourning process has various ontogenetic stages, each having particular affects connected with them. However, there are no clear delineations between the stages, one or another gradually appearing or disappearing and occasional stage exacerbations reoccurring until resolution takes place. Just as the mourning process has its own line of development, it is also part of other developmental processes. As each stage is given up, a mourning process for this stage is initiated while the new stage is already appearing.

6. The earlier ontogenetic stages of the process in adults correspond to the developmental stages of the process's appearance—though obviously of shorter duration in the normal adult.

7. The mourning process can have four outcomes: *normal resolution* which results in creative activity, creative reinvested living, creative products. Memory traces become the end product intrapsychically of the resolved and completed mourning process; *arrestation of the mourning process* at various stages; *fixations at various earlier stages* which become reactivated when a mourning process is initiated; and finally, *pathological or deviated mourning processes* that are variously diagnosed as depression, depressive states, apathy. These may result in anniversary suicides, anniversary homicides, serious delinquent behavior, psychotic decompensations, and so on.

8. A distinction that is useful and I believe essential is the differentiation of the mourning process from the effects of object loss, especially when this loss occurs during childhood or adolescence and the resulting identifications resulting from this loss.

9. Abnormal and normal mourning gives rise to varied painful affects; for example, anger, guilt, humiliation, shame, grief, psychic pain.

10. Again, mourning is a transformational adaptive process intrapsychically that has its developmental progression tied to each stage in the life cycle—from infancy to childhood. It reaches various organizations at different stages of life and is linked to other developmental processes, psychological structures, and mental apparatuses present at each of these levels.

11. There are psychosocial, cultural, and religious dimensions to the mourning process. Though extrapsychic, these external associated events and practices are intimately linked to internal psychic processes.

12. The mourning process and its stages have concomitant biochemical and physiological alterations which now can be measured. These give us additional means of differentiating the stages of the process.

13. Normal aging involves ongoing mourning processes; if one can work through via the mourning process the painful detachment of libido from a prior state of life, one has energy to invest in the present creative life.

14. In gifted individuals the successful completion of a mourning process may result in scientific discoveries (e.g., Freud and *The Interpretation of Dreams*, Darwin's idea of the

survival of the fittest) or in innovative inventions. In the realm of the arts, mourning creativity may show itself in writers, poets, musical composers (Mahler), painters (Munch, Kollwitz), sculptors. We also find mourning creativity in philosophers, founders of religious groups, and in political innovators (Lenin), and including great monarchs (Peter the Great, Elizabeth I) and presidents (Lincoln, Washington, Jackson, F. D. Roosevelt) and many important British prime ministers. These innovative, original individuals and their creative products may represent successful resolutions of the mourning process *or* attempts (not always successful) and aspects of the mourning process itself.

For those of us who are not so talented, creative living, personal growth, and further development—even in the seventh or eighth decades of life—can be an *outcome* that is indicative of the resolution of mourning. However, creative work is always part of the mourning process, even before the process comes to a conclusion.

15. The stages of mourning, though somewhat unidirectional, do on occasion oscillate and revert back temporarily to earlier stages as part of the back and forth transformational process of adapting to a new reality.

16. In some instances, for example, change, relocation, graduation, the mourning process is short-lived, nonconscious, except for affective indications, and may telescope stages of the process.

17. We find group mourning processes and/or defenses against these in individuals, groups, associations, and even nations.

18. The mourning process is very commonly seen during psychoanalytic work. In fact, one might say that the work of analysis is very similar to, and at times identical to, mourning work. This parallel was noted by others (e.g., Fenichel). In order to differentiate past from present via transference neuroses, a process of detachment and attachment occurs. This is seen in all analyses—and not just at times of separation or termination. In those individuals where there is a strong defense against mourning (e.g., childhood parent loss or sibling loss through death), activation of mourning during analysis may be necessary in order for analysis to occur (Fleming and Altschul, 1963).

Mourning reactions, present in the analyst, when resolved can be most useful in furthering the work with our patients.

19. A particularly frequent condition of arrested, fixated, or uncompleted mourning is that of anniversary reactions—there are varied variations with differing outcomes of these anniversary phenomena. I have described these in chapters 8, 9, 12, and 13.

20. In considering the mourning process we must emphasize the internal nature of the process, even though the external serves as initiator of the process. It is by understanding the depth meaning of this external trigger that we can understand what is actually lost or changed. Thus, loss of that which has value or an ideal must be distinguished from the external loss of a significant person at a critical or noncritical period in the life cycle. The internal work of mourning is the acceptance of reality. Overcoming the defenses against the mourning process must be distinguished from the process itself.

21. Finally, memorializations in various forms constitute external manifestations of internal memory traces when a successful mourning resolution has occurred.

5
NOTES ON ABANDONMENT, LOSS, AND VULNERABILITY

Over the years I have had, and continue to work with, patients, directly or through supervised analyses, who were actually abandoned* totally and permanently for critical periods of their childhood; or who were adopted at birth; who were abandoned by a divorced parent who did not obtain custody; who were abandoned when one or both parents suicided when the patient was a young child; who had a parent desert the family; who were placed in orphanages or foster homes because of economic issues; who had one or both parents institutionalized for serious emotional illness; who felt they were abandoners either by giving up newborns for adoption or having induced abortion, or who divorced; who felt they were abandoning their elderly parents by placing them in nursing homes; who gave pets up for adoption or "put them away"; or who lived with one or both depressed parents, where there was no physical separation but there was emotional abandonment or threat of this.

These latter patients usually are more damaged than when there is an actual parent loss through death, and subsequent caretakers who are involved and caring. Similarly situated are widows who find they are abandoned by their friends who suddenly see them as sexual competitors (unlike attitudes toward widowers in our society). Another example of this type is the dying patient abandoned by his or her "loved ones" in a hospital, hospice, or nursing home (decathexis before death). Then there

---

*It is important to emphasize that *separation* is not the same as *abandonment* or *loss*, although these terms are frequently used interchangeably. Following separation we can get growth, further development, and individuation, even though some loss of the prior state occurs.

Reprinted from *The Reconstruction of Trauma*. Workshop Series of the American Psychoanalytic Association, Monograph 2, edited by A. Rothstein. Madison, CT: International Universities Press, 1986.

is the abandonment of one's self, an example of which would be the mussulmen in the concentration camps, or the abandonment felt at the birth or adoption of a sibling, especially if the mother is away for a period of time. A similar situation would be the long absence of the father who is on overseas military duty, and the mother goes to visit him leaving the child with inhospitable caretakers, or placing him in a boarding school. Because of issues of confidentiality, I am unable to give many details of these clinical experiences but I will highlight a few. Through reconstructions in the analytic situation, the analysis of the transference situation and dreams, retrospective understandings and recollections, the traumatic constellations surrounding the abandonments become clear and could then be further investigated, and in many instances worked through.

In thinking about this broad subject, I arrived at the idea of a spectrum of abandonment, ranging from the actual total physical (outer) abandonment to the transitory intrapsychic (inner) "decathexis" or "deinvestment" that occurs in many normal relationships. An example of the latter would be the exhausted mother who reaches a low point of tolerance for her demanding infant and wishes it would go to sleep or "leave me alone," and who thinks this. Transitory decathexis opens up for us newer means of understanding such phenomena as detachment, forgetting, and even denial or splitting. The temporary physical or intrapsychic abandonment may be acute or chronic, a single event or chronic oscillations, temporary or permanent, external or internal. These abandonments may be related to death, divorce, desertion by a key figure, and by the resulting depression, pathological mourning, and psychotic withdrawal of the significant remaining figure.

Do these abandonments, traumatic constellations, and events have later pathological consequences? Can they be treated psychoanalytically? Do these abandonment events result in deficits and/or internal conflicts? Does it make a difference who leaves (e.g., parents, grandparents, siblings), or when the abandonment occurs? Can there be massive social and emotional abandonment, as in a concentration camp victim's experience, without consequences? When abandonment occurs, what impact, if any, do the temporary caretakers have for what occurs? Does day care, even without sexual or any other physical child abuse, help or hinder further healthy development? What about the one-parent family in terms of optimal development? We know that not all traumata are pathogenic, but some traumata do sensitize the individual to certain events throughout the life course.

CASE REPORT 1

Recently, an analytic patient of mine, whose father died when he was fourteen and who has subsequently had à lifelong anxiety reaction whenever an individual who is meaningful to him leaves even for a few days, began his session by saying, "The next week will be difficult for me . . . (pause). My son, Peter, wants to come home for Thanksgiving." (The son is in an Eastern boarding school and does not have a holiday.) "He cried on the phone. I began to sob. I thought, 'What kind of image is that for him? I guess he feels abandoned' (pause . . . tears). I feel abandoned here. (Here?) You won't be here this Friday and then next Thursday—Thanksgiving. You'll probably be with your family—all together (crying). Why does this still upset me? I know it is connected to my father—but you are okay—you'll be back—you had better be or I'll get sore. I hate you for leaving me like this and at this time."

CASE REPORT 2

Another recent clinical vignette concerns a woman in her seventies, with whom I had worked many years ago, who returned to treatment following the death of her husband from a malignant blood dyscrasia a few months before. She began her session with:

"It has been a terrible time. I am so sad—alone—I am feeling so abandoned by Michael—so many of his things I have to get rid of—so many old photos—he saved everything. Now I have to go through each little item and cry over them—weekends are the worst—damn him—why did he have to die? I had a nightmare.

"Michael and I were in our living room—he was in the chair—I was lying on our couch. Suddenly he got up and said, 'What are your favorite pre-Columbian pieces?' I said, 'These,' pointing to two death masks. He went over to them and smashed them to bits. I couldn't believe what I saw and I woke up with a start. He was so alive, so angry (pause). I guess I hate him for leaving me—the old death masks—I want to smash them—get rid of them and what they cover. You'll smash them for me (long pause). You know he killed himself. (He did?) Not actually, but he took so many x-rays—he was so hypochondriacal—always x-rays—self-medication—some doctor he was—he probably induced his blood malignancy. I hate him for leaving me (starts crying). Why did he need annual GI, chest, skull, and gallbladder X rays? We all told him he was fine. I found his personal medical diary—it is unbelievable—such an obsessive. So he killed himself trying to keep himself from dying. I was the sick one—all those years of treatment with you. I look at his picture and say, 'You goddamned fool—look what you did to me and to you.' "

CASE REPORT 3

A patient at age seven angered his father, while father was presumably drunk. The child did not know what to do. Father lunged at him, caught him, and threw him through a screen door, onto a porch. He heard the door slam and was all alone in the dark. The mother had earlier left the house in a panic. The child, shaking and cold, sat huddled in the corner all night. In the morning, a neighbor, walking her dog, saw him and took him into her house. In the analysis, his behavior initially was not intelligible. He would lie on the couch, huddled up, fearful that something would happen to him. Only in subsequent years could we understand retrospectively his anxiety, concern, reliving, and later intense rage at this experience.

CASE REPORT 4

A predental student was referred to me because of intense anxiety that began in his comparative anatomy class while dissecting a cat. He became panicky and had to leave the laboratory. An excellent student, conscientious and diligent, he went to his instructor who, after hearing about his pain, sent him to the student health service and they referred him to me. He came from Germany and as a young adolescent was caught in a Nazi net and sent to a death camp. His father was in the same camp—he only saw his father on a few occasions while he was there and was shocked at his appearance. Not long afterwards his father was killed. My patient was on a work crew that collected gold fillings from the unfortunates after they were gassed and before the bodies went to the crematorium. He managed to escape, living in the woods, and was liberated at the end of the war and came to this country. He resolved to become a dentist—the motivation was obvious—but he was not conscious of it until his analytic treatment allowed him to see this. He felt very abandoned—by his protective father, by his German government, by his God.

Interestingly, he did get into an excellent dental school and he had great anxiety in anatomy where he had to dissect the head. The next year, in physiology, he panicked at working on live dogs. In the third year, autopsies fascinated him and yet he had nightmares which directly took him back to the Nazi camp. In the fourth year, he took an elective in head and neck and oral surgery. By this time his analysis was far advanced and he had no difficulty. One of the pivotal features of this therapeutic progress was, as he put it, "You stuck with me even in the dark days. I was not alone."

CASE REPORT 5

A young pediatric resident began analysis because he found he could not comfortably enter into a meaningful relationship with a woman without becoming angry with her, even though he had no potency problems and could even feel love toward her. This pattern repeated itself sufficiently so that he recognized the problem as an internal one. Initially he was quite open in his analytic work with me, but as time went on he had severe reactions on the weekend, when we did not meet, and when I had to be away from Chicago for meetings. I had known that his mother had died when he was a child, but the exact details emerged only in the course of his treatment. When he was three, his mother developed a life-threatening pulmonary disease. His father and mother left Chicago to go to a warmer climate so that she could recuperate. From ages three to five, he heard nothing from his parents—being left in the care of a harsh governess. He feared this individual, especially when she yelled and when she spanked him for trivial offenses. When the father returned, he was told his mother had died. In addition he was never taken to see her grave. He found himself very involved with helping helpless children, but knew he had a fear of dying, of being left, and of upper respiratory illnesses. In the analysis, when I would cough, initially he would get panicky. We arrived at various understandings of his pattern and reactions to me and gradually he was able to address his difficulties.

We frequently find abandonment problems in adopted children. To be sure, there is a difference between the meaning of adoption and accompanying fantasies intrapsychically, and interpersonal strife, although there may be a connection between the two. There also may be a connection between early life abandonees who may or may not later themselves become abandoners. In psychoanalytic treatment we try to heal the wounds of abandonment. Not all adoptees have the abandonment syndrome, although in my analytic experience it is more frequently seen if the analyst keeps this possibility in mind.

In the very moving documentary film, *John*, the Robertsons (1968) show vividly the traumatopathogenic effects on a small child who was left for nine days in a residential nursery. The devastating regressions and rage even at reunion with mother apparently still had reverberations in his later life. Traumatopathogenic abandonment, depending upon circumstances of the abandonment, age of the child, prior history, and relationships, may be of importance in later outcome. Some children have a self-righting ability that makes them seem to be invulnerable. Various writers and researchers have described these phenomena in children of psychotic parents, children who survived the Nazi concentration camps, or children with severe and serious physical illness early in life. Psychological interventions are needed, may be helpful, or in some instances are not available, and the child develops with relatively minimal later psychological impairment.

In some instances we find cumulative effects of abandonment producing strain traumata. In other instances these strain phenomena can organize and strengthen an ego instead of damaging it severely. Without getting into terminologic debates, one can most frequently understand the traumatopathogenic disruption after the occurrence, as different resiliencies may protect the ego from further disruption. However, we do operate within limits, and when these are severely traversed one can assume that disequilibrium distress, disturbance, disorder, and even disease can occur, especially if there is no preventive intervention. We are now in a better position to define the limits and identify high-risk children. In the psychoanalytic treatment situation, one may get data that confirm or refute such predictions. The meanings and fantasies help us distinguish between the event itself and the meaning-fantasies of the event or events and the response to these. One also learns of the psychological homeostatic level of the internal psychic milieu and how the individual has coped to maintain this balance. The response to severe abandonment is loss, mourning, anxiety, and even deep regression requiring therapeutic intervention.

At the end of World War II, 1,000 child survivors of the Nazi Holocaust entered England. With the advice and counsel of Anna Freud, and under the direction of Alice Goldberger, some of these children lived in a home in Surrey. At the close of the war they ranged in age from three to eleven. Sarah Moskovitz (1983) has now interviewed twenty-four of these survivors. Her follow-up interviews reveal that they still suffer from loss reactions and feelings of being outsiders. They also reveal that not one of these survivors has given up. There have been no suicides, only one of this sample has been involved in drugs, only one lives in a psychiatric hospital. The rest are actively involved in communal activities and are compassionately related to others.

Despite horrendous childhood experiences, these children survived and their lives on outcome follow-up studies indicate that emotional disability does not necessarily follow early severe trauma. The survivors let us learn of their indestructibility, of their yearning for love, the tenacity of their hope, and their human resilience and resourcefulness. Some of the children came from Terezin and Auschwitz, several from orphanages, and others from hiding.

A few of the external "traumata" we observe in the spectrum of abandonment include abandonment of pets, of the elderly, through starvation, which is a form of infanticide, the ultimate child abuse. (This is effected through either overtly leaving a child alone for hours each day or emotionally withdrawing from the child, either through abrupt weaning after periods of indulgence, or through threats of death.) And yet some children do survive even after the most harrowing circumstances. Moskovitz (1983) revealed that the child survivors of the Nazi death camps were markedly aided in their adaptation to life through the heroic help and dedication of Alice Goldberger and her staff of psychoanalysts who could undo some of the effects of the severe abandonments these innocents suffered. Through their great care and understanding, some could be restored to health, and the great support of Anna Freud facilitated this rehabilitative process. As Moskovitz (1983) observed:

> [L]osses that occurred very long ago continue to reverberate deeply throughout life . . . at every life-marking event such as their own weddings, or their children's births, bar mitzvahs, and weddings, there is for all survivors the vivid, jarring encounters with those dead who should have been there [p. 227].

For some survivors, the security and certainty of belonging still eludes them, even for those adopted when they were quite young. This I also found in non-Holocaust children adopted at birth.

Moskovitz found some of the adoptees still struggling with the issue of feeling part of the adoptive family itself. Some, even as adults, still do not risk their ties with the adoptive family by asking about their biological families of origin. For those children who grew up in a children's home, there is still the feeling of being the outsider, issues of mourning, of not living up to ideals, of feeling stigmatized, of avoiding situations that could open up painful and upsetting areas that are either partly denied, repressed, disavowed, or just not accessible to memory. The sense of loss is interwoven with feelings of abandonment, diminished sense of esteem, guilt, shame, repressed and suppressed anger; feelings of uncertainty, especially as these relate to the past and the future as it relates to anti-Semitism are not uncommon. Nonetheless, Moskovitz emphasizes that among her group of interviewees there is an affirmation of life: "They have a quality of stubborn durability. They keep hoping, they keep trying to make the best of their lives. Given all they have endured, . . . no one had given up" (1983, p. 231). Enduring and surviving is fundamental and indicates the ego strength of these children. These individuals have compassion for others, wish to have families of their own, are caring and responsible parents.

Moskovitz (1983) raises fundamental questions about heretofore regarded assumptions. The first deals with the idea "that early deprivation unalterably determines the course of life" (p. 236). My own clinical experience supports Moskovitz's question and her implicit conclusion. Some outcomes are devastating; others that should be are not so. "The first 5 years seem not to have had the power to innoculate all alike for good or bad" (Moskovitz, 1983, p. 237). That some vulnerabilities remain is understandable, but "resilience, strengths, charm, and ability to get affectionate care from those nearby" (p. 236) may have kept these higher risks latent. Many losses, illnesses, or other unfortunate circumstances can increase susceptibility to late decompensations, especially if they come together en masse in time and space. Later commitment, constancy, kindness, and genuine positive feelings are protective and healing. This is seen in these children from the camps as well as in our patients and close friends and family who escaped from the direct impact of the Holocaust. Hope and faith in a future can also have ameliorative effects in facilitating integration and positive investments in the present and in the future.

Kauffman, Grunebaum, Cohler, and Gamer (1979), Adelson and Fraiberg (1980), and Werner and Smith (1982) have also written about children who, though abandoned, were able to be retrieved and restored. Let me give a few details from the Adelson and Fraiberg study as it so dramatically illustrates what can be done beneficially even with an almost impossible situation.

Adelson and Fraiberg (1980) give a treatment description of an unmarried teenage mother and her female infant "who was being starved. . . . [The mother] herself had once been a starving infant. She had been found in the streets of a war-torn country, abandoned and unfed. After an unknown period in an orphanage, she was adopted at age 2½ by an American family" (p. 222). She was pregnant before she was seventeen. The pregnancy and delivery were normal. The baby was supposed to be adopted at birth, but the young mother refused to give up her baby. Unwanted by her adoptive mother, the young mother moved into a low-cost housing facility. Unable to care for herself and the new infant because of depression, the young infant seemed to recapitulate the biological mother's own past abandonment, deprivation, and terror. The baby's condition worsened and fear was expressed for her survival. At four and a half months of age, the baby was hospitalized for more adequate feeding; the mother seldom visited. No organic basis for the baby's malnutrition was found and both mother and infant were referred for treatment and evaluation. Little was accomplished initially and the recapitulation of the biological mother's own abandonment and subsequent deprivation was in evidence—"a small baby hungered and cried and no one heard, no one helped" (Adelson and Fraiberg, 1980, p. 223). It was almost a complete identification with the abandoning mother but not with the helpless little victim.

In treatment the biological mother initially was very negative to the female therapist. By carefully acknowledging the patient's fury, disappointment, and distrust, a beginning relationship was established, although the patient made constant demands for special arrangements. The infant's condition was obviously one of great abnormality; for example, vomiting copiously, sleeping with glassy, unclosed eyes, crying. The mother could not help the baby and so left the marasmic infant alone. As the mother's "desperation and anxiety mounted during the visits, she too deteriorated; her thinking became confused, at times bizarre" (Adelson and Fraiberg, 1980, p. 224). In treatment the mother recognized the ways in which her infant was like her. The parallels were striking but the mother needed help in establishing the affective links within herself. The sensitive therapist assisted in this healing process through empathic listening to the outpouring of the painful, troubled recalling of the patient's early life, and how the birth of her baby elicited a repeat series of reactions as well as a wish *not* to repeat with her daughter what was done to her: adoption meant abandonment. The therapist was asked to help with both the crying infant and now crying mother. The mother, it turned out, was actively starving her baby by not feeding her with adequate food and only feeding her infrequently. Further neglect was in evidence in that the mother never went to the baby when she cried and did not want anyone else to hold her. One might further suggest that the identification with the aggressor was actively being acted out in a destructive fashion against the infant—the hostility to the original mother was displaced onto the innocent baby who was abused in a most fundamental way.

The therapist helped the mother learn what the baby's signals indicated, how rhythms were established, and satisfaction gradually resulted in pleasure. The therapist was treating both mother and infant simultaneously. The mother began to identify with the therapist in several ways. It seemed as if a new structure was in the process of developing; for example, both mother and infant would be nurtured with food and with psychological giving. The infant began to gradually gain weight and stop vomiting. In the eleventh session, the therapy began to aim at separating the baby from her mother's conflicts. In some ways, the paradoxical and pathological symbiosis between mother and infant was becoming accessible to division—what was done to the mother had its impact on the mother; but what was being done to the infant, though similar to what occurred in the mother's early life, was an active doing to the infant by the mother herself.

By the first birthday of the child, physical and psychological progress was very evident; for example, grossly aberrant behaviors disappeared; screaming, vomiting, and fear reactions were gone; the child could offer her mother a beautiful smile, a warm hug, and could toddle about discovering and exploring her small world. Even with these positive changes, both mother and child still remained at risk, and extended treatment continued for two more years. By the time the child was two years old she was a healthy, active toddler and there was no physical evidence of her earlier failure to thrive. Her language was advanced and well used and she could engage in inventive symbolic play. There was no evidence of pathological symptomatology. What was still lacking was harmonious reciprocity and pleasure between mother and child. The child was ready, but the mother still held herself back from full affection. In the following year many of the mother's feelings about separation, deprivation, failure, and abuse were dealt with and the mother in turn could be more empathic, protective, and nurturing to her child. A mutuality and reciprocity between mother and child was strengthened. At age three, the child was secure and dealing with age appropriate issues. The child could turn to her mother for pleasure and understanding.

There are many fascinating aspects to this excellent therapy and the ongoing follow-up and change patterns. Abandonment, even though it can and has been devastating for many, if appropriately treated can have positive results for both child and mother.

At this point I will discuss briefly the relationship of abandonment to homicide, be it infanticide or the killing of the old. Stager and Wolff (1984) have studied new evidence that indicates that child sacrifice was an ancient practice. Its origin can be traced to the ancient Israelites who had a name, "Tophet," for a place where children were sacrificed by fire on a special altar. The prophet Jeremiah (7:30–32) describes it, but there are also references in other sections of the Old Testament. A huge cemetery of sacrificed children has been found in Carthage, and in Sicily, Sardinia, and Tunisia—all connected with Phoenician settlements. Most of the 2,000 urns were probably deposited between 400 and 200 B.C. Later, burned animals were believed to be substitute sacrifices for children; however, Stager and Wolff indicate "that the demand for human infant sacrifice, as opposed to animal sacrifice, seems to increase rather than decrease with the passage of time" (1984, p. 40). Ancient writers have hypothesized that during times of crisis, massive child sacrifice was practiced to appease the gods and ward off further tragedy. The ancient Greeks followed this custom; but Stager and Wolff give evidence that this was the exception rather than the rule; mass sacrifice was rare. The commonest reason for child sacrifice was fulfillment of a vow and "child sacrifice at Carthage was largely an upper-class custom, at least until the third century" (Stager and Wolff, 1984, p. 45). The dedicants were the parents of the child or children whose remains have been found in urns and under monuments. I would suggest the possibility that these new findings may require us to reexamine the cultural practices among the Greeks at the time of the supposed abandonment of Oedipus by his biological parents. "Some Biblical scholars have suggested that child sacrifice was limited to first-born males" (Stager and Wolff, 1984, p. 47), but as we will see below, this was not true in other cultures. Stager and Wolff's evidence refutes this link between the dedication of the first-born and its sacrifice. In the fourth century B.C. most of the children sacrificed were one to three years old. This suggests that such ritual infanticide was a means of regulating population growth. Such a means of keeping the population constant was found in later times. Flandrin and Peyronet (cited in Stager and Wolff [1984]) have shown that this was the principal means of birth control in France before the eighteenth century. Langer (1974) notes that in 1833, 164,319 babies were abandoned in foundling hospitals in France and few survived. Infants today are still abandoned in garbage pails, hospitals, churches, and so on. This abandonment was a less direct form of infanticide—though its lethal outcome seems to have been what was desired.

Fuchs (1983) found that abandoned children were found among the nineteenth-century French poor. In a study of the Florentine census of 1427 (Herlihy and Klapisch-Zuber, 1985), it was found that infanticide and abandonment were relatively common, more so for little girls than boys. Hospitals could no longer provide for the great increase in the abandoned children. In 1419, the Florentine commune established a special hospital for the abandoned babies of the city. There were frequent recourse to abandonment when there was a famine, plague, or a special war tax raised the cost of supporting a family. Girls constituted 70 percent of the foundling population. A substantial number of the abandoned babies were offspring of liaisons between a master and his indentured servant. If the illegitimate child were a boy, the fathers were more inclined to retain them and rear them in their own households. Among the poor, systematic infanticide or secret abandonment was the method of disposing of unwanted children. Deserted infants frequently died, and this was a form of disguised or delayed infanticide.

Wagatsuma (1981) found abandonment was more frequent than child abuse or neglect in Japan. The age of the deserted children ranged from one day of age to three years. The "trash can" children found in the United States today are usually very young infants or newborns.

Abandonment, be it of children, of the elderly, of the seriously ill, especially of those with chronic disabilities, is a form of homicide. These homicidal abandonments may take the form of exposure to the elements, drowning, starvation, strangulation, poisoning, or suffocation. Stager and Wolff (1984) suggest that infanticide was preferable to abortion because it was less harmful to the mother physically and economic factors could play a role in the decision.

They note that

> as early as 787 A.D. the first foundling home was established in Milan, followed by hospitals in Rome, Florence, and other cities. . . . At the end of the 12th century, Pope Innocent III established the Hospital of the Santo Spirito in Rome "because so many women were throwing their children into the Tiber." London, Paris, and St. Petersburg had well-known children's hospitals [Stager and Wolff,1985, p. 51].

Many of the children died during the first few weeks and few reached the age of six. In London, by the mid-eighteenth century, it was impossible to deal with the great number of unwanted children and the institutions became houses for the dead.

The abandonment dread of the young child, even though it is repressed, may represent at its base the fear of being killed by those who should care and give life to the infant or child; and the dread continues in the adult or older adult.

Jay Katz (1984), in an eloquent and very significant volume, discusses the abandonment of patients when their physicians do not communicate or interact with them. This is especially seen when a "silent world" becomes evident in the case of a seriously ill or dying patient. There is a sense of isolation, depression, anger that is unexpressed—hopelessness, helplessness, feelings of estrangement, especially when the caretakers retreat to a position of abandonment and withdrawal. We see this in the current care of AIDS patients. Katz notes that patients feel unimportant, frightened, disregarded, ignored, patronized, dismissed from life, and untrusted (1984, p. 210).

Even in instances of cautious prognosis, faith, hope, support, and communication can help reduce the sense of abandonment that the sick individual feels. One might ask if the "silent world of the doctor and patient" exists only with very physically ill patients in hospitals. There are others who feel alienated and that they are outsiders; the physican can be an abandoning figure, too. Perhaps unwittingly we ourselves participate in this process.

How can one conclude a chapter which in some ways is only a beginning? Although some of the ideas and work had been ongoing for some time, it was only when I was a patient in an intensive care unit that I realized the unifying themes presented above. A diagnosis had not yet been made, this was my first major hospitalization, and the concerns of all who were and are very close to me were in evidence. I, too, was very concerned, felt "my body was abandoning me" and, as a result, I was in jeopardy. My caretakers were and are excellent, but the central ideas I have tried to develop kept returning. Paying close attention to my dreams, I realized that I was "in touch" with aspects of me that existed before conscious memory or willing recollection. Very shortly after my birth, my mother developed a serious septic breast abscess. She and I were separated as it was feared that I, too, might become very ill from contact with her. I was entrusted to unwilling relatives who, in retrospect, were incompetent to deal with and care for a newborn infant. In the hospitalization that I had and which culminated in a coronary bypass operation, old archaic feelings unlinked to conscious events appeared. By working at them and the accompanying dreams, I could interpret with great value to me what these meant, where they came from, and how the past was resurrected by the "present" catastrophic crisis.

The idea of temporary abandonment and noncaring caretakers came together with what I had been trying to put into appropriate perspective. Clinical data from my work with patients, supervisees, and colleagues "fit," and so I pursued the lines of scientific association wherever they led.

I wish to close by returning to my central theme: abandonment as seen from the point of view of the abandoned has many different facets. The impact will depend on various factors; for example, when the abandonment occurred, the prior emotional organization of the individual, the circumstances of the abandonment, the "replacements" for the abandoner or abandoners. It is not always easy to handle this preventively, although such factors as these can be helpful: preparation, replacement, continuity of contact with a familiar person, and facilitating discharge of feelings, be they fear, rage, or despair; and recognition and awareness on the part of the caretakers of the turmoil that is ongoing. It is the nature of human experience that man will be involved in experiences where he may feel abandoned. In some instances, however, these experiences are of such severity, chronicity, quality, suddenness, or persistence that they render the individual vulnerable to such events in later life. It is by understanding their meaning that we can then intervene therapeutically.

6

THE MOURNING-LIBERATION PROCESS AND MIGRATION: VOLUNTARY AND COERCED

I

From his earliest beginnings man was a wanderer—be it biologically based (our simian ancestors probably moved from place to place in search of food and shelter), or psychologically based (an insatiable curiosity to explore new terrain or discover new and different environments). As a wanderer, man left what he had and moved on. As psychological and social development unfolded, as the human life span increased, we came to realize that perhaps inside all of us was the push for separation and individuation as a means of defining our selves, our being. This is most notably seen as the child gradually leaves its mother and begins new relationships in new settings. It is seen in adolescence, when one has the biological and social need to move away from the family of origin, establish new intimate ties to another, and so become a person in one's own right. This step is followed by the development of a loving relationship with another that could result in the establishment of a new family unit. This is the evolutionary and psychological basis of leaving the familiar and starting something new. Yet within all of us there remain the internal and external ties to our past and to our earlier reality which may still exist. But what about the feelings that come from this leaving—be it self-motivated or, in increasing numbers, motivated by social and political upheavals that mandate migration, sometimes as a means of continuing survival? We cannot, we should not, we must not

Presented at the Third International Symposium of the American Society of Hispanic Psychiatrists, Mérida, Yucatan, March 17, 1986.

145

disavow our heritage lest we lose more than we gain. New amalgams of old and new enrich us all.

A colleague recently moved to another city, distant from his prior residence and place of work. The new post was an advancement and one he sought, although it meant leaving one of the major cities in the United States for a smaller metropolis. His wife described to me the painful adaptation required in the change. She felt lost. The familiar geographic landmarks were absent; the familiar shops and service personnel were gone; places where she and her family had many experiences (positive and negative) were memory traces which could not be reinforced by actual visits. All of these were gone, and now she and her family experienced the losses, even though they very much desired the change and new challenges. I asked about her adaptation to the changes and she very perceptively replied that being freed somewhat of what no longer was gave her the impetus to set up new networks, find new successor facilities, and not expect that identical replacements would be found for what no longer existed. The stress and resulting strain of elective leaving resulted in responses very similar to what I have described as the mourning-liberation process—a normal, necessary, universal, transformational process that permits us to adapt to change (which is loss), loss of meaningful figures, loss of home, loss of resources, loss of physical and emotional-mental health, loss of memory. The process may go on without the individual being aware of it and might conclude with new resolves, new "energy investments," and new relationships. Where there is loss of memory, as I have seen in early Alzheimer's disease, one works with the depression, the anxiety, the rage, the hopelessness, and at times one leaves the denial mechanisms in place. When the loss is due to death of a significant individual (e.g., parent, spouse, child, sibling, friend) the bereavement process follows a course that also can in many instances result in positive outcomes. When the loss, especially in children, is due to recriminative divorces, abandonments, or deaths at critical developmental periods, the effects on later personality structure can be lifelong.

In my research I have found and suggested that the more general mourning-liberation process has a line of development, beginning very early in life and becoming a critical part of the aging process. I believe aging and development are synonymous. If one cannot successfully mourn past states of the self, then one cannot accept the ongoing aging process as a natural event. The leaf in spring is a bud, in summer it is rich and full with its greenery and verdant appearance, in the fall it turns to other beautiful hues, yellow and brown, and in the winter it trembles in the wind, for its days are numbered and it will soon fall and enrich the earth that nourishes the tree, so that new leaves will come into being, each to repeat the pattern.

But to return to my research on the mourning-liberation process. The normal outcome results in life continuing with new networks and new investments. When a serious traumatic loss occurs in childhood or adolescence, the mourning-liberation process is interfered with in its development and either it stops, producing an arrest, or if it is of lesser severity, a fixation occurs. If the latter occurs, future life events and tragedies return the individual to the earlier fixation point and less developed or deviated mourning responses emerge (e.g., anniversary reactions, psychosomatic symptoms). The fourth category is that of pathological mourning or melancholia. In these instances we see gross manifestations of psychological and mental disorder (e.g., psychotic depressive symptomatology, suicides, homicides, severe alcohol and drug abuse).

We have in our time witnessed forced emigration, exile, abandonment by one's mother- or fatherland, incarceration, and death under horrendous conditions. This is not new to man, although the scope and brutality causes us to wonder if indeed we have not witnessed new levels of human degradation. People in the past were banished—a form of abandonment with the intent that as one got further and further away, one became more and more distant, in a similar fashion to the dead. As has become all too familiar to us because of recent historical tragedies, people are tortured to confess, to convert, to bear false witness against friend or relative.

When one is forced to leave one's land it is a loss and a severance, and sometimes ethnic and national identities can become intensified. Coming to a new land involves, for many, learning a new language, hearing different songs, news reports, having to participate in new sports (e.g., soccer vs. football), getting used to new foods, learning new customs, becoming immersed in new historical and cultural heroes (e.g., George Washington or Simon Bolivar), learning new forms of government, new mores, new folkways, and so on. The pain of the severance and loss of security of what one identifies with the homeland is compounded by the fears of strangers. Depressions occur and groups, even though they tend to form in the new land in order to retain some of the old and protect against the fears of the new, can cause internal splits and conflicts of loyalty. I recall a political refugee from a Latin American country telling me how much he missed his beautiful homeland, even with its tyrannies and risks. He dreamed in Spanish, even though he had been in the United States for some time and was a successful professional. He applied for U.S. citizenship, and not long before it was formally to be conferred upon him he went into a fit of despair. "It is the final break with my motherland." He knew that if he returned as long as the existing political group was in power he was in great danger of either death or permanent incarceration under most unpleasant conditions, and yet loss evoked mourning. We could talk of his complex feelings and reality. He is now comfortable with his "new land" and, even though politically life in his homeland has changed, he no longer has a wish to return there.

Over the years I have had contact with individuals who had to flee from the Nazis, from Franco's Spain, from Eastern Europe, Greece, the Soviet Union, Vietnam, and even though these individuals came from different lands there was a similarity in their ambivalent responses to having to leave. These individuals had the chance to leave, although the alternative was not a real choice. The European refugees had no choice, and unfortunately many perished because they could not escape. They were seen as aliens and they felt alienated, dehumanized, homeless, abandoned by land, nation, and their gods. Many years ago, a colleague, Percival Bailey, the eminent neurologist and neurosurgeon, told me about the plight of the Armenians. Close to one and a half million died and many others had to leave their country to escape destruction. Involuntary migration, most recently from Vietnam, Cambodia, and Laos, presents unique problems, such as anxiety, rage, depression, and basic issues of survival. Voluntary migration, though

less involved with threat to life, does involve issues of acculturation, earning a living, finding basic housing, in addition to the
leaving and loss of what was left behind. Loss of security in the
hopes of gaining greater security involves giving up in hope of
future gains. Voluntary migration is not exile, but is it not still
isolation even if the entire family migrates at the same time?
The family support system can act as a transitional source of
security from the old to the new land but there still can be
emotional sequelae, especially in the older adults who cannot
adapt as easily to the "new life." They feel estranged and at
times even in exile, in contrast to the younger members of the
family. Stein (1985) has suggested that "culture shock" refers
to the rekindling of unresolved losses and can lead to denial of
the losses through setting up structures that do not allow for
mourning to take place. I would modify this to note that shock
is the first phase of the mourning-liberation process. If one
denies the loss, one denies the shock phase and the mourning
process is stopped cold. Internally one can know that the loss
has occurred but externally one acts as if it has not taken place.
If the shock experience occurs one can then go on to the next
phase of the mourning-liberation process (Pollock, 1966, 1976,
1977a,b, 1984, 1985a,b; see chapters 4, 14, 15, 23, and 24).

Separation in and of itself is not the same as loss and need
not have a negative connotation. We separate and individuate
throughout our life course. If we did not we would remain
fixed or arrested in our development. When one individuates
and separates, a normal mourning-liberation process occurs,
and this is part of development. Garza-Guerrero (1974) wrote
about culture shock and its relationship to mourning and identity. The Pierses (1982) have also addressed this issue in a paper
that reflects their earlier experiences on being newcomers to
the United States. They point out that the United States is

> a nation of uprooted people, or of children and grandchildren
> of people uprooted under duress. . . . There were Africans,
> dragged away and sold into slavery; there were such diverse,
> hungry or oppressed, or persecuted groups as the Irish, the
> Norwegians, the Jews, various Slavic groups, various people from
> the Middle East, from Middle America and South America, from
> the Caribbean, from East Asia [p. 369].

Aside from the "culture shock," it is my contention that each individual must go through a mourning-liberation process so that there can finally be a sense of belonging without giving up ties to one's heritage that are valuable, needed, and should be transmitted. This mourning-liberation process facilitates the processes of healing the losses and allows for acculturation.

In a pioneering study of psychoanalysis in the Third Reich presented in 1975, Spiegel, Chrzanowski, and Feiner note that "Freud felt that as exemplar of psychoanalysis it was his duty to remain to the last possible moment [in Austria], that 'he could not leave his native land; it would be like a soldier deserting his post' " (p. 481). Freud had earlier written to Ferenczi that he did not wish to leave his possessions, his comforts, and the treatments for his cancer. He wrote, "In my opinion, flight would only be justified by direct danger to life" (cited in Spiegel, Chrzanowski, and Feiner, 1975, p. 481). But Freud left, and confronted his dilemma by choosing the few who could accompany him to safety, recognizing that those he left would perish. Even though he was not young, Freud's death soon after his arrival in England leaves some questions unanswered. Was his death perhaps related to his inability to mourn for all who were lost? Perhaps he had guilt about the choices he was forced to make.

II

Man probably wandered from Africa to Europe and Asia. From Asia man probably came to the Western Hemisphere by one of two routes; across the Bering Straits and then southward, and/or from Polynesia to South America. There is evidence that the Norsemen explored the eastern part of North America. But man, the discoverer, the explorer, the investigator, not only searched geographic terrains including the North and South Poles, the Moon, and the planetary system, but newer areas of thought and artistic worlds. These could be viewed from the broad perspective of self-generated migrations. When one left one's land of origin to earn a better living, to have greater freedom of opportunity, or in order to practice one's religion, this, too, was a voluntary migration. Despite the voluntary aspect of this venturing, there still were and are elements of mourning, loss, nostalgia, memories, and feelings of the past that were positive as well as negative. Such "migrants" speak of their homeland, their "motherland," their "fatherland," but no references are made to a "sisterland" or "brotherland." Fellow inhabitants (in the broad sense) may be called "brother" or "sister," but this sibling label does not extend to the land, which is parental. The "homeless" have no "homeland," and we are familiar with their plight.

In contrast to voluntary migration, we find the "forced migration" where one has to leave in order to protect oneself and one's family from destruction, torture, or incarceration. The reactions may include nostalgia, mourning, longing, but also rage, depression, and a feeling of being abandoned by one's "homeland" and also abandoning what is the familiar, the loved. Such depressive responses are similar to variants of abnormal mourning reactions. What awaits one is the new terrain, the fear of the unknown, and even fear of death, especially as it reverberates with the fear of the strange and the stranger. But the mourning-liberation process does unfold, acculturation can occur, and adaptations do take place. In the instance of soldiers conscripted for war, we find a variant of the "forced migration" phenomenon and here again the pain of loss, the fear of the unknown and death, the encouraged necessity to kill or be killed—all contribute to the pathology we see on the battle front and now in the post-traumatic stress disorders, which I believe have elements of unresolved or abnormal mourning patterns.

III

Cesar Garza-Guerrero, as early as 1972, wrote on culture shock and its relationship to the mourning process and vicissitudes of identity. Garza-Guerrero focuses on two fundamental elements of culture shock: "the mourning related to the loss of a culture and the vicissitudes of identity in face of the threat of a new culture" (1974, p.409). I would broaden Garza-Guerrero's definition of culture shock to include, basically, the loss of one's "home base," be it the abandoned or abandoning culture, family, friends, language, music, food, and culturally determined values, customs, and attitudes, or one's base of knowledge, one's profession, one's outlook on life—in other words, the loss of anything that has been meaningful and has been given up whether voluntarily or otherwise. The shock is the initial phase of this loss reaction and the adaptive acculturating outcomes and aspects of what I feel is the consequence of the successful mourning-liberation process. This "shock" phase is seen, for example, when divorce is announced to children, when a sudden death occurs, when one loses a position or job. Garza-Guerrero's division into the phases of culture shock is quite useful and applicable to the larger loss reactive process. The "new identity" that is his end point of the cultural shock crises is comparable to what I call the resolution of the mourning process, with the liberation of investments in the past, which "investments" can be used in creative and productive relationships. However, in my comparison of adults who have lost one or both parents in childhood or adolescence, who have lost one or more siblings in childhood or adolescence, who have lost a spouse, or who have lost a child, it is in the last instance that the mourning process is never fully completed—"One cannot mourn for one's future (the child), when that future is dead" (personal communication from an older adult woman whose son died in infancy and who never could complete her mourning for him). In ongoing studies comparing loss through death with loss through divorce or as a result of abandonment, significant differences seem to be emerging and these can be applied to the voluntary and involuntary migration situation. In children, the use of a transitional object helps diminish threat as a result of loss from abandonment or break in contact. We see this in young children, in adults who are threatened, in psychiatric patients who fear abandonment, or in children who fear the dark. "I am cut off from the familiar, what I see and recognize, and am left with my inner fears and fantasies that threaten me" (personal communication). And so groups cluster in the new environment—they speak their "mother tongue," they eat their original "mother food," they listen to their "mother lullabies" (music), they read their original language books and papers, and the uprooted seek to keep their roots, which helps in their internal mourning process, their transition, and the facilitation of acculturation, if not in themselves then in their children and grandchildren.

IV

Martin (1954) has noted that homesickness has been a dominant theme in the Bible, in Homer's works, in Caesar's writings. He relates homesickness to nostalgia and points out that the term *nostalgia* is derived "from the Greek *nostos*, a return home, and *algos*, meaning pining," giving us the literal meaning of "pining to return home" (Martin, 1954, p. 93). E. Sterba (1940) much earlier related homesickness to the longing for the mother's breast. Freedman (1956) calls our attention to the feelings of nostalgia seen in college students, military personnel, writers, and musical composers. (See Miller's [1956] study of Marcel Proust, and Feder's [1982] account of the nostalgia of Charles Ives.) The relationship to preoedipal gratification seems clear, be it with the mother, father, or family. Although nostalgic tendencies have been associated with an inability to mourn (Kleiner, 1970), I find this may not be so in every instance. In fact, at times, the nostalgic recall is an end-product—a memory trace that is the successful outcome of a mourning-liberation process. When nostalgia becomes a predominant preoccupation, it can be a symptom of pathological mourning — melancholia — and can, if severe enough, lead to suicide. Rosen (1975) has described such instances. Werman (1977) distinguishes nostalgia from homesickness and from fantasy. He describes nostalgia as "an affective-cognitive experience, usually involving memories of places of one's past" (Werman, 1977, p. 397). He suggests nostalgia may be a substitute for mourning and a screen affect. Nostalgia may be an aspect of the mourning-liberation process and hence seen in all reactions to losses and changes. It may also serve as a transitory attempt in affect and fantasy to recapture an aspect of the past and so be temporarily reunited with it. But the feelings and fantasies dissolve and reality takes over. One may see this in viewing family photographs, home movies, visiting sites associated with pleasant memories of the past, seeing patients that have similar associations. I have also encountered nostalgic feelings connected with certain smells, sounds, songs, holidays, and other evocative symbols of the past which may still in very transitory fashion elicit feelings of sadness and of pleasure. It is a return to a land that is no more, that may have never been as ideal as it was thought and felt to be, but where symbolically one still wishes to be on special occasions.

7

MANIFESTATIONS OF ABNORMAL MOURNING: HOMICIDE AND SUICIDE FOLLOWING THE DEATH OF ANOTHER

I

Zilboorg (1936b) has noted that the wish to join one's dead is the universal form of primitive mourning. This wish is expressed by many cultures in their religious and social mourning rituals (see chapter 12). In various behaviors that associate the mourning of the living with the dead, for example, the wearing of black clothes, the cessation of sexual and other pleasures and social activities, and prohibitions regarding work activity, the mourner's life parallels the state of "existence" of the dead person. I have related this parallel process in the mourner to what is assumed to be operative in the deceased, using van Gennep's (1908) rites-of-passage formulation as a basic consideration. Since the mourner, like the deceased, is "dead," it is assumed that the identification of the living with the dead is a basic component of the mourning process and reflects the internal emotional state of the survivor as well as the external reality situation of the deceased. The dead person is gone, and

Presented to Dr. Richard Sterba on the occasion of his seventy-fifth birthday, May 6, 1973.

This research has been assisted by the support of NIMH Grant #MH 20562; and by the Anne Pollock Lederer Research Fund and the Fred M. Hellman Research Fund of the Institute for Psychoanalysis of Chicago.

Reprinted from *The Annual of Psychoanalysis*, 4:225–249 (1976). New York: International Universities Press.

an adaptation to this change is required. In the healthy individual, mourning is the process of this adjustment.

Zilboorg suggests that "the *actively* suicidal individual . . . appears to be in mourning, but his is not a sublimated gratification of the need to identify himself with the dead; instead he reverts to the primitive pattern of mourning. A regression to the primitive impulses invades his motor system so that in *acting out* his *neurotic mourning* he actually joins the fantasied dead by killing himself, as the primitive man did at the open grave of his master" (1936b, p. 1364). This pathological identification with the dead precludes the unfolding of the normal mourning process. Thus, instead of mourning the loss with its attendant affects and process, the mourner "joins" the dead and in some instances actually dies.

Zilboorg reminds us that "joining the dead" was originally carried out passively in the form of being killed: a human sacrifice at the grave of the master. The willingness of such slaves and women to die, however, might also be called passive suicide. On many islands of Micronesia and Melanesia, the wives killed themselves or asked to be killed by one of their relatives following the death of their husbands. Extending his thinking, Zilboorg asserts, "The most dangerous type of suicidal individual met with clinically is the one who gives evidence of unconscious identification with the dead person. The impulse to die is not based on the *actual* loss of a relative or friend (father, mother, or their psychological surrogates) but on the *fantasied* loss. Even as was the primitive slave or primitive woman, the individual seems to be unconsciously impelled to join the dear dead while the body remains uninterred" (1936b, p. 1364). The death seemingly is not acknowledged, mourning does not normally take place, and, as Freud has described in "Mourning and Melancholia" (1917 [1915]), reality testing—to show that the loved object no longer exists—does not occur.

Grief suicides have been known for some time, both in history and in literature. When Dido is deserted by Aeneas, she kills herself. Cleopatra's lover and political ally, Mark Antony, commits suicide a few days before the news arrives that Cleopatra is not yet dead. Aegeus, Theseus's father, destroys himself after mistakenly believing his son dead when a black instead of white sail is hoisted on Theseus's ship. Theseus had forgotten the signal that he was to raise a white sail for victory and a black one for defeat. Robert Graves (1955) maintains that feelings of remorse about Jocasta's suicide by hanging, not guilt feelings for past crimes, are decisive in Oedipus's suicidal blinding of himself. Farber (1970) suggests that Jocasta kills herself as part of her abnormal mourning for Laius. Antigone, like her mother Jocasta, hangs herself when she cannot fulfill the mourning rituals for her dead brother Polyneices. Haemon, not wanting to live without Antigone, kills himself. While embracing the dead Antigone, he drives his sword into his side, setting forth a stream of oozing blood that falls on her pale cheek. Eurydice, Haemon's mother, stabs herself to death when she learns of Haemon's suicide by the sword. As she is dying, Eurydice remembers the other child she has lost, Megareus, who died defending Thebes (Farber, 1970). Each of these tragic suicides immortalized by Sophocles can be viewed as a grief suicide; the identification in the means of suicide can be observed in the hanging of Jocasta and of her daughter Antigone, and in death through the knife of Haemon and his mother Eurydice. For the present, the possible meaning of this identification must wait. Euripides also describes a grief by suicide in his play *The Supplicants*, in which Evadne destroys herself by leaping onto the funeral pyre of her slain husband Capaneus. The tragic suicides of Romeo and Juliet can also be seen as grief suicides. Although there is no clear evidence that Isolde committed suicide immediately after her lover Tristan's death, she does perish in her acute state of sorrow, and hers could also be considered a grief death.

Dublin (1963) has written about funeral suicides. In various cultures, among some Brazilian tribes, for example, it was customary upon the death of a chief for his retainers to kill themselves so that their souls might serve him in the spirit world. The suicide of a wife upon the death of her husband, a custom in various groups, has also been described. In the Fiji Islands, when a husband died, his wives all sought to be the first to suicide and thus become the favorite wife in the spirit world.[1]

[1] "The Fijian chiefs had from twenty to a hundred wives, according to their rank; and at the interment of a principal chief, the body was laid in state 'upon a spacious lawn,' in the presence of a great crowd of interested spectators. After the natives had exercised all the taste and skill at their command in adorning her person, the principal wife would walk out and take

The Hindu practice of suttee was based on the belief that "voluntary death was the surest passport to heaven and that by immolating herself the dutiful wife could atone for the sins of her husband, free him from punishment and open the gates of paradise to him. Furthermore, the families and relatives on both sides of the house shared in the merit of her sacrifice, and the children whose mother committed suttee gained social distinction" (Dublin, 1963, p. 93). Dublin continues:

> A wife who refused this crowning act of duty sometimes even was threatened with dire punishment. Though the word suttee has been associated with death by burning upon the funeral pyre of the husband, its original meaning was "good or faithful woman" to denote women who committed suicide in due form, impelled by high religious motives. The mode of death selected was not always cremation, but frequently was drowning, especially in the waters of the Ganges [p. 93].

The ceremonial sacrifice of widows was also common in China, although greater latitude in the choice of death was allowed. Some wives used opium, whereas others starved, drowned, or hanged themselves publicly. Great honor accrued to the willing victim and her family. Tablets were erected in the temples in memory of such virtuous and dutiful wives. In China, those who committed suicide in memory of a dead father or ancestor were considered especially "honorable." In Japan, voluntary hara-kiri (self-embowelment) took place upon the death of one's lord or master for the purpose of following him into the next world. Dublin (1963) reports that in September 1912 General Nogi and his wife committed suicide at the time of the

---

her seat near her husband's body. A rope was passed round her neck; eight or ten powerful men pulled at it with all their strength until she died of suffocation; and the body was then laid by that of the chief. This done, a second wife seated herself in the same place; the process of strangulation was repeated, and she, too, died. A third and fourth became voluntary sacrifices in the same manner; and all were interred in a common grave, one above, one below, and one on either side of the husband. The motive of this barbarous practice was said to be that the spirit of the chief might not be lonely in its passage to the invisible world, and that by such an offering its happiness might be at once secured" [Williams, as quoted in Adams, 1971, p. 228].

funeral of Emperor Meiji. For this act they were idealized to the youth of Japan as shining models.

Examples dating from prehistoric times indicate that such practices have been followed throughout man's existence. The Chou dynasty (1100–221 B.C.) nobleman's tomb contained the body of the master and those of eighteen sacrificed individuals (Treistman, 1972). In a Chinese cemetery of the fifth century B.C., the wealthy were buried in lacquered coffins placed in "underground rooms lined with wooden walls painted to simulate hanging carpets and screens. Pottery and bronze figurines were also placed there as 'retainers' intended to serve the dead for eternity" (p. 39), a humane change from the custom of burying slain retainers.

Among the Sumerians, "the provision made for the dead seems clearly to prove a belief in a future life of some sort" (Woolley, 1929, p. 38). Woolley's archaeological discoveries provided direct evidence that "when a royal person died, he or she was accompanied to the grave by all the members of the court: the king had at least three people with him in his chamber and sixty-two in the death pit; the queen was content with some twenty-five in all" (p. 57).

In another excavation, Woolley found the bodies of six menservants and sixty-eight women in a death pit. The neatness with which the bodies were laid out indicated the absence of any signs of violence or terror. Many of the women wore headdresses that were still delicate and in good order, except for the pressure of earth. Woolley suggests, on the basis of his findings, that "those who were to be sacrificed went down alive into the pit" (p. 59), concluding that "it is most probable that the victims walked to their places, took some kind of drug—opium or hashish would serve—and lay down in order; after the drug had worked, whether it produced sleep or death, the last touches were given to their bodies and the pit was filled in. There does not seem to have been anything brutal in the manner of their deaths" (p. 60).

Of the sixty-eight women in the pit, twenty-eight wore ribbons of gold. Many, if not all, of the rest wore similar ribbons of silver. The women in the pit also wore bright red, woolen garments, and many had beads at their waists. Woolley suggests that "it must have been a very gaily dressed crowd that assembled in the open mat-lined pits for the royal obsequies, a blaze of colour with the crimson coats, the silver, and the gold; clearly these people were not wretched slaves killed as oxen might be killed, but persons held in honour, wearing their robes of office, and coming, one hopes, voluntarily to a rite which would in their belief be but a passing from one world to another, from the service of a god on earth to that of the same god in another sphere" (p. 64). The afterworld was thus to be a continuation of the predeath existence.

Woolley notes that human sacrifice was confined exclusively to the funerals of royal persons. The king "did not die as men die, but was translated; and it might therefore be not a hardship but a privilege for those of his court to accompany their master and continue in his service" (p. 65).

In one of the royal Sumerian graves, a wooden chariot decorated with red, white, and blue mosaic along the edges and with golden heads of lions sporting manes of lapis lazuli was recovered. In front of the chariot lay the crushed skeletons of two asses with the bodies of the grooms by their heads. In another grave, two wooden four-wheeled wagons, each drawn by three oxen, were found. Again, the grooms lay at the oxen's heads, and the drivers reposed within the vehicles.

The most famous culture to preserve its dead, that of ancient Egypt, built large tombs and was almost totally organized around its belief in an afterlife. The afterworld was designed to deny the separation and nothingness following bodily death. The provision for a parallel existence after death, a new "space" to which one had to move, usually by some vehicle (e.g., a boat), was most fully elaborated in Egypt, although it also has been found elsewhere. The implication that death was but a change in status and place and not the end suggests that this conception of immortality made it unnecessary to mourn. There was no "loss," only a transformation.

I have relied heavily on the recently published book of Dr. I. E. S. Edwards (1972), Keeper of Egyptian Antiquities at the British Museum in London, for the following discussion of the death practices of the ancient Egyptians and the artistic and architectural developments related to these beliefs.

From very early times, before the Osirian and solar cults gained their followings, the Egyptians believed that man was composed of body and spirit and that the spirit could remain alive after physical death if the body was preserved and provided with the necessary sustenance (a belief still held by many today and the basis of elaborate embalming, funeral, and burial practices). The spirit was believed to live in a place in an underworld to which access was gained through the pit of the tomb. The conception of an afterlife closely associated with the tomb and dependent upon the preservation and sustenance of the body became the basis for the elaborate Egyptian tombs that contained every imaginable article for the use of the dead. The tomb of Tutankhamen even included regal chariots. The afterlife was envisioned as a mirror of this world. Although the physical and spiritual elements were separated at death, they were interdependent; for the well-being of the spirit could only be assured if the body were preserved intact and able to receive it. This was an additional reason for the elaborate care taken to protect the body from disturbance and decay.

The earliest Egyptian burials were in graves dug in sand. Before 3100 B.C., in order to protect the bodies from exposure resulting from the wind, a superstructure composed of brick, called a "mastaba," was built over the burial pit. Some distance from the mastaba a boat-shaped cavity was dug which was lined with brick and which contained a wooden boat intended for the use of the deceased in his afterlife. "Attendants who had been members of the owner's household were sometimes buried in small mastabas arranged in rows outside the enclosure wall of the main tomb, evidently in the belief that they could continue in his service in the after-life. They were certainly buried at the same time as their masters, but not alive as might be supposed. In all probability their death was the result of a lethal dose of poison accepted voluntarily as a duty required by their terms of employment" (Edwards, 1972, p. 27). During the Fourth and Fifth Dynasties (2686–2181 B.C.), the mastabas began to include statues of the owner of the tomb, and occasionally other members of his family as well. The stone walls were painted, and scenes carved in relief began to appear. In a Sixth Dynasty mastaba, the scenes most likely to be carved on the walls were those of servants bearing offerings of food and drink to their deceased master, harvesting, manufacturing processes, hunting, and so on. As an additional "safeguard" for the continuation of life after death, the Egyptians began to provide the deceased with an inanimate substitute for an article that it was not practicable to supply in actuality. In some Second Dynasty mastabas, dummy vases were thought to be as beneficial to the occupant of the tomb as vessels filled with actual provisions. Stone figures, of greater permanence than those made of wood, were introduced. When the principle of substitution by means of a representation had been accepted, the next step was to include not only individual objects, such as food vessels or statues, but also wish-fulfilling, composite scenes illuminating episodes in the life of the deceased and he would want to continue to enjoy in the afterlife—scenes depicting him hunting, fowling, or inspecting his estates, harvesting, slaughtering his animals, brewing, and baking.

In order to make sure that the spirit of the deceased would recognize his own statue, it was usually inscribed with his names and titles in hieroglyphs. Similarly, in the scenes carved in relief, short explanatory inscriptions were inserted as a commentary, often giving the names of the persons represented and sometimes describing in greater detail the functions they performed. These persons, who were generally relatives of the deceased or his servants, were thus also assured of an afterlife in the service of their master. Egyptian man appears to have believed that, through artistic depictions and writing, he could perpetuate his life, thought, and activities for eternity.

Gerda Frank (personal communication) has pointed out to me that eventually the magic of the written word as also furnished to nonroyal individuals in the form of texts inscribed on the inside of coffins or, later, on papyrus scrolls. Sometimes, if papyrus was too expensive for the family of the departed, a dummy scroll made out of plaster was used, in the pious belief that the gods would understand the intention and the necessity for substitution.

Eventually, the funerary stela was introduced into the tomb, to serve as a substitute for the regular supplies of fresh provisions thought essential for the well-being of the deceased.

> This stela contained a magic formula declaring that the deceased had received the daily offerings in abundance; above the formula was generally a scene, carved in relief, showing him seated at a

table heaped with offerings presented to him by members of his family. While not intended to dispense with the regular supply of fresh provisions, the stela, by means of the magic power of its written word, provided the deceased with a valuable method of re-insurance against starvation and neglect [Edwards, 1972, p. 38].

The burial of living persons was not practiced by the Egyptians of the Pyramid Age, the symbolic representations serving as substitutes.

In pyramids of the Fifth and Sixth Dynasties, vertical columns of hieroglyphic inscription completely covered the walls of the vestibule and the limestone portions of the walls of the burial chamber. These inscriptions are known as "pyramid texts." Again, their purpose was to secure a happy afterlife for the king or queen. "So powerful was the magic of the written word that its presence alone provided a sufficient guarantee that the thought expressed would be realized" (Edwards, 1972, p. 139).

In ancient Egyptian civilization, we can observe a historical progression from the actual burial of servants with the deceased master, to the burial of artistic scenes depicting their services, and finally to the almost exclusive use of written words to describe the care they provided. We see a striking progression: from the actual burial of a real person, to the burial of a primary-process thing representation, to the burial of a more symbolic secondary-process representation (words) that is still endowed with the qualities of the earlier thing-object.

The burial of boats suitable for navigation, a practice seen in many ancient cultures, may also have had several meanings. Some of the vessels may have actually been used at the time of the funeral, but others probably were intended to provide the deceased with a symbolic means of transportation in his afterlife in the afterworld. The ancient Greeks, for example, believed that one had to pay the boatman to be ferried across the river Styx to the world of the dead. The burial of boats at Sutton Hoo (England) and in ancient Scandinavian sites indicates the apparent universality of the fantasy that death is a journey from the world of the living to the world of the dead.[2]

[2] Grottskopf (1970) has described the boat burials in Sweden, Norway, and Denmark as a means of transporting the dead to the next world. Some

More than 800 years after the last royal pyramid had been constructed in Egypt, pyramidal tombs suddenly reappeared in the Sudan. In a cemetery, close to one of these later pyramids, twenty-four graves of royal horses were unearthed, each horse richly covered with silver trappings and strings of beads. "They were, without doubt, sacrificed at the time of the king's death, in order that they might accompany him to the Next World. Only one instance of a horse-burial is known from Egypt, although chariots were included in the tombs of royalty" (Edwards, 1972, p. 191).

From 300 B.C. until A.D. 350, the Egyptian kings lived at Meroë, 130 miles north of Khartoum. The kings of Meroë revived the custom of burying the royal servants with the king in his tomb, "so that their spirits might continue to serve him in the Next World. Whether they were actually buried alive or were put to death before burial is still open to conjecture" (Strabo, quoted in Edwards, 1972, p. 195). Strabo makes the following statement: "It is still the custom in Ethiopia, that when the king, by accident or otherwise, has lost the use of a member, or a member itself, all of his usual followers (those who are destined to die at the same time as himself) inflict on themselves a similar mutilation" (Strabo, quoted in Edwards, 1972, p. 195).

Rudenko (1970) has described horse burial among the ancient Siberians (2,400 years ago). The horses, killed with a blow to the head from an ax, were buried with a decorative headdress

---

of the objects found in the Sutton Hoo ship were already old at the time of their English burial and originally were brought as heirlooms from Sweden. Green (1963) mentions boat burials in Bruges and in Utrecht. Bruce-Mitford (1947) dates the Sutton Hoo burials as between A.D. 655–656. He notes that the belief held was that the individual's material requirements in the afterlife were the same as in actual life: thus, the burial of money, weapons, armor, utensils, and personal ornaments. In *Beowulf*, we learn that the Sutton Hoo burial (that took place forty-five years before the composition of the Old English epic) followed earlier rites in which the funeral ship was not buried but set out to sea.

In Eastern Sweden, a burial chamber with two women was excavated. One was richly attired, whereas the other, her servant, lay in a contorted position; she had been buried alive with her mistress and then suffocated to death. The discovery of a boat burial in Sweden in A.D. 922 revealed the body of a slave woman who was killed in order to be buried with her dead master (Brøndsted, 1960).

in a separate grave close to that of the deceased male owner. Male graves were furnished with food, knives, animal skins, and clothes, supplies that Rudenko assumed were to facilitate entrance into the next world. The custom of burying the chief with his concubine or one of his wives was persistent among the Pazyryk. The corpses were embalmed in a fashion similar to that of the ancient Egyptians. Herodotus describes in vivid detail the funeral ceremony of the Scythian kings, which is similar to Rudenko's description of the rituals of the ancient Siberians. Herodotus writes:

> [T]he corpse is laid in the tomb on a mattress, with spears fixed in the ground on either side to support a roof . . . while in other parts of the great square pit various members of the king's household are buried beside him: one of his concubines, his butler, his cook, his groom, his steward, and his chamberlain—all of them strangled. Horses are buried too, and gold cups . . .
>
> At the end of a year another ceremony takes place: they take fifty of the best of the king's remaining servants, strangle and gut them, stuff their bodies with chaff, and sew them up again. . . . Fifty of the finest horses are then subjected to the same treatment. The next step is to cut a number of wheels in half and to fix them in pairs, rim-downwards, to stakes driven into the ground, two stakes to each half-wheel; then stout poles are driven lengthwise through the horses from tail to neck, and by means of these the horses are mounted on the wheels, in such a way that the front pairs support the shoulders and the rear pairs the belly between the thighs. All four legs are left dangling clear of the ground. Each horse is bitted and bridled, the bridle being led forward and pegged down. The bodies of the men are dealt with in a similar way: straight poles are driven up through the neck, parallel with the spine, and the lower protruding ends fitted into sockets in the stakes which run through the horses; thus each horse is provided with one of the young servants to ride him. When horses and riders are all in place around the tomb, they are left there, and the mourners go away [Herodotus, *The Histories*, pp. 264–265].[3]

This last example is one of a culturally constituted anniversary reaction—involving homicide and equinicide as part of

[3] Copyright © the estate of Aubrey de Selincourt, 1954; copyright © A. R. Burns, 1972; reprinted with permission.

a cultural mourning ritual (see chapter 12). One might speculate on the specific form of Herodotus's anniversary celebration: could these riders provide further companionship into the afterworld and so reaffirm the belief in life after death? Herodotus also described how each individual reacted to the Scythian king's death: they "cut a piece from their ears, shave their hair, make circular incisions on their arms, gash their foreheads and noses, and thrust arrows through their left hands" (p. 264).

On the Ivory Coast of West Africa, the death of a king or a great chief called for the sacrifice of all of his wives and slaves. As many as a hundred persons were commonly put to death on such occasions. Moreover, every year, on the anniversary of the late king's death, his successor sacrificed a slave, an ox, and a sheep at the grave of the dead king (Frazer, 1923, p. 305).

The Nyakusa, an East African tribe, formerly buried a chief with a live son of a commoner, saying, "Let him enjoy the company of his men on the road" (Wilson, 1959, p. 63). This burial companion was usually seized secretly. A junior chief was buried with a live cow instead of a human companion. A chief's son was buried with a live black calf. In more recent times, the custom has evolved into one of taking a cow or bull to look into the grave. The term applied to this act is *burying the cow* (Wilson, 1957, p. 20). The cattle are slaughtered at the funeral feast and then eaten by the mourners.

Here we again note the transformation from human sacrifice burial—in which the deceased is joined in death—to feasting on the funeral sacrificial flesh, an incorporation and joining of the dead in symbolic form.

Hertz (1960) has noted that among the Ola Ngaju, a Dayak people in Borneo, the sacrifice of a human victim, whose head is cut off, is one of the essential acts of the funeral feast. Sacrifice is "an indispensable condition for the conclusion of the mourning period" (p. 40) and the lifting of mourning taboos.

On the day following the funeral cremation of an adult warrior, the Dani, a West New Guinea stone-age tribe, select little girls who sacrifice one or two fingers. The severed fingers are burned in the dying embers of the funeral fire, and the wound is dressed with a mixture of clay and ashes. Each girl child knows what is eventually likely to happen to her: her own mother's hands are mostly thumbs (Gardner and Heider, 1968).

The fingers are considered to be gifts necessary to placate the ghost. The symbolic joining of the dead man by a female whose amputated fingers are burned along with his body is psychologically similar to the Hindu practice of suttee. Among the Dani, however, the sacrifice is not that of a life but the symbolic amputation of the fingers of a female child.

Hubert and Mauss (1898) have described sacrifice as a communication and distinguish between expiatory, request, thanksgiving, curative, and redemption sacrifices. Some may be regular periodic sacrifices that are linked to fixed moments of time and thus independent of will and chance occurrences; others are occasional sacrifices that allow a rite of passage to be completed so that the victim can then be reborn in a divine or immortal state. In an expiatory sacrifice, the death of the deceased is reenacted; thus the control of the death and the mastery of the trauma is given to the sacrificer.

Tylor (1958) has noted that one of the most widespread rites of animistic religion is that of funeral human sacrifice for the service of the dead. "When a man of rank dies and his soul departs to its own place, wherever and whatever that place may be, it is a rational inference of early philosophy that the souls of attendants, slaves, and wives, put to death at his funeral, will make the same journey and continue their service in the next life, and the argument is frequently stretched further, to include the souls of new victims sacrificed in order that they may enter upon the same ghostly servitude" (p. 42). Tylor has described such funeral human sacrifices in Borneo. Among the Dayaks, mourning for a dead man continued until a human head was brought in to provide him with a slave to accompany him to the "habitation of the souls" (p. 43). A father who lost his child would go out and kill the first man he met, as part of the funeral ceremony. Among the American Indians, the Osage were required to raise a pole with an enemy's scalp over the buried corpse. This practice, similar to the Dayak head-hunting ritual, with the scalp suspended over the grave, like the head, allowed the spirit of the victim to be subjected to the spirit of the buried warrior in the land of the spirits.

Sacrifices at the funeral of a leader were also made in Central America. The Quakeolths, an Indian tribe of the Northwest, did not actually sacrifice the widow, but made her rest her head on her husband's corpse while it was being burned, until at last she was dragged, more dead than alive, from the flames. If she recovered, she carried her husband's ashes with her for three years, during which any levity or deficiency in expressing her grief would render her an outcast. This custom appears to be a derivative from an earlier custom of actual widow-burning at the death of the husband. Tylor describes human funeral sacrifices across Africa—East, Central, West, and South—and in India, Japan, China, Greece, Scandinavia, Germany, and Russia.

Caesar recounts how at a funeral the Gauls burned whatever was dear to the dead man—animals, much-loved slaves, and clients. Animal funeral sacrifices have already been noted. The Eskimos often would lay a dog's head in a child's grave, believing that the soul of the dog, who is at home everywhere, could then guide the helpless child to the land of the souls. The Aztecs also buried a sacrificed dog with the dead. At funerals, the Siberians sacrificed horses, the Arabs killed camels, and the Livonians sheep and oxen. "A cavalry general, Count Friedrich Kasmir Boos von Waldeck, was buried at Treves in 1781 according to the forms of the Teutonic Order; his horse was led in the procession, and the coffin having been lowered into the grave the horse was killed and thrown in upon it" (Tylor, 1958, p. 58). Object burial was also very widespread among the American Indians, Figians, and Scythians, as well as among many other groups. Funeral sacrifice and object burial with the deceased, as has already been explained, is predicated upon the notion of life after death, in which the souls and spirits of the deceased and the sacrificed will be joined in the other world. In some cultures, life after death was not the predominant belief; instead, life and death were seen as a continuum, with life being a transformation to death (see chapter 13).

In the account of the funeral of Patroclus in the *Iliad*, Homer records the slaying of twelve Trojan nobles before the pyre, along with four horses and two dogs. The slaughter was to provide the deceased with a retinue to accompany him to the other world. Achilles, who ordered the slaying and the accompanying cremation, was the chief mourner. He fasted and remained unwashed throughout the ceremony.

The Romans also sacrificed slaves or prisoners. Cumont

(1922) notes that, after the taking of Perugia, Octavius, on the Ides of March—the anniversary of the slaying of Julius Caeser—caused 300 notables of the town to be slaughtered on Caesar's memorial altar.

Frazer (1923) and Cumont (1922) note that gladiatorial combats first took place at Roman funerals and were substitutes for the slaughter of captives at the burial. The first exhibition of gladiatorial battle was given by D. Junius Brutus in 264 B.C., in honor of his dead father. Earlier, in addition to the funeral sacrifice of prisoners on the death of a king or chief, the Roman subjects assembled, tore their hair, lacerated their bodies until they were covered with blood, and then fought each other with clubs and stones until one or more of them were killed. This practice subsequently evolved into the funeral and death anniversary gladiatorial celebrations that later took on an independent significance of their own.

Thus the institutionalized practice of funeral suicide-homicide was gradually transformed into figurative symbolic activities without actual killings. These cultural-religious practices are related to, yet different from, the personal grief suicides that are of clinical interest to us. Observations of such personal grief suicides, indicating abnormal mourning, have been seen cross-culturally. Firth (1967), working with and in a Polynesian community, observed that several husbands, whose griefs were "too great" at the deaths of their wives, killed themselves soon after the death had occurred, usually by hanging, which is quick and certain. If the suicide was prevented during this acute mourning period, no later further attempts were made. Among the African tribes of the Lo Dagaa (Goody, 1962) and the Gisu (La Fontaine, 1960), suicide attempts associated with grief over the deaths of children, siblings, or spouses are common. These suicidal activities are also seen among the Eskimos, where one of the commonest reasons for self-destruction has been prolonged grief over the death of a loved one (Leighton and Hughes, 1955).

Lantis (1947) has noted that among certain Alaskan Eskimo groups (the Koniag and the Aleuts) slaves were killed as a mark of grief upon the death of an eminent person—not in order to continue to serve their dead master, but as an indication of indifference to the value of property. Among the Eskimos of the Bering Straits, scapulae and skulls of large game animals were placed on the grave of a strong hunter, and on the Diomedes a man's favorite dog was killed and placed with his body.

Guerra (1971) cites a 1526 chronicle of pre-Columbian customs prepared by Fernandez de Oviedo which describes how the Indians killed themselves of their own will when their chief died. "When some chief or principal lord died all most close to him, servants and women of his household who have served him daily, kill themselves because they believe, and thus the Tyura [devil] has given them to understand, that he who kills himself when his lord dies, goes to heaven and there he serves him to eat or to drink and remains there forever exercising the same office that he had here while he lived in the house of such a lord" (p. 54). In 1553, an Inca chronicler described how these Indians buried live women with the bodies of their dead chiefs, perhaps to tend to their needs in the afterlife. Guerra cites a 1565 edition of another Peruvian chronicler which states, "when a lord dies, they prepare a large grave and place next to him much gold and silver pieces, with some of their most beloved wives and servants; clothes, maize and wine, so that they can eat and drink until they reach the other world. This manner of funeral is used in many parts of the Indies" (p. 108). Among the Maya, a 1641 report states, "the lords were buried in certain vaults . . . along with many male and female slaves . . . and some of their most dearly beloved wives" (p. 126).

Soustelle (1970) has described the two different funeral rites used among the Aztecs: cremation and burial. "When the dead man had been a very high dignitary or a ruler some of his servants were killed, those who, of their own free-will, wished to die with him; and they were buried or cremated . . . so that they should be able to follow him in the hereafter" (p. 201). Furthermore, Aztec belief held that most of the dead went into the dark world of Mictlan, under the earth. "To help the dead man in the bitter trials that he would have to overcome, they gave him a companion, a dog, which they killed and burnt together with him. There were also offerings burnt for him eighty days after the funeral, and again at the end of a year and again after two, three, and four years. It was thought that when the four years had passed, the dead man would have arrived at the end of his journey among the shadows; for then he would have reached the 'ninth hell,' the last region of Mictlan, the place of his eternal rest" (p. 202).

If we compare the Aztec practice of dog sacrifice and burial with the dead with what has recently been discovered in the grave of a 30,000-year-old "corpse," we can see parallels and can infer the existence of a belief in immortality in Paleolithic times. A 30,000-year-old "corpse" was found in a humid cave in Spain in a most unusual state of preservation. After the grave was carefully excavated and brought to the Smithsonian Institution for preparation and conservation, the archeologists discovered the tomb contained not one set of human remains but two. The first dead man had been placed in the grave on his left side, his body extended with legs slightly bent. His head was concealed by the cast of a small hoofed animal, curled up in the way sheep are trussed for market. A larger animal had also been placed in the grave, covering his feet. Were these companions placed in the grave to guide and assist the dead man or to assure its inhabitant of an adequate food supply on his journey to another world? This grave, as well as others, contained bits of burned bone and fragments of ocher, a red coloring material. Ocher had also been sprinkled and a fire had been burned over the sealed graves. When a second body (cast) was discovered, the surprising finding was that the head had been separated from the shoulders and the lower legs had been cut off above the ankle and the stumps charred. This was then discovered to have been true of the first body as well (Smithsonian, 1972). Since postmortem mutilation is still currently practiced among living societies in order to prevent the spirit of the deceased from returning to haunt the old community and its living inhabitants, it might be inferred that Paleolithic man had a similar or related belief. The red ocher has been found in many prehistoric burials and may have been a symbol of blood and life.

Levy (1963) and Clark and Piggott (1970), discussing burial practices in many different prehistoric societies, describe the careful burial practices in Neanderthal man. For example, the flexing of the lower limbs seems to have been a widespread Neanderthal practice, having been observed as far afield as Crimea, France, and Mount Carmel in Israel. Clark and Piggott suggest that the meaning of this flexing may have been the prevention of the return of the dead to haunt the living—an explanation similar to that offered for the Paleolithic mutilations. These repeated findings give us some insight into the psychology of primitive man—he was careful in his burial practices, which were probably related to concepts of an afterlife and immortality.

Devereux's (1961) pioneering research on Mohave funeral suicides gives us an insight into the cultural evolution from what probably was actual funeral suicide to the more recent gestures by the chief mourners toward suicide that did not culminate in actual self-destruction. Because of the symbolic quality of the funeral suicide act, Devereux notes that "no recorded attempt to commit funeral suicide ever proved successful" (p. 432). The ritual consists of the mourner's attempt to commit funeral suicide by jumping on the pyre, while the society frustrates the attempt, "the whole representing a kind of tacit 'contract' " (p. 432). The fundamental character of the "grave but empty" gesture frequently indicated the current "lack of a true and generally understandable subjective and specific motivation" (p. 432). However, the Mohave attitude toward an attempted funeral suicide of a bereaved father or mother was considered more serious than a similar attempt made by a bereaved spouse. A widower received more criticism than a widow for making the suicidal gesture.

Devereux notes that actual suicide—an actual attempt or wish to kill oneself—does occur among the Mohave. Among the psychological motives seen in these suicidal gestures, Devereux mentions the identification of the suicide with an emotionally significant deceased person. Since Devereux's thesis, with which I fully agree, is that suicide is a pathological form of mourning, and that "all real suicides are more or less also funeral suicides in the sense of being mourning reactions involving an identification with someone known or unconsciously fantasied to be dead" (p. 431), we can suggest that at one time in the evolution of Mohave culture, funeral suicides actually occurred, and that only later did this self-destructive expectation become ritualized into the nondestructive gesture that is acted out as part of the acute phase of the mourning process. This gesturing, still to be seen in current-day funerals, where the survivor may throw himself on the coffin containing the deceased, is more characteristic of the acute mourning phases (see chapter 1) in the nonpathological situation. Where mourning is abnormal, actual suicide can occur much later on an anniversary occasion. Devereux does cite one example of a mourner who committed suicide at the funeral of his son "whom his nagging drove to suicide" (p. 463). In Mohave belief, "suicide is . . . the quickest and most dramatic means of achieving the reunion of the living with the dead" (p. 465). What Devereux found for the Mohave may be a fundamental motive for all suicides: through suicide, reunion and immortality are achieved. In contrast, if normal mourning occurs, it sets into motion the internal dying process that eventually results in a freeing of the mourner so that he can invest his energy in other living beings or causes.

Throughout time, all over the world, in almost every culture, funeral suicides and homicides have taken place. These, I suggest, are cultural manifestations of intrapsychic processes, in the main mourning processes, which become institutionalized in order to facilitate the personal and social adaptation to death (see chapter 20 where the psychoanalytic considerations of immortality, which are not germane to the present chapter, are discussed.)

Immortality and resurrection, though closely related, are different concepts. In those belief systems where immortality is conceived of as a journey to another place without returning, resurrection is not possible. I would suggest that this concept of the maintenance of some form of existence, despite a permanent separation from reality, is a manifestation of internal uncompleted mourning. In those belief systems where life and death are viewed as continuous states and where the dead do not leave but are constant in their transformed presence as either benevolent or malevolent spirits, the dead can one day be bodily resurrected. In both of these situations, the nothingness, internally and externally, of death is avoided, as is the mourning process.

II

Although culturally ritualized funeral and anniversary suicides and homicides are not found today, individual funeral and anniversary suicides still occur. These personal grief suicides, or melancholias, unlike ritual suicides or homicides, are manifestations of abnormal mourning closely related to the anniversary suicides seen clinically (see chapter 13). They seem to indicate a relationship to the culturally constituted rituals that originally had personal meaning.

A striking example of an anniversary homicide is that of the assassination of Robert F. Kennedy by Sirhan Sirhan on June 5, 1968, one year, almost to the day, after the defeat of the Arabs by the Israelis. Andrea Feldman, one of Andy Warhol's superstars, jumped to her death one week after toasting Marilyn Monroe's suicide with champagne (*Village Voice*, August 17, 1972, p. 52). Janis Joplin, a singer, committed suicide a few weeks after purchasing a tombstone for Bessie Smith, her ideal, on the anniversary of her death (Jefferson, 1973).

The following story appeared in a news report:

> Last March, Mrs. E. B.'s car skidded off a road onto ice on the W. River. As she and her three children tried to walk to safety, the ice gave way and her fifteen month old son, B., drowned. She underwent psychiatric treatment after the incident, and her husband said, "her spirits had been better for the last two months or so." But B.'s death still haunted her.
>
> "Everytime I go into the living room where he slept, I see my baby," she told a neighbor not long ago.
>
> On Monday, her husband left for work and she told him she planned "to do some sewing." Later that morning, a car driven by Mrs. B., again ran off the road, at exactly the same spot, and again plunged into the W. River. She and the two surviving children, Br., 5, and M., 3, drowned.
>
> The P. County Coroner, E. H. P., said Wednesday that Mrs. B. had apparently driven her car into the river intentionally. "Because of the similar circumstances and location of the March 14 incident, it would indicate that this was an intentional act," he said. "It is not an accident, and no inquest is planned" [*New York Times*, November 18, 1972].[4]

An Iowa pilot whose wife and three children were killed when their airplane plunged into Lake Michigan off Meigs Field has taken his own life. The father, who piloted the fatal plane when

[4] Reprinted by permission. © 1972/73 by The New York Times Company.

it crashed Sunday, made funeral arrangements for his family on Tuesday, and then killed himself [*Chicago Daily News*, September 20, 1972].[5]

Hilgard (1969) presents a case of suicide in a forty-three-year-old male, a successful criminal lawyer, on the day after his son reached his twelfth birthday. The anniversary coincidence is with the victim's childhood trauma: the day after his twelfth birthday, his older brother died suddenly and unexpectedly of encephalitis. The victim, who had become successful after his brother's death, felt guilty and, when an adult, said his success came only as a result of a death. He was aware of his intense jealousy and death wishes against his older, brilliant, conforming, and scholastically successful brother. At his son's birth, the suicide had said, "I probably have less than fifteen years to live." This strange reference to time, I believe, was not just a manifestation of depression, but as I have found in anniversary reactions, an indication of uncompleted and abnormal mourning.

The particular phenomenon of grief suicide following the death of a significant other may be seen in children and adolescents. One such tragic example is reported in the following news story:

The first great blow in G. C.'s young life came three years ago. His mother died of cancer.

Five months ago, his 15-year-old sister, J., accidentally shot herself while handling a gun in the family weapons collection. She was paralyzed from her chin down.

His father, P., 38, lonely and pained since his wife's death, was plunged into a mood of despair. He went to the hospital every day and often sat by the girl's bedside throughout the night.

Last Friday G. walked into his father's bedroom and found him dead—shot with one of the weapons from the collection. Nearby was a note telling of his agony since the death of his wife and the accident that crippled his daughter.

Yesterday was Veteran's Day and G. had the day off from school. He was alone in the basement apartment. The police say he went to the weapons collection, took down a 12-gauge shot-

[5] Reprinted by permission. © 1972 by the Chicago Daily News.

gun, aimed the muzzle at his head and hooked a toe up against the trigger.

At the age of 13, he shot himself to death [*New York Times*, November 13, 1973].[6]

An account by Goodwin (1966) may further illustrate an abnormal identificatory mourning reaction. He states:

> Some years ago . . . I did a cystoscopy on [a patient] while he was under anesthesia. During the minor procedure the anesthetist, looking at me with horror, said, "What are you doing to this man? He has gone into profound shock. I am having a terrible time trying to keep him alive." I stopped the cystoscopy immediately and we were able to revive him. Subsequently, a psychiatric consultation unearthed a strange story: exactly one year to the day before that episode, this man had been standing by the funeral pyre of a particularly good friend of his in India. He was watching the body be cremated. The friend had died of a urinary problem. My patient had said to himself, "I will be dead within the year." The day of my examination on which he almost died of shock was the anniversary of that occasion, and the patient, without telling anyone, had attached great significance to this [p. 516].

Zilboorg (1937) cites a clinical case report taken from a Boston newspaper: a girl, twenty-two years of age, jumped out of a fourteenth-story window. She had appeared cheerful the day before and had bought a complete new outfit. On the next day, Good Friday, she committed suicide. She was said to have had a depression about a year before, and further inquiry revealed that she was more or less always subdued in the spring. The victim's mother had died when she was eight years old, fourteen years previously, on the same day (i.e., not the same date, but on Good Friday). The girl thus had killed herself on the anniversary of her mother's death. The fact that her depressed moods usually occurred in the spring might be related to an unconscious, uncompleted abnormal mourning process. The identification of the mother with Christ, who also died on Good Friday, seems possible. Why the young woman killed

---

[6] Reprinted by permission. © 1973 by The New York Times Company.

herself is unclear, but the identificatory pattern with its reunion qualities seems indisputable.

Karl Menninger (1938), a pioneer in the study of suicide, cites a case similar to Zilboorg's. "The Countess of Cardigan . . . is reported in the press to have struggled with suicidal impulses each year on the anniversary of her mother's suicide, remarking, 'If I do not kill myself on this day, I know I shall have another year to live.' Finally, on the eighth anniversary, at almost the same hour as her mother's suicide, Lady Cardigan succeeded in her efforts to kill herself" (p. 53). Menninger also describes several examples of repeated suicides in families.

> One patient came to us at 61 on account of strong suicidal propensities which she had several times attempted to gratify. Three of the patient's sisters killed themselves in an identical manner; the patient's mother, and the patient's mother's mother had also killed themselves in the same way. Moreover, the patient's mother was a twin and the twin brother also killed himself.
>
> In another instance, a highly regarded family contained five sons and two daughters, the oldest son killed himself at 35, the youngest developed a depression and attempted suicide several times but finally died of other causes at 30, a third brother killed himself in a manner similar to that of his oldest brother, still another brother shot himself to death, and the oldest daughter took poison successfully at a party. Only two children remain living in this entire family [pp. 53–54].

Cain and Fast (1972) have recently written about the identification a child makes with the suicidal parent. In some instances they find the direct identification with the suicidal parent in a suicidal act committed by the child. These cases commit suicide

> often in a manner highly similar if not identical to the manner in which [their] parent had committed suicide, e.g., an individual who jumped from the same building at the same point in his life as did his father; an eighteen-year-old girl who drowned herself alone at night in much the same fashion and at the same beach as had her mother many years earlier; a thirty-two-year-old man who in clearly suicidal fashion drove his car off the very same cliff which his father had driven off following a similar suicidal statement of intention some twenty-one years before; a fourteen-

year-old boy who hung himself shortly after telling his younger brother and playmate that dad would feel just as rotten discovering *his* dead body as dad had been when "they found mom hanging there" . . . the identificatory aspect is patently clear, not only in the act but in the suicidal verbalizations and suicide notes or in unmistakable anniversary significance [p. 106].

It is my contention that the cases described by Cain and Fast may be regarded as variants of anniversary phenomena. Although temporal referents are the most easily detected correspondences, I have suggested that anniversary reactions need not be confined to dates, days, times, or ages. However, emotional anniversaries, not necessarily time-bound, bear the hallmark of the repetition of a significant reaction from the past and equally reflect what I believe is the uncompleted and pathological mourning. As such, what may look like identification in the suicide may be more reflective of the wish to reunite with the one from whom the separation occurred. Kohut's (1971) concept of the merger, the mirror, and the twinship applies here. In the mind of the suicide, immortality is achieved through this imitative reunion. Several of the clinical examples given illustrate this conceptualization. Furthermore, if the reunion wish resides in the mind of the suicide, there need be no grief or mourning—the separation is transient and can be erased. Again I cite a case of Cain and Fast (1972) as an illustration.

> Morton K was a twenty-five-year-old graduate student in the humanities, whose father (an eminent scientist) had committed suicide at the age of forty-three. . . . Those few who came to know him fairly intimately over the years said he spoke often of his father's death, refused to blame him or in any way begrudge his suicide. Further, he referred to himself as "star-crossed," destined for his father's fate, stated that when he died it would be by his own hand, and spoke undramatically of following his "Pied Piper" father into the water before he was thirty. . . . A few months after successfully completing his preliminary examinations, he killed himself, quietly and unerringly [pp. 107–108].

To be sure, it is difficult, without further details, to do more than make inferences from such scant data; however, the description given suggests that to this younger man following the father is a way of being reunited with him. The reunion and accompaniment motive is one that is basic to the notion of an afterlife, a heaven, a paradise, and a desire not to experience life without the loved one. It is also a component of the funeral homicides and suicides mentioned earlier. Metapsychologically, we recognize that the reunion-accompaniment wish is in opposition to the separation that occurs with actual death or meaningful loss. When something dies outside, something also dies inside. The normal reaction to loss is the mourning process that consists of various stages spread out over time (see chapter 1). The denial of death and mourning is accomplished through the belief in eternal life, transformed in space, and timeless.

I am grateful to two colleagues, Michael Basch and Ernest Wolf, who, after reading an earlier draft of the above, made several stimulating explanatory suggestions that I wish to utilize in the concluding discussion.

Basch suggests that if death is perceived not as a final but as a transformational step, then the willing self-destruction of ancient peoples could be viewed as fulfillment in the service of an ego ideal in terms of narcissistic development and in the service of the superego in the object-libidinal sense. However, if a bereavement experience occurs, it may be a manifestation of the reality appreciation of death as finality despite the mythic contrary beliefs. In other words, normal bereavement would negate the idealized self-destructive act. I would further suggest that a mourning process could still occur as a result of the change in status and being, even though it might not be a bereavement reaction. I believe mourning to be a universal adaptational process to all change (see chapter 1), with bereavement one special sub-class of this process that has as its trigger the death of a meaningful object. Thus, whereas a mourning process can occur as a response to change, the absence of bereavement might explain the self-destructive act as a merger with the idealized omnipotent figure, thus achieving a form of primitive grandiosity that encompasses the idea of immortality. Kohut (1971) has contributed much to our understanding of these early idealizing and grandiose fantasies as well as to their significance for understanding merger-reunion wishes.

Wolf has correctly pointed out the importance of further

distinguishing between various types of nonritualized suicide. He specifically adds two explanations of Kohut's. The first type are those individuals who experience great shame and envy as a reaction to "defeats in the pursuit of their ambitions and exhibitionistic aims" (Kohut, 1971, p. 181n). Self-destructive impulses, resulting from this shame and envy, "are to be understood not as attacks of the superego on the ego but as attempts of the suffering ego to do away with the self in order to wipe out the offending, disappointing reality of failure" (Kohut, 1971, p. 181n). This additional understanding, along with the more traditional explanations, may indeed allow us to construct a developmental line for suicidal behavior. I have touched upon this elsewhere (see chapter 13).

As part of an ongoing study of the mourning process as a means of adapting to change, this report has presented data that are pertinent to our understanding of some of the pathological aspects of this process as seen in the individual. Collectively, such behavior may not be viewed as deviant but as attempts to maintain social cohesiveness in a time of stress, turmoil, and transition.

Part II
ANNIVERSARIES AND TIME

8

ANNIVERSARY REACTIONS, TRAUMA, AND MOURNING

ANNIVERSARY REACTIONS AND MOURNING

In her paper "Anniversary Reactions in Parents Precipitated by Children" Hilgard (1953) observed that symptoms may be precipitated in a parent when the parent's child reaches the age at which the parent had experienced a traumatic episode in childhood. She distinguished these symptoms from those aggravated recurrently on a birthday, death day, or other fixed date. In her clinical example, Hilgard describes a mother who developed pneumonia, pleurisy, and psychosis when her daughter was six years old. The patient's father had died of pneumonia, pleurisy, and meningitis when she, the patient, was a child of six. After the father's death, the patient was separated from her mother until she was eleven years of age. Hilgard's second patient developed severe headaches, attempted suicide, became delusional and hallucinatory when his son was four years old. This patient's father died suddenly of influenza when the patient was four years old, at which time his mother had to go to work. Hilgard explains her clinical findings as the sudden eruption of the repressed with more catastrophic observable manifestations than were present in the initial reaction to the original situation. She suggests that her patients were involved in three unintegrated identifications: the child, the mother, and the father. She also discusses reasons for the underlying conflicts which antedated, but were related to, the reactions to the childhood parental deaths.

Accepting her explanation, we can view the "anniversary response" not only as an identification but as the reaction to a temporal trigger that permits the emergence of repressed con-

Reprinted from *The Psychoanalytic Quarterly*, 39/3:347–371 (1970).

flict, which may or may not have defensive qualities that can be manifested in symptoms.

In a second report, Hilgard and Newman (1959) extended the precipitating trigger situation to include the age of the adult patient as it coincides with the age of the parent who died during the patient's childhood. In some instances a double co-incidence (of patient's age with parent's age at death, and of patient's child's age with that of the patient when he lost his parent) occurred. In a large hospital sample, findings of statistical significance revealed the coincidental temporal correlation of childhood loss with first adult hospitalization dates. Several hypotheses about anniversary reactions were presented in this later paper: (1) Symptomatology may be of a neurotic or psychotic nature. (2) Death of a parent is not the only event having anniversary significance. (3) Anniversaries need not be tied to age; they may be related to time of year, festivals, holidays, or other periodicities. (4) The stage of development of the child when a parent is lost may be of decisive importance as to whether psychosis appears as an anniversary response. (5) Intrapsychic and social factors may ameliorate the traumatic effect of loss of a parent in childhood. (6) In the childhood-parent-loss cases studied, male patients included a small number of psychotics and a large number of alcoholics; female patients included a larger number of psychotic reactions and a smaller number of alcoholics.[1] (7) For women loss of the father did not tend to produce symptoms on anniversaries reflecting the father's age at death but rather when their age corresponded to that of the mother at the time of the father's death. (8) In two clinical examples there was no evidence of adequate mourning at the time of the childhood loss, but in both instances the patient had been subjected to the intense and long-continued mourning of close relatives.

In 1960, Hilgard and Fisk, studying the effects of childhood loss of a mother through hospitalization for psychosis, suggested that the loss could be handled through the introjection of the lost object with a fixation at the developmental stage reached at the time of loss. This developmental arrest, elabo-

---

[1] The authors noted: "For men, alcoholism may be in some cases an alternative to the psychotic break" (Hilgard and Newman, 1959).

rated and discussed by Fleming and Altschul (1963), results from an inability to integrate and resolve the trauma and eventuates in pathogenic defensive attempts at avoidance and denial. Some growth may occur but the patient's identification with the ill or dead parent is revived at the appropriate time in adulthood and may reach symptomatic form on the anniversary of the crisis. The anniversary is the trigger and the old relationship is transferred onto the contemporary parent-child relationship. The parent-child identifications present at the anniversary time are the "traumatized" child of old as well as the parent of old, who is expected to die.

Greenacre has written about these intrafamilial identifications in her papers on the artist. She notes that "in 1954, [Thomas] Mann was already nearly eighty years old and had passed by almost a decade, the age at which he had expected to die; i.e., his mother's age at the time of her death" (1958b, pp. 531–532). Thus this type of anniversary identification need not be limited to childhood loss, although it is more clearly seen in patients who have this past history.

In her paper "The Family Romance of the Artist" (1958a), Greenacre discusses several eminent personalities who seemingly had childhood experiences of loss that were of a traumatic and pathogenic nature. The case of Nikolai Gogol illustrates this anniversary identification quite dramatically. Greenacre reports that before Gogol's birth two siblings were born dead or died shortly after birth. Of the twelve children born to the Gogol family only five survived, Nikolai being the oldest. His only brother, Ivan, died when Nikolai was ten. "The effect on this sensitive boy of the almost endless succession of deaths of siblings has never been especially noted by his biographers, and the fact that he himself did not mention it is certainly no indication that it was not powerful, and may have been one factor in promoting his aversion to marriage" (p. 23).[2] When Nikolai was sixteen his father became ill, at age forty-three, and died two years later. On receiving the news of his father's death, he wrote his mother: "True, at first I was terribly stricken by this

---

[2] Actually Gogol did mention the death of Ivan. At age fifteen, Nikolai's first poetic efforts included a ballad, *Two Little Foxes*, in which he represents himself and his dead brother (Setchkarev, 1965).

news; however, I didn't let anyone notice that I was saddened. But when I was left alone, I gave myself up to all the power of mad desperation. I even wanted to make an attempt on my life" (Proffer, 1967). This Gogol successfully did many years later when he committed suicide through starvation at the age of forty-three. Shortly before his death he spoke of his father who "had died at the same age of the same disease."

Kanzer in "Writers and the Early Loss of Parents" (1953) has discussed identification with the dead parent and the struggle against this identification, if survival is to occur. He believes that there is a "persistent fixation of the ego on an early infantile level which is perhaps associated with actual memories of the dead parents."

In 1960, Hilgard, Newman, and Fisk identified protective and mediating factors utilized against the revived anniversary trauma of parent loss in childhood. They included (1) intactness of the home with the surviving parent assuming a dual maternal and paternal role, so that a strong ego is engendered in the child both through example and through expectations of performance; (2) support outside of the home with capacity of the parent to make use of the support; (3) the predeath relationship in the home; (4) the separation tolerance to the emergency created by death; (5) the grief and mourning that occurred at the time of the loss.

Hilgard (1969) has addressed herself to depressive and psychotic states as manifestations of anniversary reactions to childhood sibling deaths. She describes four facets of the sibling death anniversaries. First, the *saga:* the children's anniversaries belong essentially to their parents' constructions and reactions; for example, it is the parent who experiences depression on the anniversary of the child's death and this in turn affects the surviving siblings. Second, the *replacement aspect,* also described by Cain and Cain (1964), and by Cain, Fast, and Erickson (1964). The burden on the replacement child for mourning, meeting parental ideals, aspirations, and guilt is well known.[3] To discern the underlying intrapsychic factors predisposing to the guilt, such as repressed murderous rage, requires understanding of

---

[3] In some ways the survivor guilt of former concentration camp inmates parallels this phenomenon.

the individual survivor. *Excessive guilt* is Hilgard's third facet of childhood sibling loss reactions. In my experience the nature of the premorbid sibling relationship, with its underlying conflictual affects, and the meaning of the dead sibling to the surviving child are the crucial factors determining the reaction to the death of the sibling. Guilt is only one reaction, and is closely related to parental reactions to the death of the child as well as to the internal repressed conflicts of the living child. Hilgard's fourth facet relates more closely to the *anniversary reaction* itself. When children come to critical ages, critical events, or critical periods of development corresponding to the traumatic events of childhood, depression, suicide, or psychosis may occur. Hilgard suggests identification as the basic mechanism in this process.

Cain, Fast, and Erickson (1964) indicate that surviving siblings identify with the dead sibling in their belief that they will die in a similar way, but do not fully explore the underlying reasons for this identification. Siggins (1966) has summarized the different forms of identification in anniversary reactions, such as the appearance of symptoms the dead person had in his last illness, or a recurrence of the feelings that the mourner himself (or some third person, such as a surviving parent) was undergoing at the time of the loss. Such reactions may occur on the anniversary of the loved one's death, when the mourner attains the age of the lost person when he died, or the age of the third person with whom he identified. Krupp (1965) has written about identification as a defense against anxiety in coping with loss.

An earlier formulation of identification as it bears on anniversary reactions is that of Jacobson (1953), who suggests that narcissistic identification, a partial or total fusion of self and object representations in the system ego, occurs when the ego does not assume the characteristics of the love object but the self is experienced as though it were the love object. This form of identification can explain the fear of repetition that so concerns the "anniversary" patient.

Chapman's concept of nemesis (1959) is closely related to this identificatory mechanism. The patient believes he is destined to repeat in his life the pattern of a significant other person's life which ended in tragedy and catastrophe. The conviction that there is an extensive life-pattern mirroring, even in the correlation of events and ages when they occur, may persist over many years or even an entire lifetime and may form the basis of a "personal myth." The person whose pattern is being followed is usually dead or was hospitalized, almost always is the father or mother, and the loss occurred during the childhood of the patient. The "nemesis" feeling is partly conscious and is rooted in the patient's feeling of responsibility for the death or illness of the person whose life he is doomed to imitate. Guilt over hostile or competitive feelings results in symptoms that follow the path of talion principle retribution.

Related to the concept of nemesis is the fantasy of "cyclical living." According to this idea, the individual expects certain catastrophic events to occur each time the event appears in the temporal cycle. Jerome Kavka (personal communication) has reported on the significance of the twelve-year cycle in the life of Ezra Pound. Pound lost his beloved maternal grandmother when he was twelve years of age, and thereafter made changes in his life at twelve-year intervals.

The child replacement reaction described by the Cains also focuses on the defensive identification with the dead child. However, in these situations the parents impose the identity of the dead child upon the presumed substitute, and unconsciously or consciously equate the two children. This type of identification is different from that which occurs when the surviving sibling has actually had contact and conflict with the dead sibling—where the dead sibling was a "real" figure. In replacement identification there is also a mediation identification resulting from the identification with the grieving parents.

Hilgard (1969) illustrates her sibling anniversary propositions with an account of Vincent Van Gogh, who was a replacement child. He was named for his sibling predecessor, who died before his birth. The second Vincent frequently passed his brother's tombstone and saw on it, "Vincent Van Gogh." Nagera (1967) points out that the artist Vincent Van Gogh was born on the same day and month, one year after his dead sibling. And "he was inscribed in the parish register of births under the same number as his brother had been a year earlier, that is, number twenty-nine" (p. 182). Vincent, the artist, committed suicide on the twenty-ninth day of July.

To some extent the replacement phenomenon is seen in all losses. In my research I have observed replacement reactions when a parent, sibling, child, or spouse is lost. The effectiveness and success of the successor relationship depends upon many factors. Some of these include the degree, character, and adequacy of the mourning for the lost object, the ability to cathect the new object and deal with it as a different and unique individual and not as a substitute, the nature of the premorbid conflicts and relationship with the original object and the cohesiveness of the self. It is important to distinguish replacement from succession. In succession we have progression, differentiation, and further development; in replacement we have the wish to keep time and events as they are or once were. Problems of succession may bring forth problems of replacement. However, succession, unlike equivalent replacement, relates to the anticipation of the future, an important achievement of ego development and a prerequisite for later healthy ego functioning as it relates to action and fulfillment.

The anxiety signal is a manifestation of this anticipatory activity of the ego. Anxiety, a manifestation of future-oriented ego activity, is designed to assist in adaptation. The ego organizes the past, the present, the id, the superego, the self, the ego ideal, and the reality into a coherent whole that can facilitate future action in an integrated fashion. Succession and progression involve such a future orientation, whereas replacement is a past orientation that seeks to avoid the future and change.[4]

In addition to psychological manifestations, various somatic expressions of anniversary reactions have been described. Berliner (1938) writes about such an instance in his paper "The Psychogenesis of a Fatal Organic Disease." Bressler (1956) and Sifneos (1964) discuss ulcerative colitis as anniversary symptoms. In these patients the "loss" of a significant figure serves externally as the activator of underlying repressed conflicts. The external loss acts as a trigger for the release of internal feelings and conflicts as they are related to the earlier traumatic fixation points and objects, and a resultant disequilibrium oc-

---

[4] Niederland's study of the life and works of Heinrich Schliemann (1963) illustrates some of the theoretical factors just presented. He has also called attention to anniversary reactions in his studies of Schreber (1959a, b, 1960).

curs. The regression, and the attempted psychic restitution, are expressed in primitive psychosomatic symptomatology. Weiss and his collaborators (Weiss, Olin, Rollin, Fischer, and Bepler, 1957) have described coronary occlusions, hypertensive crises, and irritable colon symptoms as anniversary reactions which may be set off by birthdays, holidays, Yahrzeit commemorations, usually relating to the earlier death of a key figure with whom the patient had established a complex, ambivalent identification. Rheumatoid arthritis exacerbation (Ludwig, 1954), urticaria and dermatological reactions (Macalpine, 1952), and migraine (Giffin, 1953) have also been described as anniversary or time-related reactions.

Some additional forms of anniversary reactions are illustrated in the examples below.

I

At a dinner party, a colleague and I discussed my work on anniversary phenomena. We talked of holiday reactions, Sunday neuroses, responses to vacations, and so on. He exclaimed that he now understood the basis of his current feelings of depression, which seemingly appeared without cause: this was the anniversary of his brother's death. He was aware of previously similar responses from his self-analysis but had temporarily repressed the knowledge. We did not go into details but the periodicity and coincidence of his affective state with that of an event of twenty years ago seemed apparent. A few days after our conversation he told me of a dream he had on the night following our discussion which confirmed his insight and reconstruction.

II

A former patient whose analysis had been successfully concluded some six years earlier called for a consultation. He indicated that there was a sudden return of symptoms that previously characterized the onset of ulcerative colitis, and he was concerned lest his illness recur. He could not identify any external reason for the reappearance of his old symptoms. His sister had died of a chronic illness the year before and he had managed quite well; his business affairs were in excellent condition, and his life, though busy, was uncomplicated. As we talked he casually mentioned that he and his family were moving into a new home, larger and better suited to the family needs. Pursuing this line of thought he recalled how moving from apartments and houses in his childhood had caused him concern. He then remembered the difficulties he had in ending his analysis; there had been a sudden recrudescence of his colitis although he had been symptom-free for a long period before. I asked if he recalled when we did stop our work. At first he could not remember but then, through a series of recollections, he was able to recall the date, which coincided with the onset of the current reappearance of symptoms.

At the next consultation, a week later, he reported that the bleeding had stopped and that he had looked at his old appointment book and confirmed the coincidence of the termination date with the current reappearance of symptoms. When he "checked this out," he found that he had moved into the house he was now leaving just about the time he began his analysis. He commented that he was "leaving" spatially what was previously important to him in another way. We had no further meetings, but a later note from him reported that he was feeling fit, had no further difficulties, and that he and his family enjoyed the new home and neighborhood. The trigger here seemed to be the coincidence of two meaningful separations without conscious awareness of their significance. Both events, distant from each other in time, related to basic anxiety over separation during critical periods of early childhood.

III

A sixty-five-year-old woman came for consultation because of ever-increasing anxiety about dying, seemingly unrelated to her current physical state. She stated that at age fifty-six she had an acute coronary occlusion but made an uneventful recovery with no residual signs or symptoms. As she continued, she mentioned her brother's death five years earlier of a sudden coronary attack. To my question, she answered that he was sixty-five when he died. She then commented that sixty-five must be a magical number for her. She recalled that her mother had died of a stroke at age sixty-five. Since she had not mentioned her father, I asked about him. With a contemplative smile, she responded, "He died of a heart attack too. I was only twenty-one—it was quite a shock. I was a senior in college, due to come home for Thanksgiving; we always had a celebration then—turkey and all the trimmings. Well, I got the message about him [tearfully]—it still hurts after forty-four years. I never have enjoyed Thanksgiving since." (The date of our consultation was in October.) I asked how old her father was at the time of his death, half expecting an answer of sixty-five, but instead she said fifty-six. She caught the significance of the age and asked if this might have related to her own heart attack when she was fifty-six. She reflected that she always thought of herself as a rational person, but as she talked to me she felt ashamed of getting all involved with numbers and ages. "It sounds like astrology." She recalled how anxious she had been when her husband retired from his law practice at sixty-five; she was concerned about his inactivity and boredom. She humorously recounted her advice to his colleagues: "I told them, don't get him a gold watch. He doesn't need to watch time go by. It only points to the end." At the conclusion of the interview, she thanked me for seeing her, felt she really did not need to see a psychiatrist, and half jokingly said, "Doctor, time takes care of everything."

In this case the anniversary phenomenon was present in two forms. The association with Thanksgiving and the trauma of her father's death persisted for many years. The nonannual anniversary phenomenon of chronological identification with her father and her present anxiety regarding such a thanatological identification with her brother and mother seemed clear and could explain her anxiety about dying. Even though this patient was not seen again, these possibilities, though speculative, seem more than chance coincidence. Her internist later told me that he had not seen her since early November as she and her husband had left for an extended vacation and did not expect to return "until after Thanksgiving."

IV

In late January of 1962, a twenty-five-year-old married woman consulted me because of severe depression. She had lost a great deal of weight, slept poorly, had lost her appetite, and felt tearful without cause. Also, she had very recently had a nightmare which seriously upset her. In this dream she saw "a large St. Bernard dog who suddenly become grotesque, very silent, and when he lay down worms began to crawl out of his body." She awoke and was terrified, especially when she had difficulty in breathing; she feared she was going to die—an anxiety she had often had in the past.

As she told me of her family, she said that her father had died but she could not remember when. She thought she was about fourteen at the time but could not be certain. Her father had gone to a distant hospital for some treatment and suddenly she was told he was dead. She recalled his funeral at which she did not cry, although she was very upset "inside." She had always been close to her father. After his funeral she recalled that her mother cried constantly, but only at night. "During the day it was a pall." She never cried about him and even though she knew he was dead she did not believe it. When her mother remarried several years later she suddenly found herself crying uncontrollably and for no apparent reason. As she talked of her mother's remarriage, she began to sob convulsively. She recalled how she felt her father had moved in the coffin; she was certain he was alive. Even when they lowered his coffin into the ground, she could not believe he was dead—"at least not for me." She had not thought of her father for many years, and now this dream. When asked about the dream, she associated the warm, large, friendly St. Bernard with her father. "He was dead, yet alive—worms coming out of the body."

At the next consultation, the patient began talking about her father. He looked like a St. Bernard; she had not thought of him or his death until a few weeks before when her brother's wife had a baby boy, who was named after her father. This was the upset, she exclaimed; this was the start of her current depression. She began to pray at night to "whoever is taking care of father." She recalled how nice it was to have dinner with him, how excited she was when she heard his key in the lock when he came home at night. She mentioned that in the last week she became anxious about her husband's possible death—even though there was no reason for her concern. She recalled that when she was told of her father's death, she became nauseated, could not eat or sleep, and felt alone. She once again described the funeral and burial, mentioning that she had never visited his grave or lighted a memorial candle for him on the anniversary of his death. "I don't want him to be dead—I can't do all that goes with that. But the baby is named after him—he must be dead." As we talked she recalled that he died on a Wednesday, February 14th. Suddenly she realized that his death date was approaching—perhaps this, plus the new baby's name, had set off something inside of her. She went on to say that she was speaking of things that should have been said before—things she should have thought about but never did.

I referred this young woman to a colleague for psychoanalysis. She began her analysis on February 12, 1962; it was terminated in November 1964. The analysis revealed an elaborate fantasy life centering around play with her father; he bathed her until she was eleven years old, at which time she was uncomfortable enough to tell him to stop. The mother was more noticed for her absence than otherwise. In her thirteenth year the patient condensed three events as beginning simultaneously: menstruation, masturbation, and her father's illness. Her father died when she was fourteen and a half. Although she had little or no emotion about his death, she developed a complicated evening and night ritual in which she recalled sounds and sensations associated with him. In analysis she understood her reactions as part of a delayed mourning reaction to the loss of her father. The patient's time amnesias and distortions were clarified and there was recovery of the time sequence of events as they occurred in reality.

Following the successful termination of her analysis the patient managed well. Early in March 1969, she called me for consultation, and at this meeting she brought me up to date regarding her progress. She then told me that she had become very upset in mid-February when her sister developed acute rheumatoid arthritis requiring hospitalization and her brother developed severe migraine headaches. I asked about February, noticing that my first contact with her had been in late January seven years before. She then informed me that her father had died on February 25th; she had finally checked with her mother and this was the correct date. For years she was confused about the date but "this was it." She realized that every February she wants to see a psychiatrist; she thought of calling me at that time. I asked why she did not call her previous analyst. She replied that she had referred someone to him for treatment and did not wish to have contact with him. As she talked it became apparent that she wanted a psychiatrist "alive" and not "terminated," as she apparently felt about me. She is still fuzzy about time and seems to be unable to pinpoint events around her father's death and the circumstances surrounding it. This was confirmed when I asked her factual questions about this period of her life.

V

A patient who had completed his analysis several years ago, returned for consultation after some marital difficulty. His previous relationship with his wife had been "very good" and he was "at a loss" to understand the present problem. He said that his birthday was approaching and, unlike previous years, his wife was quite sensitive about it: she wished to avoid a birthday party although the family had always celebrated birthdays in the past. She asked him to wear a hair piece and lose some weight in order to "look younger." Bewildered by his wife's unusual behavior, and wondering if he might be contributing to it, he requested an appointment.

During the consultation, he mentioned that he had recently completed his estate plan and that while discussing his will and insurance program with his wife, she had burst into tears and run from the room; she did not wish to know of the arrangements. As she had always been a part of all financial activities, this was surprising. I asked how old he would be on his forthcoming birthday. "I'll be forty-nine. That's not old. I feel like a million. I can't understand Sally—it's so unlike her." I then inquired if the age forty-nine might be significant for his wife. He responded, "Of course, when Sally was twelve her mother suddenly died. It was quite a blow—she was on her own and she was bewildered. The older brothers and sisters were already gone . . . and her mother was forty-nine when she died."

VI

A married woman of thirty-two consulted me because of anxiety about being "abandoned, trapped, unable to get away." While this concern had been with her in manageable form for several years, she had just become pregnant for the first time and the prospect of motherhood, though consciously desired and planned for, upset her very much. Just before she had called for an appointment, she and her husband had been to see *Hamlet*. She had been very uneasy during the play and when the ghost of Hamlet's father spoke, she had to leave the theater.

When asked about her own father, the patient began to cry. He had died when she was fifteen of a heart attack; his "first coronary" occurred when she was eleven. I asked about the date of her father's death. "May 17th—I can't stand May—in May 1967 I had to see a psychiatrist. I had turned thirty and felt I was going to be alone—no husband. It helped." She and her present husband had been married for a year. In 1964 she had been engaged and was to marry in the fall. However, her fiancé developed leukemia in the summer and died suddenly. She was very upset, did not have dates for a long time, and became concerned about her own health, especially her "heart." "I feared that what happened to my father would happen to me." She did not openly mourn her fiancé, as she had not visibly mourned her father. Her mother, who did not remarry, always remembered the date of the father's death; the patient, an only child, attempted to forget. She recalled that she touched her father as he lay in his casket; "He was cold and hard. I was so shocked—I did not cry. I don't remember the cemetery—the grave—I want to forget." As we continued with the interview, the patient quietly said: "We are close to May—I am pregnant—What will happen to me?"

In this patient the anxiety was about the forthcoming anniversary date, although it is obvious that the concern had little to do with May 1969, but with what had occurred previously.

ANNIVERSARY REACTIONS AND TRAUMA

The model of symptom-formation also applies to anniversary reactions. The "anniversary" is significant as a releaser. The reaction, response, or symptom may be transitory, and adaptation and reestablishment of equilibrium may occur. However, if the regression continues to earlier fixation points (regression proper), we may find more serious pathology. The onset situation relates to the anniversary trigger. But a predisposing set must exist for this activator to have an effect. The vulnerability, sensitivity, and predisposition are in existence before the actual reaction occurs. Ritual, public ceremony, religious observances may be attempts to handle alloplastically internal reactions and readaptations, usually with only partial success.

In considering the fixations that predispose to anniversary exacerbations we must consider the role of trauma. Not all external events or injuries need be traumatic, and not all traumata need be pathogenic. It is necessary in any consideration of anniversary reactions to examine the past life of the individual, paying particular attention to previous events and conflicts involving significant figures. Knowledge of the preinjury state, the nature of the injury, the internal and external handling of the injurious situation, and the subsequent outcome are all important factors in assessing the nature of the injurious event—when and if it resulted in trauma, how the trauma was handled, and if it resulted in subsequent pathology or in pathogenic vulnerability.

In his lecture "Fixation to Traumas" (1917b), Freud said:

[T]he term "traumatic" has no other sense than an economic one. We apply it to an experience which within a short period of time presents the mind with an increase of stimulus too powerful to be dealt with or worked off in the normal way, and this must result in permanent disturbances of the manner in which the energy operated [p. 275].

He continued:

[N]ot every fixation leads to a neurosis, coincides with a neurosis or arises owing to a neurosis. A perfect model of an affective fixation to something that is past is provided by mourning, which actually involves the most complete alienation from the present and the future [p. 276].

If we postulate that an anniversary reaction in a manifestation of a previous traumatic fixation that may or may not be neurotic, we should investigate such considerations as cumulative trauma, retrospective trauma, anterospective trauma, traumatic neurosis, repetition compulsion, and psychic injury, and their relation to anniversary reactions. In addition, related issues of perception, notation registration, memory, reemergence, and time awareness become pertinent. Mechanisms of denial, disavowal, isolation, defensive hypercathexis and splitting, as well as repression and identification, must also be included in any theoretical discussion of the phenomena.

In "Inhibitions, Symptoms and Anxiety" (1926 [1925]), Freud distinguished between situations of danger and traumatic situations. These have corresponding types of anxiety: automatic anxiety and anxiety as a signal of the approach of trauma. There are different specific dangers that are liable to precipitate a traumatic situation at different times of life. Thus birth, loss of mother as an object, castration concern, loss of the object's love, loss of the superego's acceptance can all precipitate anxiety at phase specific times. Khan (1963) points out that the infant needs and uses the mother as a protective shield against trauma. The temporary failures of this maternal shield need not interfere with evolving maturational processes. Where these failures are significantly frequent and lead "to impingement on the infant's psyche-soma, impingements which he has no means of eliminating, they set up a nucleus of pathogenic reaction." This cumulative trauma concept has a complementary relationship to the concept of fixation points. Khan notes

> that though the ego can survive and overcome such strains, exploit them to good purpose, manage to mute the cumulative trauma into abeyance, and arrive at a fairly healthy and effective normal functioning, it nevertheless can in later life break down as a result of acute stress and crisis. When it does . . . we cannot diagnostically evaluate the genetics and economics of the total processes involved if we do not have a concept like cumulative trauma to guide our attention and expectancy [p. 300].

Anniversary reactions can be viewed as manifestations of accumulated trauma following injury that have strained and deformed the ego and rendered it vulnerable to later decompensation. However, when cumulative traumata exist, they may give rise to permanent distortions and subsequent rigid psychic structures. These are to be differentiated from the more circumscribed anniversary reactions which may be reverberations of a more specific event. The anniversary event is only the trigger; the repressed accumulated conflict is the motive power which utilizes or seeks out the "anniversary trigger." Thus the underlying repressed conflict can choose whatever trigger is available to it when it seeks discharge. The trigger that may be most utilizable may be the one most closely corresponding to the earlier injurious-traumatic situation. But this need not always be the case. Khan notes that cumulative trauma operates and builds up silently throughout childhood. Here we see a parallel to the apparent sudden emergence of anniversary reactions which seemingly were silent, only awaiting or seeking a cue to come on stage.

Kris (1956a) distinguished between the effects of two types of traumatic situations. The first, or shock trauma, refers to the effects of a single experience, very powerful in reality and suddenly impinging upon the child's life. The second, or strain trauma, refers to "the effect of long-lasting situations, which may cause traumatic effects by the accumulation of frustrating tensions" (p. 73). Kris indicates that "the further course of life seems to determine which experience may gain significance as a traumatic one" (p. 73). Anniversary reactions may be only retrospectively understood, and then not only as either a shock or a strain trauma but perhaps a combination of both, the strain trauma existing silently but emerging in response to the shock trigger of a single experience.

Furst (1967) points out that the degree of success that has been achieved by the ego in coping with past traumatic experiences will influence its vulnerability to later traumatization. He states: "Traumas that have not been mastered lead to massive repression; this in turn predisposes to further trauma. This is particularly true of those instances in which the later stimulus is associated with the previous traumatic experience" (p. 39). He notes that some investigators suggest that adequately mastered and assimilated traumatic experiences can serve as immunization against later trauma. He believes that the greater evidence is for the predisposing rather than the protective effects of traumatic events, but that it is difficult to say "which traumas will sensitize and which traumas will immunize, and also to what extent and in which respects they may do either" (p. 39).

Sandler's (1967) concept of retrospective trauma is also

relevant to anniversary phenomena. Retrospective trauma refers to the perception of some particular situation that evokes
the memory of an earlier experience which under present conditions becomes traumatic. Sandler differentiates retrospective
trauma from traumatic recall, wherein the trauma is not reexperienced. He believes that in the vast majority of childhood
parental deaths, a trauma in the strict sense does not occur. A
series of responses of the ego occurs with an increase in ego
strain, but not necessarily an overwhelming trauma. At a later
date the memory of the event may result in the child's being
overwhelmed with feelings with which he is unable to cope, and
a trauma could, but need not, result. While the recall of the
event many years later may become traumatic in the strict def-
initional sense, this traumatic recall, or remembrance of the
situation of injury, is not the same as reexperiencing the trauma.
Since the anniversary reaction may not be linked to what is
recalled, but reexperienced in one form or another, it is related
to the concept of retrospective trauma and the suggested differentiation of injury, trauma, and pathology.

In "Moses and Monotheism" (1939), Freud describes the
positive and negative effects of traumata. The positive effect
"attempts to bring the trauma into operation once again—that
is, to remember the forgotten experience or, better still, to make
it real, to experience a repetition of it anew, or, even if it was
only an early emotional relationship, to revive it in an analogous
relationship with someone else" (p. 75).

In this description we note an application to the understanding of public and private, religious and secular, anniversaries and commemorations. The admonition for forced
remembrance and for forced repetition may have a positive
effect, as Freud noted. However, this is totally dependent upon
the psychic structure of the involved personality. "The negative
reactions follow the opposite aim: that nothing of the forgotten
traumas shall be remembered and nothing repeated" (p. 76).
These are defensive reactions and "their principal expression
are what are called 'avoidances' " (p. 76).

We find here an understanding of the defensive nature of
the private nonconscious anniversary phenomena where there
is no recall, remembrance, and at times a disguised response
to the old trauma and injury. The contemporary reaction to

them is not conscious and, if severe, is usually relieved only through therapeutic intervention. In understanding the meaning of the anniversary phenomena, we cannot rely on the external event alone as we rarely can make an accurate assessment of what elements may be significant in the initiating reaction. Anna Freud (1967) has noted that "care has to be taken not to confuse the traumatic event with its potential result, i.e., the traumatic neurosis. . . . the traumatic event becomes pathogenic mainly through the triggering of an ordinary neurotic conflict or neurosis that has lain dormant" (p. 245).

To illustrate some of the above theoretical statements, I will briefly present a clinical situation where a trauma occurred before the patient was born—a sibling death. This tragedy evoked defensive reactions in the parents which gave rise to a second traumatic state that meaningfully affected the child's subsequent development. These two levels of trauma might be called "anterospective trauma." They are frequently observed in sibling replacement situations where the sibling died prior to the birth of the next child.

A young baby was left by the mother on the porch when she went into the house to fetch an item of clothing for the infant. In the brief interval when the mother was gone, the child reached over the railing, fell three floors onto the sidewalk, and was instantly killed. The mother was shocked, grief-stricken, and held herself responsible for the child's death. As part of her guilt-restitution reaction she promptly conceived and bore another child. This child was treated in an overcompensatory fashion as far as safety was concerned.

In the course of the analysis of this replacement child as an adult, it was discovered that the patient not only reacted to the overcompensatory safety measures of the mother but also had identified with the mother's guilt about the death of the first-born and became involved in the defensive measures that were used to alleviate these guilt reactions. The primary trauma for the parents occurred before the second child's birth, but the second child subsequently developed a defensive organization and personality structure which was related to this primary parental trauma and the reactions to it. For example, the patient had much guilt-expiation behavior: identification with the underdog, a need to give more than receive; anticipation that life would bring failure and disease, or death; and constant reiteration and distortion of external authority figures in the direction of anticipating criticism, punishment, rejection, and depression. At the same time, there was much hostility toward these authority figures because of the "unjustness of the situation." In the course of the transference neurosis, these defensive responses appeared with much feeling and particular elements were identified, reconstructed, reworked, and resolved.

Deutsch (1966) has discussed the adaptive function of post-traumatic amnesias. Her patient had an "anamnestic patch" that could clearly be demarcated in time—it extended from June to October of a certain year. Deutsch writes:

> It is doubtful whether the effect of trauma is forever removed with the recovery of an amnesia. Every traumatization creates—or increases—a disposition to repetition. Every traumatic reaction is a miniature of a traumatic neurosis; its traces can be more or less revived by a suitable provocation. A new traumatic experience, especially one identical with (or similar to) the previous one, can easily act as an *agent provocateur* for identical reasons.
>
> Whether there exists a real "completion" of an internal process, which once taxed the individual beyond his capacity, is questionable. I do not believe that any "catharsis" is able to achieve a full return to the *status quo ante* or that assimilation, adaptation, etc., can successfully end a traumatic process [p. 444].

Deutsch's statement directly bears on the traumatic aspect of the anniversary reactions seen in some of the patients mentioned above. The anniversary response is one of a repetition reaction to an old unresolved traumatic-injury situation where the current time or situation approximates significant events of the past traumatic situation. In my clinical experience resolution and undoing of such traumatic situations, manifested in anniversary reactions, can occur and successful outcomes can be obtained through psychoanalytic treatment (1964). This is particularly true where injury and trauma occurred without significant ego alteration. I believe Deutsch herself provides an explanation for the therapeutic success when she states:

> [G]enerally, traumatization means that every trauma—even when

it is managed well—leaves a residuum which constitutes a disposition. Later reactions will depend on the quantity and qualities of defenses, or the capacity for neutralization, etc., developed during the time elapsed between the traumas.

It may even happen that the consolidation of the inner world reaches a point at which a new traumatic event not only seems ineffective, but even proves fruitful and of positive value for further development [p. 449].

Amnesia as a defense against a definite trauma can be lifted, and repressed material dealt with in the psychoanalytic situation.

SUMMARY

In this paper the evolution of the concept of anniversary reactions has been reviewed, related to recent considerations of trauma, and specifically connected with unresolved mourning reactions resulting from significant losses. Clinical variations of these anniversary reactions are used to illustrate aspects of the theoretical propositions presented.

9
ON TIME AND ANNIVERSARIES

EARLY PSYCHOANALYTIC OBSERVATIONS OF ANNIVERSARY PHENOMENA

Anniversary phenomena can be traced historically to the very beginnings of psychoanalysis. In the midst of the clinical description of Fräulein Elisabeth von R., in the *Studies on Hysteria* (Breuer and Freud, 1893–1895), Freud characteristically presents us with insights that go beyond that of the topic he is discussing. He mentions ". . . traumas accumulated during sicknursing being dealt with subsequently, where we get no general impression of illness but where the mechanism of hysteria is nevertheless retained" (p. 162). Freud digresses briefly with a clinical account of "a highly-gifted lady who suffers from slight nervous states and whose whole character bears evidence of hysteria, though she has never had to seek medical help or been unable to carry on her duties" (p. 162). He emphasizes that the "woman is not ill; her postponed abreaction, was not a hysterical process, however much it resembled one" (p. 164).

Reprinted from *The Unconscious Today: Essays in Honor of Max Schur*, edited by Mark Kanzer, M.D. New York: International Universities Press, pp. 233–257, 1971.

Acknowledgment is made to Sigmund Freud Copyrights Ltd., The Institute of Psycho-Analysis, and The Hogarth Press for permission to quote from *The Standard Edition of the Complete Psychological Works of Sigmund Freud*, translated and edited by James Strachey.

Material from the *New Introductory Lectures on Psycho-Analysis* by Sigmund Freud is included with the permission of W. W. Norton & Company, Inc., and Unwin Hyman Ltd.

Acknowledgment is made to Unwin Hyman Ltd. for permission to quote from *The Interpretation of Dreams* by Sigmund Freud.

Material from F. S. Cohn (1957) is included with the permission of *The Psychoanalytic Quarterly*.

Material from M. Bonaparte (1940), reprinted with permission. Copyright © Institute of Psycho-Analysis.

From what clinical observations do these conclusions stem? Freud tells us that

> [this woman] has already nursed to the end three or four of those whom she loved. Each time she reached a state of complete exhaustion; but she did not fall ill after these tragic efforts. Shortly after her patient's death, however, there would begin in her a work of reproduction which once more brought up before her eyes the scenes of the illness and death. Every day she would go through each impression once more, would weep over it and console herself—at her leisure, one might say. This process of dealing with her impressions was dovetailed into her everyday tasks without the two activities interfering with each other. The whole thing would pass through her mind in chronological sequence. I cannot say whether the work of recollection corresponded day by day with the past. I suspect that this depended on the amount of leisure which her current household duties allowed [p. 162].

Here, the editors of the *Standard Edition* note that in this 1895 "account of the 'work of recollection' Freud seems to be anticipating the 'work of mourning' which he described much later in *Mourning and Melancholia*" (1917c).

Freud continues with his clinical account:

> [I]n addition to these outbursts of weeping with which she made up arrears and which followed close upon the fatal termination of the illness, this lady celebrated annual festivals of remembrance at the period of her various catastrophes, and on these occasions her vivid visual reproductions and expressions of feeling kept to the date precisely. For instance, on one occasion I found her in tears and asked her sympathetically what had happened that day. She brushed aside my question half-angrily: "Oh no," she said, "it is only that the specialist was here again today and gave us to understand that there was no hope. I had no time to cry about it then." She was referring to the last illness of her husband, who had died three years earlier [pp. 162–163].

Freud goes on:

> I should be very much interested to know whether the scenes which she celebrated at these annual festivals of remembrance

were always the same ones or whether different details presented themselves for abreaction each time as I suspect in view of my theory. But I cannot discover with certainty. The lady, who had no less strength of character than intelligence, was ashamed of the violent effect produced in her by these reminiscences [pp. 163–164].

In a footnote to the above clinical vignette, Freud describes the case of Fräulein Mathilde H. The anniversary of her engagement, whose dissolution precipitated her depression, proved crucial in her successful hypnotherapy and symptom removal. It is in this brief account of Fräulein Mathilde H.'s treatment that Freud uses the term *anniversary*.

Before discussing the further implications of Freud's ideas as noted here, particularly as they related to reminiscing and working through, mourning, trauma, and anniversary-holiday reactions, I wish to call attention to one aspect of Breuer's account of the treatment of Anna O., the first case in the *Studies on Hysteria*.

In this clinical report, Breuer notes that Anna O. (Bertha Pappenheim) became ill in the middle of July 1880, when her father fell ill of peripleuritic abscess.

In describing the alternation of Bertha Pappenheim's mental states, he says:

[I]n the first she lived, like the rest of us in the winter of 1881–2, whereas in the second she lived in the winter of 1880–1, and had completely forgotten all the subsequent events. The one thing that nevertheless seemed to remain conscious most of the time was the fact that her father had died. She was carried back to the previous year with such intensity that in the new house she hallucinated her old room, so that when she wanted to go to the door she knocked up against the stove which stood in the same relation to the window as the door did in the old room. The change-over from one state to another occurred spontaneously but could also be very easily brought about by any sense-impression which vividly recalled the previous year. One had only to hold up an orange before her eyes (oranges were what she had chiefly lived on during the first part of her illness) in order to carry her over from the year 1882 to the year 1881. But this transfer into the past did not take place in a general or indefinite manner; she lived through the previous winter day by day. I should only have been able to suspect that this was happening, had it not been that every evening during the hypnosis she talked through whatever it was that had excited her on the same day in 1881, and had it not been that a private diary kept by her mother in 1881 confirmed beyond a doubt the occurrence of the underlying events. This re-living of the previous year continued till the illness came to its final close in June 1882 [p. 33].

The account of Bertha Pappenheim's illness as it related to Breuer's psychic life has been discussed elsewhere (see chapters 17, 18, and 19). The present focus is on the anniversary aspects of the course of Bertha Pappenheim's treatment. Breuer proceeds to describe how these "revived psychical stimuli" of 1880–1881 made their appearance in the more normal year of 1881–1882.

[O]ne morning the patient said to me laughingly that she had no idea what was the matter but she was angry with me. Thanks to the diary I knew what was happening, and sure enough, this was gone through again in the evening hypnosis: I had annoyed the patient very much on the same evening in 1881. On another time she told me there was something the matter with her eyes; she was seeing colours wrong. She knew she was wearing a brown dress but she saw it as a blue one. We soon found that she could distinguish all the colours of the visual test-sheets correctly and clearly, and that the disturbance only related to the dress-material. The reason was that during the same period in 1881 she had been very busy with a dressing-gown for her father, which was made with the same material as her present dress, but was blue instead of brown. Incidentally, it was often to be seen that these emergent memories showed their effect in advance; the disturbance of her normal state would occur earlier on, and the memory would only gradually be awakened in her *condition seconde* [pp. 33–34].

Breuer notes that with the "verbal utterances" of the psychical events, the symptoms disappeared. Bertha herself described the therapeutic procedure as a "talking cure," or in a more joking fashion as "chimney sweeping." This discharge through verbalization of what was recalled corresponds to the importance of verbal discharge in the normal mourning process.

The questions posed by these anniversary phenomena are many, and only in recent years have we begun to consider them.

DEVELOPMENTAL ASPECTS OF TIME

In his paper "On Narcissism" (1914), Freud states that the time factor has no application to unconscious processes. He elaborates on this in 1915 when he writes, "the processes of the system *Ucs.* are *timeless*, i.e., they are not ordered temporally, are not altered by the passage of time; they have no reference to time at all. Reference to time is bound up . . . with the work of the system *Cs.*" (p. 187). In *Beyond the Pleasure Principle* (1920), he repeats this topographic conceptualization, adding, "our abstract idea of time seems to be wholly derived from the method of working in the system Pcpt.-Cs. and to correspond to a perception on its own part of that method of working" (p.28). This latter idea is reiterated in the paper on the "Mystic-Writing Pad" (1925a). In the *New Introductory Lectures* (1933 [1932]), Freud related his ideas about time to his later structural hypothesis.

> [T]here is nothing in the id that corresponds to the idea of time; there is no recognition of the passage of time, and . . . no alteration in its mental processes is produced by the passage of time. Wishful impulses which have never passed beyond the id, but impressions, too, which have been sunk into the id by repression, are virtually immortal; after the passage of decades they behave as though they had just occurred. They can only be recognized as belonging to the past, can only lose their importance and be deprived of their cathexis of energy, when they have been made conscious by the work of analysis, and it is on this that the therapeutic effect of analytic treatment rests to no small extent [p. 74].

What Freud means here is that the id, operating according to the primary process, seeks immediate present discharge and the accompanying pleasure through release—thus timelessness reigns. Freud continues: "the relation to time, which is so hard to describe, is . . . introduced into the ego by the perceptual system; it can scarcely be doubted that the mode of operation of that system is what provides the origin of the idea of time"

(p. 76). In other words, the ego with its functions of memory and reality orientation operates according to the reality principle, and the secondary processes (e.g., delay, detour) regulate discharge in accordance with adaptive needs.

Brown (1959), addressing himself to the psychoanalytical meaning of history, suggests that repression and the repetition compulsion generate historical time. He writes, "[R]epression transforms the timeless instinctual compulsion to repeat into the forward-moving dialectic of neurosis which is history" (p. 93). Fixation to the past is crucial, and one might classify this as superego-time in comparison to id-time and ego-time. We must, however, distinguish the perception of time from the retention of the past through repression and fixation.

Anna Freud (1965) has written about the different evaluations of time at various age levels:

> The sense of the length or shortness of a given time period seems to depend on the measuring being carried out by way of either id or ego functioning. Id impulses are by definition intolerant of delay and waiting; the latter attitudes are introduced by the ego of which postponement of action (by interpolation of the thought processes) is as characteristic as urgency of fulfillment is of the id. How a child will experience a given time period will depend therefore not on actual duration, measured objectively by the adult, by the calendar and by the clock, but on the subjective inner relations of either id or ego dominance over his functioning. It is these latter factors which will decide whether the intervals set for feeding, the absence of the mother, the duration of nursery attendance, or hospitalization, etc. will seem to the child short or long, tolerable or intolerable, and as a result will prove harmless or harmful in their consequences [pp. 60–61].

It is in the progression "from primary to secondary functioning that we get anticipation of the future, between wish and action directed towards fulfillment" (p. 92).

Concepts of time do not develop suddenly into final form, but follow a developmental pattern of evolution. However, as is true with so many psychic evolutions, the old patterns are not totally abandoned. Under duress, regression can occur, and earlier conceptualization referable to time may reappear; for example, loss of ability to gauge duration, to detect succession and temporal association, or to note seriation. These internal psychic processes related to time, proceeding on a developmental time axis, serve to facilitate the outward adaptation to external reality. Unlike other psychological concepts which have a tangible and material basis, however, time is one of the most abstract of all concepts. In an attempt to link it with some thing, early in development the clock or another time-measuring device becomes the base for the thought. But the abstract concept of time, involving internal and external instants, intervals, sequences, requires more advanced thinking processes, described under the rubric of the secondary process.

Boring (1936) has described five bases for time perception: (1) the child gets some perception of succession, of how stimuli follow one another, through play (e.g., running his fingers over the teeth at different rates); (2) the child acquires some perception of continuity when he observes some action continuing until it stops (e.g., a moving wheel which slows and stops); (3) the child obtains an idea of temporal length from perceiving differences in particular sensory stimuli (e.g., hearing long or short musical sounds); (4) the child learns to perceive and respond to present visceral stimuli (e.g., hunger, pain, tension—these are aspects of the immediacy associated with primary-process discharge, and biological rhythm associated with id activities); and (5) the child acquires the ability to perceive patterns of successive stimuli, to feel and respond to physiological rhythms. This latter is a more advanced stage in the developmental line of time conception than that of the id—primary process—time conception.

Lovell (1966) has called attention to the words used in primitive societies to express time. He notes that the terms used frequently reflect the main events of the day or the season (e.g., *watering time, milking time, planting time, harvesting time*). These descriptive periods deal with biological activities necessary for life adaptation. Lovell observes that time for the young child is also linked with a series of events that are task- or tension-relieving activities and biologically related.

As development proceeds, the adult concept of time gains ascendancy, and personal time becomes more closely linked to objective time which relates to events in the external world (hours, dates, holidays, anniversaries), and less linked to biological rhythms and id time. There is a gradual ability to differentiate past, present, and future; there is the acquisition of a time vocabulary that has meaning; and there is a growth of understanding of clock and calendar.

Lovell (1966) has observed that up to about age five, the child may fuse time and space, with a linkage to certain concrete objects and events. Onward from that age, the ordering of events into earlier or later begins to emerge, and the past gets structured into a succession of events. The learning and usage of time words precedes the child's grasp of differentiated time relationships. Ames (1946) found that the understanding of time words and their use came in a fairly uniform sequence which was generally the same for all children, although the age at which a particular child could understand or use a specific term varied. Children in the United States were able to use the terms morning and afternoon by four years of age, knew what day it was by about five years of age, and could tell time by seven years of age. The child could use terms like *wintertime* or *lunchtime* before the word *time* itself. Lovell suggests that a vocabulary of time words is built up by association. For example, when it is light, it is day; when it is snowing, it is winter. These linkages of words with time or season are also related to drive satisfactions and to need-fulfilling objects. Thus, breakfast and morning, sleep and night may become linked. Gradually the more global morning or night becomes differentiated and associated with certain measured time, first linked to whole hours, but later divided into half and quarter hours, and finally into minutes and seconds (Springer, 1952). What was directly associated with need tension and its satisfaction becomes a relatively conflict-free development of the autonomous ego. Time becomes a cognitive acquisition which takes on its own meaning and adaptive function.

Bradley (1948) has observed that in children below the age of nine time perspective for the past is very shallow, becoming nebulous beyond the span of a generation or so. By six years of age, however, time can be related to personal experience (e.g., morning, child's own age). By eight years there is increasing understanding of the week and of the calendar. Development progresses with increasing comprehension of the week, month, and year, until finally there is a gradual extension of the understanding of time in relation to both space and duration; for example, time elsewhere, and time between holidays. As children get older they can increasingly differentiate between objective and subjective time, and, as Lovell (1966) has demonstrated, the concept of time in its more adult form is available to the majority of children by nine years of age. It is at this age that there may be sufficient integration and consolidation of internal psychic structures to allow for conflict-free, autonomous ego activity to deal with objective time per se.

Time is one of the most complex perceptual abstractions derived from sensory data. Stimuli are ordered into the temporal properties of succession and duration. These then become conceptualized and capable of being communicated. In order to facilitate adaptation the psychic apparatus must integrate sequence and order, interval and duration. This involves the perception of the current and present, the memory of the past and the historical, and the capacity for the consideration of the future.

> Only man has an elaborately organized and systematized world of time which can be perceived and communicated directly. This taming of the merciless savage, *time*, into a refined and useful social being has enabled the human partially to liberate himself from the bondage of mortality. Language and reason, history and education, theology and philosophy, science and technology, and the arts are the spoils of man's limited but profound victories over *time* [Goldstone and Goldfarb, 1966, p. 449].

The human infant is not born with a developed sense of time and history. At birth, the human organism is little more than a physiological clock involved with the regulation of basic biological rhythms. This corresponds to id-time, which has no awareness of past or future, but is involved only in present attempts to seek discharge and tension reduction. Sleep and feed-excretory schedules appear as the initial biological temporal events which take on later social significance. The parents, especially the mother, become attuned to the infant's physiological clock, and in this way there is gradual regulation which allows for delay, postponement, and socially accepted gratification. These experiences are the beginning of ego time. The young child, through this mechanism, gradually shifts from pleasure-pain functioning to reality-principle, secondary-principle operations. Regression to the earlier primary process is always present in the most mature. When the before, now, and later can be conceptualized, we have evidence for the completion of the line of development of the time sequence. The clock, calendar, and other objective measures of time allow the adaptation to progress to the point where internal perceptions link with the outside in such manner as to permit social adaptation.

Goldstone and Goldfarb (1966) have reviewed the literature referring to children's conceptions of time from four separate points of view. First, the maturation and development of the capacity to perform temporal conceptual operations. Second, the maturation and development of the use and comprehension of temporal language. This involves the various developmental stages of the child's integration of the expression and understanding of time concepts, temporal relationships, and temporal language. The integration of succession and duration with language describing these concepts is a necessary precursor to conceptualizing historical information. Children's time concepts proceed from the specific to the general, from the concrete to the abstract, with a gradual reduction in the frequency of inaccurate tenses and inappropriate temporal expressions. This development corresponds to the gradual appearance of secondary autonomy of ego functions and the decrease in drive tensions that allows for the more abstract thinking and conceptualization. Ames (1946) has observed that words indicating the present appear first, followed by representation of the future, and finally by those indicating the past. Ames presents a detailed developmental schedule of the unfolding of this sequence of acquisition, noting the gradualness of the process, the close connection between personal activities and concrete experiences and marks of time, and the importance of understanding chronology and historical epochs which go beyond the ordinary usage of time language.

Third, the relationship between temporal conceptualization and intelligence, especially as observed in mentally retarded youngsters. The retarded child has little conception of sequence, relativity, or historical time, and cannot comprehend the world beyond his own activities.

Fourth, the relationship between temporal conceptualization and personality. Few researches have been undertaken to study this correlation. It is in this area that the child psychoanalyst can contribute empirical and clinical data which can form the basis of more systematic studies. We assume that pathogenic processes interfering with emotional development, internalization, and normal structure formation will affect temporal conceptualization. Thus, ego distortions or defects should show pathological manifestations of the temporal conceptual system. In adults with various types of psychopathology, such time distortions and disorientations occur.

Bromberg (1938) has found that the development of a time sense in children does not occur until after the age of five or six. It develops slowly until about age ten or twelve and parallels the development of abstract thinking. Children, he observes, have a better idea of age than of years. Schecter and his collaborators (1955), studying children of three to six years of age, found that in the younger age groups there is a greater emphasis on time related to immediate personal experience, at first physiological, and later on, interpersonal and play activities. With increasing age, especially in six-year-olds, external factors become more important; that is, there is an increase in abstraction with respect to the concepts of clock, days of the week, months, and years. This development regarding time sense parallels the development of the self and the ego; that is, from the autistic, pleasure domination of the infant with obscure boundaries of self and external world, to the more interpersonal, consensually validatable social world of the older child, where frustration of needs, development of routine and purpose is seen. In other words, as reality-oriented ego becomes more firmly integrated, perceptual time and conceptual time can be conceived by the child.

Cohen (1967) has distinguished between perceived time and conceived time. He agrees with other writers in differentiating three levels of adaptation to time: (1) perception of the rhythms which are set to the periodicities of nature; (2) capacity to register duration and sequence; and (3) with the aid of memory, the ability to reconstitute the succession of changes that have been experienced, and by anticipation, the acquisition of a new perspective for future activities. Piaget (1955) also distinguishes between time perception and time conception in the child. For Piaget, time as a logical concept has two aspects: the order of the succession of events (before, after, at the same time), and the duration of intervals separating successive events which can be measured in chronometric units.

CLINICAL OBSERVATIONS OF TIME PATHOLOGY

Browne, in 1874, discussed time amnesias and distortions in various mental diseases of children and adults. He presented no theoretical explanations for his observations. When Breuer and Freud (1893–1895) made observations of anniversary responses, they, too, did not link these to a theory of time perception and conception.

Stekel wrote about time and neurosis in 1912.

> [T]he significance of time for the neurotics is most clearly seen in their unconscious calendar. Their dreams betray the fact that in their minds they are continually juggling with certain numbers, especially the years of the birth of certain persons, the years of their death, the days of certain traumata, etc. Gloom and depression on certain days prove on analysis to be the anniversaries of certain important occurrences [p. 97].

Ferenczi's (1919a, b) and Abraham's (1918) papers on the Sunday and vacation neuroses relate to this theme. Freud, in the paper "On Narcissism" (1914), suggests in a footnote that "the developing and strengthening of this observing agency might contain within it the subsequent genesis of (subjective) memory and the time-factor, the latter of which has no application to unconscious processes" (p. 96). Time references seen clinically by Stekel (1912) and others did not refer to time as such, but served as a symbolic condensation, displacement, or day residue for the emergence of unconscious conflictful impulses.

As early as 1900, in *The Interpretation of Dreams*, Freud noted that there is a lack of a sense of time in the dream. In 1913 he observed (1913c) that the time of day in dreams often represented the age of the dreamer at some particular period of his childhood. Although he did not elaborate on this statement, it can be inferred that Freud meant that time and age referred to a repressed conflict from childhood, but did not relate directly to specific time perception or conception. He again comments in the *New Introductory Lectures* (1933) on the dream work's changing of temporal relations into spatial ones and being represented by these; for example, smallness and spatial distance in dreams signifying remoteness in time. Gross (1949) studied the sense of time in dreams and concluded that time references in the manifest dream were correlated with a specific thought content which involved a specific task for the dream work and did not relate to objective time as such.

Yates (1935), extrapolating from clinical observations, was one of the first psychoanalysts to write that the earliest time sense is based on bodily needs, intake, and excretory tension reductions. Later comes the need to "perform on time" (excretion), and then periodic biologic events (e.g., menses). She suggests that most fundamental to a person's later appreciation of musical time and rhythm is the sense of time and rhythm originating in the "breast period," when the body supplied the rhythm. Furthermore, she describes how one may break all contact, including independence of time, in a state of acute anxiety, by regression to an early state where there is the loss of the sense of reality and the awareness of the passage of time.

Difficulties in time awareness and discrimination may be noted in narcissistic disorders. Time for these individuals is closer to the id time and that of biological rhythms. In the transference neuroses, time awareness and discrimination are intact, although in conversion hysteria the "suffering from reminiscences" is split off from consciousness, and in the obsessional-compulsive we find time symbolically becomes part of the symptom complex in the service of control, conformity, and isolation.

I have seen individuals who can always tell time quite accurately without seeing a watch, or who can awaken at a certain time without an alarm clock. In these people the ego is constantly vigilant and, in order to avoid anxiety, anticipates and controls time perception. They usually have some obsessive-compulsive character traits. In several instances, they were quite musical, played instruments, had good pitch, and a sense of time or rhythm.

Some "accurate time-tellers" have a very competent and

secure ego which delights in its control for reasons of narcissistic gratification rather than to avoid anxiety. Such people are often very good sleepers, able to fall asleep at will at a moment's notice, and awaken, relaxed and rested, after a short nap. The more anxious group of "accurate time-tellers" are usually poor sleepers.

Schilder (1936), Straus (1947), and Oberndorf (1941) discuss disorders of time in other psychopathological states. Schilder explains the depressive's complaint that time no longer moves, as a manifestation of the attempt at inhibition of aggressive-murderous impulses. Straus explains the "stood still in time" phenomena, so often described by his depressive patients, as an inability to experience the present as a completion of the past. Thus the stoppage of time, the dragging of time, the hesitation of time seem to be manifestations of hopelessness. The present does not go anywhere, the past seems "ages ago," and the future is not contemplated or is remote. Straus writes that "every experience receives its specific significance, its special value, from its temporal position. Even in its content each moment is determined by its place in our life history. We all know that we will have to die" (p. 256). In the depressive patient, however, overwhelmed by the impact of the guilt of the past, the past is revived with its punitive judgments, and then its retribution emerges. Here the past emerges, not as objective- or clock-time, but as "the time of personal history," which the patient seeks to avoid.

Dooley (1941) has observed in her clinical work that the conscious perception of time may serve as a defense against overwhelming anxiety; that is, those who fear the retreat into the unconscious as a threat to survival of the ego cling to the concept of time as a means of preventing such a retreat. Her three skillfully described adult cases of childhood parent loss offer a mirror image of what has been found in the anniversary reactions described elsewhere. Dooley's patients watch time as a defense against ego disintegration and the emergence of threatening id impulses. Instead of denying or disavowing time, as is sometimes seen, her patients hypercathect time and reality testing as a defense. These people fear anesthesia, because it represents a loss of control of time, and they expect death and disintegration. In many ways this hypercathexis of time perception is similar to the anniversary mourning rituals where there is a hypercathexis of time and of death. Rationalized to take into account the religious beliefs, essentially what is stated is: "Be aware of the time and the event, and then you shall be safe." In other words, focusing on the external defends against the internal dangers. Several statements made by Dooley's patients are worth quoting. The first patient's mother died in childbirth when he was ten. He watched time closely. He stated, "Things have to happen in time and I must be on hand to see what happens. . . . Death and birth can't happen in the same instant. If there is time then I am alive. If there was an interval without time I wouldn't be there! If time ceased, God knows what would happen, I'd be blotted out" (p. 16). The second patient's father died when he was six years old. He said, "I have some idea that I caused the death of my father . . . and I shall be killed. Someone kills you for revenge. . . . Keep your consciousness, know what you are doing" (p. 17). The third patient's mother committed suicide when the patient was seventeen years old. The patient developed hyperthyroidism at that time. She said, "I must never forget myself for a single minute. I watch the clock and keep busy, or else I won't know who I am" (p. 17). The danger here is from the failure of repression of the internal forces that threaten the individual, the attention to time being a secondary defensive operation.

I have seen a man in psychotherapy who kept a calendar on which he entered "death days" for the entire year. To him these were more important than birthdays. When asked whose "death days" appeared on his calendar, he listed relatives, friends, and significant (to him) cultural, historical, and political figures. As a child this man had witnessed the sudden and traumatic death of his adolescent brother which consciously affected his entire subsequent life. He observed that in his conversation he frequently used the term *deadline*, to refer to time limits. Unlike the obsessional patient who uses isolation and punctuality for control of internal instinctual conflict, this patient, similar to Dooley's cases, controlled internal tensions through the hypercathexis of "death times." He did have difficulty in going to sleep, which he equated with death.

A variant of these patients who hypercathect time is the patient who is always convinced that he will not have enough time. In one such instance the roots of this anticipation were traced to the patient's childhood, when his next younger sibling was born. He felt cheated, deprived, "hurt," and the anxiety over his murderous rage toward the sibling and the mother was displaced onto time. In analysis he paid particular attention to the length of each analytic session, and the termination phase was characterized by a stormy reworking of the theme: "I have not been here long enough," "You want to fill my place with someone else," and "I want to kill you and your next patient." The hypercathexis of time and duration was a defensive maneuver designed to ward off the more basic anxiety related to his rage and death wishes at the time of the sibling's birth, as well as his feeling of helplessness.

Dooley (1941) makes a distinction between those patients to whom the fear of losing track of time means fear of loss of the world of objects, loss of a portion of the mind, loss of the body, death, being thrown back into the past where one was defenseless against internal drives, and loss of identity, and classical obsessive patients who use time defensively as part of the mechanism of isolation. Orgel's (1965) patient had to control time literally as a means of controlling life and death. This patient showed impairment in object relationships, self-observation, memory, and perception, and had to remain permanently young in order to halt time. Past and future were isolated from the present, reality-principle functioning was impaired, and the strong compulsion to repeat rather than remember served to avoid the reality of death.

Scott (1948), Eissler (1952), DuBois (1954), Eisenbud (1956), Jaques (1965), and Deutsch (1966) have described clinical aspects of time feeling, time sense, and time duration impairments as they are related to distortions in ego development. Gifford (1960) has been particularly interested in "Sleep, Time and the Early Ego." He suggests that

> the adaption of the sleep rhythm to the 24-hour periodicity of everyday life represents the first primitive experience of time, as a restriction imposed by the outer world on immediate gratification. These experiences may be the precursors of later attitudes toward time, as a stern agent that curtails pleasure and demands compliance with adult responsibilities [p. 27].

The reality principle impinges on the pleasure-discharge needs of the young infant as an adaptation to the mother's periodic availability and the quality and quantity of her care and attention. The capacity to delay and postpone the immediate need for food in the expectation of future gratification is the first differentiation of past, present, and future, and may be the earliest manifestation of memory as it applies to regulation of personal time. Chambers (1961) has approached the area of early ego-time perceptions through her study of maternal deprivation and its effect on time conceptualization in children. Her formulations, closely following Freud's theoretical ideas, also include some of Piaget's concepts. Chambers' experiments confirm her hypothesis that the group of maternally deprived children were less mature or advanced in the development of temporal concept than a parallel "normal" group.

None of these reports bears directly on anniversary phenomena as such, but do suggest that although objective time is used as a day residue for anniversary reactions, personal time linked to unconscious internal conflict is the pertinent consideration in the understanding of this exacerbation of old anxieties and defenses. The experience of time is very subjective and varied, with many different conscious meanings and attitudes attached to it. It is only through the intensive study of individual patients that we can appreciate its meaning structurally, dynamically, genetically, adaptively, and economically.

METAPSYCHOLOGICAL ASPECTS OF TIME AND ANNIVERSARIES

Philosophers and psychologists have discussed time from various points of view. Physical, objective, social, categorical, measured time is distinguished from personal, subjective, existential, experiential time (Meerloo, 1948; Eissler, 1952; Weisman, 1965). Perception of temporal duration, sequence, and other such considerations varies from person to person, and from period to period, developmentally speaking, for the same individual. In connection with this last point, mention has been made of development of a sense of time from youngest infancy to later childhood and adolescence. Jaques (1965) has written about the midlife crisis and its relationship to death. He believes that the central and crucial feature of this crisis is the "psycho-logical scene of the reality and inevitability of one's own eventual personal death [and] one's own real and actual mortality" (p. 506). Here the reality principle operates to potentially create a situation of tension and anxiety. Jaques (1965) suggests that the unconscious wish for immortality may be manifested in various ways; for example, denial of mourning, ideas of im-mortality, notions of reincarnation. He further suggests that ideas of immortality, conscious and unconscious, are the coun-terparts "of the infantile fantasies of the indestructible and hence immortal aspect of the idealized and bountiful primal object" (p. 507), with the accompanying demands for absolute perfection in behavior, as well as the omnipotent and omniscient fantasies of the object and of the self. I would suggest that, viewed retrospectively, the anxiety may not be about death and nothingness, which cannot be conceptualized, but the fear of absolute helplessness that does characterize the very early state of existence. The omnipotence-omniscience of the child and his parent is a protective device against this very threatening state. The counterpart to this early omniparent is the omnipotent, omniscient God who will take care, control, protect, and insure perpetuity, instead of separation and helplessness which hold such terrors for the child. As an extension of this idea, I would further suggest that the "immortality" fantasy is a reversal of the separation-individuation, with the wish for a symbiotic re-union with the powerful mother who gave life, direction, pro-tection, and gratification. The midlife crisis can thus be viewed as a reactivation of unresolved conflicts from infancy, child-hood, and adolescence as they relate to survival, separation, and creativity. As the adult approaches midlife, his defensive coping devices may lose their effectiveness, especially when there is accompanying failure of bodily functions and abilities. If depression occurs, suicide as a magical reunion may be at-tempted.

In Dooley's (1941) cases, cited above, we see the counter-part to the denial mechanism, namely, the hypercathexis of reality, reality testing, and especially of time. Some individuals may show the "nemesis" notion of Chapman (1959). Stein (1953) has written about premonition as a defense. In his clear and concise clinical report of an anniversary reaction which appeared with an accompanying dream during psychoanalysis, he was able to link the premonition with the temporal coincidence of the anniversary and the ongoing transference relationship to the analyst. Premonitory experiences can be used defensively to deny intolerable, conflictful, guilt-laden wishes.

Meerloo (1950) has described the "preparation or anticipation neurosis" in which one finds the traumatic episode imagined and experienced before the traumatic event is provoked. An initial primary trauma may cause a "conditioning of our memorization" by setting up memory traces or internalizations which emerge in the anticipatory fantasy. "The anxiety involved in the new trauma uses the past as defense in order to avoid future traumatic experiences" (p. 662). New defense mechanisms may overemphasize the past, or the fear of dangerous future reality may be warded off by the fantasy that it has already happened. The future, though implying danger and anxiety, is an activation of older internal traumatic experiences.

Spiegel (1966) has recently approached this topic from another avenue. He emphasizes internal anticipation rather than anticipation of external events as a means of adaptation. In his conceptualization, "the superego, when 'finally' established, significantly assists, perhaps (partially) replaces the ego as the chief internal sensory organ of the mental apparatus. . . . this assistance results in a finer calibration of the function of anticipation than has existed before" (p. 315). Related to this idea is that of Bergler and Roheim (1946), who have suggested that the "part of the unconscious personality which watches over time perception is the unconscious part of the ego, under the influence of the superego" (p. 197). According to Spiegel (1966), the superego operates along two interwoven paths: the finely calibrated internal perception of id impulses; and as "a protection of the ego against the traumatic effect of large amounts of drive energy. In these ways, it functions analogously to the protective barrier against external stimuli" (p. 317) thus achieving equilibrium. He describes a "traumatic syndrome" for a class of patients reacting as if they are traumatized, but, unlike the true traumatic neuroses, there is no indication of a recent trauma. Trauma did, at one time, play a part in the genesis of the "traumatic syndrome." The ego of the "traumatic syndrome" reacts as if a recent trauma had occurred, with a resulting psychoeconomic imbalance, but no recent trauma occurred. Spiegel's formulation may be applicable to the understanding of the anniversary reaction. The anniversary reaction can be viewed as a variant of the "traumatic syndrome." The anxiety related to the anticipatory function of the superego has a quality of futurity attached to it. In pathological forms, there is an emphasis on future impending disaster. In the anniversary reactions there is the anticipation that "this will happen because it once happened, and I am helpless to do anything about it." The reality-principle awareness seems incapable of handling the situation because the process is internal and unconscious. The anniversary date or age correspondence may serve as a trigger for the emergence of the latent repressed unconscious, which is not time bound, but related to repressed instinctual conflict that seeks discharge and resolution.

Cohn (1957) has emphasized the ego as the crucial agency dealing with the time sense. Ego functions include time orientation, coherence, relatedness, and control. "The idea, or illusion of the past, of things gone by, is often unconsciously associated with death, and the ego's effort to materialize the present" (p. 173) includes a "purging" of the past. Time psychologically reflects the assurance of life or existence. By arresting time we avoid death. Again I would consider death in this context to mean total helplessness. The ego develops a capacity to realistically discriminate time (i.e., it has a historical sense). Cohn believes that the ego

> maintains the relation to qualities of ancestral origin apparently through superego reaction. It is incessantly occupied with the "traces of yesterday." Whenever a concept is formed and fleeting experiences are thus brought to a standstill, time is conquered and replaced by form. The time quality of passing and loss is thereby reduced to a latent state . . . [and time is] brought to a standstill, stretched to infinity (unaccountability), and the pleasant illusion of eternity created. When, however, time becomes God, the threat of mortality returns (God lives forever, but Christ is man dying forever), though God can be made to take care of life in the hereafter [pp. 178–179].

God here becomes the omnipotent parent who can protect the helpless child. Through religious ritual, man betrays his qualms of doubt in his never-ending labors of worship, by which he hopes to banish fatal time to the outermost regions. . . . He also undertakes to organize the world into an unchangeable timeless pattern, and by continuously remaining in touch with his ancestors he creates a strenuous lifetime schedule that becomes a timepiece in itself. He wants to gather past and future securely in his hand. Obviously he cannot take death and annihilation for granted, and thus he lives in constant argument with the dead of his ancestral world. His rule over the times is aimed at making him the eternal survivor, and indeed, out of his narcissistic creation and manifestation of vitality in ritual arises the sublime image of universal mankind. Though his ritual was only meant to mark a standstill of time, it implicitly guarantees an endless future and the conviction of power to survive and to hold the world together [p. 180].

In other words, the rituals tend to be of an unlimited energy and variability in order to avert finality, the symbol of death, or total helplessness.

Marie Bonaparte's paper on *Time and the Unconscious* (1940) is a classical psychoanalytic study of time. In addition to the many insights she offers us regarding this topic, her discussion of time distortions and time symptoms in obsessional neurotics, psychotics, and psychopaths is quite useful. Following Freud, she writes:

[T]he negation of one's own existence has no meaning for that reservoir of our primitive instincts, the unconscious. Life can only visualize itself in terms of living; in the unconscious of each individual it is depicted as outside time, which does not exist for the unconscious, and without limitations of any kind. It has required all the power of abstraction and generalization of which the conscious human mind is capable to evolve a conception so opposed to life as the idea that death awaits all living things and to enable man to recognize that one day he himself must die [p. 445].

Among the animals, man alone knows that he must die, and the idea of death seems peculiar to man. Furthermore, as Unamuno (1954) has said:

What distinguishes man from other animals is that in one form

> or another he guards his dead. . . . from what does he so futilely protect them? The wretched consciousness shrinks from its own annihilation [p. 41]. . . .
>
> The gorilla, the chimpanzee, the orang-outan and their kind, must look upon man as a feeble and infirm animal, whose strange custom it is to store up his dead [p. 20].

I might also add, to ritualize death in order to preserve immortality. This last institutionalization through religious belief, with its bipartite division of man into body and soul, with its emphases on perpetuity and eternity, defends against the anxiety of dying or being totally helpless. The narcissistic investment in survival in this world extends beyond religious belief and practice. It includes the narcissistic investment in one's children, one's work, one's ideas, forming a basis for understanding kinship patterns, significance of names and naming, and the wish for preservation through books, theories, monuments, or memorials of many varieties. The vision of Paradise or the Garden of Eden is a thing representation of the timeless primary narcissistic unconscious. Bonaparte's synthesis clearly expresses these ideas when she writes:

> A sense of reality and a sense of time appear simultaneously in the system of perceptual consciousness alone. Neither exists for the timeless unconscious, which remains independent of the secondary process dominated by the reality principle and continues wholly subject to the primary process regulated by the pleasure principle [p. 464].

The pleasure principle takes advantage of every favorable opportunity to forget time.

> It demands the highest effort of which human intelligence is capable to induce us to pay attention to time, just as reality. Thus time does not appear to form an integral part of our fundamental nature but seems to belong solely to our dawning perception of the reality of the world outside of us [p. 465].

Maria Bonaparte undoubtedly did not become interested in the problem of time by accident. Her mother died when Marie was one month old.

Marie, who was named for her dead mother, was repeatedly told how her birth had been paid for by her mother's life. Throughout her childhood, she imagined she had really seen her dead mother. At 17 years of age she gradually became convinced, that, like her mother, she had tuberculosis and that this fact was being kept a secret from her. Her mother had died at 22, and Marie expected that she, too, would die of tuberculosis at 22. Her symptoms began to mimic TB; she lost appetite and weight, and had frequent respiratory infections. At 20, the age at which her mother married, her illness became worse; she had a bloody mucus in the throat and began to waste away. Since her mother had died at 22, Marie felt she had to pass this age before she would know whether she could live. Her sickness had the important function of discouraging her from marrying. If she did not marry, she would not become pregnant and therefore would not suffer her mother's fate. When she was 22, her father pointed out to her that it was high time she found a husband and forget her imaginary illness. . . . From then on her symptoms began to wane [Bonaparte, 1928, cited in Hilgard and Fisk, 1960, pp. 55–56].

In her 1940 paper, Bonaparte shares with us further personal information, not about her anniversary symptoms, but of her growing awareness of time and its relationship to death.

I recall an impression from my childhood years. I was perhaps eight years old at the time and was thus still possessed by the more or less shadowy notions of time characteristic of childhood. I had been taken on a visit to the mother of my father's secretary, who had expressed a desire to see me. She had just completed her hundredth year. I see her to this day, covered with wrinkles, her skin shrivelled and her eyes without lustre, holding out to me her little emaciated hands and I seem still to experience the mingled feelings of terror and respect which she inspired in me then. My mother had died in the full bloom of her youth in giving birth to me: accident! evil design! But here I was confronted with the opposite extreme, a complete contrast in the procedure of dying. To be sure, a hundred years seemed to me an eternity, but I had after all been told that I should have to make haste to go and see the old lady as she was very soon going to die. At that moment I acquired a fully developed sense of death as a natural and inevitable consequence of old age and decay, of the dread inexorable law that we must die [p. 448].

Bergler and Roheim (1946) have noted that the passage of time emphasizes the period of separation, and that timelessness may have an underlying fantasy in which the mother and child are endlessly united. The calendar becomes the symbolic representation of separation anxiety and exposure to the return to a potential state of helplessness and aloneness. This may explain the preoccupation of some patients with anxiety about chronometric instruments.

Mintz (1971) differentiates two types of anniversary reactions, only one of which, he feels, reflects the presence of the ego's unconscious sense of time. There is conscious awareness of a date or event which produces a specific ego response "which is then associatively linked to specific earlier conflict, with its revival via symptoms, behavior, dreams, and so forth" (p. 731). The conscious time symbol reawakens the repressed, unresolved earlier conflict, and the resulting anniversary reaction is a "reproduction of an adaptation to that conflict on a specific date." In the second type of anniversary reaction, Mintz suggests, there is no specific current conscious stimulus to which the ego may respond. He believes the stimulus is unconscious, and there is an unconscious sense of time which is used to initiate the reproduction of the conflict. Because of the unconscious time sense and its linkage with death, defenses are weakened, and there is a compulsion to repeat in order to master the anxiety. The anniversary response may not require an ego sensing of time, but time, age, season, or holiday may serve as a trigger which permits repressed instinctual conflict to emerge from the unconscious into the preconscious, and then gives rise to the symptoms, reactions, behavior, or affect connected with the original conflict. Various defenses may be used to avoid this anniversary emergence (avoidance or hypercathexis of potential triggers). Once the emergence occurs, it may be dealt with in a variety of ways, depending upon the integrative ability of the ego to seal, deal, or work through the disturbing situation. If the emerging forces are too strong or the ego is too vulnerable, no sealing off can occur, and regression with symptom formation takes place. Cultural and religious practices have attempted to handle such crises through various rituals and practices. These alloplastic devices may be helpful to some in coping with the situation; however, the crucial determinant is the individual's internal psychic structure.

Fundamentally the anniversary response reflects the anxiety related to the sense of absolute helplessness which can result in a nothingness or destruction to the self. It is for this reason that anniversary reactions are so frequently connected with death and mourning. Mourning is an adaptation to loss which requires internal rearrangements so that the integrity of the ego and the self are maintained at a nonhelpless level and further progression can take place.

10
TEMPORAL ANNIVERSARY MANIFESTATIONS: HOUR, DAY, HOLIDAY

For the vulnerable individual a specific time of day, a specific day of the week, a specific season of the year, or a specific holiday can serve as a trigger or activator for the appearance of a symptom related to anniversary reactions. In chapters 8 and 9, I have suggested that anniversary reactions derive from pathological or uncompleted mourning. With the resolution of intrapsychic conflicts through analysis, these symptoms disappear leaving only a memory as a memorial.

SYMPTOMS RELATED TO A SPECIFIC HOUR

A young woman in her late twenties, whose father died suddenly when she was thirteen years of age, described a daily depression each evening at 5:30 when her husband returned to the house. As the patient heard the key turn the lock, the depressed feeling would be triggered. In analysis, the patient discovered the meaning of this circumscribed reaction. As a child, she was very close to her father—his presence excited her and she waited eagerly each evening for him to return home from work. There were mutually seductive elements in the situation. After the father's sudden death, the patient affectively denied his loss and did not mourn. In analysis, she recovered her fantasies after his death, including the "waiting at the door for his key in the lock." She was able to recall a repetitive dream she had following his death—"Father was on a cross like Christ." And she was able to recognize the wish in the dream—"I believed in the Resurrection. I would see father again." In her

---

Reprinted from *The Psychoanalytic Quarterly*, 40/1:123–131 (1971).

first year of analysis, she made a slip calling Memorial Day, Labor Day. Her analysis of this slip was: "Labor Day refers to delivery of a live baby—that's better than remembering the dead." That same year, she was acutely depressed on Father's Day.

In "From the History of an Infantile Neurosis," Freud mentions the five o'clock depression in his patient:

> From his tenth year onwards he was from time to time subject to moods of depression, which used to come on in the afternoon and reached their height at about five o'clock. This symptom still existed at the time of the analytic treatment. The recurring fits of depression took the place of the earlier attacks of fever or languor; five o'clock was either the time of the highest fever or of the observation of intercourse. . . . Probably for the very reason of this illness [malaria], he was in his parents' bedroom. . . . He had been sleeping in his cot, then, in his parents' bedroom, and woke up, perhaps because of his rising fever, in the afternoon, possibly at five o'clock, the hour which was later marked out by depression. . . . When he woke up, he witnessed a coitus *a tergo* [from behind], three times repeated; he was able to see his mother's genitals as well as his father's organ; and he understood the process as well as its significance [1918, p. 37].

The five o'clock depression in Freud's example might be seen as marking the daily anniversary of his loss of the oedipal mother.

SYMPTOMS RELATED TO A PARTICULAR DAY OF THE WEEK

A man in his mid-thirties revealed during the course of his analysis a depressed feeling with anxiety that appeared each Thursday afternoon. Initially he felt apprehensive but soon thereafter was overcome by grief. Analysis of this reaction revealed that his mother had died suddenly on a Thursday afternoon when he was fourteen. He had returned home from school and entered the living room where he saw her sitting on the sofa. As he approached, he saw her mouth and her eyes open, but could not elicit a response. He screamed. A neighbor hearing the noise appeared, called the doctor, the boy's father, and then attempted to comfort the boy. The entire sequence was dramatically reenacted in the analysis.

Ferenczi, in his paper on Sunday neuroses, described symptom oscillations that occur on a particular day of the week. These "nervous conditions had developed—mostly in youth—on a certain day of the week, and had then regularly recurred" (1919b, p. 174). In his cases, the periodic symptoms returned mostly on Sundays and consisted of headaches, depressions, gastrointestinal disturbances, and oversleeping. Ferenczi also noted that his patients had a tense boredom, that those affected with it were unable to dispel it by any means of diversion, and that it was accompanied at the same time with an incapacity for work painful to them. "Laziness with qualms of conscience. . . . A laziness which you can't enjoy"—these are the expressions with which one patient attempted to characterize this state.

Ferenczi relates these Sunday symptoms to vacation neuroses, and suggests that the Sunday symptoms appear because the patients cannot allow dangerous impulses to get out of control and so the hypersensitive conscience reacts. In addition to the danger of repressed impulses breaking through, Ferenczi also suggests that self-punishment fantasies are mobilized as a result of the activation by the holiday and thus no enjoyment can occur on the day of physical and psychical rest—the day on which "we are our own masters." Ferenczi states:

> We know . . . since Freud established it psycho-analytically, that psycho-neurotics—so many of whom . . . suffer from repressed memories—cheerfully celebrate the anniversary or the time of year of certain experiences significant for them by an exacerbation of their symptoms [1919b, p. 174].

This significant statement provides us with one explanation for anniversary reactions—the time, day, date, or significant event acts as a trigger which allows the repressed to "return" and with this "return" we have symptomatic behavior, expression, or exacerbation.

Abraham (1918) also writes about an increase or temporary exacerbation of "nervous conditions" in relation to Sundays, holidays, feast days, and vacations. He observed that work or studies could be used as a defense to reinforce repression of conflictful impulses. When work was interrupted by external influences, the mental balance was upset and symptoms appeared. When work began anew, the patient felt better and was free of symptoms. When such a person was forced into inactivity by illness or accident, the outbreak of a neurosis or the worsening of an existing one was a not infrequent consequence. Work allows for the discharge of accumulated excitation instead of being overwhelmed by it.

Ferenczi and Abraham describe two related but different mechanisms for the appearance of these symptoms which are not anniversary bound. Abraham emphasized the defensive use of work, while Ferenczi mentioned the relaxation of the repression barrier which coincides with the external relaxation induced by the holiday or rest day. Neither discussed the reaction resulting from an absence from analysis on these days. The emerging symptoms might result from this break in contact.

SYMPTOMS RELATED TO HOLIDAYS

A woman in psychotherapy related that she had an abortion when she was three months pregnant. At the time of the abortion, she fantasied her child to be a boy. Following the interruption of the pregnancy the patient developed a severe reactive depression, for which she sought therapy. After two years of treatment with apparent symptom remission, the patient developed an acute depression accompanied by dreams of "babies floating about." Through a series of associations, the patient realized that her most recent depression occurred on the "fantasied second birthday" of her aborted baby. In her past history, her younger brother died at the age of two, when the patient was five years old. The brother died on the Fourth of July, the "birthday" of her aborted child. Until this "second birthday" episode, the patient did not recall particularly depressing holidays, except as a child when her family went to the cemetery to visit the brother's grave.

Cattell (1955) described the holiday syndrome as the occurrence of symptoms during the period from Thanksgiving continuing through Christmas and lasting until after New Year's Day. The reactions were characterized by anxiety and regressive phenomena including marked feelings of helplessness, possessiveness, and increased irritability; nostalgia or bitter ruminations about holiday experiences in youth; depressive affect; and a wish for magical resolution of problems. Some of these regressive phenomena were acted out with members of the family, family substitutes, or a contemporary love object. Although the patients denied the meaningfulness of the holidays, the emotional components and unconsciously motivated behavior were apparent. The holiday period between Thanksgiving and New Year's Day is a time to be with one's family, a time for giving gifts, and a time of feasting. These are special occasions of emotional closeness and intimacy with family and friends, with additional emphasis on the presence of father, God, Christ, Santa Claus, and Father Time. Cattell finds the holiday syndrome in individuals having a history of family disruption due to separation or divorce of the parents, or death of one or both parents. The patients have feelings of being unloved, unwanted, or not belonging to a family group, and react to the holiday season with the appearance of symptoms.

Rosenbaum (1962) has also described such holiday symptoms, especially in relationship to Thanksgiving—a feast that permits a regression toward the oral level. This oral regression can be used defensively against predominantly oedipal conflicts. In addition to the oral regression, hostile family interactions, especially among siblings, may be seen with the "gathering of the clan." Genetic factors may play a role in the specificity of the response. Rosenbaum explains the symptoms in the following way:

> The reality trappings of the holiday . . . function as a stimulus in the same way in relationship to the patient's productions (symptomatic or associative) as a day residue does in dream formation. That is, the patient uses the current orally oriented reality as a cover for and an expression of exciting guilt- and fear-ridden Oedipal strivings [p. 96].

Jones (1951) notes that the greatest number of festivals were held at one or another of the four cardinal points in the earth's journey around the sun. Man has always associated his aspirations and emotions with these fundamental changes relating to the source of all life, the sun. He divides religious festivals into two broad groups, happy or cheerful ones, and unhappy or solemn ones. The former indicate moods of easy conscience, the latter of uneasy conscience. December 25th was celebrated by heathens as the birthday of the sun. It was the birthday of Persian, Phoenician, Egyptian, and Teutonic sun gods. December 25th was reckoned as the winter solstice and hence as the Nativity of the Sun, when the day begins to lengthen and the power of the sun to increase. The sun was a source of security, its heat and light were necessary for life to go on. Ferenczi has also described the psychic effect of the sun bath. "The sun was a father symbol" which his patient "gladly let shine upon him and warm him" (1950, p. 365). Independent strivings were believed to best occur when the sun was at its height and greatest strength. Failing strength, impotence, old age, and death were related to the diminishing strength of the sun. The rebirth of the sun was associated with rebirth, hope, and the Deity reborn. Thus a god was periodically (annually) reborn—a central theme of many religions. Christmas, the birth of Christ and a pagan festival in its origins, may be related to the birth of the sun. Christmas has been the focus of several psychoanalytic essays. Jekels has written about the psychology and origins of this holiday (1936).

Eisenbud (1941), writing on negative reactions to Christmas, associates it with the "greatest relaxation on the part of the superego of society." Sterba (1944) emphasizes Christmas as an acting-out of childbirth in the family. He notes that the legend of St. Nicholas is associated with childbirth. Boyer (1955) has observed that depressions occurring during the Christmas season are primarily the result of reawakened conflicts related to unresolved sibling rivalries—competition stimulated by the newborn Christ, the favorite of his mother. The associated gift giving and receiving are connected with conflicts over oral drives. However, he questions the existence of the entity of the "Christmas neurosis" and regards the depressive reactions as essentially the same that exist at other times of the year. Although acknowledging that "the constellation surrounding Christmas makes it a more important holiday and a more powerful trigger for reactions in the predisposed," he still feels that the crucial factor is the internal vulnerability based upon the past history of the individual and not the holiday itself.

Inman (1948a) has written about anniversary symptoms, exacerbated by various holidays. He described a patient who developed acute glaucoma on the anniversary of his son's birthday, while discussing his own death. Three years later, on the twelfth anniversary of his wife's death, this patient went with his son to visit her grave. From that day his health began to fail, and after a fortnight's illness (acute nephritis), he died on the day appointed for the remembrance of the dead, All Soul's Day. Inman (1948b) noted the association of onset of glaucoma, conjunctivitis, and iritis with Good Friday, "the day of days for the remembrance" of misdeeds. He connects the deaths of several of his patients on Good Friday with oedipal guilt, noting that "Good Friday is the day when the Son dies to propitiate the angry Father" (1948b, p. 258).

Inman (1950) also called attention to anniversary reactions of illness and death on the occasion of national holidays, particularly Guy Fawkes Day (November 5). In 1962, Inman (1962) presented clinical reports demonstrating the association in time of increased eye disorders with anniversaries of events related to sexuality, procreation, and birth. He once more comments on Easter as the holiday connected with the "terrible unconscious solution of the Œdipus complex" (1962, p. 307). In 1965, Inman presented additional clinical reports of ophthalmic disorders associated with Armistice Day, wedding anniversaries, and sibling pregnancies. In this report Inman mentions that his own mother died on his birthday, perhaps one explanation of his considerable interest in anniversary reactions.

Inman's 1967 paper dealt with the correlation of temporally significant events with later anniversary symptom appearance of malignancy and disseminated sclerosis. Inman's data are highly suggestive of the deterministic role of the death drive in these anniversary tragedies. He implies that Winston Churchill's death on the anniversary of the death of his father, who died seventy years earlier, may be related to this "wish to die."

We can observe an extension of holiday reactions from days of religious or national significance to days and dates of personal crises associated with specific rites of passage. Thus Jackel (1966) has described situations where, under the impact of impending temporary separations due to vacations or holidays, patients express a wish to have a child. This occurs in both men and women, and Jackel believes this to be primarily a preoedipal phenomenon. It is an attempt to reestablish the mother-child unit in which the patient is both the mother and, by identification, the child, and is in this way avoiding anxiety that would be created by "desertion" by the analyst.

In the cases cited above, although there was a coupling of symptoms with specific times, dates, or holidays, the internal unconscious determinants were the significant factors; the external temporal referents served only as a trigger for the release of the repressed conflict, which appears as an anniversary reaction.

11

ON TIME, DEATH, AND IMMORTALITY

Time is one of the concepts that has engaged man throughout the ages. Philosophers, physicists, psychologists, and psychoanalysts have attempted to understand its many ramifications, yet no consistent theory of time has been presented.

Psychoanalysts, in their daily work, in content as well as in schedule, are constantly involved with time. Objective measured time is linked to the setting of definite appointment schedules for periods of forty-five to fifty minutes, four or five times a week. Units of time are measured in years of treatment. These practical considerations are intimately linked to the fee structure of analytic work. We are paid for the time we spend with our patients. The analytic situation also involves another dimension of time—subjective, personal, psychological time. Recall, remembering, reconstruction, transference neurosis, repetition compulsion, fixation, regression, genetic point of view are but a few of the clinical and theoretical constructs that differentiate past from present, therapy from reality, here and now from then and there. These differentiations as they include time perspectives are crucial for our work and our understanding. The linkages of objective measured time with subjective emotional time are important for the patient and for the analyst.

To the psychoanalyst, time is important insofar as its qualities are subjectively significant; properties that may refer to an objective structure in nature are less so. Man is situated in time and his external reality is linked to objective time referents;

Reprinted from *The Psychoanalytic Quarterly* 40/3:435–446 (1971).

Material from G. Roheim (1932). Copyright © Institute of Psycho-Analysis, quoted with permission.

Quotation from St. Augustine is reprinted by permission of Penguin Books Ltd.

however, certain temporal qualities such as duration, sequence, continuity, eternity, or progression toward death are subjectively and individually significant, especially as these have direct bearing on memory, self-concept, and differentiation.

Kermode (1968) has written that we spend our lives with time: our failures are failures to live with it, our communications depend on our respecting it, and our sanity is reflected in our power to measure it. We are born containing clocklike mechanisms, yet we spend our childhood arduously learning the nongenic tradition of time. As we age time moves faster and we think about it more and more. Our central nervous systems contain not only histories but timepieces. Our future is long and ends, as we know, with death. Our needs are much more than simple food, territory, aggression, and sex. By thinking about threats of the future, we discover the past. Speculating continually about time, we represent it as destroyer and redeemer, or are baffled by thoughts on being and becoming, permanence and change.

> Time is that without which we cannot be human, and that which denies us the eternality we feel we were meant for, but can experience only in unconsciousness, where it is a trouble to our dreams. As Heidegger remarked, "We perceive time only because we know we have to die" [Kermode, 1968, p. 379].

Meyerhoff (1955) has addressed himself to a study of time and its relationship to literature. To him the self is experienced as a continuous, internally related, and fairly unified system of thoughts, feelings, actions, memories, and intentions. The experiential links between one's own past and present become important in understanding not only the past and present, but also the goals and objectives of the future. Psychological time is private, personal, subjective, and experiential. Public, objective, and shared time may be psychologically significant, but this is to be distinguished from measured time which utilizes watches, calendars, lunar, solar, and sidereal cycles. Measured time is used to synchronize our personal experiences with a base that can reliably and validly be substantiated by others.

Saint Augustine, in his *Confessions*, was one of the first to advance an ingenious philosophical theory based entirely upon the momentary experience of time combined with the psychological considerations of memory and anticipation. What happens, happens now, he argued; that is, it is always an experience, idea, or thing which is "present." Nevertheless, we can construct a meaningful temporal series accounting for the past and future in terms of memory and expectation. By "past," is meant the present memory experience of a thing past; by "future," the present expectation of a future occurrence. As psychoanalysts, we know that the actual past of our own lives is different from our recollections of it. In the transference neurosis, however, we find nonconsciously remembered aspects of the past repeated in the present. One of our therapeutic tasks involves changes in this "memory-experiential balance." Consciously we are aware of time measurement, time order, and time direction. The metric of time is necessary for reality action and communication. However, subjective relativity of time is characterized by unequal distribution, irregularity, and nonuniformity (Meyerhoff, 1955). Time duration refers to the experience of time as a continuous flow, with successive moments and change. This psychological conception does not have an adequate correlate in the physical concept of time.

Meyerhoff (1955) notes that memory (past) and expectation (future) are vague, ambiguous, and often fuse and overlap in the future. Forgetting, repressing, distorting, projecting introduce into subjective time possible error and deception. The psychoanalyst is less concerned with the objective serial order of time than with the effects of antecedents on consequents. Since the past leaves its traces, tags, marks, or records, the analyst is involved in understanding the effects of these memories, or records, on present functioning. Since the future leaves no memory traces, future is viewed as a manifestation of the past and present. The dynamic, economic, topographic, structural, and adaptative associations of the past constitute the genetic point of view. Thus, time becomes meaningful in terms of the personal experiences of the past and present and not primarily as an objective, measurable notation. Temporal succession and sequence of different events and their residues are stored in the mind. The actual day, date, year is only a memory tag to which is coupled the subjective experience (see chapters 8 and 10). The human mind is not a passive recorder but actively perceives, registers, interprets, organizes, synthe-sizes, and stores what impinges upon it. Meyerhoff observes:

> [T]he self is experienced as exhibiting a certain quality of con-tinuity. Despite the rapid succession of different temporal mo-ments, and despite the physical and organic changes of the body, the self is not simply a convenient label attached to a bundle or collection of these elements, but seems to be a kind of structure exhibiting continuity and unity of which the individual is directly aware in calling himself the same person throughout his lifetime. Both . . . aspects are experienced as characteristic of the self, and give rise to some sense of correlation and integration among the multiplicity of heterogenous parts which we associated with per-sonal identity [1955, pp. 33–34].

This statement is in accord with more current ideas of ego and self psychology. We know that man is not just a repository of perceptions and memories, but is actively involved with self-regulative and synthetic functions which utilize relatively con-flict-free autonomous ego activities. Thus, present time is han-dled in accordance with reality testing and reality principle functioning, and, as such, is connected with the system ego, as shown by Cohn (1957) and others. The pleasure-pain principle does not take into consideration time delay or detour. Imme-diate discharge is the goal. Hence a sense of timelessness, very early described by Freud, characterizes these id-primary process strivings (see chapter 8). Memory involves a sense of past and present, a sense of time differentiation, and, as such, is a later development of mind. Though linked to objective dates, times, or days, these are of secondary importance. The anniversary reaction can be seen as a time-date-event linked response that seemingly has little to do with current objective time (see chap-ters 8 and 10). The current time-date-age acts as the trigger which allows the repressed unconscious to emerge into the pres-ent, and this in turn results in reactions and symptoms. There is a specificity of the time (date, age, holiday, event) which links to the originally traumatic situation, but the crucial factor in the pathogenic process is not the objective time measure but the repressed conflict.

Although Saint Augustine first recognized the nature of memory as a key to the structure of time and the self, he did not have available to him the concept of the unconscious and its significant associated mechanisms (e.g., repression). Saint Augustine, however, comes close. In Book X of the *Confessions*, he states:

> When . . . the memory loses something—and this is what happens whenever we forget something and try to remember it—where are we to look for it except in the memory itself? And if the memory offers us something else instead, as may happen, we reject what it offers until the one thing which we want is presented. When it is presented to us we say 'This is it', but we could not say this unless we recognized it, and we could not recognize it unless we remembered it. True enough, we had forgotten it. Or could it be that it had not entirely escaped our memory, but part of it remained, giving a clue to the remainder, because the memory, realizing that something was missing and feeling crippled by the loss of something to which it had grown accustomed, kept demanding that the missing part should be restored? Something of this sort happens when we see or think of a person whom we know, but cannot remember his name and try to recall it. If any other name but his occurs to us, we do not apply it to him, because we do not normally associate that name with him. So we reject all names until we think of the one which corresponds accurately with our normal mental picture of the man. But how can we think of his name unless we bring it out from the memory? For even if we recognize it because someone else prompts us, it is still by our own memory that we do so, because we do not accept it as a fresh piece of knowledge but agree that it is the right name, since we can now remember it. If the name were completely obliterated from our minds, we could not remember it even if we were prompted. For we do not entirely forget what we remember that we have forgotten. If we had completely forgotten it, we should not even be able to look for what was lost [Saint Augustine, 397–398, pp. 225–226].

Recollection and remembering are active, not passive, reproductions of stored memory traces or tags. Analytic work repeatedly affirms the various aspects of this process, first described by Freud and confirmed by many others. The recollection of a single, unique event only rarely allows the reconstruction of one's entire lifetime, although literary figures such as Proust have indicated the significant clue features of a single event in the unraveling of the understanding of the personality. Reconstruction of the past involves repeating, some recalling and remembering, and understanding. I emphasize this because the anniversary date, though only a single day or event, has compressed into it many antecedent, concomitant, and consequent experiences. Thus the anniversary reaction far exceeds the temporal significance of the event itself.

Meyerhoff interprets Proust as saying "that the single event remembered in all its qualitative richness and concrete reality seems to be freed from the date it originally had in the chronological order of time; and that the same holds for the self imaginatively re-created through this act of recollection" (Meyerhoff, 1955, p. 54). I would agree with this, and note that although the event is physically time-bound to a date, actually it is timeless. There is liberation from objective time (chronological order in time), but not from the elements or qualities of time on the occasion of emergence or appearance. Thus the anniversary reaction may be triggered by a time or age, but what emerges is not necessarily connected with time as such. When, in the course of analytic work, the experience is externalized, examined, worked through, and differentiated, the repression is lifted and therapeutic resolution is in order.

Thus, understanding the date or temporal age index attached to the appearance of symptoms is important in understanding the significance of this trigger. However, what emerges is not specifically time-bound in the metrical sense. Usually in our work we establish these time-day linkages after the reaction has occurred. Thus anniversary reactions are retrospectively applied labels to symptomatic responses that only on the surface are time-bound. In the unconscious the quality of the experience is preserved in a state close to its original one, relatively immune to the passage of physical time. The unconscious response or anniversary reaction, though independent of present time, is related to a past linkage of time-event and existing personality structure. Nonetheless, the repressed elements are themselves timeless. Thus, the contents of these repressed elements are not really affected by the "date they bear." They are situated outside of the scope of time, though linked to time and age (time duration). In his paper "The Unconscious," Freud (1915d) states that the events of the unconscious system are timeless. They are not ordered in time, are not changed by the passage of time, and have no relation to time. Temporal relations are connected with the workings of the conscious system. In the *New Introductory Lectures*, he expands this idea in accordance with the newer structural theory of mind (1932). In the id there is nothing corresponding to the idea of time, and no alteration of mental processes by the passage of time. Conative impulses which have never got beyond the id, and even impressions which have been pushed down into the id by repression, are virtually immortal and are preserved for whole decades as though they only recently occurred. Marie Bonaparte (1940) in "Time and the Unconscious" distinguishes three aspects of "timelessness": (1) the unconscious has no knowledge of time; (2) the unconscious is completely unaffected by the process of time; and (3) the unconscious does not perceive time. When considered from the point of view of the pleasure-pain–primary process principle, in contrast to the reality–secondary-process principle, this is quite acceptable and points to the distinction between ego and id time relations discussed in chapter 9.

The transitoriness of life, time's inexorable march to death, the progression of time in human life from birth to death, has been a preoccupation of man from the beginning of time. Unlike all other forms of life, man has a foreknowledge of his own death, even if it is only on an intellectual level. This transitoriness has given rise to the religious notion of immortality and to the dichotomy of body and soul, a precursor to the later psyche and soma division. According to this conception, the body dies and is buried, cremated, or destroyed. The soul or spirit, however, is immortal and indestructible. Thus the notion of immortality is a way of arresting or reversing the irreversible flow of time toward death. The soul is beyond and outside of time—it is eternal. In some religions, resurrection, salvation, and eternal life include the eventuality of bodily restoration; however, this optimistic hope of a world to come, where time has stopped and there is reunion and everlasting continuity, is a defense against the total helplessness associated with the "nothingness" of nonlife, be it death or the earliest states of infancy. The various death, burial, mourning, and anniversary rituals evolved in order to handle functionally this basic anxiety through public, private, and mystical means.

Róheim has related the split into body and soul to the notion of the double or doppelgänger. He writes:

> We love ourselves too dearly to comprehend or admit the possibility that we may perish, and as reality has taught us that our body is not everlasting, we desire and therefore believe in the existence of a hidden likeness of ourselves in a shape that cannot perish, eternal like a rock and full of the germs of life. But these children of our wishes, although they owe their existence to our phantasies, are yet firmly rooted in reality. It is quite true to say that we lead a double existence, that of a real man and of a hidden being [1932, p. 105].

Eliade (1959a) explains that the regeneration of time, linked intimately with rituals that govern the renewal of alimentary reserves, that is, rituals that guarantee the continuity of life in its entirety, is connected with the festivals annually celebrating the new year. Essentially, there is a conception of the end and the beginning of a temporal period that is related to the periodic regeneration of life. This implies a new creation that is periodic, a cyclical regeneration of time. Eliade describes the whole series of periodic ceremonies which involve driving out or extinguishing the old or the bad, and then starting the new. As part of these new year rituals, there are ceremonies involving the souls of the dead and their return to the houses of the living. The expulsion of demons, diseases, and sins coincides, or at one period coincided, with the festival of the new year. The abolition of the past year and past time, through these purification rituals, Eliade maintains, is the way of resuming time from the beginning. Thus, every new year is the start of "pure" time and in this way the creation of the world begins anew. This permits the return of the dead to life and maintains the hope of the faithful in the resurrection of the body. Time is suspended and then begins anew as the repetition of creation. The new year is frequently depicted as a newborn baby, whereas the old year is represented by an old man who is being swept away by the scythe of time. In Japan and in Germany, Eliade notes, the last night of the year is marked by the appearance of funerary animals and funerary gods and goddesses. In the West, the new year begins with the circumcision feast of the eight-day-old Christ child, and the Judaic new year is ushered in with the repetition of the annual reading of the Old Testament, beginning with the Book of Genesis.

Among some people, a new era begins not only with every new year but with every new reign, every consummation of marriage, the birth of every child. These are all times of regeneration with the same end: to annul past time, to abolish death, to begin creation. Viewed from this perspective, the rites of passage involve death and re-creation. Eliade discusses this idea in *Birth and Rebirth* (1958), where he recounts how initiation rites and symbols include mourning by the parents for the puberty initiate whose childhood is dead, and the return and rebirth of the initiate. In some cultures the newly initiated returns as a different person, with a new name, new role, new identity, and a new series of relationships. In order to be created anew, the old must first be annihilated. Thus we find in connection with the new year: first, the death and resulting chaos (e.g., extinguishing fires, expelling evil and sins, return of the dead); and second, the new creation (e.g., lighting new fires, departure of the dead, predicting weather for the coming year). In the scenario of initiatory rites, death of the previous state is a precursor to providing a clean new slate for the "new" being. Initiation is viewed as a rebirth or resurrection. The novice has attained another mode of existence inaccessible to those who have not undergone the initiatory ordeals—who have not tasted death. Eliade emphasizes this characteristic of the archaic mentality: "the belief that a state cannot be changed without first being annihilated"—without the child's childhood dying. In some rituals, mystical death is suggested by ritual aggressiveness when the novice is separated from his mother. Thus, among the Hottentots, the initiate is allowed to insult and even manhandle his mother as a symbol of his emancipation from her. In Papua the novice walks over his mother's body, deliberately stepping on her belly. This gesture confirms his definite separation from her. The initiate may be painted white to signify the death of his past child-self. But the dead return and so does the novice.

Reik (1961) has also called attention to death and resurrection as part of puberty rites, especially of boys, in different parts of the world (e.g., Africa, Australia, New Guinea). He attempts to show a comparison of these rites with the Isaac story, where the adolescent boy is supposed to be slain but an animal is sacrificed instead and he lives on in a new role.

Eliade (1958) parallels burial in the fetal position, certain initiation-rite fetal positions, and rebirth. The dead are regarded as undergoing an initiation, and the fetal position signifies rebirth, the start of new time. Similar practices occur in the rituals surrounding shamanic initiations. Eliade calls attention to the relationship of initiatory death rites and rebirth. This is especially found in puberty rites. He carefully explains the many specific details of these rites, as they symbolize death and resurrection in different cultures. These rites, which are socially controlled, deal with man's anxiety about death or total annihilation. The prospect of "nothingness" is so terrifying that it must be coped with through belief and ritual. Metaphor and analogy that assist man deal with the appearance and reappearance of the sun, moon, stars, seasons, plants, and so on. Something goes away and then it returns. This is the meaning of Easter. Time is the measure of the intervals between "going away" and "returning." It aids in the prediction of the non-finality of the end. Some have called this the life cycle, implying the cyclicity of end and beginning. When the beginning reoccurs we have a means of coping with aging, the bringing of the end closer, and with death.

The rites of initiatory death give man some control over what otherwise would be an overwhelming anxiety about total obliteration. In some ways fear of Alzheimer's disease relates to this—without memory and recognition one is annihilated as a person. "Death prepares the new, purely spiritual birth, access to a mode of being not subject to the destroying action of Time" (Eliade, 1958, p.136).

Lunar myths have been connected with death and resurrection, fertility and regeneration, initiation, and so on. The moon's phases measure time. Month, moon, and menses seem to be derived from the same Latin root, *me-*, which relates to the word *measure*. Just as the disappearance of the moon is never final since it is followed by a new moon, the disappearance of man is not final either.

Boas, in discussing the philosophical approach to the acceptance of time, notes that a thing which is changing has both ceased to be but is not yet anything—a transition. Since change entails the loss of something, time can be viewed as a destroyer and there is a quest for eternalism in order to attain stability. He writes:

> [W]e attempt to frustrate the passage of time by preserving the dead words of our predecessors, just as we attempt to divert the future by our last wills and testaments. One of the results of accepting time would be the admission of the reality of death, of the death of ideas, of works of art, of cultures, of people. . . . the most elaborate devices have been perfected to defeat the coming of death and to disguise it when it has come, devices running from the library and the museum to statute law and textbooks in correct grammar. The word "immortal" has become a term of high praise and we use it often simply to indicate our regard for the things to which we apply it—immortal heroes, immortal poems, even immortal deeds. It is in vain that philosophers have pointed out clearly and distinctly that no quality is changed by lasting forever. . . . The freezing of contemporary culture forever would . . . make for stability, but since we have no way of freezing it, it would appear to be more prudent to adjust ourselves to the brute fact of change. And since the change cannot come about without death, it will be necessary also to learn how to unloosen our grasp on what we have and build a philosophy of life upon the premise that nothing whatsoever is immortal [1950, pp. 258–259].

Mourning is an adaptation to change and permits planning for the future. The acceptance of time is the acceptance of change and therefore of death, but it is also the acceptance of multiplicity, growth, and further development. Perhaps this is the deeper meaning of Eliade's formulation of birth, death, and rebirth.

12

ON MOURNING AND ANNIVERSARIES: THE RELATIONSHIP OF CULTURALLY CONSTITUTED DEFENSIVE SYSTEMS TO INTRAPSYCHIC ADAPTIVE PROCESSES

CULTURALLY CONSTITUTED DEFENSE MECHANISMS

Spiro (1961) has called attention to the fact that religious beliefs and ritual may be used to resolve conflict. "It is one of the tasks of culture-and-personality to discover how . . . intrapersonal conflict is resolved in such a way that functional requirements both of the individual and of social life are satisfied simultaneously. The analysis of culturally constituted defense mechanisms offers one such avenue of investigation" (p. 491). These can protect the person and the society from disruptive consequences of his or her needs and of his or her personal defensive operations. These culturally constituted defenses serve to perpetuate the sociocultural system, and maintain the sociocultural equilibrium, when this balance is threatened by a serious crisis (e.g., death). Culturally constituted defense mechanisms integrated into a religious system that is consistent with rather than

Reprinted from *The Israel Annals of Psychiatry and Related Disciplines*, 10/1:9–40 (1972).

Permission has been granted by Barnes & Noble Books, Totowa, New Jersey, for quotations from E. O. James's (1961) *Seasonal Feasts and Festivals*, and by Stein and Day Publishers for quotations from *The Sacred Books of the Jews*, copyright © 1969 by Harry Gersh.

a distortion of "reality" serves the intrapsychic processes involved in adaptation but may not in and of themselves "solve" intrapsychic conflict.

Lessa and Vogt (1965) have considered problems about death on two levels: those which confront the individual, and those which confront the society. Both require readjustment mechanisms. Society's mourning is determined by the social and functional importance of the deceased, and the number of roles fulfilled by him. There are public ceremonies, rites, and protocol procedures in which all mourners participate. The private expressions of feeling (both internal and external) are more closely related to the actual mourning work.

All cultures have evolved ways and means of dealing with death. These coping devices are aimed at allaying the individual's anxiety about his own death, facilitating his own personal mourning, as well as dealing with concerns connected with the rupture of interpersonal group relations in which the deceased had been involved, and finding a means of keeping alive the presence of the deceased person by means of cultural institutions in order to assure one's self of one's own psychological survival after death; that is, others will mourn for us in a similar vein as we mourn for those who died. In this way we will be remembered and survive. Goethe, in his novel *Elective Affinities*, said that we all die twice: once when we ourselves die, and the second time when those who have loved us and remember us die in turn.

All cultures have developed some concept of a form of existence which goes on after death to handle these anxieties. Some belief systems are quite explicit with regards to where and how the spirit exists. The implicit belief in an afterlife stands as a universal feature of human existence.

Belief in an afterworld, though relieving an individual's fears concerning his own death, sets up the additional situation of contact to a greater or lesser extent with a host of nonmortal beings; that is, either with the spirits of the departed members of his own group or with those of all departed human beings. In many cultures people have attitudes of fear and dread regarding the spirits of the deceased. Sometimes these concerns are mild and noninstitutionalized; in other groups we find elaborate mechanisms to mollify, pacify, or to confuse and mislead the ghost or spirit. Anthropological literature is filled with many examples of devices, rituals, ceremonies, and practices—the efforts of the living survivors to ensure against the return of the spirits of the dead. The assumption is that the spirit or ghost is malevolent, even though this was not consciously felt to be the case when the individual was alive. Psychoanalysts have considered this phenomenon as a manifestation of ambivalence with the unacceptable negative feelings stimulating the fear of the external return of the dead who will seek retaliation. Ethnographic accounts of some cultures report that the ghost is considered only partially evil or dangerous and then under certain circumstances. In other cultures, spirits may be conceived of as ever-present members of the social group who have varying powers of influence, favorable or unfavorable, over the living. In these groups, ghosts may require propitiation in order to aid the living, and this forms the basis of ancestor worship. Though reverence of the dead occurs, it is not free of some fear or awe. The fear, fascination, and continued interest in ghost stories, supernatural tales, or in accounts of making life from nonliving substances, for example, Frankenstein, is an almost universal interest among peoples of all cultures. It may be that the key to the understanding of this involvement lies in the attempt to deal with intrapsychic anxieties about death and total permanent separation that is so commonly experienced by both children and adults.

Durkheim (1915) questioned the validity of beliefs which suggest that a soul is attached to a body. He states, however, that when the body is left, the simple vital principle animating the body of a man becomes a spirit, a good or evil genius, or even a deity, according to the effects with which it is charged. Since it is death which brought about this separation, it is to the dead, to the souls of ancestors, that the first cult known to humanity was addressed. Thus the first rites were funeral rites; the first sacrifices were food offerings destined to satisfy the needs of the departed; the cities were necropolises; and the first altars were tombs. Discoveries in Australia indicate that ancient Kow Swamp man (16,000–30,000 years ago) buried his dead carefully. Eight skeletons were found and in all the faces were upward with the limbs extended. The impression of a ritual burial is suggested by the presence of small pieces of

white quartz encircling some of the skeletons. The ritual significance of quartz remains a mystery; however, this kind of
stone was highly prized because the nearest natural occurrence
of quartz is about sixty miles away from the Kow Swamp site.
Ralph Solecki has indicated that Neanderthal man, at Shanidar,
may have had ritualized burials including funeral feasts, flowers, and special positions for the dead. Solecki believes these
burials took place about 60,000 years ago (1971).

Durkheim defines a cult as "a system of diverse rites, festivals, and ceremonies which *all have this characteristic, that they
reappear periodically*. They fulfil the need which the believer feels
of strengthening and reaffirming, at regular intervals of time,
the bond which unites him to the sacred beings upon which he
depends" (p. 80). If there is no periodicity, there is no cult.
Thus one can speak of funeral or mourning rites though not
of a funeral or mourning cult. "There is no cult of the ancestors
except when sacrifices are made on the tombs from time to
time, when libations are poured there on certain more or less
specific dates, or when festivals are regularly celebrated in honour of the dead" (p. 80). When funeral, burial, and mourning
rites are accomplished and the survivors have no further duties
to their no longer existing relatives, the process is completed.
The dead have ceased to exist as persons and are now in the
ranks of the impersonal and the anonymous.

Where there are no recurrent, periodic regular ceremonies, there is no cult, and the dead are decathected and cease
to exist except as memory traces. This latter process seems to
parallel the normal intrapsychic mourning adaptation process
(see chapter 1), in contrast to the continually pathologic recurrent anniversary reactions which parallel the cult organization
and indicate the lack of completion of mourning (see chapter
7).

In chapter 1, I noted "various religious rituals, when divested of their theological implications, emphasize the cultural
evolution of mores and folkways which can defensively assist
the ego in the adaptation involved in the mourning process"
(p. 31).

Since 1961, I have been studying the various culturally
constituted defense mechanisms which are parts of religious
systems, and their relation to the extrapsychic processes that in

turn may affect the intrapsychic processes. I have focused my particular attention on culturally constituted defense mechanisms found in mourning and have found they can best be studied in religious systems having detailed practices and procedures for all stages of the crises around death. As my specific area of study I have chosen Orthodox Jewish practices as they relate to death and mourning. Orthodox Judaic practices, characterized by periodic, continually ongoing obligations, both public and private, which continue throughout life, fit Durkheim's definition—as a cult of the dead ancestors with some form of deification. The laws and traditions are many and are performed in a specific order. They begin at the very moment of death and never stop for the survivors. There are specific provisions for the preparations; special regulations relating to the casket, the funeral service, the cemetery, the interment, and burial; and extensive mourning and postmourning practices, procedures, and ceremonies. The conception of an afterlife is fundamental to the Jewish religion, though the practical details of immortality are ambiguous and vague.[1] The Jewish conception of life for the deceased is one that is found in many other

---

[1] In the Talmud, "the Rabbis developed a picture of a three-layered cosmos: heaven, earth, and hell. Since the Bible has seven designations for heaven, the Rabbis reasoned that heaven has seven stories or levels. . . . Earth, too, has seven layers or strata. . . . Gehinnom, from which the term Gehanna derives, also has seven levels. The Rabbis speak of descending into Gehanna. . . . Fire is the principal feature of hell, but there is also mire. . . .

"On death, man is judged by the Great Tribunal to determine whether he will spend the years until the World-to-Come in heaven or hell. He is judged again in the last judgment."

In the Talmudic Aboth 4:29, it is stated, "They that are born will die; and the dead will be brought to life again; and they that live again will be judged . . . let not your imagination persuade you that the grave will be a place of refuge for you; for perforce you were formed, and perforce you were born, and perforce you live, and perforce you die, and perforce you will in this hereafter have to give account and reckoning before the supreme King of kings, the Holy One, blessed be He."

Gersh continues: "The Sadducees had rejected any idea of life after death; the Pharisees held as strongly to the idea of the resurrection of the dead. The Rabbis of the Talmud were in the Pharisaic tradition, but there was no agreement as to who would be resurrected" and "they also differed sharply as to the length of punishment of those souls who were sent to Gehanna" (Gersh, 1968, pp. 127–128).

religious systems. Attempts to reduce the anxiety about complete separation by indicating it does not end in a total nothingness when both of the separated parties go their separate paths—one to be a mourner in this world, the other to participate in another existence elsewhere—form the cornerstone of this belief system. In making this study, I was struck by the parallels between the process of religious practices involved in death and mourning and the internal stages of the mourning process described earlier (chapter 1). Both processes are attempts at adaptation; that is, to establish a new equilibrium related to the changed situation both outside and inside of the individual and the group. It is tempting to suggest that these culturally constituted adaptive mechanisms evolved from the individual internal stages of the mourning process, which may have been represented in primitive form in infrahuman species. Without direct evidence to support this hypothesis, however, it must remain as only an idea.

INTRAPSYCHIC ASPECTS OF THE MOURNING PROCESS

In chapter 1, "Mourning and Adaptation," I have described the sequence of the different stages of the mourning process. These stages consisted of a series of reactions occurring in a particular temporal order, having distinct degrees of acuteness and chronicity, and eventuating in a restored state of psychological equilibrium. The acute stage of the mourning process refers to the immediate phases following the loss of the object. These phases consist of shock, grief, pain, reaction to separation, and the beginning internal decathexis of the lost object. The reaction to separation brings with it anxiety as well as anger. As the acute stage of the mourning process progresses, the chronic stage gradually takes over. In this chronic stage we find an ever-increasing number of manifestations of the internal adaptive mechanisms which attempt to integrate the experience of the loss with reality and so allow life activities to continue. As time and mourning work proceed, fewer and fewer episodes of mourning occur. When they do appear they are usually acutely precipitated by specific events or items. With further mourning work, internal psychic equilibrium is restored and mourning ceases. Identification and memories remain as the residues of the completed mourning process. When symptomatic anniversary reactions occur, they are indicative of unresolved and/or pathological mourning processes. These frequently require therapeutic intervention (see chapters 7, 8, and 9).

ORTHODOX JEWISH LAW AS APPLIED TO DEATH, MOURNING, AND MEMORIALS

In Orthodox Judaism a series of practices and customs has evolved that specifically relates to death, funerals, interment, mourning, memorials, anniversaries, and immortality. These have been stated in the Kitzur Schulchan Aruch (Code of Jewish Law), and in other compilations, discussions, or tractates on mourning. Some of these laws will be presented and discussed using a psychoanalytic frame of reference.

Five Stages of Mourning in Judaic Law

Jewish law formally considers the bereaved to be those who have lost any one of the seven close relatives listed in Leviticus (21:1–3): father, mother, wife (or husband), son, daughter (married or unmarried), brother, and sister (or half-brother and half-sister). Judaic formal mourning has been divided into five stages.

The first stage is that period of time between death and burial (Aninuth). Lamm (1969) indicates that during this time when despair is most intense, social amenities and major positive religious requirements are canceled in recognition of the mourner's troubled state. This stage closely corresponds to the acute shock phase of the intrapsychic mourning process.

The second stage occurs during the first three days following burial, days filled with intense grief and pain. These days are devoted to weeping and lamentation. During this period the mourner does not respond to greetings, remains at home, and visiting the mourner "is usually somewhat discouraged, for it is too early to comfort the mourners when the wound is so fresh" (1969, p. 78). This stage closely corresponds to the grief and pain phases of the acute intrapsychic mourning process.

The third stage is the period of Shiva, the seven days following burial (this period includes the first three days).

> During this time the mourner emerges from the stage of intense grief to a new stage of mind in which he is prepared to talk about his loss and to accept comfort from friends and neighbors. . . . While he remains within the house, expressing his grief through the observance of Aveluth [the period of mourning]—the wearing of the rent garment, the sitting on the low stool, the wearing of slippers, the refraining from shaving and grooming, the recital of the Kaddish—his acquaintances come to his home to express sympathy in his distress. The inner freezing that came with the death of his relative now begins to thaw. The isolation from the world of people and the retreat inward now relaxes somewhat [1969, p. 78].

This stage corresponds to that of the acute mourning process where there is beginning internal decathexis of the lost object and where catharsis through speech is encouraged. Separation is more recognized as a reality, and the chronic stage of mourning gradually appears.

The fourth stage is the period of Shleoshin, the thirty days following burial (this period includes the preceding stage of Shiva).

The mourner is encouraged to leave the house after Shiva and to slowly rejoin society, always recognizing that enough time has not yet elapsed to assume full, normal social relations (Lamm, 1969).

The rent clothing is still worn for deceased parents, and hair cutting is still prohibited. This stage corresponds to that of the early chronic stage of intrapsychic mourning process. Greater reality awareness of the loss has taken place and slowly psychic equilibrium is being restored.

The fifth and last stage is the twelve-month period (which includes the previous stage) during which life gradually returns to the preloss state. The inner feelings of the mourner are still wounded. Entertainment and amusement is still curtailed.

At the close of this last stage, the twelve-month period, the bereaved is not expected to continue his mourning, except for brief moments when Yizkor or Yahrzeit is observed (Lamm, 1969).

The stage following the observance of the year-long mourning period, which culminates with the erection of a monument to the deceased, is one that *never* ceases. It is the period of lifelong practices and procedures that is not part of the mourning process per se. These postmourning activities are directly concerned with the anniversary memorializations and obligations that continue throughout the lifetime of the survivors. It is an outgrowth of these postmourning obligations that gives rise to later anniversaries and holidays. All commemorations are memories of what is past. What is past is dead, but relatively nonconflictual memories as well as inner conflicts may be kept alive through these anniversary observances.

Several sections of the Code of Jewish Law dealing with particular aspects of mourning will now be presented to illustrate how these obligations, practical and almost recipelike, are seemingly devoid of theology and references to God. They appear to be more of a guide to aid the adaptation of the individual mourner as well as the community and less of a religious dictate. "In this magnificently conceived, graduated process of mourning an ancient faith raises up the mourner from the abyss of despair to the undulating hills and valleys of normal daily life" (Lamm, 1969, p. 79).

As already indicated, it is surprising how closely these laws correspond to the intrapsychic mourning stages, and how much of this manifest content can be explained by psychoanalytic theory.

Laws Concerning Relatives and Minors for Whom One Must Mourn

1. There are seven relatives for whom one must mourn: one's father, mother, son, daughter, brother, and sister. A husband must mourn for his wife, and a wife for her husband.

2. For other relatives it is the custom to keep partial mourning during the first week of the death until after the Sabbath. There are degrees of mourning depending upon the closeness of the relationship, thus for the demise of a grandson, one should manifest his grief by not wearing his outer garments for the Sabbath. For a father-in-law, or a mother-in-law, and for a grandfather one must manifest sorrow by not changing one's clothes, with the exception of the undergarments. All who mourn for the

above should also observe the custom of neither bathing, nor combing their hair, nor eating outside of their house, neither at a religious feast nor at any festive gathering, but after the first Sabbath following the death everything is permissible.

3. For a child who had died within thirty days from its birth, one need neither rend one's garments nor mourn, nor keep a period of mourning. If, however, the child died after the thirtieth day, the garment should be rent and one should mourn and keep a period of mourning, unless it was already known that the child was born in the eighth month (as such a child cannot survive).

On the basis of empirical observation, it can be seen that the seven relatives for whom one must mourn are the most significant figures in the developmental and adult life of the individual. In my studies of four adult mourning situations (see chapter 2), these kinship relationships are the basic relationships which evoke the most sustained mourning reaction. Other losses can be seen as transference losses derived from these relationships.

Laws Concerning Things Which are Forbidden to a Mourner

1. He is forbidden to sit upon cushions and pillows during the seven days, but he should sit only on the ground; in the case of an invalid or of an old man, to whom sitting on the ground is painful, it is permissible for them to sit on a small cushion. The mourner may walk and stand, except in the presence of comforters when it is obligatory to sit. It is also forbidden to sleep in a bed or on a bench, only on the ground, but he may put pillows or mattresses on the ground, as he is accustomed to when he lies in bed. If the mourners are sick or have weak constitutions, they are permitted to sleep in the bed.

2. The mourner should observe some sort of enwrapping of his head, for example, to pull down the cap close to the eyes during the seven days, but not on the Sabbath because it is an overt act.

3. One is forbidden to wear a washed garment, even a shirt, during the seven days of mourning, even in honor of the Sabbath. It is even prohibited to use freshly washed sheets or bedspreads or freshly washed towels.

4. One is forbidden to wash one's garments or even to put them aside until after the seven days, because it is work.

5. If one does not change one's garments for pleasure, but out of necessity, for example, if the garments one wears be soiled, or if it be necessary for the sake of cleanliness, one is permitted to do so even during the first seven days and on a weekday, provided the clean garments were first worn by another.

6. During the thirty days of mourning one is forbidden to wear one's Sabbath garments even on the Sabbath. One who mourns for a parent is forbidden to wear new garments the entire twelve months.

7. One is forbidden to cut one's hair during the thirty days of mourning; this refers not only to the hair on one's head but also to hair anywhere else. For one who mourns his father or mother, the hair should not be cut the entire twelve months, unless it be a burden to him or if he go amongst people of different beliefs and he would be looked upon with disdain on account of his hair. If his hair grew to a size which alters his appearance so that he is unlike other people to such an amount as to arouse comment, under such circumstances he is allowed to cut his hair, but only after thirty days of mourning.

8. Just as it is forbidden to cut the hair within the thirty days, so it is forbidden to pare the nails with an instrument. It is, however, permissible to do so with one's own hands or teeth even during the first seven days of mourning.

The cessation of normal pleasurable activity as well as the identification with the deceased can be ascertained from these rules. This can also be seen in the following regulations.

Laws Prohibiting a Mourner to Marry During the Thirty Days of Mourning and Laws Concerning a Groom or a Bride Who Became Mourners

1. A mourner is forbidden to marry during the thirty days of mourning.

2. If one's wife has died, one should not marry again until three Festivals have elapsed, because on account of the rejoicing of the Festivals one will forget the first love upon nearing the second; and one should not drink of this cup and have one's mind on the first. If, however, one has not yet fulfilled the precept "Be fruitful and multiply," or if one has young children, or if there is no one to look after one, one need not wait until after thirty days. A woman whose husband has died must wait ninety days before being married again.

3. If one has prepared everything needed for one's wedding, and if one of the relatives has died, the wedding should be postponed until after the days of mourning.

4. If the relative died after the nuptial ceremony, he is forbidden to have intercourse until after the days of mourning. Since he is forbidden to cohabit, and he had no cohabitation prior thereto, the bride and groom may not be left alone without someone watching them. After the seven days of mourning, one may have a mandatory cohabitation and celebrate the seven days of the feast.

Laws Forbidding Excessive Grief

These laws are interesting in that they summarize the timetable of mourning and yet prescribe that excessive grief is forbidden. They state:

1. It is forbidden to grieve excessively over the dead. But three days should be allowed for weeping, seven for mourning, and thirty for abstaining from wearing ironed clothes and from cutting the hair.

2. If one of the family had died, the entire family should evince sorrow. During the first seven days the sword is aimed at them, and up to thirty days it is weak, but it is not restored to its sheath until after twelve months. Therefore, the first three days the mourner should consider as if the sword lay between his shoulders, from the third day to the seventh as if it was standing upright in a corner in front of him, from the seventh to the thirtieth as if it passed in front of him in the street, and thereafter during the entire year as if the attribute of justice is still aimed against his family.

3. He who does not mourn in accordance with the regulations laid down by the Sages is cruel, for it is his duty to bestir himself and examine his deeds with fear and anxiety and to repent, perchance he may escape the sword of the Angel of Death.

Specific laws requiring positive action, and not inhibition, symbolically relate to *separation* that so characterizes the acute mourning period include:

Laws Concerning the Rending of Garments for the Dead

1. One who has lost a relative for whom he is required to mourn is required to rend his garments, while standing and before the coffin is closed, when one's sorrow is still intense.

2. He must rend his garment near his neck in the front thereof; it must be rent lengthwise and not crosswise; and, in the cloth of the garment, not at its seam.

3. For a father or a mother one must rend all his garments opposite his heart, with the exception of his shirt or his occasionally worn garments (e.g., the overcoat). A woman should first rend her undergarments privately in accordance with the dictates of modesty. She should then rend her external garments so as to not expose herself.

4. It is customary to rend the right side of the garments for all relatives, and for one's father or mother the left side of the garment must be rent, for he has to expose his heart which is on the left.

5. For all relatives one may either rend his garment with his hand or with an instrument, but for one's father or mother it is with the hand that one must rend it.

6. In the seven days of mourning for all relatives, one who changes his garments need not rend those he is putting on. If, however, one who mourns for a father or mother changes his garments on a weekday during the seven days, he must rend them.

7. Garments rent for all relatives may be repaired by connecting the torn parts after seven days, and after thirty days it is permitted to sew the torn parts together, in a proper manner, but one should not connect the torn parts of garments rent for one's father or mother until after thirty days and one should never sew them together properly. One is forbidden to cut the part that was rent, and to mend the torn part with another piece of cloth. All the rent garments which one is forbidden to sew together should not be mended even by one to whom they were sold. It is therefore necessary for the one who sells them to inform the buyer thereof, and therefore they should not be sold to a non-Jew.

8. If one does not hear of the death of all relatives but a father or mother until after thirty days, he need not rend his garments; but for a father or mother, one must rend the garments he is wearing at the time when he hears of their death.

He need not, however, rend the garment to which he may change thereafter.

The rending of garments seems to symbolically signify the separation of what has occurred in reality, and what is also taking place intrapsychically. The loss of a father or mother is especially significant. Specific periods for the wearing of the rent garments relate to the various stages of grief and mourning work, with the assumption that father or mother loss is never completely healed. The anthropological and cross-cultural significance of this "cutting for the dead" will now be discussed.

In ancient Israel mourners expressed their sorrow for the death of relatives by cutting their own bodies and shearing part of their hair so as to produce bald patches on their heads (Jeremiah, Amos, Isaiah, Micah, Ezekiel). Since blood was believed to be synonymous with life, the cutting of the body with blood flowing out represented life flowing away. However, since the Hebrews believed in death as a means of passing to another existence, this blood flow, sometimes over the dead body, established a bond with the dead and symbolically served to nourish the departed on his journey to the next world. In similar fashion, hair was a symbol of life and strength. Thus the placing of hair from the living on the dead body or at the grave was a means of giving strength to the deceased. However, it clearly is also the separation and pain in the living. As such this practice can be viewed as a concrete representation of separation. Later reforms against such expressions of sorrow and practices prohibited these actions. Cutting of hair is still a current Judaic prohibition during mourning. Still retained is the custom of garment rending.

Frazer (1923) points out that cropping or shaving the hair and cutting or mutilating the body during mourning has been widespread among mankind. Variations and derivations of these practices include wounding, scarifying, or lacerating the body with the shedding of blood. Arab women, for example, would rend their upper garments, scratch their faces and breasts with their nails, and beat and bruise themselves during mourning. They would cut off their hair and place this on the grave in a variety of ways. Similar practices have been observed and described in ancient Greece, Assyria, Armenia, and Rome.

The Huns, Scythians, and Slavonic countries had comparable customs; for example, lacerations and blood shedding by both men and women. In Africa, lopping off finger joints has been described. Among the Abyssinians, in deep mourning for a blood relative, the hair was cut, ashes strewn on the head, and the skin over the temples scratched until blood flowed. Among the Kissi, a tribe in Liberia, women in mourning covered their bodies, especially their hair, with a thick coating of mud and scratched their faces and breasts with their nails. Self-laceration of the body of the mourner was also common among the Indian tribes of North America. The Snake Indians of the Rocky Mountains made incisions in all of the fleshy parts of their bodies. The greater their affection for the deceased, the deeper the cuts into their own bodies. Among the Crow Indians the mourner was bound to renew the mourning lacerations for several years every time he passed near the graves of dead relatives, and as long as a single clot of blood remained on his body he was forbidden to wash himself. Frazer described such bloody practices especially for a woman after her husband died, although they occurred as part of the mourning rituals for other relatives or chiefs.

Similar practices are described in Turkey, in the East Indies, in the Polynesian Islands including the Maoris of New Zealand, and the peoples of Tonga, Samoa, Hawaii, and Australia. Again one notes that the females seemed to be the agents of many of the bloody customs, though not exclusively. The tearing of hair, laceration of the body, and the shedding of blood were the central activities. Among some groups the "knocking out" of teeth was a popular practice for both sexes, though perhaps seen more extensively in men. In addition to these self-"destructive" activities symbolic of loss, there was frantic lamentation, wailing, and rending of the garments.

The East Indian practice of Sati was a variation of the mourning reaction expected of wives. A Sati signified a woman who was considered good and virtuous if she sought death on the decease of her husband and was burned along with his corpse. This suicide of the widow through burning on the death of her husband was declared illegal in British India in 1829.

The aborigines of Australia also evolved a timetable for mourning activities. A widower mourned his wife for three moons. Every second night he wailed and recounted her good qualities, lacerated his forehead with his nails until the blood flowed down his cheeks, and covered his head and face with white clay. If he loved her very dearly, he would burn himself across the waist with a red-hot piece of bark. A widow mourned for her husband for twelve moons. She cut her hair, burned her thighs with hot ashes pressed with a piece of bark, until she screamed with agony. Every second night she wailed and recounted his good qualities, and lacerated her forehead until blood flowed down her cheeks. Children in mourning for their parents also lacerated their brows. Parents of a deceased child lacerated themselves extensively—the father beating and cutting his head with a tomahawk, and the mother burning her breasts and abdomen with a fire stick. This was done for hours every day until the mourning period was over.

In some Australian tribes, after burning their backs, arms, and faces with red-hot brands, large ulcers appeared. When these were present the mourners flung themselves on the grave, tore out their hair, rubbed earth over their heads and bodies in profusion, and ripped open their ulcers until their blood mingled with the earth.

The identification with the dead is clearly brought out in direct fashion among Australian tribes where the mourner actually jumps into the grave before the corpse has been placed in it. In other rituals the mourner applies his severed hair or blood to the corpse directly for burial with it. While this is ongoing, the mourners cover their bodies with clay or earth. The ancient Jews also covered themselves with ashes as they sat close to the ground during the shibah period.

In general, Frazer notes that, despite variations, the basic pattern is very similar from one group to another, and these particular types of mourning rituals are found the world over and throughout time.

The mourning practices of the ancient Hebrews and the Australian aborigines show many similarities. These similarities can be observed throughout a considerable portion of mankind, from the most highly civilized nations of antiquity down to the still existing "primitives" of our times.

What is the meaning of these practices? Frazer discusses several possibilities. The first relates to the fear of the ghost of the departed and the necessity to demonstrate sufficient sorrow and grief so as to avoid offending the dead. The application of white clay to the mourner's body is manifestly an identification with the dead so as to render the mourner more conspicuous in his mourning. The second possibility Frazer discusses is the need to please or benefit the ghost through the offerings of tears, blood, hair, and lacerations. This averts the wrath of the dead, and mutual help and protection may result between living and dead. Frazer favors the third explanation which suggests that by offering hair and blood, symbols of the owner's strength and vitality, the dead are supplied with a source of energy (blood) and strength (hair) and thus continue to survive. These widespread practices of cutting the body and shearing the hair of the living seem to Frazer to be means of gratifying and benefitting the spirit of the departed. This connects with the belief in survival of the human soul after death, a belief that was the basis for the extensive death rituals of the ancient Egyptian religion. The soul is thus strengthened and made more comfortable through the activities of the living mourners. Frazer's explanations, though interesting, seem incomplete from the intrapsychic point of view.

Morgenstern (1966) has studied the rites of birth, marriage, and death among the Semites. He shows that the various rituals of the Orthodox Jews of today parallel those of the other Semites of today and of the past. In the main they deal with the basic concept that death is not the end. If the living discharge their duty at and after death, the dead may live in Paradise; if the survivors are remiss in the discharge of this duty, the soul continues on, but in a state of suffering in the "nether world." The degree of faithfulness and devotion with which the relatives perform their memorial duties determines the suffering of the soul. The dead, however, have power to enforce their demands and the living recognize and fear this power which relates to the fear of the vengeance of the ghost. The fear of the ghost, according to Morgenstern, underlies the ceremonies of death, burial, and mourning. More basic, perhaps, is the idea that death is not final—there is no end, there is no nothingness. In other words, total helplessness and nothingness do not occur. Immortality and eternity exist, but in different forms. Absolute separation does not occur.

To the psychoanalyst, the rending of the garments directly symbolizes the rent in the psychic organization as a result of the object loss. The particular objects for whom one must rend one's clothing directly refer to the pain and loss produced by the death of those objects. The length of time the rent clothing must be worn symbolizes the length of the mourning for the dead object. The anthropologists present the myths and explanations relating to the departed and their existence in another state. The psychoanalyst interprets these prescriptions from the point of view of their intrapsychic meaning. In this way, the intrapsychic meaning helps us understand the external behavior.

Jewish Ambivalent Attitude Toward the Dead

Lorand (1947) has reminded us that the Jewish practice of naming a child after a dead relative, but never after a living one, is a further demonstration of an ambivalent attitude toward the dead. "On the one hand, it expresses the longing for the deceased relative, and on the other, the tendency to expiate because of fear of revenge on the part of the deceased" (p. 242).

The name is identified with the person represented by it. By naming a child after the deceased, the soul of the deceased is kept alive. Lorand further notes that the Jewish custom of changing the name of a very sick person is intended to deceive the malevolent spirits, thus preventing further harm of the invalid by the demons. However, at times, an additional name of a benevolent ancestor is taken in order to neutralize this malevolent force, or a name addition of Chaim or Chaia, meaning life in Hebrew, is given to secure positive divine intervention. This fear of the dead among the Jews indicates the presence of afterlife in Judaic belief and is similar to religious beliefs the world over and throughout time. The internal meaning of the fear of the dead will be discussed shortly.

Identification with the Dead

The psychoanalyst, with his knowledge and appreciation of the unconscious, can see in these practices many mechanisms which are useful adaptations in handling internal tensions through external activities. Identification with the lost object is one way of retaining aspects of the lost object, through structuralization in the ego. Active mastery and control are other techniques to handle feelings of helplessness in the face of permanent separation and loss in time and space. The religious conceptions and ritual institutions fulfill critical integrative functions in the society that parallel those of the individual intrapsychically.

The identification with the object that has externally died can be seen in many of the death, burial, and mourning rituals. The identification with the deceased may proceed to the point where the survivor begins to actually resemble the lost person in one respect or another, an observation first noted by Freud. In the pathological anniversary reactions that the clinician observes, there is further evidence of the identification with the deceased or lost object and the ways in which this state may give rise to severe symptoms at specific times (see chapters 8 and 10).

In the Judaic mourning rituals we note visible evidence of this immediate identification with the dead object. The rites seem to convey the meaning that the mourner himself is dead. He is covered with ashes (earth, dust), he is cut (his clothing), he can have no pleasures, he sits and lies close to the ground, he cannot engage in earthly activities—in other words, he is made aware of the feelings related to death and what the dead may themselves experience on being removed from life. This identification reinforces the idea that death is not the end but a transitional state. Death, however, is regarded as a punishment, despite the ideas of Paradise and resurrection.

Durkheim, in *The Elementary Forms of the Religious Life* (1915), devotes a section of his monograph to mourning. He classifies the mourning rites as abstentions, interdictions, and positive acts. As already described above, the positive acts in the Australian aborigines, for example, consist of bloody incisions of the thighs, cutting of bodily hair, smearing the body with clay or cinders. Groups of men and women sit on the ground weeping, lamenting, and occasionally urinating. Specific rites vary with age, sex, kinship, and social importance of the individual. Again, the similarity of the Australian rites with some of those of Orthodox Judaism is striking, although the conscious rationale and basic explanations are different.

Durkheim believes that the mourning rites are not the spontaneous expression of individual emotion, but a duty imposed by the group. Thus one weeps not simply because of sadness but because one is forced to weep. "It is a ritual attitude which he is forced to adopt out of respect for custom, but which is, in a large measure, independent of his affective state. Moreover, this obligation is sanctioned by mythical or social penalties" (p. 443).

For example, if a relative does not mourn according to custom, the soul follows upon his steps and kills him. In other instances, society does not leave it to the religious forces alone to punish the negligent; it intervenes directly and reprimands the offender. From where comes this obligation? Manifestly the motives say the dead wish to be lamented, and by refusing them this tribute of sorrow the living offend them. The only way of preventing the anger of the dead is to conform. The psychoanalyst, again, can view these explanations of Durkheim as externalizations of the internal unconscious ambivalent motives. The mourner, concerned with his own death, wishes to be remembered, mourned, and kept within the group, and so handles this internal anxiety through external modes and means. However, culturally constituted mechanisms and practices, through derived and related to internal processes, have their own significance as well.

Melanie Klein (1935, 1940) has indicated that conflicts around aggression are always present in normal as well as pathological mourning. She postulated depressive, paranoid, and manic defenses as aspects of mourning. Aggression toward the dead person is quite prevalent even though this may be overlaid by feelings of grief. The sources of aggression are multiple and may be related to earliest developmental processes. The reproaches against the deceased give rise to internal reproaches which can be manifested by self-reproaches. If these self-reproaches are projected to the outside, the reproach comes from an external malevolent force; thus the fear of the dead, ghosts, spirits, and so on. In some ways, this fear of the dead has paranoid qualities. The dead become the potential persecutors and thus reparations are required to mollify and satisfy the dead. Thus earlier death wishes predispose the mourner to the notion that he has been responsible for the death. This gives rise to increased feelings of sorrow and guilt and the fear and need of punishment and deprivation. So deprivations may be part of the mourning ritual and ceremony, and fear of the dead a significant element of the externalization of the fear of punishment.

The social significance of mourning rites in dealing with the emotions and anxieties accompanying the loss of one of the group's members has been discussed by several writers, including Durkheim. Individuals are collectively brought together, put in close relationship to each other, share a common emotional and mental state, and in the mourning situation achieve a degree of comfort which compensates the original loss. They weep together, they hold one another, they proclaim their pain together, and the group mourning assists the group in maintaining its integrity and cohesiveness in spite of the loss of one of its members. The communication of common grief and pain solidifies the group, permits hope, and allows continuity to gradually take over. This social psychological understanding of group mourning and its adaptational significance parallels and can facilitate the intrapsychic adaptations of the internal personal mourning process.

After the mourning is over, the individual and the group, calmed by the mourning itself, regain confidence, feel relieved of powerful pressures, have a reestablished equilibrium, and life goes on. If this mourning adaptation does not occur, we may get individual and/or social pathological consequences.

As mentioned above, the life-long postmourning observances are a significant part of Judaic practices. These ritualized death anniversary remembrances are unusual in that they continue throughout the life of the survivor. Some specific laws related to this ceremony are the following.

The Laws Concerning the Fast on the Day of Yahrzeit

1. It is a religious duty to fast every year on the day when one's father or mother died in order to stir oneself to repentence, to examine his deeds on that day, and repent about them, and because of this his father and mother will be elevated in Paradise.

He must always fast on the anniversary. It is customary to light a twenty-four-hour Yahrzeit candle.

2. The fast is always on the day of death even in the first year. If a few days had elapsed between the death and the burial, the first fast is observed on the anniversary of the burial, but in subsequent years on the anniversary of the death. On the anniversary he must say Kaddish.

3. If one is unaware of the day of his father's or his mother's death, he should select a certain day to keep the anniversary thereon; but he must not encroach upon the rights of others with regards to the Kaddish.

The light which burns during the entire seven days of initial mourning, the shibah, is rekindled at every Yahrzeit—a constant reminder of the dead on the part of the living. The prayer most associated with mourning, the Kaddish, however, has little relation to the dead. Originally, it had no connection with the dead but was read at the close of theological discourse. Its theme, the surrender to the will and decision of God, alludes to Messianic hope. From the Yeshiva, the house of learning, the Kaddish passed to the synagogue where it is recited at least seven times daily. When first introduced as a prayer for the dead it was reserved for the death of a scholar after the expiration of the shibah period. In the course of time it was recited with every death, as well as during the synagogue services and after scholarly dissertations of Talmudic learning. The recitation of the Kaddish for eleven months after the death of a parent is believed to exercise a redeeming influence on behalf of the departed—the gates of Paradise would be flung open and the hope of resurrection and the coming of the Messianic are expressed.

The language of the Kaddish is Aramaic, this being the language spoken and understood by most Jews at the time of its composition. The Kaddish is recited by the son for the deceased father or mother for the full eleven-month period. Where no son remains it is not unusual for the daughter or a close relative to recite the Kaddish daily in memory of the deceased. In some communities the Kaddish is recited for a thirty-day period when one mourns a son, daughter, brother, sister, or spouse.

On the anniversary of the death, according to the Hebrew

date, the Yahrzeit is observed. The Kaddish is recited, the special lamp is kindled and burns for twenty-four hours. The anniversary mourner must abstain from all pleasures and amusements on this day as he did during mourning; some mourners also fast on that day. It was the custom for scholars to assemble on the Yahrzeit anniversary of their teacher at his graveside, to be followed later by a period of study. Yahrzeit may be observed for any relative or friend but it is meant primarily for parents. Its observance takes place in three locations: the home, the synagogue, and the cemetery. Yahrzeit observances at the home include fasting, lighting the twenty-four-hour Yahrzeit candle, the study of some aspect of religious life, and the donation of money to a charity. Yahrzeit synagogue observances include participation in all of the synagogue services for the entire day with the recitation of Kaddish at every service from the congregation. The cemetery Yahrzeit observance is the traditional time for the annual visit to the grave where psalms and special prayers are recited. Various customs have arisen regarding the proper times for visiting the graves of close relatives. These include, in addition to the Yahrzeit, days of calamity or of decisive moments, on the concluding days of shibah and Shleoshim, on fast days; for example, Tisha B'av before the High Holy Days, and on other holidays. There is no regulation as to the annual visitation and complete disregard are to be avoided.

The Yahrzeit ritual was clearly borrowed centuries ago from the non-Jewish communities in which the Jews lived. It is in fact the only Jewish ritual which has no Hebrew name (Kertzer, 1961). Gaster (1955) has pointed out that the anniversary of the death derives its name, *Yahrzeit*, among the Ashkenazic Jews from the German term *Jahrzeit*. Among the Sephardic Jews the anniversary is called *Annos* from the Spanish. Abrahams (1958) has written that the annual Yahrzeit was probably of Persian origin, but in the Middle Ages the popularity of the custom was strengthened by imitation of the Catholic masses. Aside from the fast, two principal rites distinguished this annual commemoration of the dead: (1) the Kaddish prayer, which was not due to Christian influence; and (2) the Yahrzeit light, which was kept burning for the twenty-four hours on every anniversary of the death. This light seems definitely to be of Christian origin. The very term *Yahrzeit* was used in the Church in regard to the masses in memory of the dead. The association of a flame with the soul is, however, pre-Christian.

Reik (1964), citing Reinach, traces the origin of the Kaddish as a prayer for the dead back to the Jewish colony in Alexandria, Egypt. A reference in support of this thesis is made to the second book of Maccabees, dating from 124 B.C. and composed in Egypt by a Pharisee Jew whose sect believed in saying prayers for the dead. Reik's theory about the Kaddish states that

> there was originally among the Hebrew tribes a strong ancestor worship and devotion to the dead, later for the dead, as in ancient Egypt. Those acts and rites were energetically repressed by Moses and the prophets. The old beliefs and their underlying drives did not vanish, but continued to live subterraneously and developed some activity in the darkness. Strengthened and helped by the new sojourn in Egypt, these consciously forgotten and forbidden rites returned from the repressed. As an effect of the breakthrough the new—or, rather, old—function of a prayer for the dead appeared in the transformation of the kaddish into a mourner's prayer [1964, p. 37].

Thus, "The new (or rather renewed) function of the prayer for the dead was by and by changed into the practice of a commemorative prayer" (1964, p. 38). Reik further suggests that gravestones are also related to the idea that the deceased is not completely dead, that a soul exists. Not only are tomb- or gravestones and monuments commemorative of the buried and their "dwelling place," but the stones also are a protection of the living from the envy or hostility of the dead. By putting those stones on their abode, the dead were prevented from escaping. Lehrman (1949) notes, however, that the practice of erecting tombstones by the Jews began when the Jews copied existing Greek and Roman customs. From a psychoanalytic point of view, however, Reik's hypothesis is understandable as the ambivalence toward the deceased which, if not handled internally, could require external assistance.

Beside the individual Yahrzeit ceremonies celebrating the anniversary of the date of death, there is a public commemoration of the dead known as Yizkor. The Hebrew word *Yizkor* means "may God remember" (Gaster, 1955). The Yizkor service appears to have originated in Western Germany in the twelfth century and its primary purpose was to commemorate the Jewish martyrs slain during the First and Second Crusades. The custom of commemorating martyrs by reciting their names and praying for their repose was borrowed directly from the Catholic Church which started this practice in the fourth century. In later times, the Christian prayer was called Memento after the opening word of the prayer and one that is identical to the word *Yizkor* (Gaster, 1955).

Many parallels are found between the Christian and Jewish service, which provides evidence for the adoption of this Catholic ceremony by the Jewish community. In later times the Yizkor service became connected with the redemption of the dead through charitable gifts. Gaster (1955) related this to the ancient belief that unless something was done by the living to insure the dead of their repose, the spirits would roam the earth and torment the living. Gaster interprets this to mean symbolically, that if the past be forgotten, ignored, or the connection with it negligently dismissed, the past will rise up and obtrude itself upon the present. When the dead past is fully integrated with the present, it does not threaten a return that is unwelcome. Psychoanalytically we would say the return of the repressed cannot occur if repression is fully lifted or if it never occurred.

The Yizkor prayer which begins with "May God remember the Soul of my revered"—then the Hebrew name of the departed is mentioned—"who is gone to his repose" is recited at four memorial services associated with annual festivals (Yom Kippur, Sukkoth, Passover, and Shabuoth). During Yizkor all worshippers whose parents are living leave the synagogue. However, the Yizkor prayer is said for all Jewish dead, especially parents, grandparents, mates, children, and siblings. It is accompanied by a charitable contribution to aid in the redemption of the departed when Yizkor is recited. Yizkor is recited throughout one's entire lifetime, just as Yahrzeit is observed throughout the life of the survivor. The remembrance of the dead is never relinquished. It continues on throughout life.

The resurrection of the dead is a definitely acknowledged principle of Orthodox Judaism (Sperka, 1961). References can be found to the future life. The soul is conceived as external and the Biblical expression "gathered unto his people" is an indication that death is not extinction. Maimonides had expouded on the dogma of resurrection—man's existence does not end with death, but a new eternal and spiritual life is avowed for the soul.

Not all of the Judaic laws concerning death, burial, mourning, and anniversaries of remembrance have been noted above. It will be seen, however, from this sample, that the Jewish ritual is very explicit and covers many contingencies. One may ask why there is a necessity for such detailed observances and mourning prescriptions. It is my contention that these regulations arose from an empirical base of experience and one anchored to the real need to take account of the necessity for perception, notation, and the work of the mourning process as well as the awareness of anniversary phenomena, particularly as these relate to perpetuity. Furthermore, the fact that extensive, periodic memorial services continue during the entire life of the survivors seems to substantiate the idea that in Orthodox Judaism there is a cult of the dead ancestors that parallels the anniversary reactions in the individual mourner's intrapsychic functioning, especially where the anniversary phenomena are indicative of incompleted or abnormal mourning (see chapters 8 and 10).

Although the death of a close relative or friend is a personal internal and external loss, it requires internal mourning work. It may be observed that the Judaic timetable, as described above, corresponds to the stages of the intrapsychic mourning process, including the various affective reactions accompanying each stage, that were described in chapter 1, "Mourning and Adaptation."

This cultural-religious system evolved a series of public-private externally constituted mechanisms to handle the individual crisis resulting from the death of a significant person. The cultural system, in order to facilitate this internal adaptational process and to emphasize the necessity for the mourning work, demands certain external behavior of the individuals involved in this internal adaptational process. Culturally constituted defenses through ritualization via a system of stipulated anniversary reactions individually performed in a culturally accepting environment that constantly reminds the survivor of this prior loss attempt to regulate the individual's intrapsychic tension relevant to working through of the loss. After the acute and chronic mourning phases have been "worked through" the annual anniversary commemoration responses handle, if possible, residuals of mourning that remain as well as the conscious memory of the loss and of the object. External prescriptions alone do not accomplish the internal "working through" task of mourning; however, in some instances, they may facilitate this internal process. The psychoanalytic theory of mourning allows us to understand the rationale for rituals and ceremonials and their possible adaptive significance with greater clarity.[2]

The identification of the mourner with the dead seems demonstrated by such requirements as absence of libidinal gratifications, sitting and lying on the ground, wearing of ashes, wearing clothing that is unchanged, and so on, during the mourning period. In addition to this identification with the dead object there is an awareness of the internal and external separation; for example, cutting of the clothing when mourning begins, and regulations prohibiting remarriage and marriage while mourning. Regressive behavior, culturally permitted and ordered, can also be observed in some of the rituals (e.g., the mourner's meal of hard-boiled eggs and circular lentils, prepared by others).

The anniversary, annually observed with a day of fasting, prayer, and lighting a candle, relates to separation, mourning, and survival in the present, as well as in the "hereafter"—Paradise. If one remembers, then one insures survival of the departed mother and father, and of oneself. The reality provisos facilitate the internal adaptations to the loss and seek to avoid conscious denial of it, although this can occur even in individuals who externally perform the mourning rites. That there may be unconscious denial, splitting, or disavowal of the loss and what it represents has been commented upon by a number of authors and can be seen in many clinical situations.

Krupp (1962) has noted that "cultural action patterns in

[2] Monica Wilson distinguished between ritual, which is primarily a religious action directed to secure the blessings of some mystical power, and ceremonial, which is an elaborate conventional form used for the expression of feelings and not just confined to religious occasions (1957).

the form of mourning rituals allow for intensive working through for society and individual object loss" (pp. 63–64).

He adds another dimension to the adaptive significance of public rituals; that is, a group process augmenting the individual mourning process and so facilitating social adaptation to the loss.

THE RITES OF PASSAGE AND MOURNING

Van Gennep (1908) in describing the critical stages of the life cycle of the individual, beginning with birth and going on to puberty, marriage, parenthood, and finally death, notes that though tied to physiological events, they are in fact socially defined. For example, there is a social return from childbirth, a social parenthood, a social marriage, and a social puberty, which may not necessarily coincide with the biological or physiological situation. Thus, social puberty may not occur simultaneously with physical puberty. He found that entry into and exit from these critical statuses or stages are always marked by ritual and ceremony which he calls the "rites de passage." These "passing through" rites follow a more or less standard pattern. They begin with *rites of separation*, which remove the individual from his environment or social field. He then is a participant in *transition rites*, waiting to enter the next status or social field. Finally through the *rites of incorporation*, he is accepted into a new status or role and is so confirmed by the society. The rites include elements directed to the person's success in his new status; for example, marriage rites are concerned with fertility, the ritual of birth with the safety and health of the infant and his fortunate progress through life, and the mortuary ritual with the establishment of the status of the dead person as a revered ancestor. The symbolism of transition rituals is often that of rebirth. Van Gennep writes, "Rites of separation are prominent in funeral ceremonies, rites of incorporation at marriages. Transition rites may play an important part, for instance, in pregnancy, betrothal, and initiation; or they may be reduced to a minimum in adoption, in the delivery of a second child in remarriage, or in the passage from the second to the third age group" (1908, p. 11).

The person who enters a status at variance with the one

previously held becomes "sacred" to the others who remain in the profane state. The new condition calls for rites which eventually incorporate the individual back into the group and return him to the customary routines of life. The transitional period with its rites of passage cushions the disturbance associated with the changes in the life of the individual and in the group. Van Gennep applied his system to the understanding of the periodic changes associated with natural phenomena. Thus, ceremonies which accompany the changes of the year, season, or month are also rites of passage. New Year ceremonies include rites of separation from the old (winter) and the coming of the new (spring). This parallels death and birth, as Eliade (1958) has observed. The old year is often depicted as an old dying man, while the new year is seen as a joyful, energetic infant. Van Gennep (1908) describes rites of passage associated with pregnancy and childbirth, birth and childhood, initiation at puberty, betrothal and marriage, funerals, the seasons, phases of the moon, changes in the year, and changes associated with vegetation.

For groups, as well as for individuals, life itself means to separate and to be reunited, to change form and condition, to die and to be reborn. It is to act and to cease, to wait and rest, and then to begin acting again, but in a different way. And there are always new thresholds to cross: the thresholds of summer and winter, of a season or a year, of a month or a night; the thresholds of death and that of the afterlife.

Similarities and resemblances may be noted between entire rites or specific aspects of the different "passages"—initiation at puberty, baptism, marriage, birth, death. However, a typical pattern is followed for each rite.

Eliade (1958) differentiates the periodic recurrence (the eternal present) from the nonperiodic recurrence. Every ritual has the character of happening now, at this very moment. The contemporary occurrence is not remembered, it is re-presented and becomes actual. But through this periodic reoccurrence there is a restoration to bring back time, and thus time can be created anew, it can be regenerated. The cycle continues eternally even though it has different phases. This longing for eternity parallels the longing for paradise or immortality.

Mourning is a transitional period for the survivors. They

enter through the rites of separation and emerge from this "transition" through rites of reintegration into society (rites of the lifting of the mourning). The transitional period for the living has its counterpart in the transitional period of the deceased. The termination for the one coincides with the supposed termination for the other; that is, the incorporation of the deceased into the world of the dead in the afterlife parallels the mourner's reincorporation into the society of the living.

During mourning the living mourners and the deceased mourners constitute special groups, each of which are treated in specific ways and of whom certain behaviors may be expected. How soon the living mourners leave the "special" group depends upon the closeness of their relationship to the dead and the cultural practices followed. Thus, mourning requirements differ and are based on degrees of kinship and relationship, and are systematized by each people according to the way of calculating that kinship. The rites which lift all the regulations (such as special dress) and prohibitions of mourning, are considered rites of reintegration into the life of the society as a whole or into a restricted group; they may be of the same order as the rites of reintegration for a novice during puberty.

Using the mourning rituals of the Jews described earlier, we can see specific examples of the more general observations and statements just mentioned. During mourning we have seen suspension of social life for all of those affected by it. The length of the period increases with the closeness of the relationship to the deceased (e.g., parents), and with the higher social status of the deceased (e.g., for a rabbi or learned teacher), the suspension affects the entire society with public mourning and holiday.

The funeral transition stage is divided into several parts, and in the postburial period its extension is systematized in the form of commemorations (e.g., in Jewish ritual the first three days, the first week, the first thirty days, the first year, and annual anniversaries of the death date thereafter). Thus the repeated anniversary rites are a continuation, albeit somewhat modified, of the earlier commemoration. These anniversary patterns can be seen for death, birth, weddings, and sometimes for puberty initiation rites in different societies. All are related to separation and the memory of it, through the privately constituted anniversary or the culturally constituted community holiday.

For the dead (who are also mourners and separated) there are corresponding rites of separation, transition, and incorporation or reintegration. Thus, death rituals include rites of passage for the dead as well as for the living mourners. The journey to the "other world" and the entrance into it comprise a series of rites of passage whose details depend on the distance, topography, and requirements of that world. If the deceased must make a voyage, his survivors are careful to equip him with the material objects he will need, including the magical religious amulets and signs he will require for a safe journey and a favorable reception and admittance once he arrives at his destination. Many customs are found in connection with these rites of separation, transition, and eventual incorporation of the dead into the world of the dead. The Egyptians made this a cornerstone of their religion, the Greeks a significant part of their mythology.

In the mourning process we have internal psychic work that parallels the external rites of separation, transition, incorporation, and integration of the living mourner into the world of the living. These stages have been described in chapter 1, "Mourning and Adaptation." Thus we have both private and internal and external mechanisms for the living mourner, social rites for the community, and assumed rites of passage for the deceased.

James has noted, in his monograph, *Prehistoric Religion* (1957), that prehistoric belief centered in and developed around the most critical and perplexing situations which early men confronted in everyday experience—birth, death, and survival in a precarious environment. The pressure of events in the external world and in human affairs, the perpetual struggle for existence and survival here and in the hereafter, the innumerable frustrations and awe-inspiring experiences, often completely outside of men's control and comprehension, created a tension for the relief of which ways and means had to be found. Once a ritual technique had been devised to handle the emotional strain, it became established and developed to meet new demands and maintain equilibrium in the context of a social structure and religious organization. Rituals became associated with the life-giving processes—fecundity, maternity, generative and birth events—but also with the disturbing and disintegrating phenomena of disease and death. Again these life-giving processes can be seen to be associated with change and separation—crises in the broad sense.

Through collective and personal rituals, techniques were evolved which aimed at establishing a workable relationship with the source of life, power, and abundance, to overcome the disabilities of death, sterility, and illness in the individual, and to produce stability and equilibrium in the society. By means of symbols and rites, energies were directed into activities which exercised an integrative function by enabling man individually and collectively to meet his crises with confidence, trust, and hope by assimilating life-giving strength, allaying his anxieties, and renewing his aspirations.

Thus, at critical junctures in the career of the individual from the cradle to the grave and its aftermath, and in the sequence of the seasons, especially at the turn of the year, the chances and changes of mortal life have been unified, controlled, and fortified by supernatural forces believed to govern the course of events and human destinies.

Specifically in regards to death, James (1957) notes that the cult of the dead is related to the sky religion which involves a celestial deity and afterlife. Death was not the end of life; the soul was immortal, although invisible. The fear of the dead, the elaborate efforts to preserve the corpse, and the extensive prayers and rituals dealing with the dead, tombs, and so on, all seemed to support the notion of immortality.

The rhythm of nature was a crucial factor in survival and subsistence. The food supply and means of livelihood depended upon the vagaries of the environment and its climatic conditions. Every human group lived in a perpetual state of anxiety and uncertainty lest the breeding and hunting seasons or planting times and harvests failed. From the beginning man did not rely entirely upon his own initiative and ingenuity to ensure that his needs were met. When nature appeared to be in the balance at the crucial and critical seasons, he performed the rites prescribed for the control of the growth of the crops, or the increase of the flocks and herds at regular intervals. These rituals and rites subsequently contributed to our knowledge of the world through a form of "secondary autonomy." Thus, the rising and falling of a river (e.g., the Nile), gave rise to time measurements, and these calendrical calculations were related to the phases of the moon which in turn became the times for rites. Mathematics and astronomy were thus derived from the rituals attending the crises regarding food and rebirth. James notes, in his *Seasonal Feasts and Festivals* (1961), that

> as most festivals were agrarian in origin in the first instance they were seasonal and periodic, either fixed or movable, celebrated on a certain day or days at specified times in a calendrical sequence, primarily for the ritual control of the food supply, or as acts of public worship or propitiation of the divine powers in whose honour they were held. In course of time, however, these specifically sacred purposes acquired a more secular character as games . . . and revels were added, and soon they lost much of their earlier religious significance. Moreover, as festivals increased in number and became associated with particular events or gods independent of the seasons, especially under urban conditions and State control, although many of the old rites persisted, and often were carefully preserved, they ceased to be seasonal feasts as such. New festivals were instituted commemorating national, local, religious, political and other occasions, divinities, heroes and saints. . . ." The annual festival having its origin in the seasonal ritual, myth or sacred drama relating to crises of change, separation, loss and rebirth, changed to include commemoration of profane occurrences. [p. 12]

FEASTS AND FESTIVALS

Man has many celebrations and anniversaries. They may occur on a daily, weekly, monthly, yearly, or other less regularly occurring basis. They may deal with fundamental personal crises such as birth, death, marriage, birth of children, onset of puberty, or with political-social-religious-cultural commemorations. Celebrations and anniversaries may commemorate regular predictable events, just as rites and rituals may be available to deal with less predictable crises that involve individuals or the societal group.

Feast and festival are essentially synonymous and are used to describe a religious anniversary that is observed with rejoicing and oral indulgence. More generally, "feast" and "festival" are applied to all such annual ceremonies. The word *holiday* ("holy day"), originally a religious festival, has come to be used to describe any day on which a community or individual is relieved from the obligation of work.

Major religious feasts or festivals are annual and take on an educational and social meaning in addition to their religious significance. Festivals bind a group into a unity transcending family and local ties. On the other hand, there are individual, family, and local anniversaries that have particular meaning only to the specific participants (e.g., birthdays).

In nonurban, land-oriented peoples, the start of hunting, fishing, or plowing seasons and the first-fruit and harvest times are occasions for festivals. These center around food and fertility crises. Although time-related, these occasions more likely were function-oriented. Civic holidays usually are connected with birthdays of significant leaders (e.g., Lincoln, Washington); religious leaders' births, circumcisions, or deaths; for example, Christmas, the Feast of the Circumcision (New Year's Day), Easter (resurrection), Good Friday, or with remembering the war dead (e.g., Memorial Day). In more recent years special groups are honored with special holidays, such as Labor Day, Mother's Day, and so on.

Some holidays are not characterized by specific duties or abstentions in contrast to religious holidays which may require fasting or denial of other biological gratifications; for example, the fast on Yom Kippur, the Day of Atonement, the Good Friday fast, originally for forty hours but extended to the forty-day period of Lent, and the month-long Ramadan fast—all related to penance and denial as a means of purification. Magical, ethical, and religious motivations have been described as the rationalized basis for the denial of bodily wishes and needs. Ghandi, in more recent times, used the fast as a means of political resistance. Complete abstention is rare, although in Orthodox Judaism this is required on Yom Kippur. Until very recent times, Roman Catholics were required to avoid meat in all forms every Friday, in memory of Christ's crucifixion.

Aside from the growing commercialism associated with holidays, all such events are involved with commemoration of something past, that at one time was meaningful to the religion, the country, the local group, the family, or the individual. The occasions connected with joy and pleasure are usually recalled with little difficulty, but those days or times associated with trauma, pain, grief, or anxiety are frequently forgotten or disassociated affectively. Especially prone to such forgetting are days connected with death or mourning. Perhaps this accounts for the necessity to ritualize mourning anniversaries.

Several anthropological studies have been made of anniversary mourning reactions. A notable contribution, however, is a recently published report of the contemporary Diegueno anniversary mourning ceremony held in honor of a person one year after his death (Woodward, 1968). This tradition, persisting since pre-Spanish times, is interpreted as a function of adjustability characterizing the anniversary complex.

In Mexico, the second of November is commemorated as the Day of the Dead. On the eve of it, women prepare a kind of bread decorated with a skull of sugar and the name of a person beneath it. Flowers of tissue paper are also prepared for the dead. The house is decorated with flowers. In the principal room of the house an altar is improvised, at the front of which offerings for the deceased person or persons of the family are laid. These are mainly tidbits in which predominate the dishes preferred by the deceased while living. The children of the house wander about eating "death's-heads" and skeletons of chocolate and sugar.

Shortly before midnight of the Day of the Dead, pilgrimages are made to the cemeteries. The graves are covered with flowers. Candles are lighted around them, making for a colorful night-time scene. Family groups begin their night's vigil, eating and exchanging recollections of the deceased. At midnight the women kneel down and the men begin to intone funereal eulogies of the dead, while the bell tolls for the dead. Many mournful, contemplative silences occur. Near the cemetery, a mass is celebrated in honor of the dead at the local church. If families have no dead or their relatives have been buried for more than three years, they will confine themselves to lighting candles on an arch in front of the church where they deposit their offerings. For three years, according to belief, something of the deceased remains in the grave, and so offerings are carried there. After three years, the spirit of the dead person ceases to have a personality of its own and merges into a single immense spirit, to which offerings are made in front of the church (Verissimo, 1962).

Frazer has also written of anniversary reactions. In Part III of *The Golden Bough*, "The Dying God" (1911), he describes the custom of putting the chief, king, or his proxy, to death after he had reigned for a specific period (e.g. one year). The New Year festival was the time at which this regicide occurred, or in some instances, the time when the king's power was formally renewed. There may be annual abdications of kings and their places temporarily taken by nominal sovereigns. At the close of the short reign, the nominal sovereign is not killed, but instead a mock-execution may occur—a reminder of the past when the king was put to death.

In "Adonis, Attis, Osiris" (1914) Frazer notes that the changes of the seasons were explained by the life and death of gods. By performing certain religious acts, man could aid the god in his struggle with death. Subsequently, a specific animal was killed once and only once a year as a symbolic killing of a god, even though the animal was sacrificed to a god—a pig to Osiris, a horse in Rome, a goat in Athens. These sacrifices were related to spring planting and fall harvesting.

In ancient Mexico, once a year a youth was chosen to represent Tezcatlipoca, the beautiful god of eternal youth. For an entire year, the god representation had as wives four of the loveliest virgins of the empire, all that he could wish for in material and aesthetic needs. But at the end of the year, to the acclamation of all, he went to his sacrificial death before the image of Tezcatlipoca in black stone. The Aztec executioner raised the adolescent's heart in offering and then cast it at the feet of the idol. The multitude in mystic delirium then burst into song and shouting—"beauty is never extinguished, youth never ends" (Verissimo, 1962).

Eliade has addressed himself to the topic of time and holidays from the point of view of the historians of religion and mythology. In *The Sacred and the Profane* (1959b), he differentiates sacred time, the time of festivals, from the profane time of ordinary temporal duration. By means of rites, religious man can pass with a minimum anxiety from ordinary time to sacred time. Sacred time is reversible, as it is indefinitely recoverable,

indefinitely repeatable, and thus does not "pass" as does profane time. With each periodic festival, the participants find the
same periodic time. Hence, sacred or festival time is a circular
time, reversible and recoverable. The year, though a closed
circle of time, had a beginning and an end, but could be reborn
in the form of the new year, thus time could be regenerated.
Eliade believes that the festival is not merely the commemoration of religious-mythical event, but a reactualization of the
event, a regeneration, a rebirth. The New Year coincides with
the first day of creation. The old has passed but the world is
re-created and begins anew. Thus, the sacred calendar annually
repeats the same festivals and we have what Eliade calls the
"eternal return," the sources by which "human existence appears to be saved from nothingness and death."

SUMMARY

In this presentation I have attempted to show the relationship
of culturally constituted defensive systems, manifested through
religious belief systems, to intrapsychic adaptive processes. Specifically chosen to illustrate the possibility that the former are
evolved from the latter during the course of sociocultural evolution were mourning and anniversary processes. The major
psychic trauma and external crisis related to death involves
separation in time and space and the reactions and adjustments
to it. Specific intrapsychic mechanisms in the mourning process
were presented in chapter 1; specific parallel culturally constituted mechanisms and processes related to death are presented
in this essay.

These cultural mechanisms, I believe, were probably derived from the awareness of the intrapsychic needs of the individuals, singly and collectively, and the necessity for achieved
social-psychic equilibrium through institutional regulations.

13
ON ANNIVERSARY SUICIDE AND MOURNING

It is generally accepted that living creatures are involved in two general concerns: the first is to preserve their own existence, and the second is to reproduce themselves. These concerns formed the basis of Freud's (1915) first instinct theory. The relationship between fertility, contraception, and immortality has been previously considered (Pollock, 1972) and is connected with the task of species preservation. The first concern, preserving the existence of the individual, has been discussed by many and from various points of view. Since life is precarious, a number of biological and psychological responses have evolved that serve as protections against dangers that threaten us with injury or death. One function of our sense organs and memory is to protect us from danger. Once we are alerted, protective mechanisms, designed to help us either avoid danger or deal with the effects of trauma, are set in motion. If successful, danger is avoided, coped with, or reacted to in such a fashion as to restitute—as quickly as possible and with a minimum of aftereffect—the so-called homeostatic state of well-being. Emotions and emotional conflict also play their role in this adaptive struggle.

One particular state of feeling about which much has been written but which is still incompletely understood or treated is the state of depression. One might approach the study of depression from the premise that it is a state of alerting and defending, thereby maintaining a state of psychic equilibrium,

This research has been assisted by the support of National Institute of Mental Health Research Grant MH20562 and the Anne Pollock Lederer Research Fund of the Institute for Psychoanalysis of Chicago.

Reprinted from *Depression and Human Existence*, edited by E. James Anthony and Therese Benedek, Boston: Little, Brown, 1975.

or in which withdrawal occurs defensively. Because of its discomfort, questions can be raised about the normality of depression. When one considers pain or anxiety, however, it is not difficult to appreciate the so-called normal defensive aspects of these states of feeling, even if such feelings are uncomfortable. If we can visualize depression as an indication or a symptom of altered equilibrium, we can approach depression as a manifestation of normality, albeit one that may have pathological significance under certain circumstances. Bibring (1953) considered depression an ego affective state in normal, neurotic, and psychotic depression states.

In psychiatry depression is usually considered a disease. A more fruitful approach to our understanding of this reaction may be to examine depression as an indicator or manifestation of disequilibrium and not as a disease per se. Bibring, a pioneer in this approach, notes that depression may occur when one feels helpless, hateful, destructive, lonely, isolated, unloved, weak, inferior, or a failure. These feelings may lead to a diminution of self-esteem and a state of narcissistic imbalance. Bibring writes that the tension between highly charged narcissistic aspirations on the one hand, and the ego's acute awareness of its real or imagined helplessness and inability to fulfill these aims on the other hand, gives rise to depression. Thus, according to Bibring's view, depression is a manifestation of an intrasystemic conflict in the ego and is not primarily determined by a conflict between the ego and the id, superego, or environment. Even in uncomplicated mourning, when there is an actual loss, the resulting tension from the longing and love of the lost object and the awareness that the object is realistically gone and cannot be resurrected reflects intrasystemic disequilibrium. An exacerbation of the grief response, whenever certain perceptions acutely bring the loss and the inability of its retrieval into awareness, can be seen as intrasystemic disruptions. Where there has been an uncompleted or an abnormal mourning process, the ego is vulnerable, and depressive affects may appear.

Depression, as a symptom, may have different precipitating factors; it may have varied antecedent personality configurations; and it may have different outcomes and resolutions, ranging from complete, rapid, and relatively nonrecurrent resolutions without sequelae, to conditions of total despair ending in suicide. Depression cannot be viewed as a single pathological entity, and perhaps it does not have a single unitary explanation for its occurrence. Suicide also need not be considered solely as the manifestation of disease. Just as is true of depression, suicide may be precipitated by many situations in a variety of personality organizations and may have different meanings to the victims.

Karl Abraham (1911, 1916) and Sigmund Freud (1917) very early distinguished between normal and abnormal states of depression and mourning. Their still-valid classic contributions can be summarized in the following way: in melancholia, the great ambivalence toward the introjected object does not allow for the normal instinctual decathexis when the object is lost, and frustration results, as is seen in mourning. To effect some form of resolution, the melancholic person partially regresses to an identification with the object, but a strong sadistic core still remains. In this way, the object may not be lost, and some level of equilibrium may result. In some instances melancholia spontaneously resolves itself; however, the vulnerability to recurrence still exists, and when specific precipitating circumstances reappear, the pathological state may again become manifest. In the earlier ideas of Abraham and Freud we find the suggestion that latent sadism can become manifest. When this sadism is directed against the internalized object- and self-representations, which previously were identified with the lost or frustrating object, the outcome may be suicide. In such cases suicide may be viewed as one outcome of pathological mourning. I have previously discussed the adaptive significance of mourning (see chapter 1) and have indicated that if the mourning process does not go on to completion, the arrest at an intermediate stage resembles pathological mourning. I have also suggested that anniversary reactions are manifestations of either uncompleted or deviant mourning processes. This distinction is important with regard to therapeutic management and outcome (see chapters 6, 7, and 8).

The identification inside the ego with the internalized representation of the lost or abandoning object makes the ego-self the target for the aggressive discharge, with resulting self-destruction, in the form of suicide, psychotic disintegration, or somatic dysfunction and change. The hostility and rage toward the internal object-representation and the earlier self-representations may be manifested in the feeling of self-depreciation, self-degradation, and depression. The classic explanation of suicide is the murder of the ego-self-contained object representation. Abraham, studying the self-accusations of his patients, noted their similarity to feelings that earlier had been directed against the object that the patient had internalized. One might say that the internalization that had occurred much earlier was later reexternalized and that only late in the pathological process did the feelings return to the ego-self. Freud pointed out that the actual death of a meaningful figure was not a prerequisite for melancholia, although such an event could act as the trigger of the melancholic state in the vulnerable victim. Thus the precipitating factor could set in motion a state of disequilibrium during which the underlying predisposing pathological state, stemming from childhood, emerges. Menninger (1933) described this process as a three-fold wish: (1) the wish to kill the introjected object; (2) the wish to be killed as the death penalty for the murderous wish; and (3) the wish to die. More current theoretical considerations modify this formulation to reflect our understanding of regression of the ego to early fragmented states with defective reality testing and the expression of early unneutralized aggressive impulses.

Sandler and Joffe (1965) call attention to the lack of emphasis on aggression or (I would say) hostility in Bibring's ideas and seek to link his explanations with the earlier intersystemic conflict formulations. They believe that

> the experiencing of mental pain normally mobilizes aggression which is then directed against what is felt to be the source of the pain. This aggression can be used to alter either the . . . self or . . . circumstances, so that the degree of mental pain which is being suffered is diminished . . . if the child feels impotent in the face of the pain, and cannot discharge his aggression, the accumulation of undischarged aggression may reinforce the painful state so that he is forced into a state of helpless resignation [p. 93].

These authors indicate that impotent and ineffectual rage that has not been expressed is frequently observed in depressive reactions. "It is an over-simplification to say, however, that this aggression has simply been turned against the self *via identification with the hated object*" (p. 93). More frequently observed in children is either the direct inhibition of aggression or the direction of anger against the actual self, which is disliked or hated because it is unsatisfactory. Anger with the frustrating object (or introject) and displacement of aggression from self to object and vice versa may occur. Hostility directed against the self is still consonant with the intrasystemic conflict postulated for suicide.

Friedlander (1940), classified suicidal patients into the melancholic type described by Abraham and Freud and the addictive type in whom the wish to die seems more pleasurable than tolerating the tension and despair of living. This tension, characteristic of early states of ego integration and following the pleasure principle, demands immediate discharge and gratification. Death is viewed as the pleasurable release from an unsubsiding craving and tension. Friedlander (1940) asserts that addictive suicides do not have the hostile conflicts of the melancholics but are more severely regressed in their reality operations as they relate to actions taken to secure release and gratification. Self-destruction does not appear to be the primary goal of the self-destructive action. These patients are more involved in fantasied reunions with early lost objects and not with the direct and reactive aspects of the ambivalent hostile oral aggressiveness characteristic of the melancholic suicidal patient. The particular means of suicide, as well as the presuicide communication, may give us a clue to the intensity of the desire for reunion or of the hostile destructive wish. Friedlander's addictive suicides long for symbiosis, not destruction. Instead of revenge and retaliation, they seek rejoining through retreat and regression.

Freud, in his essay "Thoughts for the Times on War and Death," written in 1915, two years before "Mourning and Melancholia" (1917), pointed out that "no one believes in his own death" and that "in the unconscious everyone of us is convinced of his own immortality" (p. 289). Thus the act of suicide may be one not of total final destruction of the self but an act manifesting early narcissistic rage and revenge vented on the internalized object- and self-representations, an act symbolizing the wish for reunion in an afterlife in which one lives on in a blissful tension-free existence, or a combination of these motives.

When a normal mourning process occurs, there is either an identification of the mourner with the deceased or, under the traumatic impact of the final separation, earlier identifications that had become quiescent or integrated into the self emerge in more unassimilated and destructive form. Freud noted:

> [W]hen a death has fallen on some person whom we love—a parent or a partner in marriage, a brother or sister, a child, a dear friend . . . our hopes, our pride, our happiness, lie in the grave with him, we will not be consoled, we will not fill the loved one's place. We behave then as if we belonged to the Asra, who must die too when those die whom they love [1915, p. 290].

This reunion with the deceased or continuation of existence after his death has been discussed in chapter 7. Friedman (1910), in his foreword to *On Suicide: Discussions of the Vienna Psychoanalytic Society, 1910*, refers to Freud's discussion of the cavalry officer who became depressed following his mother's death and suffered a fatal accident shortly thereafter. Grief, guilt, and identification were apparent in this case.

Death is primarily perceived as a separation and an instinctual and narcissistic frustration. It can reawaken old concerns dealing with need gratification, rage, guilt, unfulfillment, or idealization. These concerns vary from individual to individual, and obviously will depend upon the psychic maturity, integration, and cohesion of the mourner. However, the identification of the mourner with the mourned may be in evidence, and I believe that even without overt behavioral manifestations there is a bilateral identification. On the one hand, the mourner survives and remains, but internally something has left and is dying. Various mourning rituals and reactions seen as manifestations of this duality of identifications have been described in chapter 12.

When the ego and superego structures are functioning well, the self is relatively cohesive, and reality testing is operating in close accord with reality, the mourning process is completed without difficulty. The process of decathexis takes place, and the reality and finality of the event is eventually accepted. When ego-superego integration has been faulty prior to the death or when the self is partially cohesive and in danger of fragmentation, the mourning process cannot progress, and the identification with the lost object remains as a distinct unassimilated intrapsychic representation moving in tandem with the faulty self-representation. If there is hostile tension inside and between these psychic structures, melancholic symptomatology can appear. If narcissistic and libidinal tension predominates, the wish for regression to the earlier pleasurable symbiotic state may be sought. Either of these situations can result in suicide. When external events occur in a particular temporal-spatial-object contextual relationship that symbolically recapitulates or repeats the earlier unsuccessfully resolved traumatic state, an economic imbalance may result in the unleashing of previously bound sadistic and regressive impulses (related of course to a state of psychic disorganization). The psyche attempts to defend itself against these primitive states, and symptoms occurring at this point are due to the expression of the primitive psychic forces as well as the attempts to defend against these strivings. If these defense maneuvers fail, further regression occurs, and symptoms reflecting concern over self-destruction or actual self-destruction occur. In other words, the intrapsychic consequences of pathological or incomplete mourning precipitate states of disequilibrium that may lead to self-destruction.

CLINICAL DATA

In an attempt to obtain clinical data that might enable me to test some of my ideas about anniversary reactions, I wrote in November 1971 to every member of the American Psychoanalytic Association and to twelve selected institutions specializing in suicide studies, asking them to send me whatever clinical data they had in their records on instances of successful or unsuccessful anniversary suicides, and on situations in which there had been suicidal symptomatology in connection with an anniversary. I was very pleased to obtain 140 clinical protocols from all sections of the country. In the sample clinical reports presented below, minor changes have been made to protect the individuals' identity.

Before turning to the clinical material, I wish to mention Hilgard's (1969) case of the suicide of a forty-three-year-old man the day after his son reached his twelfth birthday. The anniversary suicide coincided with the victim's childhood trauma: the day after his twelfth birthday, his older brother had died suddenly and unexpectedly of encephalitis. The victim, who had become successful after his brother's death, felt guilty and, as an adult, said his success came only as a result of a death. Hilgard points out that he had been aware of his intense jealousy and death wishes against his brilliant, conforming, and scholastically successful brother before his death. The victim himself became a successful criminal lawyer. At his son's birth, the suicide said to a friend, "I probably have less than fifteen years to live." This strange predictive reference to time, I believe, was an indication that the fuse of self-destruction had been lit, to explode fatally on the exact day coinciding with the anniversary repetition of the victim's childhood trauma. Because there are no further data, I cannot speculate about the internal mechanisms underlying the victim's self-destructive act. However, the bipolar identification of the victim is clear. On the one side, he was his brother, who died one day after his brother reached his twelfth birthday. On the other side, he was his son, who became twelve the day before the suicide. As has been found in other anniversary reactions, it might be suggested that the victim had a latent uncompleted and abnormal mourning process that ended with his anniversary suicide.

Sadger notes that "in one family the father shot himself at a certain age; his sons grew up and at the same age, all turned to the same weapon. In such cases I always suspect . . . an identification with the father. . . . Love, or the unsatisfied need for love, remains fundamental" (cited in Friedman, 1910, pp. 75–76). Even the psychoses yield an illustration. No psychotic commits suicide without some subjectively compelling reason, which we rarely discover. It is not without reason that the suicidal psychosis, melancholia, is found frequently in the aged—people who observe their declining capacity to love and can no longer hope for love from others. When such melancholics typically complain that although they are rich they are impoverished, we know today that it is they who are right, and not the healthy people who in their arrogant incomprehension are unable to understand them. It is not money of which they are deprived but love. At this point I should like to formulate a principle based on my own experience: the only person who puts an end to his life is one who has been compelled to give up all hope of love in this life. The hope of reunion in an afterlife may still be a deep motive for self-destruction and hence tension release.

Case 1

A woman seen following her release from a sanatorium, where she had been admitted because of an ever-increasing consumption of barbiturate sleeping pills, gave her age as forty-three in the initial interview. In correspondence from the hospital, this also was her stated age. In a later interview, she confided that she actually was forty-six but told people she was younger because she was concerned about "getting older." She expressed the wish to look youthful to herself and others. The patient was the middle child and only daughter in the family; she had two older and two younger brothers. The home situation was described as a most unpleasant one because of her father's very rigid and strict moral attitudes. His suspiciousness at times seemed to take on overt paranoid qualities. As a result of this tension, the patient stated, her mother left the home when the patient was twelve, abandoning the entire family.

The patient spoke of the mother's actions in connection with this event only in such a way as to try to justify them. She had longed to see her mother but continued to live with her father out of economic necessity. At fifteen, when she could no longer tolerate the situation with her father, she ran off to find her mother, whom she located about eight months later; an older brother supported her while she searched for her mother. Even after she found her mother she could not live with her, since her mother was involved in a common-law relationship with a man and could not care for her. When the patient's mother subsequently was murdered by her lover, the patient was very shocked and upset. The great publicity that followed caused her additional anxiety. Very soon after her mother's murder, the patient, then aged sixteen, married a man three years older than herself and immediately had two children in a short period of time. The marriage ended in divorce after a few years.

Significantly, after her mother's death and after her own marriage, but in the same calendar year, her father died of a chronic disease. She recalled no mourning for her father but spoke with great emotion about her mother's murder, and this was still in evidence at the time of the interview. When asked about the ages of her parents at their deaths, she stated that the mother was forty-six at the time of her death and the father was forty-nine. The coincidence of the mother's age at death and the patient's true age was noted by the interviewer, as was the correspondence in age between the patient and her first husband, and between her mother and father.

About four or five years after divorcing her first husband, the patient had married an inadequate chronic alcoholic man. The patient masochistically tolerated this individual's demands upon her for over six years but finally separated when the situation became impossible. She did not sue for divorce and was somewhat relieved when the man died as a result of a fight that occurred while he was drunk. Although she had no contact with him and was uninvolved in this matter, she felt sorry when she heard of his death.

The year following her second husband's death, she married a much younger man, with whom she had a "fine relationship." Despite this, the patient had noticed that she was getting quite upset in the six months prior to the interview and had begun to use barbiturates very heavily, which she had started during her "horrible" second marriage. After several additional interviews, the patient's anxiety markedly increased, and hospitalization was suggested; but before hospitalization was arranged, the patient managed to obtain a sizable quantity of sedatives and killed herself. Although she was not seen in the period immediately before the suicide, it was reported to the interviewer that the patient constantly spoke about her mother and about how she had been praying to return to her even though mother was dead. Her religious beliefs reinforced this idea of reunion in an afterlife.

The temporal correspondence of this woman's age at suicide with her mother's age at death is more than a coincidence. The particular mode of orally ingesting the lethal agent seems to correspond with the regression wish to effect reunion with her mother, which she expressed overtly. The possibility that other components (e.g., rage at the mother for abandoning her and subsequent guilt) contributed to her action must be considered; however, the need to "stay young," and thus deny the fateful anniversary year, seemed strongly to indicate the importance of her unresolved mourning for her mother and her father. The identification with the mother in her unsuccessful marriages and in the time-age parameter is clear.

Case 2

A man who initially stated he was fifty-two years old, and who later corrected himself to say that he was fifty-three years old, was seen in consultation because he had developed a fear of a catastrophic lawsuit in which he would be morally degraded and lose all his money and so be responsible for depriving his family of all support. In attempts to elicit details about this possible litigation, it became apparent that these fears were unrealistic and delusional. The patient had had surgery about one month earlier and in the postoperative period became amnesic and amblyopic. He felt that during a subsequent amnesic period he may have acted in such a way as to precipitate the feared litigation, although this was without foundation. Because of complaints suggesting possible organic cerebral involvement, a neurological examination was requested; no organic pathology was discovered. The neurological consultation was obtained on a Wednesday afternoon, and the following morning the patient killed himself. His son reported that he had slashed his wrists and chest and had actually opened his abdominal cavity with the razor blades he had used. Before he died he muttered that he did not want his son to see him this way but that he felt he had to die as there was no other way out of what he knew was going to destroy him and perhaps all who were dear to him.

As indicated, his manifest reason for this behavior was the delusional fear that he had done something that had hurt or angered a particular man, who now was going to "get him." He felt, however, that he might have "imagined" all of this, since he could not recall having such thoughts before the operation.

Approximately ten years earlier he had had a "nervous break-down," from which he recovered while receiving psychother-apy. At that time, he felt he had taken undue advantage of an older man who was a business competitor. This man committed suicide, and the patient felt completely responsible. At the time of his earlier disturbance, he had felt he had to be punished, becoming depressed, self-accusatory, and suicidal. He was able to recover with psychotherapeutic assistance and returned to his activities. He had been married for twenty-four years and had three children, the oldest nineteen and the youngest thir-teen. His marital relationship had always been a good one, and there were no major financial problems.

The patient had two older brothers, one older sister, and one younger brother. His mother never remarried but sup-ported the entire family and saw to it that they all had a "good education." He spoke of his closeness to his mother and of how he had missed her after her death, from "heart trouble," about eighteen years earlier. In talking of his parents, he mentioned casually, "My father died when I was six years old. He was fifty-three, the age I am now, when he died. Although I don't re-member him and don't know what he died of, I have frequently visited his grave and have said memorial prayers for him every year." He knew his father had been ill and had died at home. The patient unknowingly spontaneously associated to the older man who committed suicide ten years earlier, after talking of his father. He then spoke of his guilt about this man, but added that he had worked things out so that he could "recover." He could not understand why these guilty and self-recriminatory feelings had now returned.

In this patient, the hostile identification with the dead father, whom he felt he had killed, actually came out in his associations to the event of ten years earlier, when he had ex-perienced an acute melancholic episode. The confusion about his age and his inability to remember his father and present actions about which he felt frightened also seem to be related to his impending anniversary suicide. After his suicide, his wife was contacted, and she stated that his father did die at age fifty-three, which was the patient's age at the time of the suicide. The cause of his father's death on the operating table was per-itonitis secondary to a ruptured appendix. Without consciously being aware of it, the patient had chosen the blade as his mode of suicide. The anatomical locale (abdomen), the perforation, and extravasation mechanisms may have been associated in his mind with his father's death. Once again, the anniversary correlation between the age of the father at his death, and of the age of the patient at the time of suicide is clear. The patient's concern with his own son just prior to his death may well have reflected the preoccupation he had about problems with his own father. The confusion about his age in the initial consultation closely resembled that of the patient in case 1.

Case 3

A twenty-four-year-old married woman was seen after she attempted to destroy herself by ingesting "sleeping pills." She felt very guilty over an extramarital affair she had had with her husband's friend. She had been married for three years and had been trying to become pregnant without success. She had been examined and told that she was not responsible, that perhaps her husband was partially sterile. The patient secretly hoped she might be pregnant as a result of her extramarital activity but became very depressed after she found she actually was pregnant and then felt that she could only "atone for her guilt" through death.

The patient was the youngest of six children, all of whom were living. When the patient was four and a half, her mother died of tuberculosis. She could not recall her mother, except that her mother was "very wonderful." After her mother's death, the patient lived with her father until age eight, then with an aunt until age fourteen, then with her father again until she was seventeen. She never liked and actually feared her father, who had an "awful temper and was brutal," and who had incestuously attacked her older sister, although he had never touched the patient. Despite her attempt to portray her father negatively, it was apparent that she was his favorite.

Prior to the patient's marriage, her husband had impregnated her, but the pregnancy was terminated by miscarriage. She believed this was a punishment for premarital sexual activity, and she viewed her infertility as further punishment for her guilt. When asked why she should be punished, she could not answer but stated that during her adolescence she had been quite promiscuous. For a long period in her teens she had carried on an illicit affair with her older sister's husband. She felt very guilty about these affairs and felt especially reprehensible when seen about her latest infidelity because her husband was such a kind, considerate, faithful man. Psychotherapy was recommended to this patient, but she preferred to return to her home in another part of the country where there were no therapists.

The patient's mother was twenty-five when she died. Although it is impossible to relate her unsuccessful suicide attempt directly to the anniversary age of her mother at death, the oedipal guilt toward her mother can clearly be inferred. The subsequent acting out of this situation in later life with her brother-in-law and the friend of her husband, plus the exposure to a seductive father, undoubtedly contributed to her guilt. The guilt based on ambivalent feelings toward her mother, reinforced by her mother's actual death, seemed insufficient to restrain the patient's sexual acting out. However, the approaching anniversary date might well have been the harbinger of the reawakened and melancholic process following her mother's death. This ambivalent identification with the mother may have been the psychological determinant of her suicide attempt.

These three patients were seen for comparatively short periods of time. Any greater discussion of their situations would have to be based in large part on inference and speculation. The identification with the deceased parent seemed clear in two of the patients. Data relating to ambivalent feelings prior to the significant parent's death were unavailable, although in each instance the parent that died during the childhood of the patient was of the same sex as the patient; the event occurred during the oedipal developmental period in two patients, and during adolescence in the third.

In the next three cases suicidal and self-destructive impulses were present but were handled, during the course of psychoanalysis or dynamically oriented psychotherapy, with successful resolutions.

Case 4

A twenty-three-year-old unmarried woman consulted an analyst because she was fearful of becoming an alcoholic. She began to drink at the age of seventeen, while still a student in high school, and had found her alcohol ingestion increasingly difficult to control. Her mother, with whom she had strained relations, had always depreciated and severely controlled her. This pattern was still present at the time she was initially seen. Her father had committed suicide when he was fifty-five, by running his car over a cliff. The patient was sixteen at the time. As subsequent information became available in the therapeutic relationship, it was clear that he too restricted the patient in regard to dating, sexual activity of any sort, smoking, cleanliness, and practically all other instinctual gratifications.

After the father's death it was revealed that he had been secretly gambling away the family resources for some time. This information came as a great shock to the family, and resulted in a severe downgrading and reorganization of their scale of living. The mother was forced to work, and the family properties had to be sold to pay the father's debts. It was in this period (after the father's death) that the patient began to drink heavily and to be depressed for prolonged periods of time. It was also at this time that the patient first began to be preoccupied with self-destructive fantasies. In all of these she characteristically destroyed herself by jumping off a tall building. These suicidal preoccupations were revealed only after four years of continuous psychotherapeutic contact. She feared talking of these ideas because she felt her therapist would disapprove of her ideas and might reject her. The transference aspects of these preoccupations emerged in various ways and clearly indicated the relationship to her father. She sometimes became deeply depressed when an appointment had to be changed. Only gradually did she permit her anger toward the therapist to emerge when such events occurred. Her destructive fantasies toward men were also slowly revealed, but on each occasion with such caution and anxiety that she would literally shake as she spoke. Vacations and other separations were very traumatic for her, even with months of discussion before their occurrence. After these events, the self-destructive fantasies increased in frequency and intensity.

On one occasion, when she was called by the analyst's secretary about a sudden cancellation of an hour, she became exceedingly frightened and anxious. She was very angry with the analyst for the cancellation but was terrified because she thought that the analyst's death was the reason for the omitted session. She feared calling the office lest she hear the "terrible news," and she approached the office for the next appointment with great trepidation. When she heard the office air-conditioner working and saw that the secretary looked cheerful, her anxiety diminished. But only when she saw the analyst did she feel relief. Her first comment to the analyst was an enraged outburst about why he had worried her so. She quickly went on to tell of her tremendous fear that he was dead and how she had been certain this accounted for the cancellation by the secretary. When asked about her feelings of anxiety, she reluctantly talked of how her suicidal preoccupations had reached their greatest intensity after the cancellation. She felt that if the analyst had died, she would also have to kill herself.

In later sessions the transference implications of this dramatic experience became clear. Her anger with her punitive and at times sadistic father actually were accompanied by conscious death wishes directed toward him. The appearance of her suicidal preoccupations after his death and the news of his clandestine gambling related to her guilt about his death and the magical fear that she was responsible for it. At a deeper level she was terrified at being left alone—a punishment meted out to her as a child. The idea of death as a punishment, as an escape, as the ultimate in isolation became clearer. Several months after the canceled appointment episode, the patient came in with great excitement and revealed that the day of the cancellation by the secretary was the same as the date on which her father had died. She had forgotten all about it until shortly before seeing her analyst at this later time.

In this patient, utilizing the transference neurosis facilitated the working out of the traumatic events relating to her suicidal preoccupations. The regression to oral gratification, coupled with the depressive self-destructive fantasies, indicated a melancholic type of mourning response to her father's death, which was chronically acted out and yet avoided through the acting out behavior. The identification with the dead parent was observed in the fantasied mode of suicide.

Case 5

A thirty-seven-year-old married woman who had been seen previously for limited psychotherapy with a successful result suddenly called for an appointment after being out of contact for many months. When asked why she decided to come in at the particular time she chose, she said that she had heard of a thirty-seven-year-old woman who had died of cancer of the breast that day and that this greatly upset her. She wondered whether she should go to the funeral and could not understand the reason for or intensity of her feeling. When asked about this situation, she immediately associated to her mother's death from carcinoma of the breast. The mother was in her early fifties at the time, and the patient had wished for her mother's death because the mother had suffered so with her disease.

One month after her mother's death the patient married and soon began to have marital difficulties. Significantly, at that time she developed the fear that she would get breast cancer and die shortly. Although very anxious, she found her concerns diminished with time. In childhood the patient depreciated her mother and admired her handsome, enthusiastic, active, seductive father, who had died suddenly of a heart attack when she was in her late teens, five years before her mother's death. Although she was very shocked at her father's death, it was only after her mother's death that she felt very guilty and depressed. Her cancer phobia started at that time.

The precipitating event that stimulated the sudden appointment request was discussed with the patient. As she talked of it, she noted the identification of herself with the dead thirty-seven-year-old woman and how this related to her previous fear of cancer and its connection with her mother's death from breast carcinoma. Several additional interviews were sufficient to aid her in understanding more fully what had given rise to the recurrence of the sudden anxiety. The anxiety about dying of cancer as her friend had done exacerbated her fear of being left. The need to have a temporary contact with the analyst was in the service of denying separation (i.e., the analyst still lived). In other words, her identification with the departed friend-mother existed along with the feelings of being left alone that occurred after her mother (and father) died. The mother's death served as an actual catapult into marriage for her.

In this situation the guilt toward and identification with the dead mother was clear. The fear that she would have a fate similar to that of her mother seemed to indicate the presence of an unconscious self-destructive impulse and her conscious reactive fear and phobia about this possible fate. There were no thoughts or attempts of suicide, but the fear of destruction through the process of internal malignancy indicated the internal self-destructive wish and fear.

The basis of the anniversary phenomenon for this patient seemed to trigger the identification processes that had been repressed. The more closely the patient's life pattern or time relationship coincides with that of the unassimilated ego-self representation of the object toward whom ambivalences are felt, the greater the possibility of the emergence of the self-destructive impulses.

Case 6

This patient, in analysis for over seven years, when first seen was extremely anxious and fearful that she had cancer that would "eat her up inside" and that she was going to die. This phobic concern so frightened her that she had been continuously involved in a process of repeated medical examinations to reassure her that she was still healthy. Initially she indicated her fear of dying from cancer started when her child was six months of age. However, as the analysis progressed, it became evident that her fear of dying actually emerged as a conscious preoccupation very shortly after she was married. When she was first seen she was twenty-seven years old, married, and had a daughter three years old. This fear of death, which started immediately after her marriage, had been getting progressively worse and was the reason she sought help. Her constant concerns undermined her marriage to the point where her husband was contemplating divorce. He felt that for the five-and-a-half years of their marriage, her active resistance to intercourse because of her fear of pregnancy, her constant preoccupation with her health, and the resulting excessive medical expenses involved in her search for reassurance added up to a situation he could no longer tolerate.

Her history as she gave it initially was that her mother had died in childbirth, when the patient was four-and-a-half years old. Her only sibling was a sister born at the time of the mother's death. Her father remarried when she was six years old, and he had no other children. The patient and her sister lived with the maternal grandmother from the time of the mother's death until after the father remarried, when they rejoined him. In talking about her sister, the patient felt that her own fear of childbirth related in some vague fashion to the birth of her own sister, although this was very unclear to her. After marriage she never intended to have a child, but her husband tricked her into the pregnancy. Her husband, wishing a child, had secretly perforated a condom, and she had conceived. Her anxiety at the time of conception and throughout the pregnancy was most intense. Her concern at the time of her child's birth was that she would die in childbirth, and she was uncomfortably surprised to find that she had survived. Her fantasy about her mother's death had been that her mother died as the result of hemorrhage in the postpartum period. Shortly after her daughter's birth, when she herself had a slight postpartum hemorrhage, she became so panicky that it required emergency sedation to calm her down.

The first part of the analysis was concerned mainly with the great resentment that she had toward her stepmother, with whom she had never established a relationship and about whom she had many competitive feelings and hostile fantasies. She had always idealized her father and could not understand his great love for her stepmother. At twenty-one the patient met her husband-to-be and married him. Her husband, like her father, was a traveling salesman for a clothing company. On her honeymoon she felt so miserable that she cried constantly and wanted to return home to "Daddy." She found sexual relationships unsatisfactory. Although a virgin at marriage, she managed to adjust so that she was able to have an orgasm practically every time she had intercourse. However, her constant fear was that if she became pregnant she would die in childbirth. She resented her husband for tricking her into pregnancy. In a somewhat magical fashion she stated that she knew she would have a daughter and felt that her death from childbirth would be from extravasation, as she had fantasied her mother's death. Despite the panic and anxiety, she managed to go through the pregnancy and give birth to a daughter, as she had predicted. After the birth the patient became increasingly anxious and depressed about pregnancy, and there gradually evolved marked restrictions as to the times that she would allow intercourse to occur. These prohibitions were specifically related to certain months, which turned out to be the months in which her mother had conceived. Intercourse was always accompanied by great caution and ritual.

The anniversary features of her difficulties were even more strikingly brought out by the fact that she was married on the day that she had established as the death date of her mother. In talking about this coincidence she stated that she set the wedding date without conscious awareness of the significance of the date. While applying for the marriage license, when asked for her mother's name she unconsciously gave her real mother's name even though she had intended to follow the practice she had established of always listing only her stepmother's name. It was only after a long period of analysis that the facts about her mother's death became clarified. Her mother did not die in childbirth of extravasation, but apparently died two weeks after giving birth to the patient's sister, from what sounded like a pulmonary embolus set off by delayed postpartum ambulation. Her sister's birthday (which the patient always knew) actually was two weeks before the date of her mother's death. The patient's daughter was born on March 25; the patient was born on March 22. The bipolar identification with daughter and mother became clearer as the significance of this coincidence emerged. On the one hand the patient was her own mother giving birth to her, and on the other she was the daughter who was born again.

As mentioned above, the patient came to see the analyst when her daughter was three-and-a-half years old. In retrospect she may already have been unconsciously anticipating a serious anniversary reaction when her daughter would reach the age that she was at the time of her mother's pregnancy and death. Analysis continued, and it was apparent that her resistance reflected the attitude of her father, which had always been to avoid talking about or recognizing the death of the patient's mother. The reconstructed anamnestic material that is presented here is a compilation and condensation resulting from the many analytic hours filled with resistance, silence, and anxiety. When the patient's daughter was born, she wanted to name her after her real mother, but feared doing this as it would infuriate her father and stepmother; furthermore, she felt that she might be condemning her daughter to die at age thirty-two, the age of her mother at the time of her death. As a compromise, she gave her daughter the middle name Hope, using the first initial of her real mother's name. The patient herself had changed her own given name about the time that she met her husband. Her mother had named her Norma, but she changed it to Helene. When asked why this change occurred, she said that it related to a movie she saw at that time. In this movie the heroine's boyfriend had gone off to war, and she waited for him. The scene she recalled most vividly was one in which Helene was "waiting for her man to return." All of the soldiers came back, with the hero at the end of the procession, blinded by the war. Helene, while crying, professes her love for him, and reunion is accomplished. Shortly after seeing this movie, the patient decided to adopt the name Helene, and she did so. She is still called Helene by everyone but her parents and old friends. She further indicated that she did not wish to have the name of Norma because she wanted to completely divest herself of her mother's influence and believed that changing her name could do this. In addition to the name change, she also tried to alter her physiognomy, hair style, and coloring, because she felt unhappy about her unattractive appearance. However, she felt more secure in that she now physically resembled her father and not, as before, her deceased mother. As the analysis proceeded, many aspects of this patient's life emerged and were worked through and clarified. A complete account of these is not germane to this presentation, but significant features and developments can be highlighted.

While in analysis the patient voluntarily became pregnant again. Significantly, her second child, whom she predicted would be a girl, was born when her older daughter was four-and-a-half years old. This child, a girl, was born several weeks before her sister's birthday. The patient stated that again she knew she would have a girl. The time interval between her daughters' births was four-and-a-half years, the same as the interval between her and her sister. Much later in the analysis, when talking about her unconscious magical activity, she stated: "I knew both times it would be a girl. I did it to test the Gods to see if I was mother. I got married on the day that I thought she died. Mother was thirty-two when she died, and I felt certain that I would never survive this age. Father was the same age as mother, and my husband is the same age as I am. It is amazing how I never realized, until we have worked this out in the analysis, how I did everything the same way as mother. I got married and tried to get away from being like mother. I changed my name, I changed my appearance, but inwardly I always felt that my fate would be exactly as mother's. I am now thirty-four years old. I passed the critical year in which I was to die only because I could work on these feelings here with you. I tried unconsciously to repeat the pattern but found that I was different and not my mother. I fought you for three years of the analysis. Nothing happened. I wouldn't let myself feel or depend on anyone as I had with my mother."

After the birth of her second daughter she again believed that she was going to die. However, even though she had some understanding, her amazement at surviving the pregnancy was remarkable. Her anxiety about death, though still present, was markedly diminished, and she could accept this child with far less ambivalence than her first.

The patient, throughout the analysis, frequently made allusion to suicidal ideas. Her marked fear of malignancy became understood as a manifestation of the fear of the wish to atone for guilt feelings through a self-destructive process, though her death would occur as the result of an internal cellular malignancy instead of an actual suicidal gesture. As her fear of malignancy lessened, her suicidal wishes increased. In the course of the working through some particularly frightening material in the maternal transference neurosis, she did on several occasions make pseudoattempts at self-destruction. These were interpreted directly, and she understood them in the context of her need to identify with mother, and her guilt and need to punish herself for her own destructive fantasies at the time of her mother's pregnancy, when she was four-and-a-half years old. The oedipal aspects of these fantasies clearly emerged.

Particularly trying periods throughout the analysis occurred when there were vacations or interruptions by the analyst. Initially, the patient began to experience a feeling of complete emptiness within her body, then became exceedingly depressed, and then various self-destructive fantasies began to preoccupy her. At first she would have symptoms that she believed indicated the presence of a malignancy. Later these changed to thoughts of suicide through the ingestion of barbiturates or by throwing herself out a window of a high building. She always associated a vacation with the time when her mother left her to have her sister and never returned. Some of her material before one of the analyst's vacations illustrates this association: "You are leaving again and will be gone on the anniversary of my mother's death. This is a bad time for me every year. Always something comes up. One year I feared that I had a brain tumor. The next year I thought that I had cancer of the stomach. Another year I feared cancer of the uterus. It is connected with your leaving. I fear your going away in the summer. This morning I thought of your dying. I know that you won't. You are not my mother. You are not going away to have a baby. Maybe your wife will. If your wife dies, I will die. This will be the punishment, but I can also in this way be your wife. In times past I used to think of death as peace. No more feelings, turmoil, no more hurting, and also if I were to die, I might be able to be with her again if there is an afterlife."

Although she was aware of the fact that her mother had died, throughout her childhood she refrained from talking about this matter to her parents. Nonetheless, throughout her childhood, and even during the first half of the analysis, she secretly maintained the fantasy that her mother existed in heaven and that she could communicate with her mother by talking to her silently in her mind. Gradually this fantasy changed and she substituted the analyst for mother. This paralleled the decrease in anxiety about her own death, which disappeared, but her concerns about the analyst's death markedly increased.

As the maternal transference evolved, she became increasingly angry with the analyst, and there followed great anxiety as she associated her anger with the magical destruction of the object against whom these feelings were directed. Then her guilt markedly increased, and she would resurrect fantasies of self-destruction. Slowly she recognized that she had wished her mother dead when the pregnancy occurred. When she herself was pregnant, she was overwhelmed by her own anxiety, guilt, and death concerns. Two dreams illustrate the therapeutic reactivations of this conflict: "I tried to come and see you. The elevator was self-service. It took me to the fourth floor but would go no higher. I wanted desperately to see you and so I walked up all of the stairs to nine. I waited to see you, but then had to go to a hospital and take an old lady there. It began to rain heavily. The old lady was a plastic bag full of bones and flesh. It moved and was alive. She was dead when I got to the hospital." The second dream, occurring the same night, was: "I was on a golf course—a man tried to show me how to play. Suddenly it was flooded. Like Noah's ark. A boat was there, and so was father." Her associations to the fourth floor related to her fourth year. If she could stay at age four she could avoid her mother's death, but she had to work in the analysis and finally recognize that her "old lady" was dead and all that remained was skin and bones. She felt that the analyst was teaching her how to play. The water in both dreams referred to her crying. She had never cried prior to analysis, and even now could only cry when she had an analytic session. She felt that all of her crying started as light rain, but gradually as her feelings about mother emerged, the tears were like the flood associated with Noah's ark. They threatened her: all might be destroyed. She went on to say that she felt as though we were in a plastic bag at times. She thought that a plastic bag was a quick way of killing oneself, and she felt that she would have had to do this if she could not realize that she did not kill her mother. The evening following her discussion of these dreams, and shortly before a separation from the analyst, she wrote the following note:

> This too shall pass—as night follows day. How long do I have to keep paying? I've paid for thirty years and am still paying for my crimes; I've paid with anxiety, tension, and depression. I've paid with my stomach, throat, ears, and eyes. I've paid with unhappiness and never enjoyed anything. I am in my own plastic bag and I can't get out. Is death the only and final payment? Who am I writing this to—my own mind? The one that is so strict and doesn't bend? The one that says "an eye for an eye and a tooth for a tooth"? I've made this little Hell all for myself and

now I am entangled in and can't get out. I am enclosed in my fears, anxieties, and angers. I wake up in the morning with this horrible anxiety—like something awful is going to happen. The only thing that happens throughout the day is punishment. I am drained of any real human feelings as I am just aware of the terrific struggle going on within me. There must be another part which is rational and knows I committed no crime—or else I would have killed myself long ago. I think of death as the final payment, yet a part of me keeps fighting to stay alive. What are my crimes? I killed my mother by wishing her dead, I wanted my father and the baby he gave to my mother. I am so angry with her for leaving me with no one to love me. But this anger doesn't come out of pure anger—it is turned inward at me. Everything is turned inward right now. All I am aware of is my hurting body and my unhappy mind. All I want is some measure of peace within myself. You are going away from me like my mother did. The one person that I love. I know it is just a vacation, but I react to it like I did thirty years ago. Only thirty years ago I didn't know she wasn't coming back. Now I know she isn't coming back. I am deserted and alone, and even now my father might leave me. I am not reacting to all this as a grown-up woman over thirty, but as a child of four. I know all this and yet I don't know it or I wouldn't feel like I do now. How long do I have to keep this up? I've paid enough—it is about time I start acting to things as they are now. It is so easy to say this but inside of me is still that four-year-old who lost everything in one day and never again was a whole person.

The reaction to the vacation of the analyst paralleled that which occurred at mother's death, but now she could write and dream of it and so could work out more feelings about the "greatest blow" she ever had. The bipolar identification of the patient with the dead mother and the surviving little girl once more was apparent.

This revealing analysis presents many features that could be discussed in greater detail than is possible here; however, we can note the close bipolar identification that she had made with her dead mother. The patient was the mother who was going to die at a particular time, under specific circumstances, and whose life had to be patterned as closely as possible after her mother's. However, this was not completely desired by her, and she did make attempts magically to alter this fate. Because of her oedipal guilt and certain aspects of pregenital conflicts not described here, she concomitantly was the object (archaic self included) who was persecuted by a punitive unintegrated maternal superego. Her suicidal preoccupations manifested themselves through active self-destructive fantasies with partial acting out, as well as anxiety about death-dealing physical malignancies. The anniversary components are clearly seen but also brought about by the patient in her need to repeat the pattern.

Psychoanalysis allowed her to understand that which was unclear for her. Each anniversary was reacted to and worked on after it occurred. The process of living through the event seemed to be essential. Her thirty-second birthday came and went, and only later did she say, with much surprise, that she was over the hurdle. The actual acceptance of reality, in addition to the experiencing and understanding of the transference neurosis, facilitated the differentiation of herself from mother as well as from other significant, though less meaningful, objects in her life.

DISCUSSION

Zilboorg (1936a), on the basis of investigation of the differential diagnostic types of suicide, concluded that

> a history of the death of a person close to the child or a circumstance bringing the theme of death into the actual life of the child at one of the two turning-points of the psychosexual development of the child [oedipus period which reaches its height at about the age of six, and the period of puberty, at which time all the conflicts of the oedipal period are revived under the pressure of physiologic maturity] makes suicide a highly probable outcome [p. 288].

In one of his cases, that of a woman aged twenty-eight, whose mother died when the patient was thirteen, the deep-seated sense of guilt resulting from hatred of her mother, with whom she identified, seemed to relate to her suicide attempt by gas poisoning. Unfortunately, the age of the mother at the time of death is not mentioned, but it is inferred that the mother at death was older than the patient's age at the time of the suicide attempt. In the course of the analysis of this patient Zilboorg was able to recognize the "severe unconscious mourning" this girl went through after her mother died. It was at this time that the identification with the dead mother was experienced. In the suicide act, she acted out this identification with the dead mother. The similarity of these data to several of the clinical examples cited earlier is striking. In another publication, Zilboorg (1936b) points out that

> the *actively* suicidal individual . . . appears to be in mourning, but his is not a sublimated gratification of the need to identify himself with the dead; instead, he reverts to the primitive pattern of mourning. A regression to the primitive impulses invades his motor system so that in *acting out* his *neurotic mourning* he actually joins the fantasied dead by killing himself [p. 1364].

Zilboorg believes that in nonneurotic mourning, the identification with the dead is transitory and self-limiting. Rituals such as dressing in black (covered with earth) and withdrawing from life action are the indicators of this normal mourning identification with the dead. I have discussed these rituals in chapter 12. In the melancholia suicidal case, there is regression to a level of ego integration at which reality awareness is so impaired that the acting out of hostile aggressive impulses occurs toward the introjected object, which is not differentiated from the self.

Identification is the basic process by which the ego and superego structures are differentiated. This process may more directly involve parents than siblings during the childhood developmental periods; hence childhood parental loss may play a more significant role than childhood sibling loss, unless, of course, the sibling has symbolically become a parental transference figure or, in instances of severe sibling rivalry, the object of destructive wishes.

The normal mourning process is a process of undoing some aspects of past identifications as well as beginning autonomous differentiation, which includes decathexis. In some ways the analytic process is predicated on reestablishing the normal mourning process with its decathectic aspects of the transference object, even when there has been no real object loss in the patient's childhood. Hence anniversary reactions are responses

that are indicative of mourning abnormality and faulty identification processes, and they may be more prevalent than we
realize. External indicators of this pathology occur when the
temporal or life situations parallel the much earlier and identifiable traumatic experience with an object that is deceased.

Only one patient of Palmer's (1941) twenty-five cases of
consecutive suicide was a sibling loss in childhood. Hilgard's
case report, cited earlier, involved a childhood sibling loss. One
of Zilboorg's patients lost an eight-month-old brother when the
patient was four years old. In general, however, the incidence
of childhood sibling loss as opposed to childhood parent loss
in psychiatric patients seems to be much less; this was also seen
in my comparative study of childhood parent-sibling loss patients (see chapters 2 and 18).

Wall (1944), in studying thirty-three patients who actually
did destroy themselves, found a family history of suicide in
eleven families, and the suicide of a near relative as the precipitant in four cases. He observed that the tendency to identify
with relatives who killed themselves was noteworthy. Moss and
Hamilton (1956), evaluating fifty patients who were seriously
suicidal, reported that they found a "death trend" in 95 percent
of all of their cases. They state: "this involves the death or loss
under dramatic and often tragic circumstances of individuals
closely related to the patient, generally parents, siblings, and
mates." In 75 percent of their cases, the death occurred "before
the patient had completed adolescence." In the remaining 25
percent, the "death trend" occurred later and precipitated the
illness. Sixty percent had lost one or both parents in early life,
the majority during puberty or early adolescence, and others
in childhood or infancy. Forty percent lost their fathers and 20
percent their mothers during this period. In every case of paternal loss, however, the patient felt a removal of the mother's
usual love and support brought about by a disruption of the
home after the father's death. Later deaths of persons close to
the patients served to reactivate suicidal preoccupations in these
individuals, of whom eleven died by suicide. Wall's study in
many ways confirms the earlier observations of Palmer about
the significant correlation of suicide with loss of a parent in
childhood. The Wall report stresses the importance of identification with the deceased relatives but does not focus on the

mourning processes of the survivors who later destroyed themselves, or on the internal significance of these early losses.

In accordance with these observations—but in addition to them—in these childhood parent-loss patients, the suicide may be triggered by an anniversary occurrence. In some of the cases cited above, it was the actual or feared attainment by the patient of the age the parent had reached at his or her death that set in motion suicidal activity. The anniversary brings back the trauma of the parent's death, and with this, the frustration, hostility, and guilt that served to feed the ambivalence that interfered with normal mourning. Instead, an identification with the dead parent was fixated. In the instances in which mourning in childhood parent-loss situations can be worked out during psychoanalysis, the potential suicidal process may be converted into the more usual mourning reaction in the context of the analysis (Fleming and Altschul, 1963).

Not every childhood object loss results in an anniversary reaction, and not every anniversary reaction ends in suicide. Probably many individuals "live through" such anniversary crises without ever being conscious of them. Some may have spontaneous resolutions of these crises without treatment, while some are helped with treatment. Others who consider treatment may not link their need with mourning. Some individuals destroy themselves as part of the melancholic or symbiotic process, and some remain chronically depressive throughout their lives.

Before closing this discussion, it may be useful to call attention to the problem of when mourning is possible for the child. Dr. Morris Peltz (personal communication) has called to my attention the controversy among child analysts about the child's capacity to mourn. Some observers consider the reactions of infants to separation from significant objects as being very similar to the adult mourning process; others have raised questions as to when a child can comprehend the concept of death, including the idea of finality. Various ages have been suggested when such a comprehension can occur, varying from the two- to three-year-old to the early adolescent. Peltz believes that most children are incapable of an adult type mourning process but instead react with a variety of affective and cognitive responses, including anxiety, helplessness, rage, somatizations, magical thinking, denial, projection, splitting of the ego, displacements, regression, and repression. I would suggest we need further study of the evolution of the mourning process, not only in the Darwinian sense but as a developmental continuum in which various ego capacities appearing at particular times eventually become integrated into what we call the adult mourning process. Fixations, arrests of development of specific ego functions, or pathogenic traumata may then predispose the vulnerable adult to later consequences of interrupted or deviated mourning processes and can eventuate in anniversary suicides.

CONCLUSIONS

Correlation does not necessarily imply teleological, causal, or direct relationship. However, it can focus our attention on two coincidental events that may have significance and thus may lead to further investigations of this linkage. Among the cases I have described in this report, there were two actual suicides and an attempted self-destruction in a third patient that corresponded in time to the death ages of the lost parents. These parents died while the patients were children. It is suggested that the suicidal actions of these patients were anniversary reactions and that they represent manifestations of abnormal or incompleted mourning processes with pathological identifications. What time-age-event relationships are selected for the anniversary suicide is significant in terms of what has been the central conflict; in the cases in this chapter, the death of the parent was the nuclear event emphasized. When one elicits anamnestically the facts of parental death or suicide during the childhood of the patient, considerations of self-destruction by the patient when he reaches the "critical age" must be considered and dealt with analytically. Many of these potentially suicidal patients are longstanding partially compensated melancholics in whom past traumata are reawakened when the temporal-age identification with the deceased parent becomes coincidental. In an attempt to avoid this coincidence of fate, there frequently may be a distortion of time or age and a wish to keep time or age from moving the victim to his presumed lethal end. The actual mode of suicide may also be related to the type of personality organization of the victim, the amount of sadism inherent in the conflict that has been remobilized, the hostile identification with the deceased object, the method of death of the childhood figure, or the addictive-symbiotic wish of the victim to reunite with his fantasied object.

Suicide can and does occur in any diagnostic category and does not depend upon any single clinical constellation—in fact, it can occur in many who would be adjudged to be "normal." However, the "anniversary suicide" patients have certain unique descriptive features, which have been the focus of this report.

Frequently an external event may occur that serves as the releaser of more primitive ambivalent feelings in these patients. It is postulated that an internal trigger of this mechanism may be set off by the coincident-external temporal correspondence that symbolizes the past conflict relationship between the patient and the previously lost object. This concomitance in time serves to reawaken in the previously compensated individual a more overt and manifest pathological state in which suicide may occur. However, these symptoms may be limited to suicidal fantasies that are either overtly self-destructive or relate to fantasies of physical death (e.g., malignancy, heart attack) and need not be acted out in deed.

It may be that many supposedly endogenous depressive episodes, though unrelated to present and identifiable precipitants, are current reflections of anniversarylike responses to previous situations in which mourning did not occur, was abnormal, or was arrested. Careful clinical investigation is needed to understand these varied outcomes and their determinants.

Part III
AGING

14

AGING OR AGED: DEVELOPMENT OR PATHOLOGY

"In my beginning is my end. In succession
Houses rise and fall, crumble, are extended,
Are removed, destroyed, restored, or in their place
Is an open field, or a factory, or a by-pass.
Old stone to new building, old timber to new fires,
Old fires to ashes, and ashes to the earth
Which is already flesh, fur and faeces,
Bone of man and beast, cornstalk and leaf.
Houses live and die: there is a time for building
And a time for living and for generation
And a time for the wind to break the loosened pane
And to shake the wainscot where the field-mouse trots
And to shake the tattered arras woven with a silent motto."[1]

According to an anonymous poem of the mid-14th century, life's span was 72 years, consisting of twelve ages corresponding to the months of the year. At 18, the youth begins to tremble like March with the approach of spring; at 24, he becomes amorous as the blossoming of April, and nobility and virtue enter his soul along with love; at 36, he is at the summer solstice, his blood as hot as the sun of June; at 42, he has acquired experience; at 48, he should think of harvesting; at 54, he is in the September of life when goods should be stored up; age 60, the October of life, is the onset of old age; 66 is dark November when all green withers and dies and a

Material from L. Vygotsky (1978) is included with the permission of Harvard University Press; quotation of J. Habermas (1979) is included with the permission of TELOS.

Reprinted from *The Course of Life: Psychoanalytic Contributions Toward Understanding Personality Development. Vol. 3: Adulthood and the Aging Process*, ed. S. I. Greenspan & G. H. Pollock. Washington, DC: U.S. Government Printing Office, 1980.

[1] Excerpt from "East Coker" in *Four Quartets*, copyright 1943 by T. S. Eliot, renewed 1971 by Esme Valerie Eliot, reprinted by permission of Harcourt Brace Jovanovich, Inc.

man should think on death, for his heirs are waiting for him to go if he is poor and waiting more eagerly if he is rich; 72 is December, when life is as mournful as winter and there is nothing left to do but die.[2]

AGING AND DEVELOPMENT: PHILOSOPHICAL AND METHODOLOGICAL CONSIDERATIONS

Various terms have been used to describe the course of life—*life cycle, life curve, lifespan, developmental stages or phases, maturational processes, growth periods, unfoldings, emergings, transitions, life seasons, turning points, life progression.* Each of these catches the notion of temporality and movement, of process and change. Most of these descriptive phrases imply the idea of ascendancy and decline with the inevitability of death. The latter observation forms the basis of a theme that has become very popular in recent years: death and dying. While raising our awareness of this inevitable ending to the life course, this theme may have done us a disservice if it has diverted our energies and concentration from what may be a more important issue: life and living.

Implicit in earlier assumptions was the idea that many, if not all, outcomes were the result of what had occurred in the earliest or earlier developmental eras. This general hypothesis was useful. It had descriptive, explanatory, therapeutic, and even predictive value. However, it was based on certain assumptions which, though still tenable, now seem incomplete. For example, the period after adolescence, described as adulthood, was rarely differentiated and distinguished into subgroups. The jump was made from young adulthood, to the climacteric period, and then to the final geriatric-senility stage. Until recent years, few attempts were made to consider the adult period as a series of progressions and at times regressions, each having unique features, developmental tasks, advantages and fulfillments, trials and failures.

Among the groups questioning this orientation is the Hu-

[2] From Emile Male, *L'Art Religieux de la fin du Moyen Age en France* (*Religious Art of the End of the Middle Ages in France*), translated by H. Wolff and B. Hudson; copyright 1949 by Pantheon Books, Inc., a division of Random House, Inc., New York; as quoted in *A Distant Mirror* by Barbara W. Tuchman.

man Development Division at the University of Chicago, a pioneering research organization that has conducted many studies on middle age and the older adult. Despite investigations, the second half of life and aging were still considered to be primarily gerontological and geriatric issues.

This orientation paralleled society's belief that aging was equated with old age and that aging was inevitably linked to sickness, disability, and deterioration. Accepting such assumptions, aging individuals frequently conformed to the status assigned to them. Those who did not were seen as deviants or exceptions. As attitudes change, we recognize that healthy aging must be distinguished from disease, particularly for individuals over age seventy. In the absence of valid and reliable data, our assumptions are increasingly being challenged, refuted, amended, and extended. We are beginning (1) to recognize dysfunctions, disorders, and even diseases that are common in one developmental group but are uncommon in others; (2) to appreciate the importance of predisposing factors which may stem from earlier periods, but which have their own unique characteristics; and (3) to identify unusual behaviors and their meanings from the viewpoint of multisystem interactions. We are considering the strong possibility that multiple psychopathologies can coexist in the same individual at the same time. From medicine we know that individuals can have several separate pathological entities simultaneously. The physician is not bound to only one diagnosis and one formulation. In psychiatry and the behavioral sciences, our goal is to find a single diagnostic designation with a unitary explanation. Multiple dysfunctions and disorders or diseases can interact with outcomes that manifest themselves in signs and symptoms, the resultants of combinations and interactions. In our considerations, we seldom attempt to analyze the products into the forms and elements that give rise to them. One assumption that has been pervasive is to consider consequents as inevitably and exclusively determined by very early antecedents. The validity of this explanation is not being questioned here; what is being suggested is that later inputs, internal and external changes, may be significant. At times, they may even assume primary importance.

Our research efforts and focus in psychoanalytic investigation emphasize early mother-infant interactions, early anaclitic symbiosis, the developmental years up to school, and the oedipal, latency, and adolescent periods. From clinical reconstructions, transference studies, and naturalistic observations, we arrive at formulations which are extrapolated, retrospectively and anterospectively, and applied sometimes in wholesale fashion to all aspects of adult life. The concepts of regression and fixation, clinically very useful and valid, serve to explain much, if not all, that occurs after adolescence. The empirical and clinical data used for such theoretical formulations are selected from the almost exclusive orientation that what occurred early is immutable and crucial and that all that comes later is to be viewed from such a perspective. Parent, sibling, and social relations have been described only in terms of early interpersonal interactions which become internalized and subsequently reemerge in later interpersonal interactions as transferences, repetitions, recapitulations, and manifestations of each conflict.

I do not disagree with this position but rather wish to emphasize the possibility that we have neglected our considerations, that we may have been reductionistic and overly simple, and that we have little data systematically and objectively collected on individuals throughout the course of life to stimulate new and additional hypotheses. For example, in research on various aspects of the mourning process and on the closely related but distinctly different area of object loss, I have become increasingly convinced that *symbiosis* is a general term that describes particular relationships throughout the course of life and is not limited to an early period of life (Pollock, 1964). Life-course symbiotic ties are focal, not necessarily total, constant, or immutable. They form the basis for positive social activity, and, although they have their roots in the earliest days of life, they do root, branch, flower, and bear fruit in different ways, at different times, and can occur with different people.

My studies of various object losses, notably childhood parent loss, childhood sibling loss, adult spouse loss, and adult loss of a child, convince me that it is necessary to describe the function, role, and meaning of the important lost "object" at different periods of the life course. One can begin to ask, "What is an object?" When viewed on a chronological axis, the significance of that which is "lost" reveals different meanings, roles, and functions at various times, phases, and eras of the life course. As this work has progressed, I have found that significant kinship relations vary at different developmental times; they have different meanings and functions during the adult periods. For example, the meaning of a spouse is different when one is in the early twenties, thirties, forties, fifties, sixties, seventies, eighties. In chapter 23 I describe the changing meanings siblings have for each other during the adult years and how these sibling relationships are related to later adult friendships. During the adult periods, parents and children change in their meanings for each other. The kinship relationships always remain, but the individuals may have different *significances* for each other at various periods of adult life. Part of our research tasks in the future should include the study and delineation of what changes occur during the various adult periods, positively and negatively, and how these manifest themselves in the present and can be articulated with past modes of coping, adaptation, conflict resolution, and antecedent pathology.

We must also be alert to the strong possibilities that newer constructions come into being which may not, need not, and cannot be solely described by what was suggested as being pivotal during the early years of life. Inner strengths, not heretofore in evidence, may emerge in adult life. These can be used to cope with change, improve interdependent relationships and friendships, facilitate enjoyment and creative activity, and deal with adversity.

Aging is development throughout the life course. Development, obviously, is not the same as growth and can include progression, regression, new contributions, remodeling, and, in some ways, decline. Aging, beginning at conception and ending with death, is to be distinguished from aged, a period of late adult life (usually after seventy-five) where changes that lead to ultimate failures become evident. Decline may or may not be regressive. If one accepts the concept of aging as presented here, several outcomes follow:

1. Some individuals can be "treated" psychologically throughout the course of life.

2. Not all psychopathology need inevitably be linked with early childhood psychopathology.
3. Early and later life experiences can and do affect later life reactions, but at times preventive intervention even at later life periods can avoid or mitigate difficulties heretofore believed to be unmodifiable.
4. We do not deal with a life cycle but with a life progression, unless we talk of an intergenerational circularity.

I wish to underline my agreement with the theoretical hypotheses and clinical observation that early experiences do affect the course of later life development. But some experiences are less crucial than others. Even in individuals having similar early experiences and traumata, unexpected and opposite outcomes are observed. The presence of many factors and the complexity of the interactions of these variables may account for differences. I am suggesting that postadolescent lifespan periods have their own developmental contributions, which need not be explained solely in terms of earlier developmental achievements or failures.

Neugarten (1979), a Chicago pioneer in aging research, has noted "that psychological change is continuous throughout the life cycle and, further, that the psychological realities of adulthood and aging are not to be understood merely by projecting forward the issues that are salient to childhood" (p. 887). She draws attention to recent studies based on actual data which allow us to delineate various periods and transitions in adult life. As we live longer, the study of different periods, heretofore not anticipated, provides us with the opportunities to learn more about these periods and about the transitions involved in moving from one to another. Van Gennep (1908) much earlier attempted such a classification in his work on the rites of passage.

Neugarten contributes to our understanding when she points out that, regardless of the number of adult life periods we define and regardless of the labels we give each period, individuals develop a concept of the normal, expectable life cycle, "a set of anticipations that certain life events will occur at certain times, and a mental clock telling them where they are and whether they are on time or off time" (p. 888). These "clock-events" show a striking similarity to Van Gennep's events. They have internal as well as external sociocultural dimensions that reinforce the psychological expectations. The biological aspects of the turning points may have a significant determining role for some psychological experiences (e.g., puberty, climacteric). Although Neugarten does not see life events as crises, others conceptualize all developmental stages as crisis periods.

Neugarten states (1979) "the themes of adulthood [and I would add of all development] are usually described in sequential order . . . , they do not in truth emerge at only given moments in life, each to be resolved and then put behind as if they were beads on a chain. Identity is made and remade: issues of intimacy and freedom and commitment to significant others, the pressures of time, the reformulation of life goals, stocktaking and reconciliation and acceptance of one's successes and failures—all of these preoccupy the young as well as the old" (p. 891). Psychological remodeling occurs throughout adult life and it is inaccurate "to describe adulthood as a series of discrete and neatly bounded stages, as if adult life were a staircase" (Neugarten, 1979, p. 891). We may now be in a better position to reexamine the general aspects of development from different perspectives.

In a world that rapidly moves toward technological imperatives, there is danger that distinctly held human values, ideals, and goals may get lost or be given diminished emphasis. It is no longer possible to ignore one or the other; it is important to call attention to this seemingly polar opposition whenever possible. The so-called scientific approach emphasizes facts, flow patterns, and the impersonal—but it can ignore the essence of what is human. We cannot, despite our concern with objectivity and precise planning, forget human contingencies. However, as we collect new information, it is apparent that we are dealing with multiple factors and complexity. Plurality and not simplicity or reductionism must alert us to keeping our perspectives open, despite our quest for single uncomplicated propositions which seemingly offer encompassing explanations.

The time is approaching when we must reevaluate our concepts and notions about development. As we learn more about genetics, prenatal organizers of personality, unique dimensions of adult and later adult functioning, we may need to revise our existing ideas about developmental progression. For example, we have firmly believed that specific consequents have precise antecedents, that later life solutions and approaches are intimately linked to earlier events. While accepting these premises, the danger that everything can be explained by the events of early life may hamper our efforts to find unique features of later life that may not be exclusively explained and tightly coupled with the traumata and resolutions characteristic of infancy and early childhood. What does not fit with our preexisting conceptions need not be labeled as deviance. Reconsiderations of developmental progress and stages or phases of development have already yielded newer concepts of development; that is, lines of development. Moving from the linear, we can now begin to think of operational fields of development with many interacting factors. These fields may gradually metamorphose into newer fields of development where certain features are less changeable and are not precisely determined by what has gone before, and where some awaken from dormant states. Unique combinations of particular elements can give rise to new configurations which then form the nucleus of newer developmental fields. The primary elements, like chemical elements, may be indivisible, but, once identified, they combine in many different ways, and yield new outcomes which then have the potential for newer organizations and structures in the present and in the future. There may even be new basic elements, as yet undiscovered, that also play pivotal roles in the unfolding field process. Some elements may remain latent until the later years when they can become active and significant. Development can be viewed as a dynamic process, having a beginning and an end, but with many intervening processes resulting in various outcomes. Deviance from established norms may be innovation, originality, or pathology. Through the study of differences and the unique settings in which they emerge, new vistas for research, theory revision, and theory extension may be possible.

Development need no longer be understood as a single continuum, as a single course or process from the beginning to the present. One may concentrate on particular periods and then compare one period with another, even though there may be discontinuities, unequal intervals between periods, and various different sequences occurring simultaneously at different rates and in different areas. There may be interactions at different points of the process that are grossly identified as unitary linear patterns. These can be analyzed into their components. These patterns may become active at different points during the course of life, and/or they may disappear at various points during the lifespan, never again to reappear. Careful observational research throughout the course of life is needed to expand our knowledge. Anna Freud pioneered this type of approach with her significant contribution of the concept of lines of development (1963).

There are fields of development in which biological, psychological, and social interpersonal components combine and/or intersect with parts of other fields of development and which can become internalized in the individual. What we observe as behaviors are the resultants of such combinations, intersections, and possible inhibitions. When particular aspects of the individual fields are given special emphasis, negative or positive, the individual developmental fields change internally. Consequently, when they intersect with other developmental fields, the resultants will differ from those of individuals having different developmental field patterns. Observational research with careful descriptions of all periods of the course of life will provide the evidence for or against this type of field formulation.

Spitz (1959) has proposed the term *force field* for the "organization of the previously undirected and unorganized discharge-seeking drives" (p. 25). He uses the term *field* as it relates to "organizers," a concept employed in embryology. The field is a means of ordering unstable entities so as to attain equilibrium. This concept of Spitz's is different from that suggested here, although the notion of "organizers" and "critical periods" has explanatory significance in considering development as an ongoing process within a temporal frame of reference. Distortions of the structure pattern of a preceding organizer may lead to the distortion of subsequent organizing processes. However, dormancies and developmental arrests may take place which may not become evident in the next period of development. Sometimes compensatory measures can delay the appearance of these dormancies and arrests until much later, when they can be triggered by external factors. In some instances they may never fully come into being.

Spitz suggests that integration, developmentally speaking, involves various modalities which are present at the particular time of the integration. When the integration takes place at the appropriate time, a firm bond is established that is not vulnerable to stress, internal or external. If key factors are missing at the time of integration, or if the timing is off, the resulting integration is more superficial and susceptible to disruption. Developmental imbalance and ego fragmentation occur more easily in such vulnerable beings. Regressions to less organized states can occur. The concept of the developmental field proposed here can encompass Spitz's concept as well as the contributions of Anna Freud on lines of development. It is necessary to recognize that, in our studies of lines, nuclei, or organizers of development, we consider these units in isolation, but the combination of the elements with one another in a field may be as significant for our understanding of development as the identification of linear or single points in time.

Retrospective reconstruction, constructions from data provided by psychoanalytic clinical situations, along with research from observations throughout the life course in different sociocultural-political economic settings, will be needed to augment the biological-genetic investigations. Psychoanalysis, though it focuses on the internal life of man, provides other means of obtaining observational data. These can complement the usual external observations of infants, children, adolescents, and adults. Simple explanations of event sequences may no longer suffice. Reductionistic elaborations focusing on one theoretical approach to another may also be insufficient to describe, explain, predict, or intervene. The narrowness of application of a theory that claims universal validity will be increasingly open to question. Internal and external observations complement reconstruction.

Habermas (1979) writes that

> a narrative describes events as occurrences that receive their significance in the framework of a history. A history is composed of interactions; it is enacted and endured by at least one person acting—the person who acts is . . . also "entangled" in it. A his-

tory falls into episodes; it is delimited by episodes with which it begins and ends. The narrated events have continuity through the meaning that they receive in the biographical and supra-subjective vital contexts of the individuals and the groups involved. Actions and events are explained with reference to situative peripheral conditions with the help of norms and values, or respectively of intentions and motives for action [p. 9].

He goes on to note that

narrative statements refer to at least two time-different events, whereby the earlier event E1 is described with reference to the later event E2. Consequently, narrative statements describe an event with attributes under which it could not have been observed. The historian [and I would add the psychoanalyst] describes an event not as an eyewitness, but as a latecomer; the narrator does not have the role of a chronicler, he uses contemporary observations only as documents. An event is described using attributes which could neither have been observed by eyewitnesses (as a presently occurring episode) nor have been told by the participants themselves (immediately after the end of the episode). Even in the . . . case of autobiography, when narrator and participant are the same person, the difference of time horizons remains; the past present, past, and future (of an earlier biographical condition) define a different narrator-perspective than the present present, past, and future (of the author as he writes his autobiography). With the change of time horizon, the narrator-perspective also shifts [p. 9].

The same cautions and concerns Habermas voices about the historian are also applicable to the psychoanalyst who attempts, by means of reconstruction, to evolve explanations regarding causation, genesis, and even normal development. Repetition of past events in the here and now provides a most useful source of data, but these must be augmented by data that are manifestations of present as well as recapitulations of earlier years. Internal and external, subjective and objective, insight and outsight observations, and observations made at one time and then repeated at a later time in systematic fashion and, if possible, using the same observer to gather data (even though this same observer is different at different times despite the fact that he or she is the same person), are methodological issues of importance. Psychoanalysts are aware of these considerations from their clinical experience.

However, it can be argued that historical accuracy is not significant for the psychoanalyst; only that which occurs in the clinical analytic situation is important. If this is so, then it should be so stated, and the extrapolation to a normal developmental sequence may be insufficient. If clinical reconstruction is augmented by cross-sectional and longitudinal observations (internal and external), the contribution of the reconstruction is greatly increased.

Habermas also suggests that

> the historian, by distinguishing between the time horizon from which he is narrating and the time horizon in which a participant has experienced the narrated history (and from which he would himself have told it), also takes into account the difference of meanings which the described event has for him as a historian and had for the one who took part in it. Thus the historian by no means assumes a neutral standpoint from which he can describe the episodes "as they were." Rather he depends on the selection of the respective frame of interpretation in which history E1 (event 1) is told. The narrative which a participant could have given after the end of the episode in which he was involved is privileged, compared with the narratives of non-participants or of later generations, only insofar as it contains eyewitness observations, and thus has documentary value. However, it has no privileged rank as a narrative. It depends in turn on the historian's decision how he ranks the various pregiven narrations of episode E1 (which relate to even different later E2, E3 . . . En), so that his own narrative is complex enough to explain both the historical event and the history of the tradition of this event narratively [p. 9].

The importance of the historian's underlying ranking, theoretical premises, and distance from the primary focus of observations is applicable to the psychoanalytic researcher who relies on reconstruction, supposed replication of an identical or closely similar occurrence in the here and now but which is believed to be a close repetition of what must have occurred "then and there." And yet, meaning changes over time for the experiencer as well as for the researcher. Insight helps the observer with internal observation and external observation.

When a pattern has been observed, internally and externally, one can reexamine past as well as present and make new observations, which in turn can expand the breadth and depth of insight. Insight can affect outsight, and outsight can affect insight. Discernment of pattern may be easier as one distances oneself from the event or events, but in this distancing, the advantage gained by historical perspective may be diluted by newer meanings given at the later time than was true when the event first occurred.

These arguments notwithstanding, there is a continuity of a history, as there is of a life course. The narrated episodes are unified in such fashion that one life course can be compared with other life courses. Differences, deviations, similarities, and changes give opportunity for charting convincing universal patterns. "History is an objective life context that is not 'theoretically' constructed for the first time by the history writer" (Habermas, 1979, p. 10) or by the psychoanalytic reconstructionist. The developmental or hierarchic order may have a deterministic frame based upon interpretative reference orientation of the observer. The observer decides what is to be regarded as a period in which relevant events are understood as elements of a single continuity. If based on empirical observations, the ordering can provide the theoretical base that will allow other observers to confirm or refute that which was postulated. The role of theory is to describe, explain, predict, and hence intervene, and the object of science is to find universals in reality. These universals may be of limited scope or may be of more general applicability. In psychoanalysis, we often arrive at theoretical statements that deal with past events but rarely with conditional predictions of events that will occur in the future. We can, however, make the latter forecast or correct conjecture in the area of life-course development and behavior, assuming certain constancies in the changes in human development.

> Every reference-event E2 lies after the depicted event E1, but before the time of the narrative itself. The choice of the frame of interpretation, i.e., the decision to narrate a particular history among many possible ones about E1, is . . . dependent on the narrator's interpretation of the future, i.e., on his expectations of future events. The narrator's anticipations are not part of the

narrated history, but of the situation of the hermeneutic point of departure. The horizon of expectations guiding the narrator's interest cannot at the same time determine the construction of a history and be its content. The narrator's anticipations are of significance to the narration perspective, but the history itself remains retrospective [Habermas, 1979, p. 10].[3]

We can anticipate future events, but these are predictions that can be tested. These future events are not historical. History limits itself to reconstruction of the past. For history to have prognostic or predictive content, hypotheses must be stated beforehand. These forecasts must be made independent of outcome, lest knowledge of outcome bias or interfere with the testing of the prediction. The scientific study of development allows us to make predictions of long- and short-term outcome. The greater the availability of data about the significant variables to the predictor, the greater the possibility of accuracy of the predictions. The reconstruction of a life, pathological or normal, is a narrative. It may be used as an example or even as evidence in support of, or as refutation of, a particular hypothesis, but it is not predictive in and of itself. Surprises, new observations, new insights, and discontinuities are found in clinical experience. These may not be predictable, as are the regularities and constancies. Discontinuities do not fit into what is expected by existing theory. These newer observations form the basis for theory change (i.e., extension or refutation), and so, in one sense, are "scientific"—they begin the process of seeking new realities, new regularities, new understandings, new testing, and they form the basis of new predictions.

We must be ever-mindful of the unique and the random as well as of the regular and the predictable. Otherwise, stagnation will take over without opportunity for new discovery. In considering development, Habermas rejects the idea of evolution as a causally unfolding lawlike process. Instead, one must consider the concept of contingent causality, where there may be leaps and transitions from one level to another in ways that

[3] I document Habermas's position with extensive quotation because he so clearly and succinctly presents a position which has applicability to the present discussion.

may not be orderly unfoldings but which have certain boundary limitations (e.g., biological progressions).

APPROACHES TO DEVELOPMENT

A comprehensive survey of theories and schemata of development is not a feasible undertaking, given limitations of space and the fact that the interested reader can go to original sources and learn firsthand from individual contributors about their work. Some researchers have focused on particular "stages" of development; others have attempted to formulate a particular theoretical approach and follow it throughout life-course periods; still others have presented theoretical models for the functioning of mind and have attempted to correlate these models with the progressions of life. Wolff (1960), comparing the contributions of Piaget with those of psychoanalysis, used Werner's propositions regarding development to delineate the major issues which every developmental theory should consider, regardless of the research methodology employed in its formulations or testing; for example, longitudinal studies, comparative investigations based on cross-cultural or cross-species observations, or reconstructions based on narrative accounts, dreams, and transference understanding.

Wolff, discussing Werner's 1947 paper on "The Concept of Development from a Comparative and Organismic Point of View," presents five principles of development.

1. The orthogenetic law. Whenever development occurs, it proceeds from a state of relative globality and lack of differentiation to a state of increasing differentiation, articulation, and hierarchic integration.

2. Uniformity versus multiformity of development. Development may, depending on the species, or on the type of activity, involve either differentiation of partial patterns from a global whole, and their integration . . . or the integration of originally juxtaposed, relatively isolated global units which now become differentiated parts of a newly formed pattern.

3. Continuity versus discontinuity of development. The increase in differentiation and integration are the forms and processes which undergo two main kinds of changes: (a) quantitative changes which are either gradual or abrupt; (b) qualitative changes which by their very nature are discontinuous.

4. Unilinearity versus multilinearity of development. The co-existence of unilinearity and multiplicity of individual develop-ment must be recognized for psychological just as it is for biological evolution . . . this polarity opens the way for a devel-opmental study of behavior not only in terms of universal se-quence but also in terms of individual variation, that is, in terms of growth viewed as a branching-out process of specialization or aberration.

5. Fixity versus mobility of developmental levels. All higher or-ganisms manifest a certain range of genetically different oper-ations. There is, so to speak, not only a "horizontal differentiation," but also a "vertical differentiation": the more mature compared with the less mature individual has at his disposal a greater num-ber of developmentally different operations (Wolff, 1960, pp. 29, 32).

Wolff includes one additional developmental principle: the polarity of maturation versus learning. These two poles are not independent variables as "every new behavior pattern which is differentiated as the result of experience acquires develop-mental significance only after it is integrated into the innate organization. Maturation enters as the organism's fundamental tendency to organize and integrate all experiences which can be assimilated; learning enters as the means of introducing new experiences into the organization so as to alter behavior in ac-cordance with reality" (Wolff, 1960, p. 35).

These general principles can be applied to the sequences of the life course in early life as well as in the second half of life. Wolff's perspectives help us to reconceptualize existing ideas and more fully appreciate the idea that aging throughout the life course is an ongoing process.

Our Russian colleagues have also contributed to an un-derstanding of development from a perspective that has pur-sued a course different, yet in some ways parallel, to the psychoanalytic conception of developmental processes. The studies of two of their outstanding researchers are briefly de-scribed in order to familiarize the reader with their work. The first contribution comes from the germinal investigator and theoretician, L. S. Vygotsky (1978). Vygotsky wrote many sig-nificant papers and books and founded a school of Soviet psy-chology that has extended his ideas into newer areas. Vygotsky's early death in 1934, at age thirty-eight, cut short a promising career. Some of his works are now being translated into English by a group of American psychologists and linguists including Michael Cole, James Wertsch, and their colleagues.

Vygotsky was critical of theories which claimed that the properties of adult intellectual functions arose from maturation alone—just simply waiting for opportunities to manifest themselves.

He stressed the social origins of thinking and language and was a pioneer in suggesting the mechanisms by which culture becomes a part of each person's nature. Using a Marxist theoretical framework, he held that

> all phenomena be studied as processes in motion and in change . . . the scientist's task is to reconstruct the origin and course of development of behavior and consciousness. Not only does every phenomenon have its history, but this history is characterized by changes both qualitative (changes in form and structure and basic characteristics) and quantitative. [He] applied this line of reasoning to explain the transformation of elementary psychological processes into complex ones [in the course of development] [Vygotsky, 1978, pp. 6–7].

Vygotsky's "developmental" approach is differentiated from a theory of child development in that it relates external changes in society and material life to changes in consciousness and behavior. The internalization of tool and sign systems, which are culturally produced, brings about the behavioral changes and bridges early and later forms of individual development. Using experimental methods in some ways similar to those of Werner, Vygotsky ingeniously devised means of "telescoping the actual course of development of a given function" (p. 12). This approach, when augmented by the intensity of individual behavior over long periods, as is done by psychoanalysis, can provide complementary ways of devising and testing developmental hypotheses. In some ways, like Piaget, Vygotsky "sought to reconstruct the series in intellectual operations that normally unfold during the course of the child's biographical development" (p. 13). Vygotsky's ideas about internalization of higher psychological functions should be noted. He writes that the process of internalization consists of a series of transformations:

> (a) An operation that initially represents an external activity is reconstructed and begins to occur internally.
>
> (b) An interpersonal process is transformed into an intrapersonal one. Every function in the child's cultural development appears twice: first, on the social level, and later, on the individual level; first between people (interpsychological) and then inside the child (intrapsychological). . . .
>
> (c) The transformation of an interpersonal process into an intrapersonal one is the result of a long series of developmental events [pp. 56–57]. Functions develop gradually. Their transfer inward is linked with changes in the laws governing their activity: they are incorporated into a new system with its own laws [p. 57].

From the psychoanalytic perspective, this last transformational process can give rise to autonomy and independence and make possible and reexternalization of the intrapersonal (intrapsychic) in transferential interpersonal relationships, such as the psychoanalytic situation. Much more can and will be said about Vygotsky's theories and psychoanalysis as we have the opportunity to study his work.[4]

El'konin (1971) addressed the problem of stages in the mental development of the child and patterns of transition from one stage to the next. He stated that the existing conception of developmental stages was open to question. It is noted that P. P. Blonsky, in 1930 and 1934, as mentioned in El'konin, questioned the immutability of the stages of development. The processes of mental development being subjected to changes in the external world. Childhood was seen as different at each stage of evolution and of mankind's own historical development. Thus, adolescence and youth are "by no means a universal human characteristic" (p. 540). When there were unfavorable conditions, growth and development ceased at puberty. Blonsky's idea can be applied to aging and the aged. When people

---

[4] Of unrelated but historical interest is the fact that Vygotsky and his student, A. R. Luria, wrote the foreword to the Russian edition of S. Freud's "Beyond the Pleasure Principle," published in Moscow in 1925.

died at much earlier ages, there were few opportunities for studying aging and the aged. As man lives longer as the result of society's improved medical, nutritional, and social conditions, we can expect new data and new theories to emerge. Newer developmental progressions and natural declines may be observed which previously were not seen.

Blonsky, who "considered child development to be primarily a process of qualitative transformations accompanied by sudden breaks and leaps" (El'konin, 1971, p. 540), wrote in 1930, "these changes . . . may occur in the form of sharp crises, or they may take place gradually, almost imperceptibly. Let us agree to call those times in a child's life that are distinguished from one another by larger or smaller crises, 'periods' and 'stages' respectively. Further, let us refer to those times in a child's life that only flow into one another as 'phases' " (p. 540). Blonsky's suggestions apply to adult as well as to child development; he suggests that we are dealing with continuities as well as with discontinuities. Some discontinuities are predictable; others are not. The concept of crisis is consistent with the recent work on catastrophe theory, which I will shortly discuss.

In the early 1930s, Vygotsky also wrote on the problem of age. He stated:

> We may provisionally define psychological age as a specific epoch, cycle, or stage of development, as a definite, relatively self-contained period of development whose significance is determined by its place in the general developmental cycle and within each of which the general laws of development are expressed in a qualitatively distinct fashion. . . .
>
> In the transition from one age level to another we find the emergence of new structures that were absent in earlier periods; we can see a reorganization and alteration of the very course of development. Thus the development of the child is but a continuous transition from one age level to another, accompanied by developmental changes in the child's personality. The study of child development is the study of the child's transition from one age level to another and of the change in his personality within each age period as these changes occur under concrete sociohistorical conditions [El'konin, 1971, p. 541].

Vygotsky also observed that "only internal changes in the

course of development itself, only sharp breaks and turning points during development, can give us a reliable foundation for determining those basic epochs in the formation of the child's personality that we call 'ages' " (pp. 541–542). These ages of stability are interrupted by ages of crisis.

Before continuing with a description of El'konin's work, let me suggest that the recently described catastrophe theory of Thom may have applicability to the idea of crisis and discontinuity in development. Catastrophe theory is a new way of thinking about change. Although the name suggests disaster, it is applied to nondisaster situations where mathematical models are used to predict abrupt crises resulting from discontinuous change. Its utilization in studies of development, as yet unknown to me, suggests the applicability of such research to aging crises where prediction and preventive intervention may be possible (Thom, 1975; Woodcock and Davis, 1978).

Both Blonsky and Vygotsky conceptualized development, as we still do, in terms of stages. Leont'ev (1965), as cited in El'konin (1971), felt "that each stage of mental development is characterized by one dominant relationship of the child to his environment, by one dominant activity within that given stage" (El'konin, 1971, p. 544). Leont'ev's formulation, similar to that of Erikson, has no reference, however, to unconscious or internalization processes. Vygotsky, in the 1930s, emphasized the necessity for considering the development of affect and intellect as a dynamic unity, a unity not emphasized by Piaget. Nonetheless, there exists a dualism despite Vygotsky's ideas—"mental development . . . is seen to follow two basic and parallel lines: the line of development of the need-motivational [affective] sphere and the line of development of the intellectual [cognitive] processes. It is this dualism and parallelism that we must overcome in order to understand the mental development of the child as a unitary process" (El'konin, 1971, p. 546). El'konin observes that Piaget's theory of intellectual and cognitive development is different from Freud's theory of development as it related to the need-affective sphere. Piaget's child's adaptation is to the "world of things," and Freud's theory deals with mechanisms for the child's adaptation to the "world of people." El'konin transforms these two independent systems into one unified system through a formulation that emphasizes the "child in society" or child–social object. Using internalization or a special form of learning, the child relates to the physical properties of the object as well as to the human meanings of objects and their behavior. The adult is the bearer of certain types of social activity, the performer of certain tasks, an individual who exists in various relations to other people. "The ends and motives of an adult's activity are not outwardly visible from the activity itself. Outwardly, the child sees that activity as the transformation and production of objects" (El'konin, 1971, p. 551). There is a unitary process contributing to personality formation; that is, child–social object–social adult. Important from the psychoanalytic point of view is El'konin's statement that "in the process of learning an action, the action seems to become detached from the object on which it was originally learned: the action is transferred to other objects that, although similar, are not identical with the original object. In this fashion, actions are generalized" (p. 554). Put into a psychoanalytic frame of reference, this description is similar to the concept of displacement which has emotional meaning and is not always externally observable, even though it is present unconsciously. El'konin again writes that "Interpersonal relations can be, and are, built on the basis not only of mutual respect but also of complete trust and a mutually shared private, inner world" (p. 557). This inner world is related to the inner unconscious system of relationships, aims, values, ideals, conflicts, defenses, and sublimations.

El'konin's developmental scheme consists of "periods characterized chiefly by the assimilation of the objectives, motives, and norms of human relations and, on that basis, by the development of the need-motivational sphere, and . . . of periods characterized chiefly by the acquisition of socially evolved modes of action with objects and, on that basis, the formation of the child's intellectual and cognitive powers, his operational and technical capabilities" (p. 560). El'konin discriminates two sharp transitions in children's mental development. The first is termed the *three-year-old crisis*, and the second is referred to as the *puberty crisis*. A comparison of the behaviors of these two transitions reveals a great similarity between them. His schema of development consists of three periods: early childhood, childhood, and adolescence. Each period is divided into two stages: infancy and early childhood, preschool and early school, and early and late adolescence. Each stage in turn has two phases, the second one involved with transition. El'konin sees the process of development as an ascending spiral rather than as a linear progression, with transitional periods and stages that link succeeding periods and stages with antecedent ones. No reference is made to adult development.

In contemporary psychoanalysis, we find related issues similar to those of El'konin; for example, Settlage at the 1979 International Psycho-Analytical Congress suggested that "throughout developmental progression, each stage confronts the same generic issues, namely: new intrinsic phase-specific biological changes and developmental tasks; new extrinsic demands for adaptation—with related interpersonal conflicts; new intrapsychic conflicts" (Settlage, 1979, p. 6). There may also be particular satisfactions and masteries associated with developmental progression, and these may play a role in facilitating progression onward. Development is continuous and cumulative, but it is also discontinuous, and certain aspects may appear, disappear permanently, or reappear at a later time. Continuity may not be a sine qua non for later developmental progressions. Explaining the meaningfulness of traumata "after the fact" may be useful to our understanding but may deter us from fully understanding why some traumata are pathogenic, while others are not. Making an a priori prediction, if possible, about the importance of a traumatic intervention in development gives greater credence to the significance of the trauma, employing it as an explanation after outcome is already known. A priori prediction is not always possible, but, as an ideal, it is worthwhile to strive for its attainment. Several predictive studies have been reported in the psychoanalytic and psychosomatic literature; for example, Benedek and Rubenstein (1942), Alexander, French, and Pollock (1968), and Pollock and Pilot (1970). Life-stress events can adaptively result in regressive behavior throughout the course of life, but such events even in later adult developmental periods can be progressive, creative, and fulfilling. Erikson has recently suggested that life cycles are embedded in generational cycles and that generativity has a procreative libido beyond genitality. Generational renewal is linked to cultural renewal (1979). This perspective creatively forms a new linkage that will become increasingly important—that of cultural evolution and immortality.

Neubauer (1979) has noted that the life cycle and the developmental point of view rest on our knowledge of phase organization and of processes of differentiation and dedifferentiation. The distinction between "dissection of psychic material and reconstruction of past events," as seen in adult psychoanalyses based on direct observation of the ongoing development of children in treatment, is very useful, but it should be added that one can observe internal and external developmental unfoldings in adults. In discussing developmental phases, Neubauer correctly emphasizes that phases overlap, are not clearly delineated one from the other, coexist with earlier phase derivatives, and may be in evidence in later phases. He asks if there might not be numerous variations in development; for example, some progression or regression sequences in cognition, maturation, or libidinal organization. He asserts that, while variations occur, "there is a core constellation from the earliest years which seems to coexist next to the progressive processes" (1979, p. 14). This is similar to the coexistence of memory and memory traces within the psychic apparatus from all periods of development. Neubauer suggests that one can have continuity and discontinuity simultaneously coexisting in different areas and in different fields. His current thinking extends our conceptualization of development and is consistent with what has been presented above.

CLINICAL STUDIES

General Considerations

In the first part of this chapter, the focus was on normal aging or developmental processes and concepts. In this section, the concentration will be on clinical phenomena. My data derive from two sources: personal and clinical. My own personal contacts with aging or developing individuals at various points of the adult life course include colleagues who shared their feelings and reflections with me and others who were relatives and friends. My insights into my own aging processes have also been very useful. The processing of my self-observations undoubtedly reflects my own subjectivity. I have tried to objectify some of these experiences and compare them with those of others. My clinical data derive from an increasing number of middle- and later-age patients referred to me for consultation and treatment.

Since there is already an increasing body of clinical data on middle age, I shall not emphasize that period here but shall report on my work with older adults. More recently I have undertaken intensive psychotherapeutic work, including psychoanalytic treatment, with patients in their sixties, seventies, and eighties. There have been few reports of such depth in psychological therapies in the literature, although more such work is being done by clinicians.

Earlier psychoanalysts who have treated older individuals have reported substantial successes. Even in fairly late maturity, there can be important personality changes. Significant transformations, shifts, modifications, and newfound "freedoms" after intensive therapy can result. The death of a restrictive parent or spouse can result in personal creative happiness, even growth. But in the therapeutic situation, internal freedom and growth are possible without such external events. In some gifted individuals, truly creative ideas, productions, and innovations can appear. Certain personality organizations obviously are not amenable to such change in treatment. However, some unfortunate persistent situations need to be examined carefully before attributing immutability to aging per se. The fixity of certain pathological characteristics may not be true for other ones. Such rigidities, if they are indeed rigidities, when evaluated from the psychoeconomic, psychodynamic, and psychoadaptive reference frames, may prove to be reversible through treatment. Unpredictable behaviors and symptoms should also be examined carefully to ascertain what might be responsible for their emergence and the effects they may have on subsequent development through therapy.

Kohlen (1959) studied changing motivations during the life course. He suggests two broad contrasting motivational tendencies: expansion and restriction. The need for continued expansion (achievement, sense of significance, and ongoingness) he suggests is more frequently evident in the expansive earlier years, while the increased need to defend against anxiety due to physical and social losses becomes increasingly evident in the latter part of adulthood. Both expansion and restriction may be seen throughout the life course. Esteem needs exist at all times, although the means of satisfying such needs vary throughout life. Losses and anxiety are similarly seen throughout life and, in some instances, may be more intense and debilitating in earlier life than in the later years. The older one gets, the greater the likelihood that life disruptions and life crises can occur. Some of these produce changes that are externally unchangeable. The reactions to these life events, however, need not yield psychical incapacity, especially if the traumata and changes can initiate a successful mourning-liberation process. Significant positive changes can occur in the advanced years and after painful losses, frustrations, or upsetting disruptions. Successful adjustment in old age is more likely to be seen in those who have positive self-images and age identifications, are busy, and occupy significant interpersonal roles (e.g., employed, married), have varied social contacts and activities, and are oriented toward the future in a positive fashion. Health and socioeconomic status are also important factors (Kohlen, 1959, p. 893).

Chronological age is a convenient means of ordering developmental and observational data on an easily identified temporal axis. This allows us to compare different individuals who are at the same point in time but whose psychical constructions vary.

Psychoanalysts are connoisseurs of dynamic psychopathology. Extrapolating from the clinical, they have formulated hypotheses about normality, now buttressed by actual observations of children of various ages. However, the reference base is still that of childhood. Although few would disagree with this emphasis, the necessity for obtaining internal and external observations from individuals throughout the course of life is imperative if we are to understand normal aging development. Constructions, reconstructions, and transference data are not our only source of information about adults of all ages. Data obtained from other sources can be of great value when compared with these clinical data. The phrase "course of life" is used here as it refers to the individual. Life cycle seems more appropriate for a generational perspective. Cyclicity implies a return to an original point of beginning, and for the individual the life course begins at conception and ends with death. There is no "starting over" again. During the life course, various complex forces shape the individual. Differentiation and dedifferentiation, separation and return to the earlier holistic state, individuation and its prior deindividuated state occur regularly and may be nonpathological (e.g., sleeping and dreaming). It may be reductionistic and oversimplifying to identify only one focus and link it to an entire age period. We deal with complexity, pluralistic and multiple variables all operating at the same time, although one or another may be more clearly observed at a single time or age range. We may see shifts that are rapid or slow, permanent or transitory, reversible and irreversible (especially in the biological sphere). Deviations from the norm may or may not be pathological. Freud opened the realm of the unconscious for us, and this has added another world to our complexity, that of the inner life. At times, for purposes of communication, scientific discourse, and study, we have to work with single or isolated variables, keeping in mind that we are still dealing with complex interreactions, which can influence and alter the many coexisting operating variables.[5]

Abraham (1919) believed it was "incorrect to deny *a priori* the possibility of exercising a curative influence upon the neuroses in the period of involution" (p. 313). Some of his most successful cures occurred with middle-aged patients. He concluded that the age at which psychoanalysis was begun was of lesser importance than the age at which the neurosis first manifested itself. After Abraham's report, few papers were published on the psychoanalytic therapy of middle-aged and later-life adults. Jelliffe (1925), Kaufman (1937, 1940), Atkin (1940), Grotjahn (1940), and Gitelson (1948) all indicated the possible successful outcomes of therapeutic work with patients in these age groups. In 1955, Grotjahn reported on the analytic psychotherapy of the elderly, and Segal (1958) published the account of her analysis of a man in his mid-seventies. For the

---

[5] In examining the published literature on intensive psychotherapeutic work with older adults, the Boston group has been in the forefront. The works of M. Berezin, S. Cath, R. Kahana, S. Levin, and N. Zinberg are especially to be noted.

next twenty years analytic communications were either non-existent or very sparse. Since the mid-1970s, we have begun to see a reversal of this situation. I specifically refer to the works of Boland (1972), King (1974, 1979), Guntrip (1975), A. M. Sandler (1978), and Shainess (1979). We will undoubtedly find an increasing number of publications on the topic of the psychoanalysis of middle-aged and later-aged adult patients in the future.

The reluctance to undertake intensive therapeutic work with individuals in later life may have reflected a bias on the part of the therapist. Freud wrote about the difficulties in analyzing older individuals. In the *New Introductory Lectures on Psycho-Analysis* (1932), he suggested that among the various factors which cramped the therapeutic effectiveness of psychoanalysis was the amount of psychical rigidity correlated with age. As people get older there is "a general stiffening of mental life; the psychical processes, to which one could very well indicate other paths, seem incapable of abandoning the older ones" (p. 154). Fenichel (1972) suggested that the optimal age for psychoanalytic treatment is between fifteen and forty and that, after that time analysis might be counterindicated; however, other briefer and less intensive forms of psychotherapy might be preferable. In his paper, "The Aims of Psychotherapy," Jung wrote:

> It was with the older patients that I had the greatest difficulties, that is with persons over 40. . . . It seems to me that the basic facts of the psyche undergo a very marked alteration in the course of life, so much so that we could almost speak of a psychology of life's morning and a psychology of its afternoon. As a rule, the life of a young person is characterized by a general expansion and a striving towards concrete ends, and his neurosis seems mainly to rest on his hesitation or shrinking back from this necessity. . . .

Jung continued:

> The life of an older person is characterized by a contraction of forces, by the affirmation of what has been achieved and by the curtailment of further growth. His neurosis comes mainly from his clinging to a youthful attitude which is now out of season.

Just as the young man is afraid of life, so the older one shrinks back from death. What was a normal goal for the young man becomes a neurotic hindrance to the old. It is natural that neurosis, resistance, repression, transference, guiding philosophies and so forth, should have one meaning for the young and quite another in the old, despite apparent similarities [1936, p. 66].

Jung noted that about a third of his older-age patients were not suffering from any clinically definable neurosis but from a feeling of the senselessness and aimlessness of their lives. He suggested that this might be called the general neurosis of our age. He went on to state that two-thirds of his patients were in the second half of life, were socially well adapted, and often of outstanding ability. Most importantly, Jung suggested that people in the second half of life no longer needed to educate their conscious will but needed to experience their own inner being. Social usefulness was not an aim for them; indeed, the goal was to acquire an inner stability and a new trust in themselves. This goal seemed more appropriate to the second half of life, to those who have already achieved a shape and a resolution of their sexual and incestuous problems.

My own experience is at variance with that of those who were skeptical about treating older adults with depth psychological methods. The latter half of life is a very long period—it can begin in the early thirties and extends to death. In my experience, this span of life seemingly has various phases, stages, periods, or whatever grouping one uses. Each of these has its own stage-phase-period specific developmental issues. Many different spheres of influence interact at different times of the life course, and these have been called the developmental fields. These fields include the many forces operating on the individual. The fields, integrated and combined in characteristic ways, form a whole life-course pattern. Retrospectively viewed, they almost seem like a life strategy that has been enacted. At various critical transitions, individuals may return to earlier developmental fields.

The life revision that occurs, consciously or unconsciously, as each stage is entered into and a new integration brought about, gives the process (life) a spiraling or helical character. Because each of the points at which there is a necessary turning involves fairly fundamental revision . . . each (can be designated) as a "life crisis." . . . At the time of these critical transitions there is an "unfreezing," a disorganization during which established patterns are loosened. The reorganization follows. In the period of disorganization a revision occurs which provides a potential challenge to develop new patterns for all strands, not only the one in which the transition occurs. For example, when an individual marries, his patterns of heterosexual and family relationships, his orientation to work and career, his pattern of involvement in peer group activities and his other life interests are all likely to be affected [Rapoport and Rapoport, 1975, pp. 20–21].

My own work on change suggests that crises and reorganizations are facilitated by a transformational adaptive process which I call the mourning-liberation process and which has a creative outcome (Pollock, 1977b). The Rapoports divide the later adult life span into various phases that are linked to social role, e.g., the three phases of later life are: preretirement (50–60/65); retirement (60/65–75); and old age (75 +). Each phase has its preoccupations, potential problems, and potential rewards. The earlier adult phase between twenty-five and fifty-five, called the establishment phase by the Rapoports, includes three subphases, each relating to children and school (e.g., early establishment—preschool children; midestablishment—children at school; late establishment—children out of school). The empirical research of the Rapoports is one scheme for classifying the period loosely called the second half of life.

We are familiar with Erikson's contributions on the identity cycle (1959). His "epigenetic" scheme describes the development of health or mental vitality in age-correlated stages. Erikson notes that each stage becomes a crisis as incipient growth and awareness of a new function go together with a shift in instinctual energy. This may cause a specific vulnerability in the self at that transition stage. Erikson's stages of the life cycle pose stage-specific polarities which include the major task or the then-current actual issues of psychic equilibrium. Polarities from other developmental stages, though not central, are present but are of less significance.

Particular stages in the life course carry a specific importance for particularly vulnerable individuals, but some have special meaning for almost all who are in that state of their life.

In 1965, Jaques published what is now a classic paper entitled "Death and the Mid-Life Crisis." Jaques suggests a developmental crisis around the age of sixty-five. We should note that his focus is on specific crises or transition points in the life course that have singular importance. Biological aging, cross-cultural, and cross-socioeconomic variables are additional dimensions we face in assessing the psychological status of an aging adult. Do we find psychological reactions to biological changes that usher in various stages of adult development? My answer is "yes"—the ego can sensitively pick up cues of biological change even before they are grossly in evidence. In similar fashion, one might suggest that biological reactions can occur in response to psychosocial changes. The vulnerable individual can have psychological and emotional responses, some quite severe, to these biological alterations and conversely biological responses to emotional alterations. Some reactions may be psychoemotional reactions without reference to a biological stimulus. Empirical findings from individuals who lost parents or siblings in childhood illustrate the importance of earlier pathogenic traumatic occurrences which predispose such an individual to a severe reaction to a later life change or loss.

Classifications of Dysfunction and Disorders

In all developmental periods there are dysfunctions and tensions during transition periods, whether these change periods are sudden or gradual. When dysfunction or disorder accompanies such transitions, the possible specific meanings of the presenting signs and symptoms need to be understood. Developmental tensions, including their behavioral and emotional expressions, need not be indicators of deviancy or pathology. However, as the elderly begin to show dysfunction which can lead to disorder and/or disease, even though these processes may be "normal" for individuals of a given age, they still may appear pathological when we use as our basis for comparison an image that is unrealistic. For the older adults, our fantasy may be based on the idea that elderly equals disease. Although older people may be more vulnerable to stress, this does not represent disease but may be a manifestation of development during that part of the life course. Emotional decompensations secondary to physical illnesses may be the norm and not pathological for this age group. The slowing down, lack of memory, and deficits in vision, hearing, and mobility can curtail the ability to deal with environmental challenges, stresses, and strains. This is to be distinguished from exacerbated earlier psychic conflicts, regressions to earlier fixation points, newer psychopathological constructions, or serious reactive responses to loss. For example, as the postparental and retirement stages are ushered in, involuntary social isolation, role loss, loss of social support systems and networks, and loss of outlets for aggression or libido may become contributory stressful factors that can give rise to symptoms. In addition to the usual stress disorders, depressions, suicidal attempts, alcoholism, drug abuse, hypochondriacal reactions, paranoid suspicions, anxiety, obsessions, and regression to confused, restless, and incontinent behaviors can occur. As already mentioned, reactivation of earlier conflicts which had been kept repressed may emerge in more blatant form. Understanding the meaning of these various symptoms can be a perplexing diagnostic problem.

Underlying, reemerging, or compensated ongoing neuroses, psychoses, or personality disorders may be seen as reactive to decompensations socially or biologically, and their true significance may remain undetected and so untreated. Instead, institutional isolation may be recommended. Psychoanalytical treatment is not indicated for many of these diseases, but careful psychological assessment and diagnosis are useful.

Specific reactions to midlife (thirty-five years and upward) and maturity (sixty-five and upward) crises usually have unconscious meaning. Manifestations of tension may be related to particularly frightening specific transitions. As a result of earlier traumata, such as childhood parent or sibling loss, the individual may be vulnerable to sudden life-course changes. These transitional stresses, seen in adolescence, in early adult life, at menopause, when newer status roles and sexual tensions can occur, give rise to serious psychic disruptions. Similar event-related stresses may serve as the trigger for reactions to aging throughout the life course; for example, anniversary responses, special problems resulting from bodily changes, changes in appearance, isolation and aloneness, reactions to losses, especially of spouses and friends, and retirement. Problems of retirement result from diminished self-esteem, isolation, diminished social significance, increased aggression which cannot be discharged in one's work, economic insecurities, increased helplessness and dependence, and fears of illness and disability. Memory erosion, diminished capacity for new learning, protective conservatism against change, and diminished sexuality complicate the diagnostic picture.

Butler and Lewis (1973) have classified the factors affecting subjective experience, overt behavior, and level of adaptations in the elderly into environmental or external factors and intrinsic factors. In the former category, we find personal losses of loved and significant figures, and social-economic adversities, unwanted retirement, and cultural devaluations with accompanying feelings of uselessness, therapeutic pessimism, forced isolation, and segregation. Internal factors include personality organization; physical illness including brain and perceptual damage; age-specific changes, such as changes in body size and appearance, losses of speed in understanding, and experiences of bodily dissolution and approaching death (p. 29). Gradually there is a loss of energy, mental acuity, sense of humor, the sense of freedom and autonomy. The individual shifts from being an active participant *in* life to a passive viewer *of* life. Mastery, play, fantasy, and enthusiasm gradually evaporate, and if the individual "listens to his mind," he becomes more fearful and psychically debilitated. There is depression, exhaustion, and sleeplessness which can further isolate the individual and make it uncomfortable for children and friends who begin to avoid the aging person. Fear of residential care meshes with the guilt of the caretakers (spouse, children), and further avoidance and alienation occur. The wish for contact and the rage at being betrayed by one's body, family, fate, or even by one's religion compound the already difficult situation. When restrictions of diet, drinking, activities, and mobility are imposed, a further stress appears, and death is welcomed—not feared.

Gutmann (1979) has observed that the geriatric psychiatrist sees older patients as terminating instead of aging, and the generalization is frequently made that the aging individual is a dying person. We know this is not so. It is as if we play the finale when there are still one or two movements left in the life symphony. In some ways, the death and dying movement, though focusing on an essential aspect of the life course that we previously avoided, has focused more of our attention on the end instead of on life and living. Gutmann correctly notes that "the ubiquitous application of the depletion doctrine may lead theorists and therapists to misdiagnose some important strengths of the elderly, and even to code them as weaknesses, that is, as further evidence of loss."

In my own experience, the completion of the mourning-liberation process in the aging or even the aged person, accomplished through intensive therapy, can result in creative freedoms, further development, joy, and the ability to embrace life. Gutmann has called our attention to role exchanges between men and women in the mid- and postmidlife period. These, too, can result in anxiety, fears of passivity, diminished self-esteem in males, while women may be threatened by their new roles and new strengths and experience anxiety about the shifts in their relationships with their partners and children. Both passivity and activity in men and women can give rise to tensions when they are not anticipated and when they require a restructuring of an established, adult, symbiotic relationship.

In 1964, I suggested that symbiotic unions are part of all meaningful human relationships throughout the course of life. These symbiotic balances reflect the past states of psychoecological equilibrium, as well as current balances of relationship. Development at all levels occurs in a field in which there is a connection between innate and early maturational forces, later forces, and environmental and social fields in which the individual is situated. There can be different levels of symbiosis, different qualitative and quantitative aspects of the symbiosis. When changes occur in the symbiotic field, as occur in and after midlife, we find that shifts in the field may cause tensions, reawaken old buried conflicts, and stimulate anxieties. These may also be part of the pathological pictures we observe in our patients. Such shifts in symbiotic unions, however, can give rise to more creative relationships, once relative stability in the "new" union is established (Pollock, 1964).

Some of the diagnostic problems one confronts in the aging and the aged individual have been discussed. The importance of patience, sincere caring, and careful attention to process and personality is essential, if one is to avoid therapeutic nihilism and prejudice and if one is to be of assistance to those who otherwise might not be cared for.

Treatment

The treatment modalities used for the aging and the aged patient will be determined by the diagnosis of the patient's problem, the understanding of the psychopathological processes, the ability, feelings, and interest of the therapist, the availability of support systems which can assist the patient, and the attitudes of the family and of society. Residential care, medical treatments, and pharmacotherapy are not discussed here, although each can be important, and each has psychological significance. What I wish to focus on in this portion is the individual depth psychotherapy and psychoanalysis of the aging and aged patient. As already indicated, one must understand the individual, the presenting problems, as well as the meaning of the symptoms. Complete resolution of the psychopathology is not always possible for any patient—improvement of functioning, increased comfort, and a greater ability to deal with present and future, however, are possible and well worth the therapeutic investment of patient and therapist. We frequently encounter in work with aging or aged patients the same outcome considerations as seen in therapeutic work with younger individuals.

King (1974) observed that an important reason for her patients seeking treatment was their increasing awareness of changes brought about by the physical, psychological, and social effects of aging on themselves. When they could no longer deny these realities, there was an undermining of the effectiveness of their narcissistic equilibrium. The prospect of aging was threatening, and they feared fragmentation or disintegration. King noted that threats in the life situation of middle-aged patients bring a dynamic and urgent sense to their analyses, and this motivation assists in establishing and consolidating a more productive therapeutic alliance than one may be able to establish with young adult patients with similar character structures. Where therapy is successful, such patients may begin to find new forms of creativity within themselves, as well as new satisfactions with life, their friends, and their families.

There are a variety of methods by which an individual can deal with suffering. The simplest and perhaps most basic is to withdraw oneself from the source of the pain. This flight reaction is well known to all of us. It is the counterpart of the fight reaction, which describes the active attempts to master the uncomfortable situation. What determines whether "flight" or "fight" will be the predominant mode of response is complex. My intent here is to call attention to these contrasting methods of defense which, though external, have their internal psychological meaning; for example, depression can be seen as a "flight" response, whereas aggression may be a "fight" equivalent. In "flight" responses there may be a turning against the self as a symbolic means of dealing with conflict. When this occurs, splitting may be the mechanism used. The individual is sufferer as well as persecutor or attacker of himself. The alien part of the self may be perceived as foreign or external to the self. In this way, externalization, or viewing the bad as coming from the outside, allows for displacement to the outside and can be viewed as a form of the fight-flight mechanism. This mechanism of defense used in the middle- and later-age person can too frequently be ignored, misunderstood, or viewed as a serious indicator of pathology. Through insight, it can be understood by the patient and then disappear, as the underlying conflict is resolved. The above mechanism was presented as an illustration of how defenses can be used in later life when people confront newer and later stresses that may be age-specific, even though a serious defensive pattern is used.

In my analytic work with middle-aged or elderly patients, I follow the principle of analytic neutrality but may make exceptions in instances where minimal contact with the patient's physician is indicated; for example, where the primary-care physician prescribes medication. I rarely do the prescribing, but I want to know what drugs the patient is currently using and for what purpose. Usually my patients, like those of King and others, are motivated to work hard in their treatment. They are less likely to feel shame and guilt about the past, but these affects can and do appear in the transference situation. The recrudescence of symptoms, conflicts, memories, and feelings, seen in the termination phase of an analysis and in follow-up studies of analysis, is similar to the reworking characteristic of the mourning process but also to the life review observed in the reminiscence of the elderly.

In the elderly, where reminiscence is common, there is a particular and special therapeutic benefit from remembering, free association, dream recollection, and fantasy elaboration. Memory can be used to rescue people, places, and events from insignificance. These patients feel in control, have a sense of self-esteem by being able to do what is requested, achieve some relief from the cathartic expression of their feelings and concern, and have a diminished sense of isolation and loneliness; and when they can establish linkages between inside and outside and past and present, they find direct evidence that insight helps and gives relief. Therapeutic progress stimulates hope and facilitates the process even further. Older patients understand the difference between reality and transference. In several instances I have observed what I call the "son" or "child" transference. In this situation, the elderly patient relates to the analyst as if the analyst were the "son" or "child" who understands, is interested, is trustworthy, is protective and supportive, and who has regular, constant, and frequent contact. The patient shares his or her concerns which are not ignored or insensitively dismissed. The analyst does indeed fill these wished for needs to some extent but also uses interpretation to achieve insight, sees as his major therapeutic goal the relief of tension through understanding and the establishment of maintenance of a therapeutic connection. The many levels and meanings of the "son" or "daughter" transference can be analyzed quite profitably. Nonetheless, the reality meaning of an adult "child" who helps the older person cannot be overlooked and gives us information about the meaning of a child to an elderly parent. Analytic patients in the earlier middle years require little or no modification of classical analytic technique. They are and can be analyzed, and I have had successful therapeutic experiences with individuals in their late sixties and early seventies.

Parameters are more common with patients in their seventies and eighties. In working psychotherapeutically with the elderly, countertransference attitudes and feelings are of great significance. These sensitive patients can detect the therapist's mood and his ability to differentiate therapeutic issues from biological, psychosocial, emotional, and external reality problems. At times, encouraging patients to participate in social groups can be helpful. On other occasions, educational approaches can be therapeutic in addition to being supportive.

In dealing with aging issues, I have found the focus on the mourning-liberation process to be of great importance. The basic insight is that parts of self that once were, or that one hoped might be, are no longer possible. With the working out of the mourning for a changed self, lost others, unfulfilled hopes and aspirations, as well as feelings about other reality losses and changes, there is an increasing ability to face reality as it is and as it can be. "Liberation" from the past and the unattainable occurs. New sublimations, interests, and activities appear. There can be new relationships with old "objects" as well as new "objects." Past truly can become past, distinguished from present and future. Affects of serenity, joy, pleasure, and excitement come into being. Many mechanisms are involved in the therapy of the elderly. Kohut (1966) has called our attention to the transformation of narcissism into humor, wisdom, and the capacity to contemplate one's own impermanence. These qualities may be found in some individuals who have made peace with themselves while in the twilight of their existence. This ideal state, not guaranteed, is possible through successful therapeutic work.

Learning comes from insight, improvement from support and relationship, but also from identification with the therapist. This at times opens up areas for special analytic exploration which may include envy of or competition with the younger therapist who can do what the patient no longer can do but what he or she can contemplate. The wish to help or share experience with the younger therapist can be an outcome of resolution. Particularly sensitive areas relate to sexual longings in transference. There may be exacerbations of the infantile oedipal neurosis, castration, and mutilation anxiety, fear of helplessness and abandonment, as well as the earlier anaclitic, narcissistic, and preoedipal conflicts, wishes, desires, and needs. Libidinal overflows may evoke autoerotic activities that must be carefully handled and understood in the context of past as well as present. The reappearance of libidinal strivings in reality, in dreams, and in fantasies has positive implications for "investment in life." In a few instances, the reestablishment of sexual relations was not only a reinstitution of past but a new creative freedom in the present; pleasures previously unattained came into being.

Role reversals of parent-child occur in analysis. These can be interpreted without much threat or shame, if there is an effective therapeutic relationship. In some instances the natural children, very pleased to be freed of the responsibility for the psychological well-being of their aged parents, are more capable of providing significant support of the treatment and of the patient. Social contacts between children and parents are reinstituted, and in some instances more harmonious relationships exist than did previously. Acceptance, understanding interpretation, and insight are of critical importance when anger and greater assertiveness appear. Acting out such impulses can threaten the family. In the very few instances where there has been direct contact between analyst and family, this has been by telephone. Children who have a deep ambivalence about their aged parent may at times be harsh with him or her, especially if the parent is less capable of defending himself or herself. This has not been a major problem in my experience. The wisdom and insight achieved by the aging patient relieves these tense situations. One can open up the future without annulling the past. The aging analysand recognizes what he or she has done to alienate or affect the child who is now adult and that some things cannot be undone.

Termination problems are special situations. In some instances, there can be no complete severance of contact—a marked reduction of sessions with the option of infrequent meetings is often realistically sought and agreed to. In some instances, no further association with the patient occurs after termination. However, if biological failure occurs, home or hospital visits may be indicated. Awareness of countertransference feelings is of great significance when this "parameter" is employed. Especially important is the recognition of the shame and humiliation experienced by the very ill former analysand, who previously was more independent and competent.

I have encountered atypical situations that are different from what is encountered in the analysis of the middle-aged or younger adult patient. For example, the nursing home decision may necessitate talking with spouse and/or children as well as working with the patient; the mourning process of the entire family when a fatal illness is diagnosed; the unique problem of preparation of a will, and the attendant feelings of fear, depletion, loss, or insecurity as it relates to death.

In recent years, several "new" problem areas have appeared which require special attention: the premenopausal woman who continues on with analysis through the completion of the menopause; the middle-aged male patient who has had a myocardial infarction or a "successfully" treated malignancy; the individual in his or her sixties whose living and healthy parents become a social burden; the middle-aged mother or father who discovers that their child is homosexual or, if heterosexual, has decided to have no children. Earlier infantile, childhood, and adolescent unresolved intrapsychic conflicts frequently are exacerbated by such situations, but the reality of the external stress can produce its own strain which adds to other aging-process tensions and intrinsic psychopathology.

As with child and adolescent analysis, it is possible to make many observations during the course of the psychoanalytic treatment of middle-aged and later-aged analysands. What has been particularly illuminating is the opportunity to make observations on the internally changing meaning of significant figures at different periods of the life course. For example, as mentioned before, a spouse takes on different importance as life moves forward. The same is true for siblings, children, and parents. There are changing roles, changing meanings, and changing functions. As children establish their own families, their parents, siblings, and grandparents assume different meanings and importance, and contacts with them change. These changes can and do contribute to the stress-strain of aging and become woven into the therapeutic situation.

All individuals in their fifties, sixties, seventies, and eighties cannot be treated with psychoanalysis or insight psychotherapy. However, many more may be able to be helped than was previously thought possible. Increasingly, psychoanalysis can and will play a role in prevention. The knowledge gained from clinical work, longitudinal research, observations in various settings, cross-cultural studies, experimental investigations, and the use of cross-sectional techniques will allow us to understand, describe, explain, and predict core issues confronting individuals in the course of life; when such predictions can be made, and if proven correct, interventions can be considered. This truly can be a major contribution of psychoanalysis. Some problems, if detected early, can and are dealt with in a fashion that reduces later pathological effects. But there are some life events that, even when predicted, still have their traumatic effects, and there are some life events which cannot be predicted. Prior analytic treatment can help the aging individual to deal more effectively, less traumatically, and with fewer pathological consequences when such life events overtake the individual or affect those who are meaningful and significant to him or her. When such traumatized people enter intensive treatment, they can often more quickly form an effective therapeutic alliance, pick up pertinent past patterns that may be exacerbated, and be less threatened by the emergence of unconscious material in the therapeutic situation. They are sensitive to transference and can differentiate these issues from more realistic concerns, even though they may have transferential meanings. A preventive prior psychoanalysis is not being advocated, but attention is called to the author's experience with analysands where this has occurred. Underlying neurotic, borderline, and/or narcissistic disturbances previously untouched may quickly come onto center stage, or they may be embedded in concerns over more current issues and become clearer only as treatment continues. The role of psychoanalysis in prevention of disability should be explored more fully for individuals, young or old.

Creativity

Some individuals find their aging years rewarding, liberating, enjoyable—a time for personal growth, creativity, accomplishment, and pleasure. Some cultures provide possibilities for regenerating and continued meaningful development in later adulthood. No simple explanation has been offered to account for this successful adaptation in the later years. It is clear that adjustment in old age is related to adaptations earlier in life, but aspects of old age may be unique and ontogenetic for that period of life. There are sequences in development that are unique to the period of middle and later life. There may be the release of hitherto unexpressed potentials for creative behavior. Earlier adaptive patterns can affect structure, constrain, or facilitate the emergence of later life adaptations and creativity. One account of the later years of three great writers—Leo Tolstoy, Henry James, and W. B. Yeats—by Edel (1979) emphasizes the close relationship between aging and creativity. Edel calls this linkage "creative aging."

He suggests that "aging is a way of crystallizing and summarizing the life of art and the achievement of art. And when—amid the new despair that aging brings—the artist has experienced fulfillment of certain old unfulfilled needs, then he finds an expanding power of mind and utterance that can bring him to the supremacies of art" (p. 212). There have been some individuals who have surpassed themselves as they grew older; for example, Goethe, Rembrandt, Leonardo, Picasso, Michelangelo, Titian, Tintoretto, Bach, Beethoven, Verdi, Coleridge. We find orchestral conductors working until they reach advanced ages; for example, Stokowski, ninety-five; Toscannini, ninety; Stravinsky, eighty-eight; Walter, eighty-five. Aristotle and Freud are also excellent examples of the creative genius whose excellence progressed almost in parallel with their course of life.[6]

Longfellow wrote a poem to commemorate the fiftieth anniversary of his Bowdoin College class of 1825. I wish to quote a few lines from the poem, *Morituri Salutamus*.

It is too late! Ah, nothing is too late
Till the tired heart shall cease to palpitate.
Cato learned Greek at eighty; Sophocles
Wrote his grand Oedipus, and Simonides
Bore off the prize of verse from his compeers,
When each had numbered more than four-score years.
Chaucer, at Woodstock with the nightingales,
At sixty wrote the Canterbury Tales;

[6] The roster of contemporary women and men who have continued distinguished careers in the arts far into their advanced years also include Marc Chagall, Arthur Rubenstein, Aaron Copland, Georgia O'Keeffe, Martha Graham, Norman Rockwell, George Abbott, Alfred Hitchcock, Ruth Gordon, Eubie Blake, Eugene Ormandy, Robert Graves, Luis Buñuel, Josef Albers, Andres Segovia, and Henry Moore. It may be that in the arts, unlike the sciences, age is less a barrier to creativity (Livesey, 1978).

> Goethe at Weimar, toiling to the last,
> Completed Faust when eighty years were past.
> These are indeed exceptions; but they show
> How far the gulf-stream of our youth may flow
> Into the arctic regions of our lives . . .
> For age is opportunity no less
> Than youth itself, though in another dress
> And as the evening twilight fades away
> The sky is filled with stars, invisible by day.

We can learn much from studies of creative women and men, but such opportunities are also available in our work with less talented individuals. Some individuals who do not produce "works" are more talented than those who do, and some creative people have little talent. This idea will not be developed here. The creativity may be expressed in more personal ways—in creative dreaming—in creative living through a fulfilled life for self and for others. Although we are not knowledgeable about many aspects of creativity in the middle- and later-aged individual, we can study this area which involves us all. My own approach to the questions has been through the focus on the mourning-liberation process, but I recognize this as only one avenue, perhaps among many, that can lead us to more insight and understanding of the problem under discussion.

In prior research, I have suggested that one can observe the attempts or results of the mourning-liberation process in the works of the gifted. For example, some of the music and texts of Gustav Mahler are attempts to deal with his many childhood sibling losses, the loss of his mother, and the loss of his daughter. Käthe Kollwitz, in her art, was involved in attempting to work out her mourning process first for her baby brother, who died when she was a child, and later the death of her own son in the First World War. After the death of the woman who was his model, mistress, mother of his two sons, and later his wife, Claude Monet underwent a change of both personality and painting style. Soon after the death of Camille, Monet painted gray and white ice scenes of the Seine. But then, as his grief was beginning to lift, Monet's painting changed to color. His style also changed. Gone were the cheerful, gay, even playful themes which so often featured Camille in many roles in the same painting. Now Monet concentrated less on figures and more on color for color's sake (Southgate, 1979). One can speculate about the meaning of these changes in content, style, and color, but I will refrain from doing so and just call attention to the obvious connection of the mourning process to the change in the creative product.

Similar creative attempts linked to mourning, some successful and some not so, can be found with the work of writers, poets, philosophers, sculptors, political and religious leaders, and scientists. The mourning process is not the primary cause of the creative inspiration, the creative elaboration, or the creative medium, but it may give direction and content to the creative attempts and outcomes. Just as there is a relationship between creativity and the mourning-liberation process, so, it is suggested, is there a relationship between aging, developmental forces, and creativity. The mourning-liberation process is present in all of us throughout most of our life course. There are many paths that aging takes, but they all lead to the same destination. When one approaches that terminus, one is no longer dealing with creative aging; one is, it is hoped, coming to a peaceful and painless close, in some ways a liberation in itself.

CONCLUSIONS—SOME TENTATIVE AND SOME FIRM

In this chapter, several issues were discussed which bear upon general concepts of psychological development during the course of life. Aging was equated with development, and an attempt was made to focus on some aspects and unique features of the adult periods of the life span. Specifically discussed were the middle-age, later-age, and older later-age periods.

The sequences of the life course need not be seen as linear, even though life begins at conception and ends with death. The author suggests that developmental sequences can be conceptualized as fields of development. The field concept attempts to encompass many variables; for example, biological, psychological, sociocultural, and economic. Developmental progress can be viewed as gradual transformations of existing fields into different combinations which constitute new fields of development. In discontinuities or crises, shifts may be more rapid, may be primarily intrafield, with or without developmental progression. These disrupted fields or crises can be viewed as traumatic disturbances. If interferences with field reconstitution or field progressions take place, the traumatic has become the focus for pathological or deviated progression of aging. It is important to study how and what variables appear and combine, when there is a coming together on a time axis, and the fate of these constellations throughout the life span. Some features are predominantly associated with particular age/time periods of the life span. As these become more clearly defined, described, and related to a sequence of appearance, they become predictable expectations. These expectancies, when described for various life-course periods, provide the baseline data for definitions of the boundaries of normality. If deviation from normal base lines appears to be present, preventive and restorative measures can be instituted to return the individual to the normal course of development.

We should aim to identify the components associated with all life-course sequences. The evolving patterns are complex, even though our current discussions and formulations appear to be relatively simple. Although core stabilities appear to be relatively immutable from the earliest years of life, discontinuities and transformational processes occur and may influence core stabilities. Newer studies of prenatal and neonatal periods at one end of the life course and investigations of middle and later life periods at the other end of the life course are expanding our fields of inquiry and understanding.

Concepts of critical times, critical periods, or crisis periods refer to turning points or periods during which an organism can be influenced in significant ways by psychological, biological, or interpersonal events that can affect future development. If certain events do not occur at particular times, future development may be affected. If other events occur at particular times, future development may be affected. Dosage and quality of the events are also significant in development. We deal with multisystem functioning, where one system affects the others and conversely is affected by each of the other systems, singly or in combination. For purposes of study, one or another thread, strand, or seam is investigated, but in our overall assessment, the whole fabric must be considered as well as the parts, some of which may be more significant than others.

On the basis of research into the mourning-liberation process, four outcomes have been described:

1. The successful completion of the process with freedom to follow newer creative paths. These liberations can result in creative living as well as in more contributory creative work by the gifted.
2. Arrests in the development of the mourning process, which require special therapeutic management to allow the process to continue developing in a normal fashion.
3. Fixation at various points in the evolving mourning process. Regression to these earlier fixation points can result when at later developmental times various stresses and strains tax the integrative capacity of the organism.
4. Pathological mourning with the appearance of abnormalities and serious difficulties. In order to age successfully, the individual should be capable of mourning past states of self-organization, of reorganizing the reality of what is no more, and of successfully accepting present and future realities. Unsuccessful and pathological aging may be reflective of unsuccessful mourning-liberation processes and so constitutes a basis for aging or development pathology or deviance.

Individuals beyond the age of forty can successfully participate in intensive psychotherapeutic or psychoanalytic treatment. The capacity for developing a transference neurosis is present even in the elderly. Catharsis, confrontation, interpretation, working through of resistance, conflict resolution, dreaming, sublimatory transformations, the attainment of insights into past and present situations can occur in suitable individuals, even in the elderly periods of the life course. Creative living as an outcome of therapy does occur in individuals in middle, older, and late elderly periods of the life course. Hope of eternal life is not a treatment objective, despite the hidden wishes of some individuals. Alleviation of pain, resolution of conflicts with the appearance of new patterns of coping, and the achievement of insight can and do appear within the matrix of the interpersonal treatment situation. Aging can have its satisfactions, comforts, joys, and productive outcomes. When one recognizes and accepts that what is past is truly past, the present and future can be dealt with in a more realistic fashion. New investments in life, love, and sublimations can take place, as well as the capacity to meet the unpleasant challenges ahead. Life and living, change and transition, newer creative realignments are possible for the aging individual and in some instances for the aged as well. A critical aspect of the therapeutic process involves a working through of a mourning-liberation process.

Techniques of adult observation, comparable to those of child observation, can be used throughout the life course. These observations, both internal and external, can provide us with a data base for understanding development and its deviations. The transference situation encountered in therapeutic work with adults in the second half of life allows for the reenactment and understanding of prior unresolved intra- and interpsychic conflicts. It also affords us the opportunity to observe details of behavior associated with developmental progressions and tensions related to the specific age-development group in which the individual exists currently. The therapeutic situation becomes the "observational laboratory" in which to formulate new hypotheses, test existing theories, and conceptualize the chain of living.

Significant intimate human relationships change throughout the course of life. The kinship label is no guarantee that function and significance remain the same throughout life. Further studies are required in this new area of inquiry.

We can learn much from our work with aging throughout the course of life and from work with the aged. We can help this group of individuals, and in turn we ourselves can be helped with our own aging processes. We are not immune from that with which we are working and studying. Socrates put it well when he stated:

> I consider that the old have gone before us along a road which we must all travel in our turn and it is good we should ask them the nature of that road, whether it be rough and difficult, or easy and smooth [Plato, *The Republic*].

15
REMINISCENCES AND INSIGHT

In the elderly (but also in children and in some middle-aged adults), one can observe repetitive themes in the narratives, stories, and reminiscences communicated to the researcher. In the elderly, these frequently are dismissed as manifestations of senile change or unfounded fantasies. Even if these reminiscences are not of real events, they do have meaning, and this meaning is of significance to our understanding of such aged individuals.

My own experience leads me to conclude that such repetitions may be important to the individual in various ways, as adaptational attempts, relational-communication attempts, or self-therapeutic attempts. The recollections or fantasies of the past expressed in reminiscences help the elderly maintain a sense of continuity between past and present and between inside and outside. The events, relationships, and feelings recalled also maintain a sense of "me-ness." These recollection-reminiscences bridge time and maintain the sense of individual personality, especially when there is an inner awareness of diminishing ego intactness and competency. In some individuals, the frequently repeated tales of the past are similar to the repetition, remembering, and working through sequences observed in the psychoanalytic treatment situation. In some, the obsessive reiteration-and-recounting is similar to mourning work where recalling-and-expressing is part of the self-healing process. In some elderly, the recounting allows the investigator to observe the consistencies of the accounts as they are restated. Even if inaccurate in all details, they are accurate in their re-

Supported in part by the Anne Pollock Lederer Research Fund of the Institute for Psychoanalysis of Chicago.

Reprinted from *The Psychoanalytic Study of the Child*, 36:279–287. New Haven, CT: Yale University Press (1981).

flections of the intrapsychic state of the individual. When the psychoanalytic researcher notes content and context in which certain accounts are given, and is aware of the transference meanings of the communications, these additional data allow insight into the present and past mental and emotional life of the person. Again, the purposes of the reminiscence may be many, varied, and complex. I have found that reminiscence is a way of returning to the past, especially to periods of life when satisfactions and mastering took place. In some, the return is to past traumatic situations where attempts to "work through" these past, but still present, intense mental and emotional disturbances seem clear. The insight of the psychoanalytic observer allows for understanding the meaning of what is otherwise considered "the ramblings of old men and women."

In my own personal experience and in my work with others who have had psychoanalytic treatment, insight or "reinsight" can come relatively quickly in rediscovering exacerbated unresolved conflicts, the return of old defensive patterns, and their repeated transference manifestations. With such insights one can understand and rework the past as it is manifested in the present. As I shall show, insight and work go hand in hand.

I now turn to clinical data to illustrate and elaborate some aspects of how the therapist gains insight. A ninety-year-old man, Mr. A., quite intact physically, had to be placed in a residential nursing facility after the sudden death of his wife. She had, up to the time of her death, cared for him in all ways and had, at times, felt quite distressed by his failures of memory. He was initially bewildered at the time of his loss, but gradually reestablished a psychological equilibrium through the support of his children and grandchildren. He spent several months in his own home with a housekeeper caring for him—but this was costly and in addition quite isolating. The painful decision on the part of his children to move him to the residential home exacerbated their own mourning processes for their mother, their increasingly incapacitated father, and the "breakup" of the family home with the dispersal and disposition of many possessions, each of which had emotional meaning to them.

Mr. A.'s initial adjustment to the new "home" was uneventful. He spoke little of his wife's death (they had been married for close to sixty years), and adapted to the routine of the institution. Gradually he began to talk about Russia, his birthplace, and his family of origin, most of whom were now dead. The vividness of his descriptions and the constant repetition of certain stories, though uncomfortable to the listeners, took on a pattern.

Mr. A. wished to see his sisters, his parents, his paternal grandfather. This latter figure had been especially important to him as he was the replacement for the mother, who died when Mr. A. was an adolescent. The association between myself and the bearded grandfather was clearly in evidence. In resurrecting this material figure of the past, Mr. A. seemingly attempted to replace the lost mother and the lost wife with the now reinstated grandfather who was embodied in the present. At times he would treat me as a son, tearfully talking about how it was so wonderful to have family. This compensated old man had no insight into his transference reactions, although the meaning of his repetitive reminiscence presented a pattern which allowed me to have insight into Mr. A.'s defensive and adaptational structure.

When Mr. A. was angry and upset, he talked about the inhumanity of the Czar's government which suppressed Jews. As he felt better, he would shift and talk about the greater equality that the Communist regime had instituted. Lenin was seen as the good father who wanted the best for the helpless people. Stalin, described far less glowingly, was seen as the "strong man" who saved Russia from the tyrannical Nazis. Although Mr. A. was aware of Stalin's activities, he did not see Stalin as a tyrant.

In the course of his reminiscences, spontaneously related, he slowly and in bits and pieces told his life story. Each recollection had meaning in terms of current transference reactions as well as past history. His father, as a little boy, fell from a tree. Because of inadequate medical care, the father's fractured leg was improperly set and the father became crippled. The father's mother, a strong and dominating matriarch, opened an inn for travelers in the small Russian village in which they lived. The father had two sisters. These women, who never married, identified with their domineering mother.

Into this household came Mr. A.'s mother, a young woman who was orphaned early in life and who came from a distant village. A marriage was arranged, and the docile young woman came under the control of the matriarchal household. At least eight children were born in quick succession, and then the mother died. Her father eventually left Russia to live and die in Palestine.

Mr. A. had been the third child and first son. He described how his demanding father frequently beat him in order to "teach" him to be an upright and dutiful son. In late adolescence he finally ran away from home, came to Odessa, and then made his way to the United States, where his two older sisters and several of his younger siblings lived. He received no support from his paternal grandmother and his paternal aunts. They, like his father, were harsh, cruel, and at times also physically brutal.

Upon arriving in Chicago, Mr. A. taught himself English and through self-education and hard work became a pharmacist. He was shy, socially inept, and a "loner." His sisters helped him and arranged a marriage to a kindly, depressed young woman. This woman had previously wanted to marry another man, but her father had rejected this man. All of Mr. A.'s adult life was characterized by hard work, anal compulsiveness, identification with helpless people, and a political orientation to the left. He did not beat his children, but lectured them and tried to teach them to be upright and conforming. The identification with his father and paternal grandmother and aunts was clear but never verbally acknowledged. The course of this man's life had a tragic quality to it—he repeated patterns of his own family that he had found so painful in his own childhood. He attempted to justify and rationalize all of his behavior and values in terms of doing what was right and just, and yet he was unaware consciously of what he was actively doing to his wife, whom he tried to dominate and with whom he fought, and to his children, whom he intimidated in frightening ways.

Yet he was always overly generous to his customers. Interestingly, his shop was located in a Slavic neighborhood where he was beloved by his customers who revered him as he had revered his saintly grandfather. This figure was described as a kind, giving man who removed himself from his family as Mr. A. had with his own family. Throughout most of his adult life in Chicago, the patient did not write to his remaining siblings in Russia and rarely, if ever, talked of his childhood. In the nursing home, however, the reminiscences that emerged went back over his life of eight plus decades. No attempts were made actively to interpret his behavior. He seemingly wanted to tell his stories to anyone who would listen and understand. He demanded little and still attempted, even though enfeebled, to be as independent as possible, feeding himself and moving on his own without assistance.

The patterns of his life were clear; the methods of defense and coping were understandable; the relations he established were explainable. Yet he had no insight into them. His dreams of being in Russia, seeing his mother, playing in the village as a little boy, paralleled the reminiscences. Evidences of intra-psychic conflicts were present but not confronted or dealt with. He seemingly had made his adjustment with life, although the barrenness and solitude had persisted for almost ninety years. What I have addressed here is the issue of insight in the observer, not the patient. The "therapist" could understand, but had no reason to intervene.

Hollós and Ferenczi (1925), in their classic study of the psychic disorder of general paresis, have described how psychoanalysis helped to understand insightfully the meanings of the psychotic symptoms of patients with this disease, especially the delusions that were so commonly observed. Anatomical-pathological changes in the brain had been seen as causal. Hollós and Ferenczi, however, had insight into the importance of endogenous psychological factors in determining the content of the delusions and were not content to consider only the exogenous, toxic features of the disease. In analogous fashion, I am suggesting that the psychic content of the reminiscences of senile individuals also has internal psychic meaning. This does not suggest that there are no cerebral pathological factors at work, but rather implies that the psychic contents of these productions have significance in different ways; that is, psychic meaning related to much earlier times as well as to current situations. In several other instances I have, on carefully exploring the memory deficits of the elderly, also found psychic meaning to their lapses, which seem akin to what Freud (1901) described as slips of the memory. Psychological investigations of such symptoms, usually attributed to organic changes in the elderly, can yield insights into the psychological organization of the individual. Psychic determinism may be found even in the so-called organic psychological manifestations of aging and the aged.

Hollós and Ferenczi found that paretics wish to repress their insight into their disease, even though their concealed self-insight can be ascertained from the understanding of their delusions, from their dreams, and from their poems. The idea of insight repression can be found in other types of patients who presumably have discovered their deeper patterns but cannot deal with them. This suggests that insight or discovery is not sufficient for therapeutic change. Instead, additional working through of what one has learned is required if there is to be meaningful therapeutic success. The discovery of meaning in personal phenomena is different from the determination of cause and effect or antecedent-consequent linkages. This distinction highlights the important difference between inductive understanding derived from the transference repetition in the psychoanalytic situation and deductive understanding arrived at by reconstruction. Reconstructive insight is less likely to be demonstrable than inductive insight. Both types of insight, however, have their place in psychoanalysis.

At particular times repetitive stories and reminiscences may change in emphasis and even in detail. When this occurs, I examine the discrepancies and try to understand them either from a transference point of view or from a frame of reference that includes external stresses. An example of this was observed in an eighty-three-year-old woman. Mrs. B., whose husband had a transient cerebral ischemic attack which incapacitated him for a period of time. Where previously he cared for his wife's needs, now she had to support and assist him. She herself was anxious about the possibility that a similar illness might afflict her. Where previously she spoke in glowing terms of her father—he had been very successful in business, caring for his wife and family, taking them on trips to Europe and the Far East, and so on—after her husband's illness she began slightly to shade the stories and bring out some of her father's faults; for example, he would go on business trips, leaving the mother to care for the children; he would take her brothers but not

Mrs. B. to the ballgames. I asked why she was emphasizing features of her father that she had previously not discussed. Initially she was perplexed, but then with great insight she wondered if it had anything to do with her husband's condition. As we talked further, she jokingly said, "Important men abandon me—even you are going off for a long vacation." Freud (1906) suggested that if an analysand is asked to retell a dream, additional aspects may be recalled and worked with. In a similar fashion, changes in reminiscences are significant. The discovery of their meanings may open new areas for the therapeutic work.

Mrs. C., a seventy-five-year-old widow, in talking of her reactions to the sudden death of her husband five years earlier, described how during the bereavement period a friend paid her a condolence call. The friend asked, "How old was Mr. C. when he died?" She looked at him and said, "Mr. C.? Mr. C.? Who is he?" After an interminably uncomfortable silence, she exclaimed loudly, "Oh, my God—I must be senile!" In the course of our work, she added, after telling me of this episode, "I don't think I was senile—I think I was so shocked that I blocked everything out, including the name of my husband. Do you think I might have also had some hostility to him?" This question stimulated productive self-examination and reflection about many issues—some extending back into her early childhood.

I wish to emphasize that many may have insight into aspects of their functioning which they have had to push away for a variety of reasons. The psychoanalyst can facilitate the rediscovery of that which was removed from awareness—or perhaps the uncovering of that which was buried but which had and can still have vital importance. But discovery is not enough, just as insight is not enough for the analysand. Insight is the creative beginning of understanding at many levels for the psychoanalyst—of the communications of the analysand, of the psychological state of the analyst, of the fit between the clinical and the theoretical, of the more general scientific value, and even as a means of more carefully delineating one's own world view and value system. If insight is discovery or inspiration (Kris, 1950, 1956b), then elaboration, working through, and further detailed investigation are necessary complements to consolidating the gains attainable through "opening the door" to new realms of awareness.

Rather than summarize my position, I wish to raise questions about additional aspects of the subject of our consideration for possible discussion and examination:

1. Is insight a process that has several components, each with their own lines of development but which converge in time to yield new knowledge?
2. Can we identify the developments of the capacity for and the utilization of insight throughout the course of life, before, as part of, or after psychoanalytic treatment?
3. What is the relationship of insight to ways of observing and learning?
4. Are there levels and types of insight which can be examined and differentiated over the course of a psychoanalytic treatment, and which may be similar or different for the psychoanalyst and for the analysand?
5. What is the relationship of insight to creativity?

Doris Grumbach, a contemporary novelist, has recently written an essay on "Creativity: Flights of Fancy and Leaps of Faith" (1979). In conclusion, I wish to quote a few passages from her work. Perhaps in reading this, we might substitute "insight" for "creativity" and achieve a new level of insight into insight.

> Creativity is the synapse between what is known and common and accepted, and what is unknown until now, uncommon and unexpected. It is the leap between the surmise and the conviction, the conjectural and the inevitable. It is the guess made certain.
>
> Every solver of problems and difficulties is creative: the person who studies a question, or the cause of apparent failure, examines alternatives; considers even absurd, contradictory, and incredible solutions; and then, in a prodigy of choice, changes failure to success, doubt to certainty, ignorance to knowledge. A solver of problems, in Sigmund Freud's words, is one who disturbs the sleep of mankind [p. 64].

Insight does this initially, but the subsequent sleep, as a result, will be more sound, more restful, more refreshing.

16

IDEAS ON THE INNER LIFE OF THE OLDER ADULT: WITH SPECIAL REFERENCE TO PSYCHOANALYTIC PSYCHOTHERAPY

I

Cicero, the famous Roman orator and philosopher wrote an essay "On Old Age" in 44 B.C. The form chosen by Cicero is a dialogue, a form used and seemingly preferred by both the Greeks and the Romans. The imaginary conversation is like a play or even a dream in that the various speakers represent the author's points of view and his questions. In some ways one can hear in the text Cicero the lawyer and lawmaker addressing his colleagues and the judicial bodies. Since the words and the ideas are those of Cicero, one can infer that they are reflections and externalizations in language of what his inner concerns, messages, and thought related to. In this essay, two younger men pose their questions to the wise elder who shares his experiences and observations with us, his readers. In the theater of Cicero's mind, the lives of the participants represent his internal dialogues.

Cicero (106–43 B.C.) wrote "On Old Age" at the age of sixty-two, the year before he was killed, although he sets the discussion in the Rome of 150 B.C. The main speaker, Marcus

A version of this paper appears as "The Mourning-Liberation Process: Ideas on the Inner Life on the Older Adult." In: *Treating the Elderly with Psychotherapy: The Scope for Change in Later Life*, edited by J. Sadavoy and M. Leszcz. Madison, CT: International Universities Press, 1987, pp. 3–29.

This work was supported in part by the Anne Pollock Lederer Research Fund of the Institute for Psychoanalysis of Chicago.

Procius Cato, aged eighty-four at the time of the imaginary conversation, was much admired by Cicero. In this work, Cicero anticipates much later gerontological research. Grant notes that "Cicero's reflections on immortality come from the heart because of the recent death of his beloved daughter Tullia" (1982, p. 212), who died in childbirth. Since Cicero may have also been distressed at the idea of retirement, he may have wanted to show that he was still very capable of writing about a more important concern of man in a positive way.

Although Cicero was not part of the group involved in the assassination of Caesar on March 15, 44 B.C., he approved of the deed. He delivered a series of speeches critical of Antony, and Antony's agents set out to destroy Cicero. When they found him in December 43 B.C., the centurion in charge of the group killed him with his sword. But let us turn to the essay "Cato the Elder on Old Age."

Scipio, aged thirty-five, opens the conversation by saying to Cato: "I have never noticed that you find it wearisome to be old. That is very different from most other old men, who claim to find their age a heavier burden than Mount Etna itself" (p. 214). Cato responds:

> A person who lacks the means, within himself, to live a good and happy life will find any period of his existence wearisome. But rely for life's blessings on your own resources, and you will not take a gloomy view of any of the inevitable consequences of nature's laws. Everyone hopes to attain an advanced age; yet when it comes they all complain! . . . Old age, they protest, crept up on them more rapidly than they had expected. . . . who was to blame for their mistaken forecast? For age does not steal upon adults any faster than adulthood steals upon children. . . . I follow and obey [nature] as a divine being. Now since she has planned all the earlier divisions of our lives excellently, she is not likely to make a bad playwright's mistake of skimping the last act. And a last act was inevitable. There had to be a time of withering, of readiness to fall, like the ripeness which comes to the fruits of the trees and of the earth. But a wise man will face this prospect with resignation, for resistance against nature is as pointless as the battles of the giants against the gods [*Cicero: Selected Works*, pp. 214–215].

In a most informative document prepared by the American

Association of Retired Persons and the Administration on Aging of the U.S. Department of Health and Human Services, *A Profile of Older Americans: 1984*, we are told that persons sixty-five years or older numbered 27.4 million in 1983.

> They represented 11.7% of the U.S. population, about one in every nine Americans. The number of older Americans increased by 1.7 million or 6% since 1980, compared to an increase of 3% for the under-65 population. . . . Since 1900 the percentage of Americans 65+ almost tripled . . . and the number increased more than eight times. . . . The older population itself is getting older. In 1983 the 65–75 age group . . . was over seven times larger than in 1900, but the 75–84 group . . . was 11 times larger and the 85+ group . . . was 20 times larger. . . . In 1983, there were 16.4 million older women and 11.0 million older men, or a sex ratio of 149 women for every 100 men . . . the sex ratio increased to a high of 241 for persons 85 and older [p. 1].

It is anticipated that the older population will continue to grow in the future and by the year 2030 there will be 65 million older persons, two-and-one-half times their number in 1980. Furthermore, by the year 2000, persons 65+ are expected to represent 13 percent of the population, and this percentage may climb to 21.2 percent by 2030 (p. 2). These statistics are most impressive and call attention to a pressing area deserving of our attention and one that we in psychiatry, psychoanalysis, and the mental health field have overlooked or ignored. Related issues deal with mental status; for example, widowhood, living arrangements, geographic distribution, income and poverty, housing, employment and retirement, and health care, especially problems in mental and psychological health. Most older persons have at least one chronic condition and many have multiple difficulties. "The most frequently occurring conditions for the elderly in 1981 were: arthritis (46%), hypertension (38%), hearing impairments and heart conditions (28% each), sinusitis (18%), visual impairments and orthopedic impairments (14% each), arteriosclerosis (10%), and diabetes (8%)" (p. 13). Although emotional and mental disorders per se do not appear in this list they constitute an important element in the reactions to stress and strain induced by ill-health, psychosocial disruptions, exit and entrance events, transitions and diffusing of structures which gave the individual support and boundaries. The same demographic patterns found in the United States are reflected worldwide and in developed countries some of the socioeconomic problems related to an increased older population are similar to patterns we observe in the United States.

The shifts in population seem to be reflected in the number of individuals who are specially trained to care for older adults. In 1980 there were approximately 600 physicians identified as geriatricians. It is estimated that by 1990, there will be a need for 9,000 geriatricians. Moeller has noted that even though older people utilize physicians and health services more than younger adults, they do not use them inappropriately and probably underutilize both health and social services. Most older persons living in the community, even though they have some chronic condition, have few serious limitations in their daily activities. However, "among all persons 65 years and older, approximately 10–15% have marked mental health problems, and about 25% have serious difficulties caring for their daily tasks" (Moeller, 1985, p. 13). This is especially true for individuals over eighty years of age—the number of individuals with physical and mental difficulties nearly doubles in comparison to those between the ages of sixty-five and eighty. I will not discuss the fiscal implications of these figures except to underline what Dr. Moeller has noted, namely, "the means (public or private) of paying health care expenses has little effect on either the incidence of medical problems or death rates. Rather the organization of health services appears to be a critical variable in the quality of health care, and consequently planning becomes an essential aspect of the efficient delivery of a geriatric health system" (p. 13). How mental health fits into this system is a significant question that we must address despite our previous avoidance of this issue.

The problems of the elderly that we encounter professionally may be depression, paranoid reactions, anxiety reactions, and the fear of helplessness and isolation if there are no family or other available support systems. In chapter 14 I discussed the question of aging and aged and how this should be viewed as an issue of development or pathology. Without a data base for normal development in the older years it is too easy to equate aging adults and/or aged adults as incompetent, ill, or incoherent. We know this is not so. We have extrapolated our experiences with the decompensated elderly to all or most elderly and thus perpetuated the myths of mental illness in older adults. We need more demographics and research on aging (gerontology), as well as on geriatric medicine, including the psychiatric, psychological, and psychoanalytic components. Perhaps as we obtain the data from the well and the ill, we will be able to plan preventive and rehabilitative, as well as therapeutic, programs, including appropriate individual treatments for those who need this care.

An important distinction should be made for all developmental stages; namely, normative or normal developmental "crises" that are predictable, anticipatable, and universal. These developmental crises can be traumatic without being overwhelming and usually the stress-strain they induce can be coped with by individuals who have sufficient "strength," "energy," and integration. Of course, some decompensations may occur and these may require supportive treatment in order to help the individual to return to a homeostatic level that allows for comfortable functioning and further progression. In contrast to normal crises, we have the so-called "catastrophic crises." These include the unexpected, the overwhelming, and disruptive events, the sudden or even gradual situations that slowly build up to a breaking point, the frightening and disorganizing situations that affect the individual as well as the family. Examples of such catastrophic crises include severe physical illness (e.g., acute malignancy, cardiac or stroke attacks, automobile accidents, Alzheimer's disease, and/or severe psychological illnesses, such as schizophrenia, manic-depressive disorder, severe depression, or anxiety-panic attacks). These catastrophic crises may require professional interventions of various kinds, including individual or family psychotherapy, pharmacotherapy, or hospital-based treatment.

II

Recent comprehensive statistical reports regarding Americans aged eighty-five or older revealed that as a group these "old old," "oldest old," or "extreme aged" are growing in numbers more rapidly than any younger segment of the population

(Collins, 1985). Furthermore, the individuals in this group are less frail, less likely to be institutionalized, and more independent than previously believed. The increase in numbers of the eighty-five and older group is engendering new concerns that relate to their impact on the economy, the health care and maintenance system, and the family and other support structures. Nonetheless, these individuals have great powers of survival and study of them can provide us with information that can be useful to younger generations and to the institution of preventive measures. In some ways these older adults can be likened to the invulnerables and lower-risk individuals who are now attracting our attention. What "self-righting," survival, and positive equilibrium maintenance factors do they possess that permits them to thrive? Confronted by the data we now have, it is necessary to reexamine our biases, preconceived notions, and obtain additional data to extend and test newer hypotheses.

The U.S. National Institute on Aging is inviting proposals to study those eighty-five and older. At the same time, we must begin to treat and share our clinical findings as they come from individual psychoanalytic psychotherapy with people in this group and those in the even "younger old" groups, persons in their fifties, sixties, seventies, and eighties, as well as those in their nineties. I have had successful clinical experiences with people in this age range and can attest to the feasibility and positive outcomes of intense treatments. Not all in these chronological, sociological, and psychological groupings are amenable to such treatment, but this is also true of people in their twenties, thirties, and forties.

When the lives of the older members of our community are considered, contrary to popular beliefs, increasing numbers of this age group are actually adapting well. According to the 1980 U.S. Census, eight out of every ten of those Americans over age sixty-five (80%) describe their health as good or excellent compared with that of their contemporaries. Two-thirds of them are living in homes that they own free and clear, and in fact only 5 percent live in nursing homes. The question of why and how these people are so well adapted is now being investigated by Dr. Gene Cohen, Director of the National Institute of Mental Health Program on Aging, who is studying a community of healthy, affluent, independently functioning older people living outside of Washington, DC. This research will yield valuable information and help dispel the myth that assumes erroneously that when one is old, one is sick. Sufficient baseline data are needed to tell us what is normal for different aging cohorts; also much more must be studied about people as they age (i.e., the aging process itself, which is developmental throughout the life course). This issue of normalcy is important in studying the lives of people of all ages (see chapter 14).

There are many dimensions in the process of aging that require examination. For many different reasons the meaning of aging, despite its inevitable presence, has not been sufficiently explored. Introspective studies of what it feels like to move on in the life course are rarely undertaken—perhaps because of inherent bias against studying older adults, an undertaking which can be threatening to younger investigators, perhaps because of the preponderant interest in infancy, childhood, and adolescence which has attracted investigators to these age groups.

My work in the psychoanalysis of individuals with manic-depressive disorders has led to the conclusion—which is not a radical but a rather obvious one—that two or more diseases of the emotional psychic system can be present at the same time in the same person, each requiring a different kind of intervention or treatment. It is well known that two or more physical diseases can be present at the same time. Similarly, it is not unusual for a multiplicity of problems to occur in the psychic system. Patients, who primarily would have never been considered for psychoanalytic treatment, now can have their manic-depressive symptomatology controlled enough to permit them to lie on a couch, five days a week, and be analyzed. Underlying pathology that was previously undiscovered can now be examined. With the knowledge that patients can have more than one kind of depression at the same time, it is also possible to deal with one kind of depression with the judicious use of certain medications, and to use psychosocial means of treatment for the other disorders. The newer conceptualizations bring increasing opportunities to the treatment situation and widen the horizons for psychic care.

In parallel fashion, one may have normative developmental crises as well as catastrophic crises at the same time. The understanding and treatment that is instituted requires careful diagnostic and sensitive therapeutic handling. Aging is a developmental crisis that may be less acute, hence the need for normal baseline data in assessing normality and pathology. Recognition that one must look at any aspect of human life in terms of its complexity rather than its simplicity can be valuable, especially regarding the question of aging. The aging process occurs throughout the life course. As the individual ages or develops there are other components that concomitantly develop and age as well. All the family members are aging, new members are introduced and sometimes are met with stranger-anxiety responses, the relationships and lives of siblings may shift, and work may end with retirement. Hence, aging needs to be approached, not as a single isolated entity, but as a process composed of multiple dynamic systems, all of them moving, all of them impinging upon the individual and each other, and all of them capable of being studied as discrete entities, as specifics, as well as interacting with each other.

In addition to these developmental and catastrophic crises, chronic and physical illnesses may also be present. This adds further complexity to the situation. Emotional illnesses, affective disorders, mental disturbances, and memory dysfunctions all may occur simultaneously. Drug intoxications, allergies, degenerative phenomena, the depletion of energy, sleep disruptions (a major area of pharmacologic research today), problems with hearing, sight, skin, arthritis, and pain are also associated with aging. As many changes are ongoing at the same time, at different rates, internally and externally, in socio-cultural-religious-gender contexts, these changes require adaptational mechanisms to facilitate continuity and adaptation.

The constant changes in this complex, interconnected mosaic confront the individual with stress, strains, and the need to accommodate to repeated losses.

A very crucial element for successful aging is the ability to mourn for prior states of the self. When one can accept aging and its changes, and mourn for the past, the result can be a liberation, a freeing of energy for current living, including planning for the future. One frequently sees this in individuals who have experienced serious physical illnesses and then have a "rebirth" with new life perspectives. They are able to feel and say to themselves, "Okay, this is behind me, and I can now see many things ahead of me for which I can begin to plan constructively." When this mourning-liberation process has not taken place, the pathological aspects of aging emerge with the obvious and expected symptomatology. I am suggesting that for those individuals who cannot accept the normative crises of aging, impaired mourning is a central dynamic in old age pathology (e.g., depression). When catastrophic crises are superimposed on the normative crises, one must distinguish as best one can between them and institute appropriate treatments. *Depression* is itself so global a descriptive term that imbedded within it can be both the normative and catastrophic reactions.

In addition to my clinical work of varying intensity with elderly persons, some of my observations about childhood and adult losses have been extended to include data on the meaning of significant kinship relationships throughout the life course. An illustration: an eighty-year-old mother does not mean the same to her sixty-year-old daughter as she did twenty or thirty years earlier. Consequently, even though one uses the same kin terms, *mother* who is eighty has a different psychological meaning than *mother* who is forty, or *mother* who is twenty-five. The same holds true for *father*. In working with older adults it is possible to begin to study some of this changing, internal psychosocial meaning. The changing intrapsychic needs also shift the meaning of children, parents, spouses, and siblings as the life course moves on.

The meaning of children to their parents changes. One of the most devastating psychological traumata I have encountered clinically is that of losing a child. Of all the loss experiences that I have studied, this is the one in which there is seldom a complete mourning resolution, particularly for the mother. However, work with people in their eighties and their nineties often reveals that the loss of a child does not have the same meaning that it did earlier in life. Further research on the changing meanings of loss, who is lost, and the consequences of loss, are most important if we are to extend our knowledge of the inner life of the older adult.

Sibling relationships also change as life courses on. Though the family of origin dissolves as each of the siblings moves out and establishes his or her own family, as that family in turn matures, moves away, and establishes its own generation of familial nuclei there is a return to the initial sibling relationships and the nuclear family of origin, assuming that the sibling relationships were previously satisfactory. Those sibling relationships to which one returns may become the underlying basis for friendship with sibling surrogates in later life. The return to original sibling relationships can serve to renew positive ties of past when change is occurring, or they may be social regressions, or they may be attempts to avoid mourning, loss, and emptiness. Here again new research data can help us understand these observations.

The dynamics of friendship throughout aging is an area that has not been adequately addressed. There are types of change and loss, in each of these relational spheres, that are inherent in the process of aging. The normal process needs to be understood in order to better aid those whose processes are amiss.

Similarly, spouses at eighty-five do not have the same meaning for each other as they did at twenty-five or thirty. The social, sexual, supportive, mutualistic, and altruistic aspects of spouses throughout the life course are in need of further study. An example: a woman in her late seventies, married, husband alive, and in relatively good health, presented such concerns. She felt increasingly unfulfilled in her relationship with her husband to whom she was married for fifty-five years. In the course of work she made a very important discovery: the man she had married was a substitute for her mother and was not someone whom she genuinely loved. As she began to explore these feelings and talk about the lack of fulfillment in many areas of her life, tears came to her eyes and she said, "At this point of my life, I can't make changes; nor would I want to. I must adjust." It was a very painful experience for her, but adjust she did, and she was able to benefit from psychotherapy in this transitional process. As she became free of some of the emotional shackles of her earlier life, she returned to university studies as a later-life scholar, received her degree, and is now pursuing her interests in art and the theater with great verve and enthusiasm.

David Gutmann (1979) has written about the role shift that often occurs in the relationships of older couples. Females in later middle age become more active and more assertive, whereas males have a tendency to remove themselves and become less active and a bit more passive. This role shift is not pathological. It is a normal aspect of change in later life, and an important one to bear in mind. This is an illustration of the kind of normative developmental data that previously would be seen as pathology. If conflict occurs over these developmental changes, we may see their becoming the focus of "catastrophic crises."

There are many individuals who become quite creative in later life—pursue interests in the arts, music, literature, and the theater. Political leaders are also often productive well into the later decades. There are countless examples of individuals who seem to have a remarkable ability to reach out to life with joy and enthusiasm throughout a long life span, to cultivate flowers, inspire young people, write poetry, learn new languages, travel, or whatever. Why this takes place will require more study; however, in my research up to this point I see a successful mourning-liberation process for the past as playing a significant role in these creative activities. The painful detachment internally from ideals, goals, objectives, and individuals who no longer exist realistically results in an acceptance of the reality principle of functioning. With this traditional accomplishment, freedom to view the world and oneself in it serves as a stimulus for regeneration. Although bereavement is a specific subclass of the mourning adaptational process, it is not the only or the most frequent precipitant of mourning. Mourning is a process that is continually ongoing throughout life. A disappointment, a promotion that does not come through, a baseball game that is lost by one's favorite team, a broken romance, a lost opportunity are all examples of disappointments and losses that must be mourned and relinquished. Most of these mourning-liberation processes go on unnoticed—just as we accept aging and change without notice unless we have conflict. When a major loss or catastrophic change occurs we find the mourning-liberation process becoming a more consciously painful experience, at times requiring professional intervention.

New work in the area of psychoimmunology, for example that of Schleifer, Keller, Meyerson, Raskin, Davis, and Stein (1984), has now come to the fore which bears upon research in the mourning-liberation process. There are indications that the process can be monitored by studying certain immune mechanisms and markers; for example, T-cell changes. Prenatal and infant research has also provided new insights and new clues (e.g., the fetus can discriminate between strong light and weak light, among rock, waltz, and jazz music). These adaptive mechanisms suggest that these intrauterine adaptations to outer stimuli may be the precursors for the mourning-liberation process. The great controversy as to whether mourning-liberation is finally achieved at adolescence or can occur much earlier is becoming resolved as more and more evidence is accumulated that even the four-month-old fetus is already adjusting to the outside world of light, heat, sound, and gravity. The physiological concomitants of the psychological adaptational process may be able to provide us with biological markers that will help us monitor the psychological process in and out of treatment.

If the capacity for discrimination and differentiation is present from such an early age, then it suggests that people are continuously mourning something that once was, and adapting to what is present. This is an epigenetic process—if it is missed or negotiated poorly at an earlier stage of life it will be negotiated poorly at a later stage. It is in this area that psychotherapy may play a key role in getting the mourning-liberation process back onto an adaptive track.

Let me summarize some of my conclusions in a somewhat telegraphic form. In an etiological perspective one has to consider the following issues in working with the older adult:

1. Antecedent psychopathology, either manifest or latent, compensated or pathologically defended, detected or undetected as a result of favorable life situations.
2. Situational crises, acute or chronic, that strain the ego's ability to maintain equilibrium. Age, physical health, and intactness of support systems are but a few of the variables one must keep in mind as contributing to signs and symptoms of psychic distress or illness.
3. Organic illness (neurological and other bodily systems) which can increase reactive symptoms such as depression and psychosocial needs. Helplessness, isolation, fears of loss of basic controls, hopelessness, are a few of the emotional anxieties that I have observed. There

can be regressions to earlier fixations, and if the reality disruptions are severe and persistent these regressions can become chronic and return the individual to very early levels of functioning.

4. As Abraham (1919) observed, age in and of itself need not preclude psychoanalytic treatment. I believe indications for, and anticipations of, successful psychoanalytic treatment depend upon the individual's psychological construction as well as the nature of the subsequent psychic distress. In my successful work with middle-aged and older adults, some in their eighties, I have found:

   a. The capacity for and utilization of insight.
   b. The capacity for and utilization of therapeutically induced transferences.
   c. The capacity to dream and the ability to relate these dreams and fantasies to the therapeutic process as well as to one's past.
   d. The mobilization of motivation to change, to examine goals and values anew, and to make new social relationships or restructure those of the past in more positive ways.
   e. The capacity for self-observation in the present as well as a retrospective view more or less objectively of how one handled significant life relationships in the past and how these can be changed in the present. Retrospective introspection assists in current retrospective activities, as well as in prospective planning.
   f. The mobilization of libidinal and constructive aggressive "energies" in ways that make life more creative, satisfying, and allow the individual to face the inevitable traumata ahead with less anxiety, depressions, and pain.
   g. The institution of a mourning-liberation process that allows past to appropriately become past and allows for "investment" in the present and future.

I wish to emphasize that although this picture is not one that can apply to all older individuals, it can be applied in selective instances (as is true of all patients), and we should not a priori be therapeutically nihilistic about what can be accomplished with psychoanalysis. There are differences in style, approach, preferred topics, specific concerns, appealing theories, and personal sensitivities among psychoanalysts as among all other people. Each investigator pursues his or her work in ways that are most personally fruitful or meaningful. The orientation of the psychoanalyst, however, can be of critical importance in treating the older individual.

In discussing the clinical report of a colleague, we assess what his chosen mode has led him to discover or investigate—his data, his arguments, his interpretations, his illustrations, his theoretical framework, and the universality or specificity of his findings. There is no one and only correct way of interpretation—a number of possible perspectives allow one to proceed in different ways. A brief clinical account does not allow for the elaboration of the many therapeutic nuances that may have been crucial in the therapeutic process.

Let me now illustrate my approach and understanding of a case Norman Cohen (1982) described. The patient first saw Dr. Cohen, when he was in his late forties, after his therapist of a few years died. He seemingly denied feelings of grief or bereavement at that time. The contact with Dr. Cohen at that time was brief. The patient seemed to have reestablished a manageable level of equilibrium. The patient returned when he was in his middle fifties in a state of panic and anxiety. This time the external precipitating circumstances again dealt with loss—the death of his father and the threatened loss of the patient's homosexual partner. The loss response and the uncompleted or pathological mourning-liberation process seems clear to me to be present in both episodes of the initial consultations with Dr. Cohen.

We learn that a baby brother was born when he was three years of age and died suddenly when the patient was six or seven. His mother was very depressed at the time and subsequently so over-invested in him that she was perceived to be intrusive. In research on the effects of childhood sibling loss (see chapters 2 and 24), I have discussed this particular trauma as well as the special relationship of the depressed mother to her surviving son. The guilt, fear, choice of "love object," sexual preference—all can be related to this trauma constellation and could be seen as attempts to defend against more serious, overt pathology. We might suggest that the patient could no longer defend himself against the strains of his earlier pathogenic trauma, especially that his aging ego could no longer manage the later loss of three significant males—therapist, father, and lover. The possible significance of his forthcoming retirement from his work can also be seen as a "loss," one that is psychologically similar to the loss of a significant other, but one that comes at a time when one's aging ego cannot deal with this trauma effectively in the "high risk" individual. He may have turned to a male analyst as a possible replacement for his lost objects and to reestablish a manageable equilibrium. This may have been so. He had "great hopes that he would be cured" and indeed "his distress quickly disappeared" once he established a tie with Dr. Cohen.

This patient's pathology could have emerged at any time and is not specific for middle or later age. The vulnerability to the death of a significant other stemmed from his childhood experiences with loss—of the brother, and of his depressed mother. Issues such as survivor guilt, interfered development, defenses against anxiety, narcissistic vulnerability, mourning, etc., were either repressed or handled alloplastically. The early fear of death that he had after his brother's death is frequently seen in children where there has been a parent or sibling loss through death. Later loss events served to re-open the vulnerable wound; when healing cannot occur pathology emerges. Being an "only child" could also be seen as an additional factor in his "loneliness." I will not further discuss Cohen's very interesting case, as I hope what I have said illustrates my overall thesis: one's orientation can determine the clinical data collected and selected, one's interpretations, how one views the analytic process, as well as outcome. My approach deals with the mourning-liberation process, the effect of childhood object loss on later pathology, which vulnerability exists even before one is middle aged. Psychoanalysis can help in the rehabilitation of such individuals.

In our work with middle- and older-aged adults, we deal with complexities. In our understanding of the normal aging process, of the psychopathology of latter day life, as well as in our understanding of the more severe pathology of middle and later aged adults, we must not be satisfied with simple answers or with theoretic reductionism if we are to be therapeutically effective. My caution is to avoid saying "it can't be done," because others may have said it, based on incomplete or faulty understanding.

The goal of psychoanalytic treatment is to make more of people available to themselves for present and future creative and satisfying life experiences. We all know that psychoanalysis is a humanizing force which allows an individual to be in touch with parts of himself or herself that have been forgotten, neglected, or pushed away and yet continue to exert important influences upon the individual. During analysis these parts become alive, old emotional allegiances are revived, passions and rages reawakened, paths overgrown walked upon anew. The past is mourned and self-investigation allows for freedom and liberation to occur. Life enjoyment ensues and the ability to confront the inevitable traumata of later life events is enhanced. Alienations that are draining get resolved and intensely private past experiences, still alive, gradually are worked through and become appropriately syntonic with one's being. Energy is released for new investments in life, in the inner as well as in the outer ambience in which one lives alone and with others. This can occur in individuals who are middle aged, older aged, or in the younger group of analysands.

III

The organism attempts to cope with the internal and external strain of psychosocial disruption using a number of biological, psychological, emotional, social, cultural, and religious mechanisms. Psychiatry and psychology are on a new frontier that will be able to monitor these changes, just as the response of the body to an antibiotic in fighting infectious diseases can be monitored by watching the number of white cells decrease until they approximate a normal level. It is conceivable that in the very near future biological markers will be developed that will monitor various psychological processes as well and demonstrate how effective psychotherapeutic interventions are and what kinds of therapeutic interventions are appropriate.

We have new perspectives on the diagnosis and under-standing of the basis of pathology. By differentiating between normative and catastrophic crises, we can further understand the maladaptations to aging, as well as successful aging. More precise treatments and interventions will be possible. Under appropriate circumstances, the possibility of combinatorial ther-apy must be considered: supportive psychotherapy, insight-oriented psychotherapy, psychotherapy that is designed to con-dition the individual to certain types of responses, and formal behavior modification. For example, supportive-educational counseling may be useful in dealing with minor concerns over aging crises. Late-life paranoia or severe depressive reactions may be helped with intense psychotherapy and/or pharmacoth-erapy. The physical changes and illnesses of aging cannot be ignored, particularly when dealing with older adults. Bowel and bladder problems, sleep problems, weight problems, adequate nutrition, drug sensitivity and drug interactions, fatigue, bore-dom, the use of sedatives, tranquilizers, and sleep medications must all be considered and their impact assessed on the ongoing psychological portrait of the patient.

It is necessary to emphasize also that psychotherapy is ex-tremely important and is not to be overlooked. Psychotherapy is of enormous value in aiding the individual to get back on track with the course of mourning and circumvent the patho-logical outcome of loss. All people, including and especially older people, want to talk about themselves, and this is part of mourning therapy. Reminiscences, life reviews, and nostalgic recollections all serve the cathartic function of discharge and detachment while also forming the basis of the more intimate psychotherapeutic relationship with the therapist. An illustra-tion: when I asked one of my older patients about himself, he suddenly began crying. I paused. "You are the first person who has asked me to talk about myself," he said. "My kids are in different parts of the country; my grandchildren call me on Father's Day or other holidays. We see each other at weddings, funerals, and graduations. I want to talk about myself. I am alone; I feel lonely." And he began to talk; the affective and reminiscence catharsis was the beginning of the liberation pro-cess. I became a transference figure representing the children and grandchildren but I also helped him see past as past, and to recognize and see present and future. His dreams gave us data that confirmed the ongoing changes. The relationship with me facilitated the mourning-liberation process. People who are in a state of acute bereavement have a need to talk, talk, and talk, which can be constructive and lead to resolutions. If aging must be met with mourning in order for liberation to ensue, then the process of intimate talking must be encouraged. The first therapeutic task is to allow the patients to talk about themselves and to be genuinely and sufficiently interested in what they say.

The process of psychotherapy with the elderly involves the establishment and working through of transferences, though these may be somewhat different from those of younger patients. As a younger analyst working with people in their sixties, seventies, and eighties, the author frequently observed that patients developed a son transference. They would begin to have expectations of the therapist similar to those they would have of a son who was not fulfilling some of their special needs at this time in life. This transference may be seen as a reversal of old parental transferences; however, in many older adults this is not so. There is an expectation that one has of one's children and this gets placed upon the analyst. The fact of frequent contact over a long period of time may be seen as a form of gratification, but this may apply to individuals of all age groups who are in analysis. By working with transferences, fantasies, dreams, and symptomatic acts, the entire spectrum of what we see in psychoanalytic treatment, the patient develops insight, identifies with the analyst, and change occurs.

Patients become very upset with their therapists' vacations. Sometimes they cry; sometimes they become furious. Sometimes they have dreams and fantasies that would go back to earlier disappointments, losses, and changes. By carefully encouraging them to bring out their full range of feelings they were helped to develop a feeling of security instead of abandonment. This process could be called mourning therapy. They mourn what they never had but wanted, or what they had and no longer have.

In working with older adults, one must also consider the question of liaison with family, with other physicians, with lawyers, brokers, and social workers, because this is also part of therapeutic diagnostic responsibility. It is also necessary to come to terms on occasion with a change of where treatment takes place (i.e., house calls). This is true for the family practitioner, for the psychiatrist, and some day soon for the psychoanalyst as well. Social workers have always been involved in making home visits; these are often very therapeutic and allow firsthand observation which is of diagnostic value. I have personally found this interesting, useful, and quite helpful in inclement weather when older patients are at risk of falling and injuring themselves. Health care people (and they are called health care, not disease care, people) should begin to think very seriously about prevention. There are many factors to consider, including the importance of exercise, physical therapy, particularly with people who may be homebound, nutrition and diet, the use of alcohol, no matter how judicious, the monitoring of medication, the permission for sexual gratification, be it auto-erotic or whatever. All these factors influence the quality of life as one ages.

Elsewhere I have written about the spectrum of abandonment (see Chapter 5) and have tried to describe the many situations in which this occurs—from the transitory internal feeling of abandonment to the actual permanent abandonment of a child by its parents, either through death, divorce, or a permanent leaving. These experiences can constitute catastrophic crises that may be of minor consequence or have a serious life-long impact on personality development. We find such "abandonments" in immigrants, in survivors of concentration camps, in prisoners, in individuals placed in hospitals for long periods, in retirement, in families where suicide has occurred. In other words, the abandonment experiences, coming at crucial times, and existing in overwhelming quantities, may result in the high-risk, highly vulnerable individual. The mourning-liberation process is a necessary adaptation to undoing these pathogenic consequences of earlier traumata. Intensive psychodynamic treatment, when indicated, can facilitate this healing process. Psychotherapeutic intervention in earlier life, closer to the time of pathogenic trauma, can help and prevent later decompensation when life with its inevitable crises presents situations that can trigger more serious responses.

Also of great importance is the establishment of a trusting

relationship with the person who is the caregiver, because older people, like children, are especially sensitive to being patronized. It is also necessary, in considering the role of psychotherapy, to consider countertransference in broad terms. There is the need to consider: Why am I working with this patient? Why am I involved with this age group? What attitudes do I have? What is the benefit to me? Is this autopsychotherapy as well as work with my patient? One sees these countertransference reactions in younger colleagues and students who may either perpetuate existing myths or for personal reasons have the need to defend against the emerging behaviors, attitudes, and feelings of their older patients.

Plato put it well when he has Socrates say, "I consider that the old have gone before us along a road which we must all travel in our turn and it is good we should ask them the nature of that road, whether it be rough and difficult, or easy and smooth" (Plato, circa 375 B.C.). By working with older adults we will learn about that road, and in doing so it will be smoother for us and we will make it smoother for them.

SUMMARY

It is difficult to summarize an essay in which various ideas have been briefly presented. In my own clinical work with adults beyond the age of fifty, with women and men in these age categories and with individuals who come from various backgrounds, I have attempted to distill some of my thinking and my current findings regarding aging and aged. These have dealt with normal aging as well as some pathological entities. In my considerations, I have differentiated the normal crises of aging from the unexpected crises that disrupt the equilibrium of the individual and various members of the family. The distinction just made may not be as precise as the conceptualization. For example, what is a normative crisis for one person can be catastrophic for another. If one's childhood and early life was filled with personal illness, chronic disability, the death or abandonment by a parent, or serious life threatening disasters, such an individual is highly vulnerable to changes and normal developmental crises. On the other hand, we increasingly find individuals who, despite such serious earlier crises, seemingly are not at risk and might even be impervious to serious disruptions. When we see change sensitivity or change resistance, especially in the later years, e.g., when change or threat of alteration of the status quo results in major anxieties, depressions, regressions, somatizations, or paranoid reactions, one must consider the possibility of psychological disturbance that warrants therapeutic intervention. For some of these disorders I have found psychoanalytic-psychodynamic psychotherapy very useful and the treatment of choice. In my own work the significance of the mourning-liberation process in aging has been found to have important significance.

DATE DUE

MAY 7 2002			